ULRIK WAGNER
RASMUS K. STORM
KLAUS NIELSEN

(2017)

WH€N
SPORT
M€€TS
BUSIN€SS

capabilities, challenges, critiques

Book has a European focus to examine
how sport & business come together.

⑤SAGE

Los Angeles | London | New Delhi
Singapore | Washington DC | Melbourne

Los Angeles | London | New Delhi
Singapore | Washington DC | Melbourne

SAGE Publications Ltd
1 Oliver's Yard
55 City Road
London EC1Y 1SP

SAGE Publications Inc.
2455 Teller Road
Thousand Oaks, California 91320

SAGE Publications India Pvt Ltd
B 1/I 1 Mohan Cooperative Industrial Area
Mathura Road
New Delhi 110 044

SAGE Publications Asia-Pacific Pte Ltd
3 Church Street
#10-04 Samsung Hub
Singapore 049483

Editor: Matthew Waters
Assistant editor: Lyndsay Aitken
Production editor: Imogen Roome
Marketing manager: Catherine Slinn
Cover design: Francis Kenney
Typeset by: C&M Digitals (P) Ltd, Chennai, India
Printed and bound by CPI Group (UK) Ltd,
Croydon, CR0 4YY

Preface and editorial arrangement © Ulrik Wagner, Rasmus K.
Storm and Klaus Nielsen 2017

Chapter 1 © Rasmus K. Storm, Ulrik Wagner and Klaus Nielsen
2017
Chapter 2 © Anna Gerke and Maureen Benson-Rea 2017
Chapter 3 © Sine Agergaard 2017
Chapter 4 © Johannes Orlowski, Manuel Herter and Pamela
Wicker 2017
Chapter 5 © Koen Breedveld and Jeroen Scheerder 2017
Chapter 6 © Thorsten Dum and Ulrik Wagner 2017
Chapter 7 © Harry Arne Solberg 2017
Chapter 8 © Simon Chadwick, Nicholas Burton and Cheri Bradish
2017
Chapter 9 © Bastian Popp and Herbert Woratschek 2017
Chapter 10 © Mathieu Djaballah 2017
Chapter 11 © Klaus Nielsen and Rasmus K. Storm 2017
Chapter 12 © Jan Pieper 2017
Chapter 13 © Arnout Geeraert 2017
Chapter 14 © Larissa Davies 2017
Chapter 15 © Wladimir Andreff 2017

First published 2017

Library of Congress Control Number: 2016934713

British Library Cataloguing in Publication data

A catalogue record for this book is available from
the British Library

ISBN 978-1-4739-4804-4
ISBN 978-1-4739-4805-1 (pbk)

At SAGE we take sustainability seriously. Most of our products are printed in the UK using FSC papers and boards.
When we print overseas we ensure sustainable papers are used as measured by the PREPS grading system.
We undertake an annual audit to monitor our sustainability.

TABLE OF CONTENTS

About the Contributors   viii

SECTION A: THE NEW SPORT ENVIRONMENT   **1**

1 When Sport Meets Business: A Brief Introduction   3
   Rasmus K. Storm, Ulrik Wagner and Klaus Nielsen

   The effects of commercialization   3
   A focus on Europe   4
   The target groups   5
   Book structure and content   6
   References   10

2 The Expansion of the Sport Goods Industry   11
   Anna Gerke and Maureen Benson-Rea

   Introduction   11
   Historical and recent developments   12
   Contemporary and future challenges   15
   Contemporary and future critiques   19
   Case study 2.1: Decathlon – The expansion of a European sport goods player   20
   Conclusion   26

Recommended further reading   26
References   27

3 When Globalization and Migration meet National and Local Talent Development   30
   Sine Agergaard

   Introduction   30
   Historical and recent developments   31
   Challenges, options and capabilities   33
   Case study 3.1: Talent development in times of immigration   34
   Case study 3.2: Dual career support in times of globalization   35
   Conclusion   37
   Recommended further reading   39
   References   40

4 The Commodification and Commercialization of Elite Athletes   43
   Johannes Orlowski, Manuel Herter and Pamela Wicker

   Introduction: Historical and recent development   43
   Contemporary and future challenges, capabilities, and critiques   46
   Case study 4.1: The Klitschkos   49
   Conclusion   53
   Recommended further reading   53
   References   54

5 The Business of Running   57
   Koen Breedveld and Jeroen Scheerder

   Introduction: Historical and recent developments   57
   Challenges and critiques   58
   Case studies: Running   59
   Case study 5.1: Amateurism and commercial influences in sports   66
   Case study 5.2: Three waves of running events   67
   Conclusion   68
   Recommended further reading   70
   References   71

SECTION B: SPORT MARKETING AND MEDIA   **73**

6 The Commercial Growth of Sponsorship SBM 2017   75
   Thorsten Dum and Ulrik Wagner

   Introduction   75
   Broadening the sponsorship scope: Marketing and beyond   76
   Addressing target groups, setting objectives and planning the
   strategic sponsorship process   79
   Present and future challenges, capabilities and criticisms   82
   Case study 6.1: Topdanmark – using a sports sponsorship as an HRM instrument   84

Case study 6.2: BASF and Sportclub 2020 – demonstrating CSR
through regional sports sponsorships   86
Conclusion: Rationalising sponsorship opportunities through the lens of social trends?   87
Recommended further reading   89
References   89

7 The Battle for Media Rights in European Club Football   92
   Harry Arne Solberg

   Introduction   92
   Historical and recent development   93
   Contemporary and future challenges   97
   Case study 7.1: The sale of the international media rights of the Spanish
   LaLiga for the period from 2016/17 to 2019/20   101
   Conclusion   104
   Recommended further reading   105
   References   106

8 Ambush Marketing in Sport SBM2017   108
   Simon Chadwick, Nicholas Burton and Cheri Bradish

   Introduction   108
   Historical and recent development   108
   Contemporary and future challenges   112
   Case study 8.1: Caught with their pants down?   115
   Conclusion   117
   Recommended further reading   118
   References   119

9 Sport, Social Media and Online Communities   120
   Bastian Popp and Herbert Woratschek

   Introduction: Historical and recent development   120
   Contemporary and future challenges, capabilities and critiques   125
   Case study 9.1: Anti-RB Leipzig activism   130
   Case study 9.2: Anti-Wiesenhof activism   131
   Conclusion   132
   Recommended further reading   134
   References   134

10 Corporate Social Responsibility in Sport CSR- SBM2012   137
   Mathieu Djaballah

   Introduction   137
   CSR and sport, a relationship of both proximity and distance   138
   Contemporary and future questions of sport-CSR   141
   Case study 10.1: French Tennis Federation – A 'genuinely strategic' CSR 142
   Conclusion   147

Recommended further reading   149
References   149

SECTION C: SPORT AND FINANCE   **151**

11 Profits, Championships and Budget Constraints in European Professional Sport   153
    Klaus Nielsen and Rasmus K. Storm

    Introduction   153
    Win optimization rather than profit maximization   154
    Persistent losses but a high survival rate   156
    Soft budget constraints – theory and practical relevance   158
    Soft budget constraints in European professional football   159
    Institutions and social and emotional attachments   161
    Case study 11.1: Soft budget constraints and rescue operations in Spain   162
    Case study 11.2: Soft pricing and subsidies in Denmark – The case of Viborg F.F.   163
    Conclusion and further perspectives   164
    Recommended further reading   164
    Notes   164
    References   165

12 Financial Fair Play in European Football   167
    Jan Pieper

    The need for regulation in European Club Football   167
    What the FFP regulations are about   168
    Why clubs overinvest in playing strength   168
    Do the FFP regulations bite?   177
    Case study 12.1: Bayer AG as a true investor at Bayer 04 Leverkusen   178
    Case study 12.2: Roman Abramovich as a pure success-seeker at Chelsea FC   179
    Conclusion   180
    Recommended further reading   181
    References   183

13 Corruption and the Governance of Sport   186
    Arnout Geeraert

    Introduction   186
    Systemic trends that provide motive for corruption   187
    Organisational variables that provide opportunity for corruption   189
    Case examples: FIFA scandals and other cases of ISF corruption   192
    Conclusion   195
    Recommended further reading   196
    References   197

SECTION D: SPORTING EVENTS   **201**

14 Sustainable Urban Legacies of Hosting the Olympic Games   203
    Larissa Davies

    Introduction   203
    Historical overview of the Olympic Games and urban development   204
    Contemporary and future challenges, capabilities and critiques   208
    Case study 14.1: London 2012   210
    Conclusion   214
    Recommended further reading   215
    References   216

15 The Cost of Hosting International Sports Events   219
    Wladimir Andreff

    Introduction   219
    The winner's curse, the sports economy and mega-sporting events   219
    Case studies: the Olympic Games   224
    How to hedge against the consequences of the winner's curse
    when hosting sports events   227
    Conclusion   231
    Recommended further reading   232
    References   233

Index   234

ABOUT THE CONTRIBUTORS

Sine Agergaard is a social anthropologist and an associate professor at Aarhus University. Her research focuses on migration issues within sport and is published in a wide range of peer-reviewed journals. She has contributed to and edited several books, including: *Women, Soccer and Transnational Migration* (Routledge, 2014). Agergaard sits on the editorial board of *International Review for the Sociology of Sports* and *SportsWorld: The Journal of Global Sport*. She is a co-founder and manager of the International Network for Research in Sport and Migration Issues.

Wladimir Andreff, Professor Emeritus at the University Paris 1 Panthéon Sorbonne, Honorary President of the International Association of Sports Economists and the European Sports Economics Association, Honorary Member of the European Association for Comparative Economic Studies, former President of the French Economic Association (2007–08), President of the Scientific Council at the Observatory of the sports economy, French Minister for Sports, sits on 12 editorial boards and acts as a reviewer for 30 other economic journals, and has achieved 44 missions for international bodies (UNDP, UNESCO, UNIDO, ILO, EU programmes, Council of Europe) and foreign governments. His scientific publications cover international economics, economics of transition and sports economics (403 articles, 29 books). His last books in the latter area are: *Disequilibrium Sports Economics: Competitive Imbalance and Budget Constraints* (ed.) (Edward Elgar, 2015) and *Mondialisation économique du sport. Manuel de référence en Economie du sport* (De Boeck, 2012).

Maureen Benson-Rea is a Senior Lecturer in the Department of Management and International Business at The University of Auckland Business School, New Zealand. With an undergraduate degree in European Studies, an MBA and a PhD in Marketing and International Business, Maureen has held academic positions in the UK as well as several international policy roles with a major UK business organisation. She has published extensively in the areas of international business, strategy and marketing. Her work has appeared in *Sport Management Review*, *European Management Journal*, *Industrial Marketing Management*, *Public Administration*, *Journal of Business Research* and *Multinational Business Review*, among others.

Cheri L. Bradish is the Loretta Rogers Research Chair in Sport Marketing with the Ted Rogers School of Management at Ryerson University. A sport marketing professional, her area of research interest is with regard to sport marketing and sponsorship, and sport and social impact, including broader global sport for development concerns. She has further developed a special related focus examining the management and marketing of the Olympic Games, including ambush marketing-related issues. Among a number of conference proceedings and publications, her research has appeared in the *Journal of Sport Management*, the *International Journal of Sport Management and Marketing*, the *Sport Management Review* and the *Sport Marketing Quarterly*. Cheri also has significant experience in the sport industry, including work with the Florida Sports Foundation, Nike Canada Inc., Florida State University Department of Athletics (NCAA), Vancouver Grizzlies (NBA), and most recently with the Vancouver Organizing Committee for the 2010 Olympic and Paralympic Games (VANOC). She has been acknowledged for her teaching, receiving the 2013 Brock University Faculty Award for Excellence in Teaching; and in 2011 was chosen as the Canadian Olympic Committee's representative to attend the International Olympic Academy (IOA) Session for Educators of Higher Institutes of Physical Education in Ancient Olympia, Greece.

Koen Breedveld is managing director of the Mulier Institute and professor in sport-sociology at Radboud University. As such he has published widely on the issue of sport participation, sport policies, on trends and developments in sports and on their relationship with broader social and cultural changes. Koen Breedveld has published numerous books and scientific articles, including the book *Running across Europe* with Jeroen Scheerder as co-editor. In addition he is the (co-) author of a great deal of policy reports on sports, for the Dutch government as well as for the European Commission. He is the present coordinator of the European Sociological Association's *Research Network for Sport & Society,* and was, in 2010, with Jeroen Scheerder and Remco Hoekman, the initiator of *Measure*, the European network on sport-participation research.

Nicholas Burton is an Assistant Professor with the Department of Sport Management at Brock University. His research focuses on the strategic and managerial implications of international sport marketing, with a specific interest in ambush marketing, sponsorship relations, athlete branding, and entrepreneurship. Most recently, his research has examined consumer behaviour and football fan motivation, as well as media representation of ambush marketing and post-legislative interventionism in sponsorship management. Nick's work has been published and covered widely across academic and professional media, including *Thunderbird International Business Review*, the *Journal of Sponsorship*, *The Economist*, the *Financial Times,* and the *Wall Street Journal*.

Simon Chadwick is 'Class of 92' Professor of Sports Enterprise in the Centre for Sports Business at Salford University, UK, and Director of Research at the Josoor Institute, part of Qatar's Supreme Committee for Delivery and Legacy, the body charged with organising the 2022 FIFA World Cup. Simon's research and teaching interests lie in the areas of sponsorship, sport marketing and commercial strategy in sport. Having previously worked at the Universities of London, where he was the founding Director of the Birkbeck Sport Business Centre, and the University of Leeds, where he was Programme Director for the MA in Advertising and Marketing, Simon is the founding Editor of *Sport, Business and Management: An International Journal* and a former Editor of the *International Journal of Sports Marketing and Sponsorship*. He also recently created and edits the highly regarded academic website *The Scorecard*.

Larissa Davies is a Reader in Sport Management at the Sport Industry Research Centre, Sheffield Hallam University. She has over 15 years' experience teaching and researching in the discipline areas of sport management and geography. Larissa has a PhD in the field of sports economics and specialises in the area of sport, events and urban regeneration. Her research interests include: the role of sport in economic development and regeneration; the economic and social impact and legacy of sport and events; and the tangible and intangible impact of sports stadia. She has published widely around these themes in various international journals including: *European Sport Management Quarterly*; *Sport Management Review*; *Leisure Studies*; *International Journal of Event and Festival Management*; *International Journal of Sports Marketing and Sponsorship*; *Sport in Society* and *Managing Sport and Leisure*. Larissa is currently working on research relating to measuring and valuing the social impact of sport.

Mathieu Djaballah, PhD, is an Associate Professor at the Department of Sport Science, University Paris-Saclay, where he is also the co-coordinator of the Master's degree in Sport Management. He is affiliated with the research team *Complexity, Innovation, and Sport Activities* (CIAMS). His research focuses on the economic, social and environmental impacts of sport events as well as corporate social responsibility in sports.

Thorsten Dum is Lecturer at the Duale Hochschule Baden-Württemberg (DHBW) in Mannheim and Heilbronn (Cooperative State University Baden-Wuerttemberg) and specialises in marketing and service marketing, especially communication, sports marketing and sports management. As a graduate from the German Sport University Cologne (DSHS Köln), his research interest specifically is sports management (with a focus on sports sponsorship) and organisation, as well as knowledge management. Thorsten has presented and participated at several international and national conferences and published research articles and papers in his area of expertise. He has also many years of experience as a project- and sponsoring manager in professional service firms within the event and sports marketing business.

Arnout Geeraert is Post-Doctoral Fellow at Leuven International and European Studies (LINES), University of Leuven, Belgium. He develops the Sports Governance Observer for Play the Game/Danish Institute for Sports Studies. His current work explores the role of the European Union in international sport through different theoretical lenses and looks into elements of good governance in sport organisations in general. He is the author of *The EU in International Sports Governance* (Palgrave, 2016).

Anna Gerke has obtained her PhD from the faculty of sport sciences at the University of Paris-Sud. Her work analysed the influence of interorganisational linkages and behaviour on innovation in sport industry clusters. Today, she is Assistant Professor at Audencia Nantes School of Management at the Parisian campus. She teaches courses in sport management and marketing and manages the specialised Master's programme in the management of sport organisations. Anna's research interest are cluster theory, interorganisational linkages and behaviour, strategy, innovation and the sport system. She has published in peer-reviewed journals including *Sport Management Review, European Sport Management Quarterly* and *Multinational Business Review.* Anna is a regular attendee of international conferences such as EURAM, EASM, NAASM and WASM. In 2015 she was nominated Programme Chair for the SIG Managing Sport at the EURAM conference.

Manuel Herter, MSc, is a Research Assistant at the Department of Sport Economics and Sport Management, German Sport University Cologne, where he also completed his Master's degree in Sport Management. His Master's thesis was on professional football in Germany.

Klaus Nielsen is Professor of Institutional Economics at the Department of Management, Birkbeck, University of London, where he is a member of Birkbeck Sport Business Centre. He teaches research methods, innovation, business in the European Union and economics of sport. His current research areas include varieties of capitalism, innovation, social capital, elite sports and the economics of sports. He has coordinated several research projects about Danish elite sports, sports participation and economic aspects of sport. His work has been published in several books and in journals such as *International Studies of Management and Organization, Journal of Economic Issues* and *European Sport Management Quarterly.*

Johannes Orlowski, MSc, is a Lecturer and Research Associate at the Department of Sport Economics and Sport Management, German Sport University Cologne. His predominant field of research is the economics of sports participation. Further, Johannes is involved in a research project investigating labour market conditions and drivers of labour migration amongst elite sport coaches. He is currently working on his PhD which is related to the monetisation of intangible benefits associated with active and passive sports participation. He is a member of the European Sport Economics Association (ESEA) as well as the North American Association of Sport Economists (NAASE). His work has been published in journals such as *Voluntas: International Journal of Voluntary and Nonprofit Organizations* and *Journal of Behavioral and Experimental Economics.*

Jan Pieper is a Professor of Business Administration at the International University Bad Honnef, Campus Berlin, Germany. Jan holds a Master's degree in Business Administration from the University of Greifswald, Germany, and a PhD in Management and Economics from the University of Zurich, Switzerland. His research interests lie in strategic management issues, which he empirically and theoretically explores in contexts of professional sports. He has published in *Schmalenbach Business Review* and presented papers at multiple international conferences.

Bastian Popp is Senior Research Fellow Sports Business and Marketing at Carnegie Faculty, Leeds Beckett University, UK. Moreover, he is Visiting Senior Lecturer at the University of Bayreuth, Germany, where he contributes to an MBA programme in Sport Management. He is a member of the European Association for Sport Management (EASM). His primary areas of research are innovative media and consumer behaviour, value co-creation and service-dominant logic, brand management, identification, loyalty, quality management and fan behaviour. Together with Herbert Woratschek and Chris Horbel (2014) he developed the sport value framework which integrates alternative models of value creation into traditional sport management approaches. His work has been published in journals such as *European Sport Management Quarterly*, *Sport Management Review*, *International Journal of Sport Marketing and Sponsorship* and *Journal of Strategic Marketing*.

Jeroen Scheerder, PhD, is Associate Professor in the Department of Kinesiology and head of the Policy in Sports and Physical Activity Research Group at the University of Leuven, Belgium. His research focus is on sport governance and sport participation. So far, he has (co-)supervised ten PhD projects in the fields of sport governance, sport sociology and sport marketing. He has also (co-)authored more than 60 papers in peer reviewed international journals and books. Between 2005 and 2007 he was a guest professor of sport sociology at the Faculty of Political and Social Sciences at the Ghent University, and in 2010 he co-founded MEASURE, which is a European research network on sport participation and sport governance. Since 2014 he has been the president of the *European Association for Sociology of Sport* (EASS).

Harry Arne Solberg is Professor of Sport Management/Sports Economics at Trondheim Business School at the Norwegian University of Science and Technology (NTNU), and he also holds a 20 per cent position at Molde University College. His research interests have covered economic impacts from sport and sport activities, including sporting events, sport and the media and team sport economics. He has published the book *The Economics of Sport Broadcasting* together with professor Chris Gratton, and also more than 50 articles in scientific journals and books.

Rasmus K. Storm, PhD, holds a position as head of research at the Danish Institute for Sports Studies. Moreover, he is Adjunct Associate Professor (10%) at Trondheim Business School. He has managed several research projects on Danish elite sport, edited and co-edited four books on sport, and has published in a variety of international sport science and sport management journals such as *European Sport Management Quarterly*, *International Journal of Sport Management and Marketing*, and *Soccer & Society*. He is regularly interviewed in the Danish media, and gives a large number of public lectures. Furthermore, he writes regularly in Danish newspapers.

Ulrik Wagner, PhD, is an Associate Professor at the Department of Marketing and Management, University of Southern Denmark, where he is also coordinating the BA programme in Sport and Event Management offered at the Slagelse Campus. Ulrik is affiliated with the research team *Management of People*, and he is a member of the European Association for Sport Management (EASM). He has been working with research on organisational changes related to international anti-doping efforts and sport scandals, and he is currently involved in several projects that focus on sponsorships from an organisational sociology and critical management perspective. His work has been published in journals such as *European Sport Management Quarterly*, *Sport Management Review*, *International Review for the Sociology of Sport*, *International Journal of Sport Communication* and *International Journal of Drug Policy*.

Pamela Wicker is a Senior Lecturer and Researcher at the Department of Sport Economics and Sport Management, German Sport University Cologne, where she obtained her PhD in 2009 and her Habilitation in 2014. Her main research interests include sport economics (e.g., economics of sport consumer behaviour, league and labour market economics, health economics, economics of physical activity), sport finance (e.g., financing non-profit sport clubs, player and coaching salaries; CVM research), and sport management (e.g., sport club research, organisational capacity and resources). Pamela is Associate Editor and Social Media Editor of *Sport Management Review* and a member of the Editorial Board of another five scientific journals (*Journal of Sport Management*, *European Sport Management Quarterly*, *International Journal of Sport Finance*, *Managing Sport and Leisure*, and *Journal of Sport & Tourism*).

Herbert Woratschek is Professor and Head of Department in Service Management at the University of Bayreuth where he is also responsible for BA, MA and MBA programmes in Sport Management. Herbert was extraordinary professor at the University of Trondheim, Norway, and visiting professor at the University of Calgary, Canada, La Trobe University, Melbourne, Australia and at the University of Auckland, New Zealand. He was also Vice-President of the European Association for Sport Management from 2009 to 2015. His main areas of research include the service–profit chain in various contexts, service-dominant logic, service quality, and sport management. Together with Chris Horbel and Bastian Popp (2014) he developed the sport value framework which integrates alternative models of value creation into traditional sport management approaches. His work has been published in several journals including *Journal of Service Research*, *European Sport Management Quarterly*, *Sport Management Review*, *Journal of Strategic Marketing*, *Marketing Theory* and *Journal of Relationship Marketing*.

MADE IN
EUROPE

ISBN-13: 978-1-473-94805-1

9 781473 948051

SECTION A

THE NEW
SPORT
ENVIRONMENT

WHEN SPORT MEETS BUSINESS: A BRIEF INTRODUCTION

RASMUS K. STORM, ULRIK WAGNER AND KLAUS NIELSEN

The effects of commercialization

What happens when sport meets business? This is the central question in this book. One answer is that sport becomes commercialized. During the last decades sport has undergone momentous change. One of the most in-depth processes of radical and rapid societal reshuffling has been the process of globalization. Increasing international trade and investments, more open national economies, new communication technologies and increasing mobility of labour and citizens have together been driving a process of commercialization of sport (Horne, 2006).

Commercialization has supplemented existing activities and added new activities that did not exist before. In many respects, commercialization has assisted mass sports in a positive way. One example is the development of the fitness sector. Another is the new ways of motivating people to exercise by providing specialized fitness or running apps for smart phones or the development of equipment or clothes designed for movement. Commercialization has also given elite sport a central position as an entertainment product by disseminating athlete performances through increasingly diversified media.

Sport has become an important economic sector in itself with increasing revenues and high growth potential. This has prompted the European Commission to engage researchers and experts in a joint effort to develop a robust way of measuring sport's contribution to national Gross Domestic Product in the EU member states. The provision of improved data of sport's economic impact may foster new forms of commercialization and shape new growth strategies and development patterns (European Commission, 2013).

However, the impact of the meeting between sport and business is not always positive. Commercialization of sport does not only benefit society, athletes, fans and mass participants. The impact of making sport a business may hamper qualities ascribed to sport, such as emotional attachment, interpersonal relations or personal expression and wellbeing. The following examples illustrate the ongoing in-depth transformation of European club-based sport, which has not only positive consequences, but also produces new problems:

- Revenues in European professional football grow at a high rate, supported by valuable television rights deals and capital injections by investors, often from outside Europe. However, players' salaries and transfer fees increase even more and very few professional clubs are managed in order to provide profits or maintain economic balance (Storm & Nielsen, 2015).
- Meanwhile, athletes in some Olympic sports are struggling to maintain momentum in a global arms race for medals (De Bosscher, Shibli, Westerbeek, & Van Bottenburg, 2015). Many athletes train and perform as professional athletes but have financial conditions as amateurs (Wicker, Breuer, & von Hanau, 2012).
- The financial crisis from 2009 has urged some firms to evaluate their use of sponsorships, but simultaneously athletes, clubs and national federations have become even more dependent on external corporate funding (Wagner & Nissen, 2015).
- The claimed positive impacts of hosting major sport events (such as city branding, catalyzing economic growth, or stimulating sport-for-all initiatives) are used politically to legitimize and intensify the focus on and financial support for events and bidding for events, even though there is only limited evidence regarding the benefits (Storm & Asserhøj, 2015; Zimbalist, 2015).
- The expansion of social media provides an opportunity not only for new businesses, but also a forum for resistance to the commodification by offering an alternative path for organizing sport.

These developments, their benefits and negative side-effects, are some of the themes that this book aims to analyze, mainly in the context of teaching programmes specifically targeting future scholars and employees of European business enterprises in the field of sport, as well as voluntary organizations dealing with sports-related business enterprises.

A focus on Europe

The process of commercialization has been shaped in different ways depending on context. In Europe, sport has strong roots in civil society. It has traditionally taken place predominantly in voluntary organizations. This provides a barrier for rampant commercialization. However, even in Europe sport has been commercialized to such a degree that it is now a billion dollar industry with a large impact on national economies, culture and patterns of mass participation.

When Sport Meets Business takes a European approach in dealing with the identified development processes and problems. The book has its focus on the specificities of the European context in order to examine how business and sport comes together here. Although Europe is by no means a homogeneous unit, most countries in Europe have common features that distinguish them from North America, Japan, the BRICs (Brazil, Russia, India and China), and other countries. This is linked to specific features of sport and business in the European institutional and cultural context: the predominance of voluntary sports clubs and associations, open professional leagues, the high level of popular sport participation, high but relatively stagnating incomes, and a high level of education and skills based in a fairly regulated capitalist system. All these specificities affect how sport and business work together compared to other parts of the world.

Most of the phenomena covered in this book are global and not only of relevance for the relation between sport and business in the European context. However, some phenomena of sport and business have specific European characteristics, and in order to distinguish these characteristics the book contrasts Europe with other contexts, for example the US. For instance, European football has its own characteristics, such as the open league system, which makes it extremely difficult for other than a few top clubs to profit from its activities. A comparison with non-European nations reveals similarities and differences regarding organization, culture and tradition, which subsequently affect the relation between sport and business.

The target groups

The book is first and foremost meant for students, but is not limited to students as a target group. The content and structure as well as the presentational style are meant to support the learning experience of students. The chapters are designed for application in student courses, e.g. undergraduate and postgraduate programmes in sport marketing, sport management, sport economics or the sociology of sport.

The book covers the most central themes about the relationship between sport and business. Its focus is topical rather than disciplinary. It covers various perspectives relevant for understanding the interactive, transformative, self-reinforcing and conflictual relationship between sport and business.

Its primary target group is university students. However, we believe that it will prove useful for practitioners and researchers as well. Each chapter springs from the author's most recent research and is directly related to contemporary developments and discussions within the respective topics.

For practitioners working in the areas covered by the chapters, or students following courses on sport and business, the book can thus be used for gaining new insights and understandings about the multiple contemporary aspects of the relation between sport and business. It is also useful for academics and researchers who seek updated reviews and want to explore new (sub)fields of potential interest.

In order to clarify and make the book accessible for multiple audiences, the chapters all use case material to exemplify the presented issues in detail in practical contexts. Further, recommendations for further reading are added at the end of each chapter.

Book structure and content

The book is structured in four sections, each covering topics related to the theme headlines and the book's overall subject: The New Sport Environment; Sport Marketing and Media; Sport and Finance; and Sporting Events.

It also takes a cross disciplinary approach. The authors cover a broad range of social science disciplines, such as economics, management, marketing, sociology and cultural studies. Most chapters apply a common template: after the introduction and a section on historical and recent development there follows a section on contemporary and future challenges, capabilities and critiques. Thereafter are the main case(s), the conclusion and recommendations for further reading.

Section A: The New Sport Environment

The first section includes chapters that analyze the consequences of the increasing commercialization of European sport.

The opening chapter, written by Anna Gerke and Maureen Benson-Rea, deals with the expansion of the sports goods industry. It introduces the global sport goods industry as an empirical field in sport management research, and stresses the importance of the industry using recent research findings and examples of sport goods companies in Europe. It then identifies the main drivers of growth in the sport goods industry and outlines the future challenges for European sports goods firms in an increasingly globalized market. The case study illustrates how a French sport equipment manufacturer has dealt with the challenges of this new environment.

The second chapter, by Sine Agergaard, takes a critical look at globalization and more particularly labour migration. The focus is on the effects on national and local talent development. Recent migration trends create new challenges as well as new opportunities for sport governing bodies at both local and national levels. The chapter also discusses the moral and political implications of cases in which local and national sport policies for talent development appear to be out of sync with broader globalization and migration processes.

The third chapter, written by Johannes Orlowski, Manuel Herter and Pamela Wicker, concerns the impact of commercialization – and the additional commodification it entails – on the lives of athletes. It introduces key terms, such as 'commodification', 'commercialization', 'brand endorsement' etc. and outlines how these affect elite athletes in a historical perspective. A comparison of commercialization and commodification of sports and athletes' lives in Europe and the US follows in order to identify what characterizes the specific European context. Further, the chapter reviews recent research on the commercialization and commodification of sport in general and athletes' lives in particular. The main case study illustrates both the advantages and disadvantages of becoming an 'elite sport commodity' as far as athletes' careers and personal lives are concerned.

In the final chapter in this section, Koen Breedveld and Jeroen Scheerder describe how running has become one of Europe's most popular sports, with a focus on the role of running events and the running industry in this process. The chapter provides statistics for 11 EU-countries and the EU as a whole, with regard to the size and growth of the running market, in terms of number of participants, expenditures, and number of running events. It analyzes the running market in terms of motives and preferences of runners, the rise in women running, and the predomination of individuals with higher education, as well as the apparent preference of runners not to join athletics clubs. In addition, the authors discuss the implications of informal and commercial running for social capital, and the role running plays in sport-for-all-policies.

Section B: Sport Marketing and Media

In the second section of the book the focus shifts from the general trends of commercialization to the role of media and marketing with regard to sport.

The first chapter, by Thorsten Dum and Ulrik Wagner, deals with sport and its relation to sponsorship. It analyzes the commercial growth of sponsorship and argues that the range of sponsorship deals has grown steadily in recent years. More and more individuals, groups of individuals, and organizations such as associations and federations or organizers of events, offer potential organizations – and most notably commercial corporations – a collaboration in form of sponsorship requests and proposals. The increased sponsorship portfolio has intensified the competition among sponsored entities and led to a progressive over-commercialization and professionalization of the business of sponsorship. The chapter provides examples of sponsorships that focus on human resource management and corporate social responsibility, in addition to examples of the contemporary use of sponsorships which highlight some of the challenges and capabilities involved.

The second chapter in this section, written by Harry Arne Solberg, analyzes the role of media rights in European club football with special attention given to the five leagues that are the biggest in the world measured by revenue. The relevance of the subject is testimony to the fact that media rights have become the biggest source of revenue for those at the top of the financial ladder in European soccer. Besides outlining the revenues stemming from the media rights, the chapter focuses on the forces behind the growth in media rights fees, both in domestic and external markets. It also analyzes the factors that influence distribution of revenue, both between the clubs within the same leagues and between the leagues in different nations.

The third chapter, by Simon Chadwick, Nicholas Burton and Cheri Bradish, argues that few industries or marketing communications activities mark out sport as a unique and specialized business as effectively as sponsorship does. However, in line with the development of sponsorship as a strategic sport marketing tool, challenges to official sponsorships in the form of ambush marketing have emerged too, offering brands the opportunity to go above and beyond the legal and contractual rights of official partnerships in an effort to leverage against the ever-increasing value of sport in marketing. This has presented sponsors, commercial rights holders, event organizers and consumers alike with important challenges. The chapter outlines the history and development of ambush marketing and provides examples of its strategies and counterstrategies, while also discussing future directions and implications for ambush marketing and sport sponsorship.

The fourth chapter, by Bastian Popp and Herbert Woratschek, focuses on social media and sport. It outlines the rise of social media and other recent developments and offers a typology of social media activities in relation to sport. Furthermore, it highlights the multifaceted influence of social media on the sports business, outlining its role as a venue for positive sport-related interaction and co-creation where sports brands can improve their value in a collaborative process involving the sport property, its customers, fans and potential consumers, as well as the operator of the social network site and other actors. However, the chapter also addresses possible negative outcomes including the loss of company control, anti-brand activism, and negative effects on sponsorships. In order to illustrate how social media can be used in anti-brand activism, two European cases are provided. The implications for sport brands of anti-brand communities illustrate some of the less well-known implications of the process 'when sport meets business'.

The final chapter in this section, by Mathieu Djaballah, analyzes the trend towards corporate social responsibility (CSR) practices in sport since the beginning of the last decade. It examines the specificities of CSR in sport and gives a description of general CSR issues and debates. It also analyzes a case of a national sport organization, which envisions the range of CSR activities as well as the different rationales behind these activities. As a conclusion, the chapter offers a critical perspective on CSR practices, which can sometimes be used merely as instruments to pursue brand image or reputation objectives, without achieving genuine social benefits. In addition, the ambiguity of these practices is highlighted.

Section C: Sport and Finance

The third section of the book includes three chapters that relate to the economics of sport.

The first chapter of this section, written by Klaus Nielsen and Rasmus K. Storm, discusses the peculiar business of European professional team sports. The characteristics of the specific European context of professional football are outlined by means of a comparison with the North American major leagues. Whereas profit maximization prevails in North America, European football is often seen as characterized by win maximization with a break-even constraint. The chapter challenges this view by identifying the effects of soft budget constraints in the European context, explaining why European football clubs operate with persistent losses but survive anyway. It also identifies the institutional framework of European leagues and the social and emotional attachments to teams as contributing reasons for the prevalence of soft budget constraints in the European context.

The second chapter in this section, written by Jan Pieper, takes its departure in the contemporary discussion of financial fair play in European professional football. European professional football is characterized by financial problems and growing debts among the clubs. This has prompted UEFA,[1] to take regulatory action in order to push the clubs towards balancing their books. To be admitted to the UEFA club competitions (Champions League and Europa League) each club now has to meet not only a series of defined sporting, infrastructural, personnel and legal standards, but also financial quality standards as well. The chapter argues that the FFP regulations in general restore the incentives for 'good club management' in an industry that has degenerated into a 'zombie race' with an ever-increasing number of technically bank-rupt participants. Thus, FFP seems to fulfil its task even though the full effects of its implementation are still not clear.

In the final chapter in this section, Arnout Geerart discusses whether commercialization of sport explains the increasing problems related to corruption and match fixing in international sport. The chapter briefly outlines the depth and impact of these phenomena that have resulted in a legitimacy crisis. The author argues that in order to counteract the problems the institutional design of international sport federations needs to change. By drawing on a number of empirical examples, he shows how corruption, concentration of power and lack of effective-ness constitute a breeding ground for threats to the integrity of sport. By introducing a principal–agent model, he analyzes how the governance of sport in a range of international sport federations deals with the 'power of money', and outlines proposals as to how a sounder development guided by principles of good governance can be met.

Section D: Sporting Events

The final section of the book includes two chapters about the economic and other effects of (mega) sporting events.

In the first chapter, Wladimir Andreff describes how international sporting events are nor-mally hit by 'a winner's curse'. Legacies stemming from (especially mega) sporting events are a potential that does not necessarily materialize in the intended fashion. In fact, the examples of cost overruns in mega events are overwhelming, according to Andreff. One of the central problems is that it is easy to convince local politicians and decision makers that it is advanta-geous for their country/city to host international mega sports events. Usually ex ante studies of the economic and social impacts exhibit a net benefit. However, it is nearly impossible to succeed in hosting a mega sporting event at the expected costs and benefits. The underlying cause of this paradox lies in the process of awarding such events by following an auction-like procedure, which then triggers a winner's curse. Through case studies of Summer and Winter Olympics, the chapter exemplifies these problems and touches upon how to counteract this winner's curse. It also includes recommendations for how cities or nations can become better at managing the hosting of international sports events.

In the last chapter of the book, Larissa Davies elaborates on some aspects of the issues presented in the previous chapter. Her focus is on the urban legacies of international sports events. She utilizes examples from various European cities to examine the potential of lega-cies, and reflects in more depth on the concept of event legacy and its relation to sustainable urban development in order to define and examine the success factors for creating positive urban legacies from sports events at both micro and macro levels. She also provides historical evidence from a range of Olympic cities with a focus on the London 2012 Olympics, and examines the importance of legacy planning in creating an urban legacy development, arguing that commercially viable, business-oriented post-event venues are critical to sustain positive urban legacies. The importance of monitoring and evaluating legacies for maximizing the prospects of longer-term urban change is also stressed.

Note

1   Union of European Football Associations.

References

De Bosscher, V., Shibli, S., Westerbeek, H., & Van Bottenburg, M. (2015). *Successful Elite Sport Policies: An International Comparison of the Sports Policy Factors Leading to International Sporting Success (SPLISS 2.0) in 15 Nations*. Maidenhead: Meyer and Meyer Sports.

European Commission (2013). *Sport Satellite Accounts: A European Project*. New Results. Brussels: European Commission.

Horne, J. (2006). *Sport in Consumer Culture*. New York: Palgrave Macmillan.

Preuss, H. (2015). A framework for identifying the legacies of a mega sport event. *Leisure Studies*, (January), 1–23. http://doi.org/10.1080/02614367.2014.994552

Storm, R. K., & Asserhøj, T. L. (2015). The Question of the trickle-down effect in Danish Sport: Can a relationship between elite sport success and mass participation be identified? In R. Bailey & M. Talbot (Eds), *Elite Sport and Sport-for-All* (pp. 41–56). London: Routledge.

Storm, R. K., & Nielsen, K. (2015). Soft Budget Constraints in European and US leagues – similarities and differences. In W. Andreff (Ed.), *Disequilibrium Sport Economics: Competitive Imbalance and Budget Constraints* (pp. 151–171). Cheltenham: Edward Elgar.

Wagner, U., & Nissen, R. (2015). Enacted ambiguity and risk perceptions: making sense of national elite sport sponsorships. *Sport in Society*, *18*(10), 1179–1198. http://doi.org/10.1080/17430437.2015.1024234

Wicker, P., Breuer, C., & von Hanau, T. (2012). Is it profitable to represent the country? Evidence on the sport-related income of funded top-level athletes in Germany. *Managing Leisure*, *17*(2–3), 221–238. http://doi.org/10.1080/13606719.2012.674396

Zimbalist, A. (2015). *Circus Maximus*. Washington, DC: The Brookings Institution.

THE EXPANSION OF THE SPORT GOODS INDUSTRY

ANNA GERKE AND MAUREEN BENSON-REA

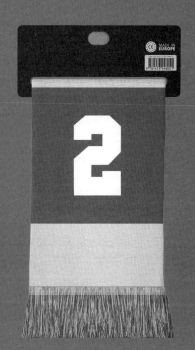

Introduction

The importance of sport in the European countries has increased significantly over the last decade. Sport has become more relevant economically and socially for various reasons. Social aspects include sport participation, sport for health and economic activities directly or indirectly related to sport (Breedveld et al., 2013; Dolles & Söderman, 2011). European sport policy initiatives such as the *White Paper on Sport* (Commission of the European Communities, 2007) or the *Study on the Contribution of Sport to Economic Growth and Employment in the European Union* (SportsEconAustria, 2012) show an increasing interest in sport from a political perspective.

This chapter focuses on one major economic aspect of sport – the sport goods industry. It consists of three sections, a case study and conclusions. The first section gives definitions for sport, sport industry and sport goods industry. The chapter then follows the expansion of the sport goods industry in Europe over the last five years (based on MarketLine (2015a) industry reports). This expansion is analysed by comparing the market value of the sport goods industry within Europe and the US. We look at the value of trade in the European sport goods industry and also compare the sport goods industry with other sport industry segments. We then discuss the major drivers of growth in the European sport goods industry and different firm-level strategic approaches. The third section discusses contemporary and future critiques. Our case study explores the expansion of a large French sport goods retailer and manufacturer. We close with reflections on the case.

Historical and recent developments

Definitions

In its revised 'European Sports Charter', the Council of Europe (2001, p. 3) defines sport as 'all forms of physical activity which, through casual or organised participation, aim at expressing or improving physical fitness and mental well-being, forming social relationships or obtaining results in competition at all levels'. This definition includes physical activities for competitive, recreational or convalescence purposes. Furthermore it includes organised and informal forms of sport at an individual or group level. Although this definition dates back more than a decade, it remains valid and is commonly-used. We build on this to define the sport industry and more specifically the sport goods industry.

National statistical offices typically define industries and sectors using standardised classifications and categories according to their related economic activities. In the European Union (EU) the NACE standard is used (*Nomenclature statistique des activités économiques dans la Communauté européenne*, the statistical classification of economic activities in the European Community). However, the only NACE category covering sport is 'operation of sports facilities' (NACE 92.6) and hence this statistical definition covers only a small part of the sport industry, and ignores entirely the sport goods industry. The NACE definition should be extended twofold. First, the definition of sport industry should include industries that produce goods or services necessary to perform sport (e.g., sport shoes, rackets, dance lessons). Second, the term sport industry should include all industries for which sport is an important input or precondition for the production of their goods and services (e.g., television broadcasting, hotels for people doing sport) (SportsEconAustria, 2012). The former definition includes the focus of this chapter – the sport goods industry – and is defined in more detail in the next paragraph. Figure 2.1 illustrates the different aspects of defining the sport industry.

Consumer expenditure		
Goods and services conditional on doing sport		
Veterinarian	Dietary supplements	Sport bets
Health services	Hotels, restaurants (sport tourism)	TV broadcasts
Doing sport (according to the statistical definition)		
Stadiums	Swimming pools	Professional sports
Goods and services necessary to do sport		
Racing horses	Sport shoes and clothes	Sport weapons
School education	Sport cars, motorbikes	Fitness centres
Watches, clocks	Sailing equipment	Dancing schools

Figure 2.1   Definitions of sport industry © European Union, 1995–2016

Source: SportsEconAustria, 2012

We use the MarketLine industry reports (2015a) to illustrate the expansion of the sport goods industry in Europe[1] over the years 2010–2014, using the example of sport equipment (excluding sport apparel and shoes). The definition for sport equipment used in these market reports includes ball sports, adventure sports, fitness, golf, racket sports, winter sports and other sports. While this definition is only partly congruent with the United Nations' definition (UN Statistics Division, 2015), it covers a broad range of sport goods and is therefore useful here (SportsEconAustria, 2012). Market values cited are based on retail sales prices in the respective countries and currency conversions have been calculated using constant annual average 2014 exchange rates.

The European sport equipment market

This market is valued at €28,873 million with an annual increase of 4.2% in 2014. Ball sport equipment represents the largest segment accounting for 24% of the total market volume, with the UK as the largest market (21%). Sport management research identifies football in England as an important case to illustrate the increasing significance of sport in economic and social terms. Chadwick (2009) shows how participation in the game of football increased in England during the industrial revolution as people's leisure time increased.

The European sport equipment market experienced a steady compound annual growth rate (CAGR) of 1.7% between 2010 and 2014. However, the expansion of the industry in Europe differs from country to country and from sector to sector. The UK market, for example, grew by 5.6% per year while Germany recorded only 1.1% growth. Similar growth in the European sport equipment market value is forecast for the years 2014–2019, with a CAGR of 1.8% (MarketLine, 2015a). Table 2.1 shows the major European sport equipment segments and their market shares. After ball sport equipment, fitness is the second strongest sport equipment segment with a 20% market share. Adventure sport equipment comes third in Europe but is valued as the largest sport equipment industry segment globally. That is due to the strong presence of adventure sport equipment in the US where it is the largest segment (39% of the total US market value).

Table 2.1 European sport goods market shares per type of sport in € million, 2014

Category	2014	%
Ball sports equipment	6,979	24
Fitness equipment	5,765	20
Adventure sports equipment	5,469	19
Winter sports equipment	4,266	15
Golf equipment	3,769	13
Racket sports equipment	2,625	9
Total	**28,873**	**100**

Source: MarketLine, 2015a

Table 2.2 shows country comparisons of sport equipment market values in Europe. France and Germany closely follow the UK in market size though there is a significant gap between these three main markets and the rest, with Italy in fourth place (9%) and Spain in fifth place (6%). These five countries represent over 70% of the European market, even as much as 87% when compared on a per capita basis (SportsEconAustria, 2012; Worldbank, 2015). A comparison of the European market with the US shows that the European sport equipment market values are almost as much as those in the US, which accounted for €29,359 million in 2014 (MarketLine, 2015b).

Table 2.2   European sport goods market shared per country in € million, 2014

Geography	2014	%	per capita	%
United Kingdom	6,167	21	94	27
France	4,923	17	74	21
Germany	4,885	17	60	17
Italy	2,543	9	41	12
Spain	1,654	6	36	10
Rest of Europe	8,700	30	46	13
Total	**28,873**	**100**	**352**	**100**

Source: MarketLine, 2015a

EU trade in the sport goods industry is important. By the early 1990s Europe had a strong position as a trading bloc in the sport goods industry compared with North America and amongst major Asian countries (Andreff, 2006). Export statistics on selected sport goods show that about two-thirds of sport goods exports from European countries stay in Europe but are traded amongst European countries (SportsEconAustria, 2012). The main exporting countries are France and Austria, with Austria exporting more to other European countries, while France exports evenly to EU and non-EU countries (SportsEconAustria, 2012).

Sport goods and other sport industry segments

We compare the sport goods industry with other sport industry segments using the SportsEconAustria (2012) study and the data provided there. The operation of sport facilities and activities related to organised sport (e.g., sport clubs, events, public venues) accounted for €28,160 million in the EU (27 members as at 2012). When including the first extension of the definition – all industries producing goods or services to perform sport – the sport industry market value quadruples to €112,179 million. When including the second extension – all industries for which sport is an important input – the sport goods industry grows by 50% to €173,855 million market value. These figures show the importance of the sport goods industry compared with other sport industry segments. The sport industry segment, comprising sport goods and services to perform sports, is the largest, with sales of

€84,019 million compared with €28,160 million for the operation of sport facilities and activities related to organised sport and €61,676 million for industries using sports for their final product or service as important input (SportsEconAustria, 2012).

Contemporary and future challenges

The EU context for strategy

The global drivers for the growth of an industry are: market drivers, competitive drivers, cost drivers, government drivers and the potential of the industry to globalise (Yip, 1995). The creation of a Single European Market (SEM), which eliminates trade, legal and administrative barriers to the free movement of goods, capital, labour and services among the Member States, has had both a competitive effect and a restructuring effect. The competitive effect led to some downward pressure on prices and costs and increased competition has led to a reorganisation of industrial sectors and individual companies. Further, the SEM created new business opportunities for firms of all sizes, access to other markets within the EU, cross-border foreign direct investment (the share of inflows into each of the 15 members of the EU from other members rose from 53% in 1995 to 78% in 2005) and trade integration – intra-EU trade relative to GDP rose by 30% 1992–2010 (Business Europe, 2010). The international growth of the European sport goods firms has been driven by the competitive dynamics of the European market. The removal of cross-border barriers to building large European businesses in the SEM enabled economies of scale, and made concentration, through acquisition and mergers, a viable strategic option. The effect of EU market integration has been to move strategy from a country-market level to a European and global view. An example is Adidas – a German company that has grown from a family business to becoming not only a European player but also a global player in the sport goods industry. The SEM has stimulated similarities in the strategies of firms, although Europe retains elements of discrete territories (particularly in language and culture). There is no single unified mix of strategies for the EU market but firms have developed strategies which balance complete centralisation across Europe and localisation within each country market. Successful firms deploy Europe-wide objectives with market-by-market adaptation and coordination at a European level.

Growth drivers in the sport goods industry

The industry-level drivers of growth for sport goods are closely related to the general drivers of sport and its rising significance for social reasons, health aspects and economic activity (Breedveld et al., 2013). There are other drivers specific to the sport goods industry such as: innovations in material, function or design; the development of new sport practices; and the democratisation of sports through cheaper production and increased accessibility of sport products and lessons (Desbordes et al., 2004). We now discuss these general and specific drivers and analyse changes in the structure and configuration of actors in the sport goods industry and how these influence growth. Finally the different strategic approaches employed by sport goods firms of different sizes and specialisations are outlined before the third section, Contemporary and Future Critiques.

Social drivers. Social aspects as drivers for sport include: the level of sport participation, the availability of sport infrastructure, good governance of sport organisations, sport to foster social integration and inclusion, sport as a means of education, sport against racism and violence, and sport club participation and volunteering (Breedveld et al., 2013). Of these aspects the general participation level in sport is the most important driver for the sport goods industry because any participation in sport requires sport goods. Sport club participation and sport as a means of education are also drivers of sport goods consumption because these stimulate general participation in sport.

An example of how sport participation stimulates sport goods consumption is the recent growth of participation in lifestyle sports. These are often characterised as new forms of sport such as skateboarding, surfing, wakeboarding, kite- and windsurfing and snowboarding. These sports focus less on the competitive aspects as in traditional sports and replace these with the pursuit of virtuosity, speed, risk, fun and freedom. Lifestyle sports are referred to as alternative, extreme, adventure or action sports (Hennigs & Hallmann, 2014; Kellett & Russell, 2009). With the rapid increase of participation in such sports, sport goods markets have also grown. An ISAF (International Sailing Federation) (2012) report on kitesurfing as a discipline in the Olympic Games reveals that for 60,000 new participants in kitesurfing per year 180,000 kites and 75,000 boards are sold every year. These numbers are forecast to grow 10% annually.

Health drivers. Health is an indirect driver of the sport goods industry. Sport for health also aims at increasing sport participation which in turn stimulates demand for sport goods and services to perform sport. The World Health Organization (2003) confirmed the positive effects of sport and physical activities on health for numerous reasons. Regularly practising appropriate sport and physical activities provides physical, social and mental health benefits to individuals of all ages and genders, and those with disabilities. Sport for health is a cost-effective method for a nation to foster disease prevention and general public health improvements. However, currently an estimated 1.9 million deaths globally are due to physical inactivity and 60% of adults do not pursue enough physical activity to achieve health benefits. Therefore sport infrastructure, equipment and services need to be widely available and affordable and participation in physical activities and sport should be promoted as a human right (World Health Organization, 2003).

Economic drivers. Sport stimulates many direct and indirect economic activities. The sport goods industry itself is an economic activity that results directly from sport activities since sport goods are indispensable to perform most sports. Services directly related to sport such as lessons to learn or improve a particular sport are also sport goods industry drivers. Sport lessons require sport products to be carried out (except for theory aspects) and participants are likely to purchase sport goods after the lesson. There are economic activities indirectly related to sport which correspond to the second extension of the definition of the sport industry, such as television broadcasting based on sport and hotel accommodation provided to athletes or spectators (SportsEconAustria, 2012). Economic activities that are indirectly related to sport have only a minor impact (if any) on the sport goods industry since the realisation of these activities does not require additional sport goods or services. The diffusion and mediatisation of sports might, however, encourage adults and children to play mediatised sports. Few insights are available on the impact of mediatised professional sport on amateur sport participation and more research is required on this topic.

Innovation drivers. Innovation is an important driver of the sport goods industry. To clarify and reinforce this we take a more differentiated look at sport goods. Sport goods can be differentiated into 'trite' sport goods and 'equipment-intensive' sport goods (Andreff, 2008). Trite sport goods can be used for various sport practices such as sportswear or some sport shoes. Equipment-intensive sport goods are quite specific goods to be used in a single sport like cross-country skis or windsurfing boards (Andreff, 2008). The evolution of sport goods, especially in the equipment-intensive sport goods segment, has led to numerous innovations in materials, design and technology. Developments in materials usually allow for higher performance in increasingly extreme conditions in terms of human limits, weather, speed, height and distance (for example, ocean racing technology now permits single-handed Atlantic crossings). Changes in design can lead to new ways of using sport goods and hence to the emergence of new sports (e.g., snowboarding). Developments in technologies can add new or replace extant systems (for example, binding technologies in skis and snowboards). New emerging needs of particular user groups lead to the development of new technologies and systems. Existing technologies are replaced when the new technology fundamentally changes (and improves) the sport good for any user (e.g., safety systems in kitesurfing). Having identified different types of innovation and their impact on existing sport goods it may be argued that innovations in material, design or technology can stimulate additional purchases of sport goods in order to achieve a better performance (material innovation), to participate in a new sport (design innovation) or improve the personal suitability of sport goods or general quality of the product (technology innovation) (Desbordes et al., 2004; Gerke, 2014).

Innovation drives the sport goods industry indirectly by fostering the development of new sport practices. However, socio-cultural and socio-economic factors play an important role in the emergence of new sports. Using the example of lifestyle sports, in many cases new lifestyle sports were adopted initially by younger generations, sometimes in opposition to traditional sports (for example, snowboarding and skiing or kitesurfing and windsurfing). The emergence of a new lifestyle sport is often the result of youthful resistance expressing a rebellion that relates not only to traditional sports but also to the values, beliefs and attitudes associated with those traditional sports. The emergence of new sports not only has an impact on sport goods consumption it also creates playgrounds for social frictions, collective identities and conflicts between generations, genders, ethnic groups and social classes (Heino, 2000; Kellett & Russell, 2009).

Besides the social aspects of the development of new sports there is a spatial dimension. When a new sport emerges which uses the same territory as an existing sport (e.g., ski slopes for snowboarding) that territory and its use need to be redefined (Heino, 2000). This is especially important once a new sport becomes more accessible and hence more widespread. As a new sport ages and gains more participants over time sport-specific cultural capital evolves. This includes norms of how to dress, the language to use, and how to interact during or after the sport (Heino, 2000). A new sport develops into a mass sport when lessons to learn the sport become available and goods to perform the sport become affordable. This democratisation of a new sport to a mass sport is especially relevant for equipment-intensive sports (Desbordes et al., 2004). In conclusion, the democratisation of sports increases the demand for sport goods and can hence be confirmed as a driver of the sport goods industry.

Firm-level strategies

Small and young firms are key to economic growth, employment, poverty reduction and in economic interactions. The export performance of small and medium-sized enterprises (SMEs) is an important measure of economic progress (OECD, 2013). There is no consensus on a definition of SMEs, but they are distinct from multinational company (MNCs) subsidiaries and their size is generally measured by employment numbers – fewer than 250 in the EU (European Commission, 2014). Small firms generally have fewer than 50 employees, with micro-firms having fewer than 10, and medium-sized firms between 50 and 249 employees (OECD, 2013, p. 380). In most OECD countries the majority of exporting is done by firms of 250 employees or more, and in most OECD countries fewer than 10% of firms are exporters, with the smallest accounting for anything between 3% of exports (in Norway) and 17% (in Denmark) (OECD, 2013, p. 36).

Many SMEs begin their internationalisation with export marketing (Root, 1998), followed by gradual, incremental expansion as they commit more resources to international operations (Johanson & Vahlne, 1977). An example is the New Zealand brand Icebreaker that produces technical sportswear based on natural merino fibre. Gradual internationalisation was undertaken by exploring the European market first, followed by the US and China in incremental steps (Lassiter & Heath, 2006). Small firms which gradually internationalise can pursue innovation, an entrepreneurial orientation and commitment (Deakins et al., 2013) to sustain their positions in export markets. More recently, rapidly and early internationalising firms have been identified as international new ventures (Oviatt & McDougall, 1994; Zahra, 2005) or born-globals (Chetty & Campbell-Hunt, 2004; Gabrielsson et al., 2008; Knight & Cavusgil, 2004) that seek to internationalise rapidly from the stage of a start-up.

Regardless of the rate of firm growth, most internationalising SMEs pursue innovation and niche differentiation (Chetty & Campbell-Hunt, 2004), and a differentiation strategy (Tolstoy, 2014) is one of the best predictors of successful export performance (Baldauf et al., 2000; D'Angelo et al., 2013). Many SMEs grow within domestic boundaries, only serving local national niches or becoming acquisition targets when their growth becomes limited or their innovation becomes attractive to a more resource-endowed MNC. Examples from the sport goods industry are Millet – a French backpack manufacturer – that was acquired by Lafuma in 1995 after more than half a century of family business, and Salomon – a French ski manufacturer – that was sold first to Adidas in 1997 and then joined the Amer Sports Group in 2007.

Exporting is the major strategy (D'Angelo et al., 2013) for SMEs to grow, particularly when constrained by a domestic market which is still developing (Boso et al., 2013) or small (Casey & Hamilton, 2014). The hockey equipment specialist OBO is an example of this: since the New Zealand hockey market was too small from the outset, local sales have never exceeded 5% of its sales (Benson-Rea & Shepherd, 2010). Firms with an export market-orientation are often in a better position to 'develop understanding of market players, exploit this knowledge and adapt to existing market demands' (Boso et al., 2013, p. 58). Successful exporting firms, as measured by growth, financial performance, or survival (Abouzeedan & Busler, 2004), depend strongly on product innovation. Product innovation is important in explaining export performance as innovative

SMEs are best able to sustain competitiveness in international markets (D'Angelo et al., 2013). An ability to respond to change in export customer needs and competitor actions is essential and a major determinant of export performance (Boso et al., 2013).

Competition-based strategies (Ohmae, 1986) have been enabled by the liberalisation of EU regulatory frameworks which has accelerated restructuring across industries and borders. Customer-based approaches to EU markets increasingly use relationship marketing (Ohmae, 1986). Firms build relationships with customers through understanding their needs and, consequently, building new European and global brands (e.g., the case of Decathlon). The multi-domestic growth of European firms with distinctive specialisation within their national boundaries meant that these had to be integrated at European level for firms to achieve economies of scope and scale. The transfer of traditional capabilities of European firms across international boundaries was accelerated by the free movement of goods, capital, labour and services in the SEM. Access to more sources of capital and the consequent changes to the European social model of ownership and joint determination have enabled corporate-based acquisition and growth strategies (Ohmae, 1986). Many more mergers and acquisitions, in which European companies have become more ambitious and aggressive, have led to the emergence of new European MNCs (e.g., Amer Sports Group, which is a Finnish headquartered sport goods company including brands like Salomon, Wilson, Atomic, Arc'teryx, Mavic, Suunto, Precor, and Demarini Bic Sports), which increasingly involve companies from different European countries. One of the key strategic options for firms is collaboration in joint ventures and strategic alliances, which lower cost and risk, especially when carried out with well-established and complementary partners. These collaborative arrangements can build into clusters of SMEs (e.g., Sporaltec, which is a cluster dedicated to accelerate innovations in sport-sector companies in the Rhône-Alpes region) or global production networks for large MNCs (e.g., Adidas) (Menzel & Fornahl, 2010).

Contemporary and future critiques

The sport goods industry has benefited from EU enterprise policy which has aimed to build a system of open and competitive markets. This has speeded up adjustment to structural changes, encouraging a favourable environment for entrepreneurial initiatives, more cooperation among firms, better exploitation of innovation and focusing on technology and research and development (R&D). These factors continue to define the challenges and opportunities for European business. In the steadily growing sport goods industry firms that are traditionally very small enterprises or SMEs orient their strategies towards cooperation and collaboration to cope with competition from large corporate groups. In a survey of industry views of Europe's attractiveness as a business location (Ernst & Young, 2010) the top measures respondents identified to stimulate growth were support for SMEs, high-tech industries and innovation. The same survey saw Europe's world-class features as its research and innovation capacity (85%), its emphasis on green business (83%), the diversity and quality of its labour force (81%), and development of world-class business clusters (73%). The sport goods industry and the sport industry overall in Europe have taken initiatives to develop sport clusters as a means to further exploit sport as economic sector (EU4SportsClusters, 2015).

The internet is a key challenge for firm strategy since it 'blurs the notion of geographical boundaries' (OECD, 2000, p. 207). Some argue that the internet 'is destructive of the distinction between domestic and international' (Kobrin, 2001, p. 700) and is 'disrespectful of national borders and renders geography irrelevant' (Grant & Bakhru, 2004, p. 95). To build an effective digital strategy for brands, firms need to align the online and in-store experiences, since consumers take multi-device pathways to purchase (Marketo.com., 2014) across tablets, pc/laptops and smartphones. This has been referred to as omni-channel strategy (Marketo. com., 2014) and is an increasingly important challenge, especially for sport industries that cut across sport participation, events, media, tourism and, of course, sport goods.

Case study 2.1: Decathlon – The expansion of a European sport goods player

The French sport goods market

The French sport goods market is valued at €4,923 million. Market growth was moderate between 2010 and 2015, and the outlook is moderate due to forecasts of decreasing sport participation. France is the second largest sport goods market in Europe after the UK and almost even with Germany with a 17% market share. However, in the comparison of per capita value the difference between the French and German market becomes clearer. The winter sport goods sector is the largest market segment accounting for almost 24% of the national sport goods market, closely followed by ball sports goods (23%) and fitness equipment (19%) (MarketLine, 2015c). France is home to numerous SMEs and several large sport goods firms that are often clustered in locations that provide favourable conditions for particular sports (e.g., Rhône-Alpes for mountain sport equipment or Aquitaine for surfing equipment) (Gerke, 2014). These firms include a number of French sport goods manufacturers with a national, European or global market reach and reputation. Examples are Gitane (bicycles), Salomon (originally French but bought by German Adidas in 1997) (skis), Beneteau (sail boats), Oxbow (snow and surf boards) and Millet (bought by French company Lafuma in 1995) (backpacks) (Desbordes, 1998). Besides sport goods manufacturers, sport goods retailers play a crucial role in the French sport goods market.

French sport goods retailers

There are several types of sport goods outlets in France: general merchandisers/supermarkets (e.g., Carrefour), department stores (e.g., Galeries Lafayette), specialist sport goods retail chains (e.g. Decathlon), small specialist niche sport retailers and sport goods manufacturers' own stores (e.g., Nike) (Gasparini, 2004). All of these different types of retailers are in direct competition. While sport goods retailer chains were the main outlet for sport goods in the past, the forward integration of sport goods manufacturers and the integration of sport goods into general merchandisers' product ranges has provided consumers with a larger choice of points of sales (MarketLine, 2015c). Specialist websites for general sport goods such as Private Sport Shop (www.privatesportshop.fr) or specialist sport products such as Flysurf (www. flysurf.com) are increasing the competition in sport goods retailing even more. This explains why general merchandisers (e.g., www.carrefour.fr), specialised retailers (e.g., www.decathlon.fr) and sport goods manufacturers (e.g., www.nike.com/fr) also offer online sales platforms, to respond to all customer preferences in terms of shopping experience.

While sport goods manufacturers have engaged in forward integration, specialist sport goods retailers have integrated backwards by starting to develop and manufacture their own products. In some cases this has been so successful that internally-developed products are overrepresented in the product offer compared with sport goods manufacturers' products. This is the case for the sport goods specialist retailer Decathlon which is the subject of this case study.

Decathlon in France and abroad

Decathlon was founded in 1976 with the vision of offering 'all sport under one roof' (MarketLine, 2015c). The company describes itself as 'a network of innovative retail chains and brands providing enjoyment for all sports people' (Decathlon, 2015a). Decathlon employs about 63,000 people, generating €8,200 million turnover in 2014. Figure 2.2 shows the development of sales turnover between 2008 and 2014 (Decathlon, 2015a).

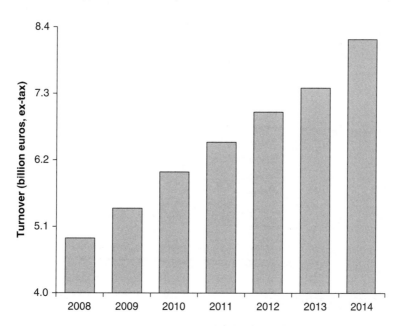

Figure 2.2   Development of Decathlon's sales turner between 2008 and 2014

Source: Decathlon, 2015a

(Continued)

(Continued)

More than 60% of revenues are generated outside France while the majority of retail outlets are still in France. International expansion of Decathlon covers not only geographically and culturally close countries such as Spain and Italy (numbers 2 and 4 in number of stores), but also distant markets such as China and Russia (numbers 3 and 6 in number of stores). Table 2.3 shows the number of stores per country (Decathlon, 2015a).

Table 2.3   Number of Decathlon's retail outlets per country

Rank	Country	Number of stores
1	France	288
2	Spain	129
3	China (Taiwan: 6)	120
4	Italy	101
5	Poland	44
6	Russia	25
7	Portugal	24
8	Germany	23
9	Belgium	22
10	India	20
11	Brazil	19
12	United Kingdom	17
13	Hungary	16
14	Romania	13
15	Turkey	10
16	Czech Republic	9
17	Netherlands	5
18	Bulgaria	4
19	Morocco	2
20	Croatia	1
21	Slovakia	1
22	Sweden	1
	Total	**894**

Source: Decathlon, 2015a

Decathlon's business activities

Decathlon's business activities are divided into retail, brands and services. Decathlon's retail business sells own brands and other branded sport goods in 894 retail outlets in 22 countries, of which 16 are in the EU. Besides retail outlets under the Decathlon store brand, the company offers online shopping in 10 languages. The company's own product brands (which they call 'Passion Brands') are only available in Decathlon outlets and online shops. There are currently 20 brands in the multi-brand family, with each brand representing 'a sports universe' relating to one or more sports (Declathon, 2015b). Table 2.4 show the list of Decathlon brands with their respective sport(s).

Table 2.4 Decathlon's 'passion brands'

Decathlon brand	Sports universe
DOMYOS	Fitness, dance, gymnastics & combat sports
BTWIN	Cycling
Kipsta	Team sports
Tribord	Nautical and water sports
Nabaiji	Swimming
Quechua	Mountain sports
Wed'ze	Skiing, snowboarding
Simond	Climbing and mountaineering
Kalenji	Running
Newfeel	Walking
Artengo	Racket sports
Inesis	Golf
Geologic	Darts, archery, boules
Caperlan	Fishing
Solognac	Nature & Hunting
Fouganza	Horse riding
Oxelo	Urban skate sports
Aptonia	Sports nutrition and health
Geonaute	Electronics
Orao	Sport optics

Source: Decathlon, 2015b

The third business activity of Decathlon is various services that complement the retail and product divisions. Currently there are nine different services offered, each represented by a different brand. Those services are either linked to the purchase of a product (e.g., funding solutions, insurance), to after-sales-service (e.g., servicing and repair, personal coach) or to interact with the customers (e.g., hockey social network). Table 2.5 lists the different service brands and the services offered by the brands.

(Continued)

(Continued)

Table 2.5 Decathlon's service brands

Decathlon brand	Service
Alsolia	Funding solutions
Atelier	Servicing, repairs, customisations
Hockey Community	Hockey social network
Decathlon sports insurance	Insurance
Jiwok	MP3 personal coach
Skimium	Ski renting
Sowego	Active mobility
Sporeka	Gift cards
Decathlon Villages	N/A

Source: Decathlon, 2015b

Innovation at Decathlon

From the beginning of Decathlon's development and production of its own products, innovation was one of its top priorities. To build the 'passion brands' Decathlon had to change customers' mind-sets that associated lower quality with Decathlon's own branded products than with specialist sport goods manufacturers of the same type. This change was done by establishing independent business units by 'sport(s) universe' that were located close to where the sports were practised. This was so that staff in each business unit could live the sports and hence perform better in the creation and innovation of new sport goods. At the same time local opinion leaders and heavy users could play a role in product development. High autonomy for the passion brand managers and their teams has been key to Decathlon's success across a wide variety of sports (Kapferer, 2012).

Decathlon has two innovation objectives. First, innovation should make sport easier for people who use the products. Second, innovation should be accessible to the maximum number of customers and users. Innovation is primarily driven using internal firm sources. Decathlon mentions as the main source of innovation the observation of customers and the passion of the company's employees. Incentives for employees to drive innovation are the yearly innovation awards that are held amongst the different passion brands. Other initiatives to drive innovation in Decathlon's passion brands are dedicated, shared resources for innovation. These include an internal research centre (Oxylane), an industrial division and a design department that all work with and for the passion brands (Decathlon, 2015c).

The research centre was founded in 1990 by hiring a researcher which was followed by a significant increase in investment in R&D activities. This research unit concentrates especially on upstream innovation, i.e. inputs into sport products which compete with established technological labels such as Lycra or Goretex (Kapferer, 2012). Today the Oxylane research centre comprises 50 researchers and a worldwide network of scientific laboratories, research organisations, universities and industrial partners that together register about 40 patents per year (Decathlon, 2015c).

The industrial division was created in 1996 and consists of 500 employees in France and another 2,100 in different production countries. This support unit aims at providing the passion brands with efficient components and product solutions according to the different industrial processes. Those result in more than 3,000 prototypes every year that are tested in workshops. This cross-divisional support unit accelerates the design process of innovations and product testing by letting employees and customers play a crucial role in the innovation process and keeping costs down through shared resources. The design unit was created to provide space for innovation project groups. These groups are formed to observe users – whether on the field, in stores or online – and obtain insights and information that will lead to inspiration, ideas and finally new products (Decathlon, 2015c).

Decathlon's values and ethical commitments

Decathlon's company culture is built on two values: vitality and responsibility. Vitality relates to the company's employees and their attributes (e.g., positive, full of energy, enthusiastic, innovating). Responsibility refers to any decision taken within the company and ensuring that actions are taken based on those decisions. It is about responsibility within the company, towards colleagues and employees, and outside the company, not only towards customers but also society in general (Decathlon, 2015d).

Decathlon is committed to sustainable development through fundamental principles that guide the company's actions. These principles and commitments include: responsibility on a daily basis; anticipating and acting upon future trends; long-term value creation; improvement of human and social conditions; entrusting responsibility and diversity; respecting the environment; security of products, retail outlets and services; and transparent communication. An example of the implementation of these principles and commitments is a social charter created in 2003 to assure human responsibility in production throughout the value chain. This charter is a contractual document that is signed by Decathlon's suppliers prior to any commercial relationship. It covers aspects such as: no children on work sites, no forced labour, a healthy and safe work environment, no discrimination, no abusive disciplinary practices, respect of working hours, respect of employees and compliance issues (Decathlon, 2015d).

The information stated above reflects the perspective communicated by Declathon. However, some researchers indicate that there is a flipside to the coin in Decathlon's business model and human resources policy and in the sport industry more generally. Firms in the sport industry can take advantage of their natural attractiveness to young and sport interested people. More radically speaking sport firms can manipulate customers and employees by using values that are associated with community life and sport in their business. Imitating a friendly and associative atmosphere within the firm and amongst the employees, as in a sport club, the sport firms are able to employ highly motivated people at lower salaries than in comparable jobs (Gasparini, 2003). A major reason for the success of this strategy is that work and passion get mixed up, and hence managers are able to exploit their employees' passion for the purposes of the sport business (Gasparini, 2004). Some researchers even go as far as postulating that competences in sport are even more valued than competences in sales when recruiting a sales person or manager for a sport equipment retailer (Gasparini & Pierre, 2008; Hidri & Bohuon, 2008).

(Continued)

(Continued)

Decathlon – A European leader in the sport goods industry?

Decathlon is the 10th largest sport goods distributor in the world (Kapferer, 2012). The company has grown locally in France over three decades but is now heavily internationalised with over half of business revenues coming from abroad. Decathlon's branches abroad function like start-ups. Country managers act independently and adapt to local markets. In China, for example, Decathlon's passion brands' recognition is low, so prices must be low to attract Chinese customers. Decathlon's success in European countries varies. While it has a significant presence in Spain and Italy, the company has a weak presence and positioning in other EU countries such as Germany, Belgium and the UK. Decathlon has only just started developing its presence in Eastern Europe, so it has a long way to go to design a pan-European strategy. Furthermore, how will other sport goods retail chains such as Intersport or Go Sport react? How will the further development of online shopping influence consumer behaviour in Europe and beyond?

Conclusion

This chapter describes the current size and scope of the European market and trade in sport goods, analysing the major producers and patterns of demand within Europe. We highlight that industry trade and segment definitions remain to be clarified as current data do not include all relevant sport-related goods and services. The expansion of the European sport good industry has been stimulated by a number of general firm-level strategy drivers, relating to the market, competition, costs, government policy and globalisation drivers as well as a number of drivers specific to the industry. Some specific drivers – social, health and economic aspects – may be seen as defining characteristics of the industry.

Specific firm-level growth drivers in the sport goods industry include: innovations, new sport practices and sport democratisation. We highlight some of the specific features of the European economic, social and regulatory context within the EU Single Market, which have stimulated and enabled the expansion of its sport goods industry. Sport goods firms in Europe have grown within national contexts and built on those national markets through collaboration, internal growth and mergers and acquisitions, to become international players. One of the most critical contemporary issues is access to customers through multiple channels: retail stores, online shops, combinations of these and enabling customers to experience brands across multiple devices. The Decathlon case study brings these issues to the fore and illustrates many of the trends and features described in the chapter. We suggest future areas of study should include analysis of non-European competitors' global manufacturing and logistics and supply chain strategies.

Recommended further reading

For those interested in the sport goods industry and its management, we suggest reading sport management and marketing textbooks as well as scientific articles from relevant academic journals. Recommended textbooks include:

Andreff, W. (2009). 'The Sports Goods Industry.' In W. Andreff & S. Szymanski (Eds), *Handbook on the Economics of Sport* (2nd edn, pp. 27–39). Cheltenham: Edward Elgar.

Hoye, R., Smith, A., Nicholson, M., Stewart, B., & Westerbeek, H. (2009). *Sport Management Principles and Applications* (2nd edn). Amsterdam: Elsevier.

Pitts, B. G., & Stotlar, D. K. (2002). 'Fundamentals of Sport Marketing.' In B. G. Pitts, D. K. Stotlar, J. DeSensi, & S. Inglis (Eds), *Sport Management Library* (pp. 1–36). Morgantown, USA: Fitness Information Technology, Inc.

Slack, T., & Parent, M. M. (2006). *Understanding Sport Organizations – The Application of Organization Theory.* Leeds: Human Kinetics.

Recommended research articles include:

Shilbury, D. (2012). 'Competition: The heart and soul of sport management.' *Journal of Sport Management*, *26*(1), pp. 1–10.

Slack, T., & Thurston, A. (2014). 'The social and commercial impact of sport, the role of sport management.' *European Sport Management Quarterly*, *14*(5), pp. 454–463.

Note

1   In Europe MarketLine covers: Austria, Belgium, the Czech Republic, Denmark, Finland, France, Germany, Greece, Ireland, Italy, the Netherlands, Norway, Poland, Portugal, Russia, Spain, Sweden, Switzerland, Turkey, and the UK.

References

Abouzeedan, A., & Busler, M. (2004). 'Typology analysis of performance models of Small and Medium-Size Enterprises (SMEs).' *Journal of International Entrepreneurship*, *2*(1–2), pp. 155–177.

Andreff, W. (2006). 'International Trade in Sport Goods.' In W. Andreff & S. Szymański (Eds), *Handbook on the Economics of Sport* (pp. 59–67). Cheltenham: Edward Elgar Publishing Limited.

Andreff, W. (2008). 'Globalization of the sports economy.' *Rivista di diritto ed Economia dello sport*, *IV*(3), 13–32.

Baldauf, A., Cravens, D. W., & Wagner, U. (2000). 'Examining determinants of export performance in small open economies.' *Journal of World Business*, *35*(1), pp. 61–79.

Benson-Rea, M., & Shepherd, D. (2010). 'OBO: Global Success in a Niche Niche Business.' In I. Hunter & K. Morris (Eds), *New Zealand Case Series: Innovation and Entrepreneurship* (pp. 176–187). Auckland: McGraw-Hill.

Boso, N., Cadogan, J. W., & Story, V. M. (2013). 'Entrepreneurial orientation and market orientation as drivers of product innovation success: A study of exporters from a developing economy.' *International Small Business Journal*, *31*(1), pp. 57–81.

Breedveld, K., Gratton, C., Hoekman, R., Scheerder, J., Stege, J., Stubbe, J., & Vos, S. (2013). *Study on a Possible Future Sport Monitoring Function in the EU.* Utrecht: Mulier Institute.

Business Europe (2010). *Go for growth – An agenda for the European Union in 2010–2014*, 4 February. Retrieved 08 June 2015, from http://www.businesseurope.eu/content/default.asp?PageId=875

Casey, S. R., & Hamilton, R. T. (2014). 'Export performance of small firms from small countries: the case of New Zealand.' *Journal of International Entrepreneurship*, *12*(3), pp. 254–269.

Chadwick, S. (2009). 'From outside lane to inside track: sport management research in the twenty-first century.' *Management Decision*, *47*(1), pp. 191–203.

Chetty, S., & Campbell-Hunt, C. (2004). 'A strategic approach to internationalization: a traditional versus a "born global" approach.' *Journal of International Marketing*, *12*(1), pp. 757–781.

Commission of the European Communities (2007). *White Paper on Sport*. Brussels.

Council of Europe (2001). Recommendation No. R (92) 13 REV of the Committee of Ministers to Member States on the revised European Sports Charter 752. *Meeting of the Ministers' Deputies / 16 May 2001*. Strasbourg: Council of Europe.

D'Angelo, A., Majocchi, A., Zuchella, A., & Buck, T. (2013). 'Geographical pathways for SME internationalization: insights from an Italian sample.' *International Marketing Review*, *30*(2), pp. 80–105.

Deakins, D., Battisti, M., Perry, M., & Crick, D. (2013). *Understanding Internationalisation Behaviour*, New Zealand Centre for SME Research, Massey University, Wellington, New Zealand, 7 June.

Decathlon (2015a). Who are we? Retrieved 04 June 2015, from http://corporate.decathlon.com/en/who-are-we/about-us/.

Decathlon (2015b). Our brands. Retrieved 04 June 2015, from http://corporate.decathlon.com/en/our-brands/retail-formats/decathlon-2/.

Decathlon (2015c). Our innovation. Retrieved 05 June 2015, from http://corporate.decathlon.com/en/our-innovations/research-and-development/.

Decathlon (2015d). Our commitments. Retrieved 04 June 2015, from http://sustainability.decathlon.com/en/page/our-commitments.

Desbordes, M. (1998). *Diffusion des matériaux, changement technologique et innovation: analyse et étude de cas dans l'industrie du sport instrumenté* (Docteur). Université Louis Pasteur, Strasbourg.

Desbordes, M., Ohl, F., & Tribou, G. (2004). *Marketing du Sport* (3rd edn). Paris: Economica.

Dolles, H., & Söderman, S. (2011). *Sport as a Business*. Basingstoke: Palgrave Macmillan.

Ernst & Young (2010). 'Waking up to the new economy: Ernst & Young's 2010 European attractiveness survey.' Downloaded from: http://www.ey.com/GL/en/Issues/Business-environment/Ernst—Young-attractiveness-surveys.

European Commission (2014). 'What is an SME?' *Enterprise and Industry*. Retrieved 08 June 2015, from http://ec.europa.eu/enterprise/policies/sme/facts-figures-analysis/sme-definition/index_en.htm.

EU4SportsClusters (2015). 'Innovation in the European Sport Sector'. Retrieved 21 October 2015, from http://www.clustercollaboration.eu/eu4sports

Gabrielsson, M., Kirpalani, V. H. M., Dimitratos, P., Solberg, C. A., & Zucchella, A. (2008). 'Born globals: propositions to help advance the theory.' *International Business Review*, *17*(4), pp. 385–401.

Gasparini, W. (2003). 'La forme et le fond. Participation et exploitation chez Décathlon'. *Regards Sociologiques*, *24*, pp. 91–102.

Gasparini, W. (2004). 'La face cachée de l'industrie du loisir:nouvelles formes de domination au travail dans le champ de l'offre sportive commerciale.' *Loisir et Société / Society and Leisure*, *27*(1), pp. 45–67. doi: 10.1080/07053436.2004.10707641.

Gasparini, W., & Pierre, J. (2008). 'Vendre et se vendre. Dispositions et compétences des vendeurs d'articles de sport'. *STAPS*, *4*(82), pp. 43–56. doi:10.3917/sta.082.0043.

Gerke, A. (2014). *The relationship between interorganisational behaviour and innovation within sport clusters*. Unpublished doctoral dissertation, Paris-Sud University, Orsay, France.

Grant, R. M., & Bakhru, A. (2004). 'The limits of internationalisation in e-commerce.' *European Business Journal*, *16*(3), pp. 95–104.

Heino, R. (2000). 'New sports: what is so punk about snowboarding?' *Journal of Sport & Social Issues*, *24*(2), pp. 176–191. doi: 10.1177/0193723500242005.

Hennigs, B., & Hallmann, K. (2014). 'A motivation-based segmentation study of kitesurfers and windsurfers.' *Managing Sport and Leisure*, *20*(2), pp. 117–134. doi: 10.1080/13606719.2014.979554.

Hidri, O., & Bohuon, A. (2008). 'Faire du sport pour être embauché ? Logiques et pratiques de recrutement du personnel commercial chez Décathlon.' *STAPS*, *4*(82), pp. 57–70. doi:10.3917/sta.082.0057.

ISAF (2012). 'ISAF Kiteboarding Format of trials.' In Events Committee (Ed.), *Technical Report*. Santander, Spain: ISAF.

Johanson, J., & Vahlne, J.-E. (1977). 'The internationalization process of the firm – a model of knowledge development and increasing foreign commitments.' *Journal of International Business Studies*, *8*(1), pp. 23–32.

Kapferer, J.-N. (2012). *The New Strategic Brand Management: Advanced Insights and Strategic Thinking* (5th edn). London: Kogan Page.

Kellett, P., & Russell, R. (2009). 'A comparison between mainstream and action sport industries in Australia: a case study of the skateboarding cluster.' *Sport Management Review*, *12*(2), pp. 66–78. doi: 10.1016/j.smr.2008.12.003.

Knight, G., & Cavusgil, S. T. (2004). 'Innovation, organizational capabilities, and the born-global firm.' *Journal of International Business Studies*, *35*(2), pp. 124–141.

Kobrin, S. J. (2001). 'Territoriality and the governance of cyberspace.' *Journal of International Business Studies*, pp. 687–704.

Lassiter, J. B., & Heath, D. (2006). *Icebreaker: The China Entry Decision*. Harvard: Harvard Business School (9-806-195).

MarketLine (2015a). 'Sports Equipment in Europe.' In MarketLine (Ed.), *MarketLine Industry Profile*.

MarketLine (2015b). 'Sports Equipment in the United States.' In MarketLine (Ed.), *MarketLine Industry Profile*.

MarketLine (2015c). 'Sports Equipment in France.' In MarketLine (Ed.), *MarketLine Industry Profile*.

Marketo.com (2014). Retrieved 08 June 2015, from http://blog.marketo.com/2014/04/the-definition-of-omni-channel-marketing-plus-7-tips.html.

Menzel, M.-P., & Fornahl, D. (2010). 'Cluster life cycles – dimensions and rationales of cluster evolution.' *Industrial and Corporate Change*, *19*(1), pp. 205–238.

OECD (2000). *VI. E-Commerce: Impacts and policy challenges*. OECD Economic Outlook 67.

OECD (2013). *Entrepreneurship at a Glance 2013*. OECD Publishing, Paris. Retrieved 08 June 2015, from http://dx.doi.org/10.1787/entrepreneur_aag-2013-en.

Ohmae, K. (1986). *The Mind of the Strategist: Business Planning for Competitive Advantage*. London: Penguin Business Library.

Oviatt, B. M., & McDougall, P. P. (1994). 'Toward a theory of international new ventures.' *Journal of International Business Studies*, *25*(1), pp. 45–64.

Root, F. R. (1998). *Entry Strategies for International Markets*. San Francisco, CA: Jossey-Bass.

SportsEconAustria (2012). *Study on the Contribution of Sport to the Economic Growth and Employment in the EU*. Brussels: European Commission, Directorate-General Education and Culture.

Tolstoy, D. (2014). 'Differentiation in foreign business relationships: a study on small and medium-sized enterprises after their initial foreign market entry.' *International Small Business Journal*, *32*(1), pp. 17–35.

UN Statistics Division (2015). SITC Rev.3 code 849.7. Retrieved 04 June 2015, from http://unstats.un.org/unsd/cr/registry/regcs.asp?Cl=14&Lg=1&Co=894.7

Worldbank (2015). 'European Union'. Retrieved 21 October 2015 from http://data.worldbank.org/region/EUU

World Health Organization (2003). *Health and Development through Physical Activity and Sport*. Geneva, Switzerland: WHO Document Production Services.

Yip, G. S. (1995). *Total Global Strategy: Managing for Worldwide Competitive Advantage*. Englewood Cliffs, NJ: Prentice Hall.

Zahra, S. A. (2005). 'A theory of international new ventures: a decade of research.' *Journal of International Business Studies*, *36*(1), pp. 20–28.

WHEN GLOBALIZATION AND MIGRATION MEET NATIONAL AND LOCAL TALENT DEVELOPMENT

SINE AGERGAARD

Introduction

Despite the ongoing debate on how to define globalisation, most scholars agree that it can be understood as an increasing global connectedness both in geographical and imaginary terms (Palmer, 2013). Sport is a brilliant example of this. Sport is practised and consumed across national and continental borders, and international sport events contribute to the imagination of a global community. This happens although not all nations are represented, and although international sport events are also used to reinforce our sense of belonging to nation-states and local communities. The contribution of sport to imagined and lived forms of global connectedness is also reflected in the increasing migration of athletes and sport personnel across national and international borders to pursue a transnational professional career (Agergaard & Ryba, 2014).

Sport labour migration is currently increasing in extent as well as in geographical scope (Maguire & Falcous, 2011). The phenomenon of sport labour migration is much larger than reflected by the media coverage of official transfers of famous male football players, who are primarily recruited into and between the Big-5 leagues in Europe: England, France, Germany, Italy and Spain. Footballers also migrate into lower divisions and other countries, and athletes from other sport disciplines than football migrate too. Recently, researchers have also brought attention to female athletes migrating to pursue international professional careers (Agergaard, 2008; Agergaard & Tiesler, 2014; Botelho & Agergaard, 2011; Eliasson, 2009; Engh, 2014).

This chapter aims to direct the attention of sport students and researchers to the ways globalization processes and more particularly sport labour migration create new challenges and options for local and national sport governing bodies. Particular focus will be on the ways in which sports labour migration affects domestic talent development in national federations and local clubs. Case studies will be used to describe and discuss two questions:

1. What are the *challenges and options* for national and local talent development in periods with considerable immigration of athletes from abroad?
2. How is the *capability* of specific European approaches to developing talented athletes as 'whole persons' to also cover migrating athletes?

The chapter will end with a discussion of the possible moral and political implications of cases in which local and national sport policies do not appear to be synchronised with globalisation and more particularly with migration processes.

Historical and recent developments

Historically, talents have been identified and developed as an integral part of organised sport in local clubs in many Western countries (Holt, 2002). Thus, this de-centralised and asystemic system rests on the chances that local talents develop and find their way into bigger clubs and national teams. Recently, efforts to identify and develop local and national talents have intensified as part of 'the global sporting arms race' (De Bosscher, 2008). To increase the possibilities for winning medals in international competitions, Western countries, starting with Australia and Canada in the 1970s, have developed more goal-oriented elite sport policies and been inspired by talent development systems from Eastern European and Asian countries (Bergsgard, 2007; Green & Houlihan, 2006).

In the Scandinavian countries, talent development still takes place primarily in sport clubs rather than specialized sport schools or high performance centres (Andersson & Ronglan, 2012). Due to a continuous adherence to the de-centralized and asystemic talent development model, player migration may significantly influence domestic talent development in these countries. Thus, talent development in the Scandinavian countries still heavily depends on the effort of local clubs compared to other parts of the world where centralized governing bodies in sport play a more prominent role in facilitating national talent identification and development (Green & Oakley, 2001).

The European Union (EU) law ensures free mobility of workers across member-states. This rule has also been enforced to apply to sport following the Bosman case in 1995 (Frick, 2009). The Bosman case has become a symbol for professional athletes moving freely and working across European member-state borders. Attempts have been made by some international federations such as UEFA, the European football governing body, to introduce barriers to the free mobility of athletes. This became apparent in the 'home-grown rule' introduced during the seasons 2006–2009.[1] The rule states that all teams participating in international competitions should name eight players in their team of 25 players; of these four players should have been trained in the club for at least three years between 15 and 21 years of age, while four players should be association-trained, complying with the same rule in a cooperating club.

Still, the number of expatriate players in European premier league clubs is increasing, when surveyed as the squad members who play outside of their home national association.[2]

The Scandinavian countries adhere to cultural values believing that the individual elite athlete should be given the opportunity to develop as a 'whole person' (Bergsgard, 2007). Thus, Scandinavian countries appear to be at the forefront in establishing programmes to support elite athletes in dual career development, at least when it comes to national athletes. The European Commision has also argued for the relevance of supporting athletes' dual career development. In the period 2009–2011, the EU supported a number of dual career projects as part of the preparatory actions for funding the development of sport (European Commission, 2012). Subsequently, the *European Guidelines on Dual Careers* were made and enacted to reflect the variety of concerns related to this field in Northern and Southern European countries respectively.[3] Most recently, the EU has issued a 'call for tenders' to investigate whether the guidelines have been implemented in all European member-states.[4] The results of this investigation are expected to be published in 2017.[5] Still, the guidelines represent a rather soft power that encourages the member-states to support athletes' dual career development without enforcing them to do so (EU, 2012).

Moreover, when reading the EU documents it is made clear that their focus is on national governing of the dual career issue (European Commission, 2012; EU, 2012). Each European member-state is encouraged to ensure that their domestic athletes receive support to develop a dual career. Still, the documents show that the EU is aware that European athletes often face difficulties in accessing the education system in other member-states. Efforts are made to enhance the options for accessing educational institutions in other European member-states and adapting European education programmes to athletes. However, the EU documents hold very little reflection on the position of non-European athletes. Meanwhile, it is a fact that some athletes (e.g. from African countries) often face even bigger difficulties in gaining access to the European education system. Moreover, these athletes are often recruited to European clubs as international professionals with little thought of the need for local and national sport governing bodies to support their dual career options.

Thus, the humanistic ideal of supporting athletes' development of a dual career seems merely to apply to Europeans. The lack of attention given to international athletes in EU documents may not be intentional, but simply caused by no European member-states having raised a moral and political discussion of this issue. The international football governing body, FIFA, has expressed concern for the education of underage athletes in their regulations for international transfers of players (FIFA, 2014). These regulations state that the international transfer of players below 18 years is only allowed if complying with three requirements. Firstly, a player's parents moved to the country in question for reasons unrelated to football (that was for instance more or less the case in Lionel Messi's transfer to Barcelona). Secondly, transfers of underage athletes must take place within the EU or the European Economic Area (EEA) followed by a number of minimum obligations including academic and/or school and/or vocational education and/or training. Thirdly the player's journey to the club must involve less than a 100 km distance over a border (FIFA, 2014, p. 17). Dual career development plans for football players above 18 years are not part of these regulations.

Challenges, options and capabilities

Even though globalisation and migration processes are not new to sport, the increasing flow of athletes and sport personnel causes governing bodies in sport to be faced with new challenges and options. As mentioned above, the limited capability of the existing policies is illustrated by the lack of political support given to migrating athletes' dual career development. The critical issue of keeping local and national sport policies aligned with the newest development is also related to the fact that the impact of globalisation is ambiguous. For instance, the immigration of athletes from abroad may be seen both as a severe challenge for local and national talent development and an option for exchanging skills across national and international borders. The variety of ways in which national governing bodies relate to global migration processes can be illustrated by what is happening outside Europe in women's football.

At one end of the range of possible approaches is the national protectionist strategy. National sport governing bodies' development of this strategy may be illustrated by the evolvement of regulations for recruitment to the women's football league in the US from 2013. The American, Canadian and Mexican FA all support the US league so that up to 24, 16 and 12 of their national team players/talents respectively are guaranteed a position in one of the US clubs. This strategy makes it more difficult for players from outside North America to migrate into the US league, and it appears to be an attempt to protect national resources in the shape of a well-established professional league, educated coaches and skilled female football players. The US women's football national squad coach Tom Sermanni found at that time that it would be easier to gather the national squad and ensure that all players were undergoing qualified training.[6] However, Sermanni also mentioned that in his experience, American squad members playing abroad were confronted with other playing styles and thereby would develop new football skills and prepare themselves for the level in international football competitions. Thus, a national protectionist strategy does not appear to be the solution in a global sport world (Agergaard, 2015).

At the other end of the range of approaches from national sport governing bodies towards global migration processes is the strategy of outsourcing. An illustrative example here is the Japanese Football Federation supporting their best women's football talent to play in clubs in Europe and the US (Takahashi, 2014). This appears to be a deliberate strategy based on the rationale that the conditions for player development are better in Europe and the US than in Japan – a strategy that possibly contributed to Japan winning the World Cup in Women's Football in 2011. The same calculation for development of younger talents seems to be the background also for other national FAs to support showcases helping young female players from Trinidad and Tobago to be recruited by American colleges (McCree, 2014).

This strategy may be described with the concept of outsourcing defined as where an organisation moves parts of its in-house functions out of the country (Kumar and Eickhoff, 2006, cited in Lee, 2010). Lee uses this definition to describe how European football clubs outsource their talent production by buying players from abroad rather than developing local talent (Lee, 2010). In the case of migration in women's football it is national governing bodies that outsource their talent and player development to places outside of their borders. This strategy is followed by the risk that some talented players may not return to perform for the national squad, and in some cases the players will decide to settle and become citizens of their new destination. However, this may lead to establishing a bridge-head of players (Elliott & Maguire, 2008) who will facilitate the migration back and forth of fellow players and coaches.

Thus, national protectionism and outsourcing strategies appear as outer markers along a continuum of options for dealing with the challenges and options of sport labour migration. EU law does not support the national protectionist strategy, while the benefits of outsourcing for European federations may be limited as Europe (together with North America) is the centre of many sport disciplines. Still, it appears critical for local and national sport governing bodies in Europe not to give in to a public understanding that sport labour migration poses a severe challenge to domestic talent development. The real challenge is to understand and develop the options following athletes' migration into local and national settings. The case studies presented below will illustrate the ambiguous challenges and options following globalisation.

Case study 3.1: Talent development in times of immigration

What follows is a closer examination of cases in Europe, more particularly in Scandinavia, where emerging professionalization and globalization process are followed by immigration of players from abroad: cases where local and national talent development is probably influenced and at least challenged by the reality of global sport.

Handball is mainly played in European countries and there are no national quotas for the recruitment of players from abroad, either from EU or non-EU member-states. The Scandinavian countries have been among the leading nations in international handball, particularly women's handball. Throughout the 2000s, there was a remarkable increase in the professionalization of women's handball clubs in the Danish league, that were followed by higher salaries that were attractive not only to national players but also to players from abroad (Storm & Agergaard, 2014). Within a few years the percentage of international players grew from 15% in 1999/2000 to 40% in 2007/2008 (Agergaard & Andersen, 2008). This percentage then dropped at the beginning of the financial crisis so that the number of players from abroad in 2014/2015 has decreased to 17% of the players in the Danish women's handball league (Olsen, 2015).

When this development peaked public opinion was that the immigration of players from abroad destroyed national talent development.[7] A quantitative study supported this, reporting that while the percentage of players from abroad increased considerably in the Danish women's handball league, the number of goals scored by immigrant players even more clearly surpassed their share in the number of league players (Hjort, Agergaard, & Ronglan, 2010). Further, the quantitative study used goal scoring as a proxy indicator of players' importance in matches, reporting that junior national team players were more influenced in their match participation than established national team players, who appeared to remain the same in terms of access to and importance in matches in the years where there was remarkable growth in the number of international players (Hjort et al., 2010).

Nevertheless, so the ways in which sports labour migration challenge local and national talent development also seem to depend on the social learning conditions and structures within elite sport teams. A qualitative study showed that immigrant players quickly gained legitimacy in Danish women's handball clubs, compared to domestic talents who needed to work their way up to a place in the starting line-up (Agergaard & Ronglan, 2015). Nevertheless, the presence of immigrant players may not only increase the competition within the elite sport team and decrease the opportunities for national talent to participate in matches, it may also contribute to the development of skills and experiences in younger players. Contrary to public opinion it appears that players from abroad are not to blame for the changing conditions for talent development in Danish women's handball; rather challenges and options for local and national talent development must be considered in relation to the total presence of professional, experienced senior players as well as in relation to the ways in which local clubs and national sport governing bodies structure the organisation around domestic talents (Agergaard & Ronglan, 2015).

Recently, the economic recession has caused many international players to leave Danish women's handball. This could be seen as a new way of strengthening possibilities for young domestic talents to receive more playing time and gain more responsibility as a team. Yet fewer experienced players from abroad could also lead to a weaker league, with less opportunity for domestic talent to learn from experienced players and less teams being competitive at international top level.

However public opinion seems to have changed.[8] Representatives from national sport governing bodies and league club coaches are now expressing their concern that when international stars leave Danish women's handball the conditions for local and national talent development will be impaired. Further, this concern also includes cases where some of the best Danish national team players have left the country to play in a club abroad. This indicates that there is a need for a more thorough discussion of advantages and disadvantages following players migrating to and away from national leagues. Rather than considering migration as a simple linear process, transnational migration studies suggest that migration is a circular process by which domestic as well as migrating players may be able to benefit from exchanging skills and gaining international experiences (Agergaard, 2015; Elliott & Weedon, 2011).

Case study 3.2: Dual career support in times of globalization

While it is predominantly players from other European countries who migrate into Danish women's handball, the following case will direct attention to non-European athletes. Europe and the US are the centres for many sport disciplines and are thus often recruiters of athletes from countries in the Global South. The following case will illustrate the limited capability of local and national sport governing bodies to support athletes' dual career development and to include international migrating athletes in these attempts.

(Continued)

(Continued)

The particular case here is from Scandinavian women's football, which is interesting since processes of globalization, professionalization and commercialization of the national leagues are emerging in these years (Kjær & Agergaard, 2013). Denmark, Norway and Sweden all have well-established women's football leagues (Hjelm & Olofsson, 2003; Skille, 2008; Trangbæk & Brus, 2003) and international players have been recruited to these leagues since the early 1990s (Botelho & Agergaard, 2011). Swedish women's football clubs in particular have recruited athletes from abroad. One of the largest groups of migrant players in the Swedish top league is made up of African female football players (Engh, 2014).

Due to the emergence of professionalization in Scandinavian women's football and sparse financial resources, international players are about the only full-time professional players in Scandinavian women's football, while much of the national talent and players are supported in developing a dual career. The Danish, Norweigan and Swedish players are paid part-time and/or supported financially to be able to engage in gaining an education or a job while playing football at top-level. Therefore in this case Scandinavian women's football clubs, often situated at relatively remote geographical locations with few relevant jobs and institutions of further education, have started recruiting international players, who are among the very best in their discipline and who have often played professional football in their home country before migrating. The same team consists of Scandinavian girls engaged in often quite advanced university programmes, while the international players are recruited to play football. This case challenges the scope of the humanistic ideal of the Scandinavian sport system to develop all elite athletes as whole persons through support to develop a dual career.

Based on studies of the migration of South African and Nigerian women footballers into Scandinavian leagues, publications have already directed attention to the African women footballers' changing descriptions of their post-career plans (Agergaard & Botelho, 2014). Over five years repeated interviews have been conducted with key informants. One of these key informants has provided insight into her changing considerations and experiences in combining sport and education in the setting of Scandinavian sport clubs.

Cathy arrived in Scandinavia when she was quite young. The club supported her in attending language classes and finishing what was equivalent to the ninth grade level from a language school. After that Cathy went on to vocational training, but the organization of the training was not adapted to elite athletes. After participating in an international tournament, She was asked to repeat a three-month vocational job training. She opted out of the vocational training since she also viewed this as not being relevant to the job options she would have in her home country when returning. Moreover, she had few options for getting access to advanced youth education:

> So things here wouldn't get me anywhere back home so it was like a waste of my time. I can't get into the gymnasium[9]... it bothers me a lot because I really want to move forward with my education and I can't really do that here that's one of the reasons why I sometimes feel like I should leave. My next option is to go to the US. I could maybe get a scholarship and maybe play for a school and study. But for real I really want to get an education, it bothers me a lot, because education is important. I could feel like I'm losing my brain like [laughs] I want to have contact with my [brain] you know, it's been a while. (Cathy)

The quote above illustrates not only the difficulties that non-European athletes face in entering the education system in European countries, but also their experience of what appears to be one-sided and isolated dimensions of everyday life as a professional athlete in a Scandinavian sport club, where most fellow players are simultaneously involved in education programmes. Cathy dreams of going to the American college system where sport and studies are supposed to supplement each other.

There is of course huge variety in the extent to which athletes are keen on focusing merely on their sport or on pursuing dual-career development. Nevertheless, the Scandinavian elite sport policy is based on the cultural value/political ideal that it is beneficial for all human beings to be engaged in various training and activities. The case above illustrates that even if the Scandinavian sport club attempts to support their international players' language training, it cannot change the fact that it is difficult for non-European athletes to enter the education system in Europe, and that the national sport policies are often set up to support athletes' participation in advanced youth education courses rather than vocational training. Similarly, this is also a challenge for athletes from ethnic minority background in Denmark (Gregersen & Østergaard, 2009).

As described in the introduction, the cultural value of supporting athletes to develop as whole persons is still emphasized in the Scandinavian countries and even encouraged in a broader part of the EU. Nevertheless, the case study above points to the fact that Scandinavian national sport policy appears mainly capable of supporting dual-career development for athletes of a certain national heritage and with an educational background directed towards advanced youth education. It seems that national and international dual-career policies primarily support an elite of European youngsters moving towards higher education programmes.

Notwithstanding there may be a number of other possible outcomes of migration such as economic gain, social networks, skills exchange and, not least, the opportunity to fully focus on your sport. However, the ambiguity of being engaged in a *labour of love* has been pointed out (Botelho & Agergaard, 2011; Roderick, 2006). Sport is a short-term career with a transient character where injuries and a change in club management may end career options for athletes abruptly. At the end of their career, non-European athletes are left without rights for residency and social services unless they fulfil specific national demands for length of stay, ability to pass tests etc.

Thus, the transition to a career after being a professional athlete appears to be even more challenging for international athletes. The critical issue is not only to re-locate in physical terms such as finding a new place to live, but also in broader terms to find another job and often also another social arena. The options for non-European athletes to transfer into sport-related jobs in coaching and the media are often limited due to their level of language skills and limited insider knowledge. A very few successful athletes would have gained enough economic resources to support themselves for the rest of their life. From the humanistic perspective that versatile development is relevant for all human beings, dual career support to non-European athletes at all levels appears relevant to persue further.

Conclusion

This chapter has focused on ways in which globalization influences local and national efforts to promote domestic talent development. Particular attention has been given to the learning conditions for national talents in situations where there is immense immigration from abroad, and to the capabilities of national and European sport policies to promote dual-career support not only for national and European talents but also for non-European athletes.

The review of the historical and recent policy development in relation to sport labour migration has shown that there is still very little regulation of the flow of athletes into Europe. There is even less discussion of the degree to which European countries' political ideals and privileged position to support athletes' dual-career development will also in future encompass non-European athletes. Further, the ambiguity of challenges and options in recruiting players from abroad is described with attention given to the strategies of North American and Japanese national federations to protect or outsource national talent development.

The case studies in this chapter are both taken from Scandinavian sport club settings in which talent development follows a relatively decentralized and asystemic model. Even if increasing attempts are made to standardize and centralize talent development, it is still primarily the local sport clubs that are responsible for developing local talents and recruiting players from abroad. Thus, this setting appears particularly interesting for studies of how local and national sport governing bodies are influenced by globalization in the shape of sport labour migration.

The first case study refers to Danish women's handball where immense immigration developed within a few years in the first decade of the 2000s. The ambiguous relationship between migration and talent development was pointed out. On the one hand, quantitative studies showed that the immigrating athletes increased not only in number but also in their importance in matches in the national leagues. Young talent (here defined as the junior national team players) seemed to be particularly influenced by holding less significant roles in matches in years where the number of migrating athletes was high. On the other hand, qualitative studies demonstrate that there are also a number of options for exchange of skills when domestic talents are surrounded by leading international players. Thus, the case study concludes that the local and national organization of sport is highly important for turning possible disadvantages into advantages in sport labour migration.

The second case study refers to the situation where non-European athletes are brought into Scandinavian sport clubs. Referring briefly to the narrative of an African female football player, the study highlighted the challenges for non-European athletes in accessing the education system in Europe. It also illustrated the difficulties in finding an education programme/type of vocational training that was adapted to the career of elite athletes while also meeting non-European athletes' post-career expectations. Thus, the case study demonstrated that even if Scandinavian clubs and spectators increasingly recruit and consume international players, they do not seem to be considered according to the same moral and political standards. As a result the humanistic values of supporting versatile development do not seem to be applied to non-European athletes. It appears that further moral and political discussions are necessary to update the capability of local, national and European sport policies with regard to the situation where an increasing number of athletes from the Global South spend most of their early years in Europe.

It is remarkable that official governing bodies do not appear to take the global dimension of sport fully into account. In other political situations related to for instance the allocation of sport events, it has become apparent that even if the relevant governing bodies do not react, globalization may also raise public political protest. Following Arjun Appadurai's perspective on globalization processes, it is not only the global flows of people that connect us, but also flows of finance, ideas, technology and the media (Appadurai, 1996). The development of communication technology and social media has made it possible to exchange with ideas about the consequences and options for non-European athletes engaged in sport labour migration. If the treatment of 'the player product' appears unacceptable, consumers may react and start creating social protest movements (Harvey, Horne, & Safai, 2009). But to begin with, we need more knowledge about the career trajectories of transnational athletes through studies that systematically inquire into the issue of (lacking) dual-career development and the post-career transition.

Recommended further reading

There is still limited literature on the various ways in which globalization and more particularly sport labour migration are related to current challenges and options for local and national sport governing bodies. The various strategies for national federations to outsource or protect their talent development are described in some of the chapters in the edited book:

Agergaard, S., & Tiesler, N. C. (Eds) (2014). *Women, Soccer and Transnational Migration*. London: Routledge.

Further, Richard Elliott and Gavin Weedon have described the ways in which the relation between talent development and migration is not only a disadvantage but also an advantage for the exchange of skills between domestic and international players etc.:

Elliott, R., & Weedon, G. (2011). Foreign players in the English Premier Academy League: 'Feet-drain' or 'feet-exchange'? *International Review for the Sociology of Sport*, 46(1), 61–75. doi:10.1177/1012690 210378268.

The last recommendation for reading is currently the most comprehensive book including a number of contributions about sport labour migration in diverse disciplines and areas of the world:

Maguire, J., & Falcous, M. (2011). *Sport and Migration: Borders, Boundaries and Crossings*. London: Routledge.

Notes

1   Retrieved 7 June 2015 from: http://www.uefa.com/news/newsid=943393.html
2   Retrieved 5 November 2015 from: http://www.football-observatory.com/IMG/swf/da2015_v01_eng.swf
3   Retrieved 15 June 2015 from: http://eur-lex.europa.eu/legal-content/EN/TXT/?uri=CELEX:52013XG0614(03)
4   Retrieved 15 June 2015 from: http://ec.europa.eu/sport/calls/2014/18-eac-2014/specifications_en.pdf

5   I am thankful to PhD student Mads de Wolff, Loughborough University, for sharing his great insight into the European Union's sport policy development.
6   Interview with Tom Sermanni at Algarve Cup March, 2013.
7   "Dansk kvindehåndbold lider under udlændinge."Fyns Stiftstidende 01.09.2007, retrieved 10 January 2015 from: http://apps.infomedia.dk:2048/Ms3E/ShowArticle.aspx?output Format=Full&Duid=e0bb2727
8   Retrieved 24 February 2015 from: http://play.tv2.dk/programmer/sport/haandbold/super matchen/studie-21-februar-1650-95468/
9   A three-year educational programme for 15–19 year-olds followed by the majority of Danish youth. The programme gives access to university study programmes.

References

Agergaard, S. (2008). Elite athletes as migrants in Danish women's handball. *International Review for the Sociology of Sport, 43*(1), 5–19. doi: 10.1177/1012690208093471.

Agergaard, S. (2015). Current patterns and tendencies in women's football migration. Outsourcing or national protectionism as the way forward? In R. Elliott & J. Harris (Eds), *Football and Migration. Perspectives, Places and Players* (pp. 127–142). London: Routledge.

Agergaard, S., & Andersen, L. V. (2008). Udenlandske spillere i dansk kvindehåndbold. In R. K. Storm (Ed.), *Dansk håndbold. Bredde, elite og kommercialiseringens konsekvenser* (pp. 125–143). Slagelse: Bavnebanke.

Agergaard, S., & Botelho, V. (2014). The way out? African players' migration to Scandinavian women's football. *Sport in Society, 17*(4), 523–536. doi: 10.1080/17430437.2013.815512.

Agergaard, S., & Ronglan, L. T. (2015). Player migration and talent development in elite sports teams. A comparative analysis of inbound and outbound career trajectories in Danish and Norwegian women's handball. *Scandinavian Sport Studies Forum, 6*, 1–26.

Agergaard, S., & Ryba, T. V. (2014). Migration and career transitions in professional sports: Transnational athletic careers in a psychological and sociological perspective. *Sociology of Sport Journal, 31*(2), 228–247.Retrieved from http://search.ebscohost.com/login.aspx?direct=true&db=s3h&AN=96995014&s ite=ehost-live

Agergaard, S., & Tiesler, N. C. (Eds) (2014). *Women, Soccer and Transnational Migration.* London: Routledge.

Andersson, S. & Ronglan, L.T. (2012). *Nordic Elite Sport: Same ambition, Different tracks.* Frederiksberg: Samfundslitteratur.

Appadurai, A. (1996). *Modernity at Large: Cultural dimensions of globalization.* Minneapolis, Minn.: University of Minnesota Press.

Bergsgard, N. A. (2007). *Sport Policy: a comparative analysis of stability and change.* Oxford: Butterworth-Heinemann.

Bosscher, V. de (2008). *The Global Sporting Arms Race: an international comparative study on sport policy factors leading to international sporting success.* Aachen: Meyer & Meyer.

Botelho, V. L., & Agergaard, S. (2011). Moving for the love of the game? International migration of female footballers into Scandinavian countries. *Soccer and Society, 12*(6), 806–819. doi: 10.1080/ 14660970.2011.609681.

Eliasson, A. (2009). The European football market, globalization and mobility among players. *Soccer & Society, 10*(3), 386–397. doi: 10.1080/14660970902771449.

Elliott, R., & Maguire, J. (2008). 'Getting caught in the net': Examining the recruitment of Canadian players in British Professional Ice Hockey. *Journal of Sport and Social Issues, 32*(2), 158–176. doi: 10.1177/0193723507313927.

Elliott, R., & Weedon, G. (2011). Foreign players in the English Premier Academy League: 'Feet-drain' or 'feet-exchange'? *International Review for the Sociology of Sport, 46*(1), 61–75. doi: 10.1177/1012690 210378268.

Engh, M. H. (2014). *Producing and Maintaining Mobility: a migrant-centred analysis of transnational women's sports labour migration: PhD dissertation.* Aarhus: Aarhus University, Department of Public Health, Section for Sport.

EU (2012). *EU Guidelines on Dual Careers of Athletes. Recommended Policy Actions in Support of Dual Careers in High-Performance Sport.* Brussels.

European Commission (2012). *Towards an EU Funding Stream for Sport: Preparatory Actions and Special Events 2009–2011.* Luxembourg: Publications Office of the European Union.

FIFA (2014). *Regulations on the Status and Transfers of Players.* Switzerland.

Frick, B. (2009). Globalization and factor mobility: The impact of the 'Bosman-Ruling' on player migration in professional soccer. *Journal of Sports Economics, 10*(1), 88–106.Retrieved from http://search.ebsco-host.com/login.aspx?direct=true&db=s3h&AN=36027960&site=ehost-live

Green, M., & Houlihan, B. (2006). *Elite Sport Development: policy learning and political priorities.* London: Routledge.

Green, M., & Oakley, B. (2001). Elite sport development systems and playing to win: uniformity and diversity in international approaches. *Leisure Studies, 20*(4), 247–267. doi: 10.1080/0261436 0110103598.

Gregersen, M. T., & Østergaard, S. (2009). *Måske foregår den vigtigste kamp uden for kridtstregerne. En rapport med fokus på spillere med anden etnisk baggrund i dansk ungdomselitefodbold.* Retrieved from København.

Harvey, J., Horne, J., & Safai, P. (2009). *Alter globalization, global social movements, and the possibility of political transformation through sport* (Vol. 26): Human Kinetics Publishers, Inc.

Hjelm, J., & Olofsson, E. (2003). A breakthrough: Women's football in Sweden. *Soccer & Society, 4*(2), 182–204. doi: 10.1080/14660970512331390905.

Hjort, R. L.-N., Agergaard, S., & Ronglan, L. T. (2010). *Spillermigration og talentudvikling. Et komparativt studie af udenlandske spilleres betydning for unge nationale spillere i dansk og norsk damehåndbold.* Retrieved from Institut for Idræt, Københavns Universitet.

Holt, N. L. (2002). A comparison of the soccer talent development systems in England and Canada. *European Physical Education Review, 8*(3), 270–285. doi: 10.1177/1356336X020083006.

Kjær, J. B., & Agergaard, S. (2013). Understanding women's professional soccer. The case of Sweden and Denmark. *Soccer & Society, 14*(6), 816–833.

Lee, S. (2010). Global outsourcing: A different approach to an understanding of sport labour migration. *Global Business Review, 11*(2), 153–165. doi: 10.1177/097215091001100203.

Maguire, J., & Falcous, M. (2011). *Sport and Migration: borders, boundaries and crossings.* London: Routledge.

McCree, R. (2014). Student athletic migration from Trinidad and Tobago: The case of women's soccer. In S. Agergaard & N. C. Tiesler (Eds), *Women, Soccer and Transnational Migration.* London: Routledge.

Olsen, K. (2015). *Migration og talentudvikling efter finanskrisen. En mixed methods analyse af udenlandske spilleres aktuelle andel og betydning i dansk kvindehåndbold.* Speciale, Sektion for Idræt, Health, Aarhus Universitet.

Palmer, C. (2013). *Global Sports Policy.* London, England: SAGE.

Roderick, M. (2006). *The Work of Professional Football: a labour of love?* New York, NY: Routledge.

Skille, E. (2008). Biggest but smallest: female football and the case of Norway. *Soccer & Society*, *9*(4), 520–531. doi: 10.1080/14660970802257598.

Storm, R. K., & Agergaard, S. (2014). Talent development in times of commercialization and globalization: The pros and cons of international stars in Danish women's handball. In B. Saltin (Ed.), *Women and Sport*. Stockholm: SISU Idrottsböcker. doi: http://www.sisuidrottsbocker.se/Global/Kvinnor och idrott/WomenAndSport_1_3.pdf

Takahashi, Y. (2014). International migration of Japanese women in world soccer. In S. Agergaard & N. C. Tiesler (Eds), *Women, Soccer and Transnational Migration*. London: Routledge.

Trangbæk, E., & Brus, A. (2003). Asserting the right to play – women's football in Denmark. *Soccer & Society*, *4*(2), 95–111. doi: 10.1080/14660970512331390855.

THE COMMODIFICATION AND COMMERCIALIZATION OF ELITE ATHLETES

JOHANNES ORLOWSKI, MANUEL HERTER AND PAMELA WICKER

Introduction: Historical and recent development

Sport has included commercial components since its early years. Already in 590BC when Greek athletes were competing for Olympic victories the winners were financially rewarded (Harris, 1964). In medieval tournaments participants were rewarded with valuable prizes and in the 19th century the first professional cricket players could be found in England (Mandle, 1972). However, the commercialization and commodification have never been faster than in the 20th and 21st centuries and have reached previously unknown dimensions. Today sport is a major business and events like the Olympic Games or the Football World Cup represent a culmination of the relationship between sport and the economy.

The economic sociology literature defines commercialization as a process of 'transforming into saleable objects social phenomena which were not previously framed in that manner' (Slater & Tonkiss, 2001, p. 24) or the introduction of 'monetized exchange for the purposes of profit' (Williams, 2005, p. 14) where it did not exist before. The term 'commodification' is used interchangeably in this context. Subsequently, only the term 'commercialization' will be used to avoid misunderstanding. In the context of sport, commercialization can be illustrated best by the economic development of institutions such as the Union of European Football Associations (UEFA) Champions League or the Summer Olympics. Further, the ongoing commercialization process taking place in the sports business can be illustrated by the rapid development of athletes from pure athletes towards omnipresent media personalities.

When the first European Cup took place during the 1955/56 season, 16 teams from all over Europe participated. From day one the competition generated huge public interest and popularity and it became a platform for Europe's best football teams, with entry limited to the national champions of each country. However, the financial benefits were modest and limited to gate revenues from the teams' home games. For instance, in the first season of the European Cup, the Scottish team Hibernian generated £25,000 (approximately €34,000) in revenues by reaching the semi-finals (King, 2003).

Back then players were all but top earners. For example, in Germany salary regulations were quite strict: players were not allowed to earn more than DM400 (approximately €205; equivalent to €820 in 2015 Euros) a month until 1963 and were obliged to have a regular job besides playing football (*Der Spiegel*, 1963). One of Germany's all-time greatest, Gerd Müller, was working as a furniture mover when he started playing for Bayern Munich in 1964 scoring 33 goals in his first season (Süddeutsche, 2010). In 1963, the maximum monthly salary was raised to DM1,200 (approximately €614; equivalent to €2,455 in 2015 Euros) with only a few exceptions. One of the German star players at that time, Uwe Seeler, playing for the Hamburger SV, was among the top earners with a monthly income of DM2,500 (approximately €1,278; equivalent to € 5,110 in 2015 Euros) (*Der Spiegel*, 1963). In 1972, the salary caps were removed and players' revenues developed accordingly (*Die Welt*, 2008).

The growth of television as a major medium for football consumption and the development of new broadcasting technologies led to exponential growth in the revenues for clubs and consequently players. Following these changes the financial dimensions of European football changed tremendously. The new media environment had a critical impact on the transformation of football in the 1990s, as the financial imperatives of these companies have transformed the economic structure of the game. After almost 40 years of the European Cup remaining unchanged, UEFA reconsidered both the commercial and sporting aspects of the competition. As a consequence, the European Cup was transformed into the UEFA Champions League in 1992, a competition comprising group (round robin) and knock-out stages with an increased number of participating teams. The reason behind this transformation was the desire amongst clubs and broadcasters for a greater number of guaranteed games within the competition to generate more revenues.

Also, UEFA managed to increase its revenues from the European Cup dramatically and developed the continental competition into a global brand. As a consequence the competition was renamed 'The Champions League' and the selling of exclusive sponsorship or broadcasting packages was introduced. Additionally, elements such as key symbols, house colours, and an anthem were introduced to highlight the distinctiveness of this competition. The major European clubs gained significant financial benefits from this restructuring of the competition format. When the Champions League was first introduced for the 1992/93 season, a team shared a pool of £15 million (approximately €20 million) with the other teams. This sum steadily increased as the competition expanded. When Real Madrid won the competition in 2000, they earned approximately £18 million (approximately €25 million) from the event. The whole competition produced £240 million (approximately €326 million) in revenue in the same year (King, 2003). Fourteen years later Real Madrid earned roughly €57.4 million by winning the

Champions League. In the 2013/14 season, the 32 participating teams received €904.6 million (UEFA, 2014). Following these changes in the revenues generated through sporting competition, the lives of professional players have also changed accordingly: top players' salaries and endorsement revenues are now comparable to the income of sport celebrities from US major sports such as baseball, basketball, or American football (Frick, 2007).

Similarities to other sporting events such as the Olympics can be detected. Since the first modern Olympics in 1896 the pressures of increasing media coverage, expanded technology, and commercial profit have eroded the classical Olympic ideals (Stokvis, 2000). The commercialization within TV broadcasting started with the 1960 Summer Olympics in Rome when television rights were sold for the first time: the North American Broadcasting station Columbia Broadcasting System (CBS) paid $394,000 (approximately €360,000) to broadcast the Games in Italy (Billings, 2007).

Ever since the broadcasting revenues have increased steadily and in 1984 television rights and sponsors became the two most important financial pillars of the Games. A new financial landmark was reached in 1995 when the National Broadcasting Company (NBC) sealed the first-ever deal that included both the Olympic Summer and Winter Games for 2000 and 2002, respectively, for $1.25 billion (approximately €1.14 billion). Even more remarkable were the most recent contracts between NBC Universal and the International Olympic Committee (IOC). NBC agreed to pay $7.75 billion (approximately €7.07 billion) for the exclusive broadcast rights to six Olympic Games from 2022 to 2032 (Sandomir, 2014). In the period between 2009 and 2012, the Olympic Movement marketing revenue accounted for more than $8 billion (approximately €7.3 billion). Of this total revenue about 47% was money gained through broadcasting rights, followed by 45% through sponsorships, only 5% through ticketing, and 3% through licensing (Olympic Movement, 2014). These numbers provide an understanding about the financial dimensions of sporting mega events and it is hard to disagree with the following statement: 'today, Olympism is a commodity that can be bought and sold on the global consumer market' (Roche, 2000, p. 16).

Athletes inevitably became caught up in the commercialization of the Games. The transformation of sport into an entertainment and show business culture led to an increasing emphasis on individual stars such as Usain Bolt or Michael Phelps – athletes who were transformed into sporting celebrities. Making use of sporting heroes and role models in terms of achievement can be considered an authentic and credible way of promoting the Olympic brand (Rahman & Lockwood, 2011). Athletes represent marketable brands and earn millions of dollars from sponsorship or brand endorsement contracts. McCracken (1989, p. 310) defines a celebrity brand endorser as 'any individual who enjoys public recognition and who uses this recognition on behalf of a consumer good by appearing with it in an advertisement'. Approximately 14 to 19% of advertisements that aired in the US in recent years featured celebrities who endorsed products and brands with the number being even higher in foreign markets (Creswell, 2008). In the context of sport, Nike alone spent around $909 million (approximately €833 million) on athlete endorsements in 2013 (Abbruzzese, 2013). Celebrity endorsement research in the context of sports began to evolve during the mid 1990s when Michael Jordan became omnipresent on and off the basketball court (Kellner, 1996).

However, the most outstanding European athlete in terms of commercialization might be David Beckham. He is an example of how an athlete has turned into a sports brand that has several sports products under its corporate umbrella. In addition to playing football in Europe and in the US, David Beckham has used his popularity to market his own brand of aftershave. The key for him to become a true global sports brand has been the successful leveraging of his multiple brand personalities. In a unique way Beckham has shown how a sportsman can transcend his sport by crossing over into the realms of entertainment and fashion (Vincent, Hill, & Lee, 2009).

Contemporary and future challenges, capabilities, and critiques

The commercialization of sport has significantly influenced the lives of many professional athletes. Through increased public interest and the growing financial dimensions of sport, athletes have many new opportunities to earn money both on and off the pitch. However, besides many positive aspects of the commercial trends in sports in general and in athletes' lives in particular, there are various challenges associated with the progressing commercialization of sports. The next paragraphs critically discuss three specific areas in the context of commercialization: first, the physical and psychological exploitation of athletes; second, the issue of doping; and third, match fixing.

Regarding physical and psychological exploitation, Connor (2009) describes the position of elite athletes as subjects or widgets. Further, he argues that this has not always been the case, but that sport shifted from play and entertainment to a money-making business. Today sport has to be seen from the viewpoint of a capitalistic world where commercialization shaped the way we see sports today. In general, sport is an environment of extremes where not only very wealthy, but also very poor individuals or teams exist. While many athletes playing in the top European soccer leagues or in the four major leagues in the United States earn millions of Euros, other athletes are not (really) able to make a living from their sport although they are elite within Olympic sports. A German study shows that elite athletes in non-professionalized sports earn a monthly gross income of €1,919 on average (Wicker, Breuer, & von Hanau, 2012). Despite increased commercialization some athletes take part like professionals, but remain financial amateurs. Thus, not all athletes benefit equally from increased commercialization.

The internal driver for athletes is the rewards promised by sporting success. The goal of sporting success and associated wealth is only achieved by a few athletes and even for those it is hard to maintain. However, the successful life of a few leads to a Marxist-inspired idea that having a reserve army of potential employees (athletes) allows for greater exploitation of the few successful ones. Additionally, there is not just the exploitation of elite athletes; the majority of those who do not reach the sporting top tier suffer too (Connor, 2009). Like David Beckham himself, who left school at 16 and grew up as the son of a kitchen fitter, many athletes come from the working class, leave education with no degree, but do not end up playing for achieve Madrid. As mentioned earlier even for those who achieve wealth it is not a given that they maintain that wealth: for example, it was found that 75% of NFL retirees were unemployed and bankrupt within two years of retirement (Pierce, 2006).

Connor (2009) suggests considering wider social forces when explaining athletes' exploitation. According to him, athletes are not willing participants, but have to conform to the dominant narratives of sport, e.g. play when injured, giving one's all for the team, and being honoured to represent the team or the home country. Elite athletes suffer from external pressure by fans, media, and coaches – the latter being subject to pressure themselves. Connor acknowledges that 'athletes have become a business input and as such, managers, coaches and administrators seek to exploit that input as much as possible' (2009, p. 1369). Thus, the exploitation of elite athletes occurs through commercialized structures of sport with a must win endeavor that rewards the outcome and not the process that produces that outcome.

A special case of exploitation of athletes and a direct consequence of the commercialization of sport is the trafficking of young players. The problem of human trafficking in sport became apparent in many European countries at the beginning of the 1990s, mainly in professional football (Arnaut, 2006). European top tier clubs outbid each other in recruiting under-aged talents for their youth academies. The core problem football is facing is that young players may often end up being abandoned by both their agent and club in a foreign country. Especially the exploitation of young African football players in their pursuit of football stardom has become increasingly problematic. It is estimated that up to 15,000 young African players are taken abroad every year under false pretences (Homewood, 2013). Coaches as well as European and Arab middlemen haggle over the best players, signing children as young as seven years old. Agents basically buy them from their families with tightly binding pre-contracts and the hope of making thousands of Euros selling these under-aged talents to clubs in Europe. Those agents often use fake business cards allegedly issued by European clubs, promising the players and their families a lucrative contract abroad in exchange for a fee ranging between €3,000 and €10,000. There is a risk of both illegality when the player has no legal working permit and exploitation with regard to working conditions (Homewood, 2013). It is questionable if the current football regulatory framework is sufficiently equipped to deal with this issue.

Second, the relationship between commercialization of sport and doping is a frequently discussed issue (Boudreau & Konzak, 1991; Hoberman, 2007). Generally speaking, the culture of sport has gone through a process of scientification and medicalization. As a consequence athletes are increasingly seeking the support of new scientific advances and technologies that will give them a competitive advantage. Athletes are convinced that science-based disciplines such as clinical medicine, physiology, biomechanics, and psychology are one of the keys to a world class performance (Stewart & Smith, 2008).

The increasing commercial interest in sport has added more pressure on athletes to perform in order to maintain sponsorships and to acquire as much wealth as possible during their brief and risky sporting career. Nowadays, the media–sport–business relationship has made winning more important than ever before, not only for intrinsic reasons, but also for economic reasons as well, since prize money and sponsorship revenues have reached astronomical highs.

This has led to a commercialized sporting culture which sets incentives to do whatever it takes to gain a competitive edge even if this is immoral, against the rules, or even illegal. Under these conditions, the use of performance-enhancing drugs becomes a possibility for athletes to win championships or medals – or to simply survive and stay in the game, as some of the recent positive drug tests among road cyclists revealed with regard to marginal riders.

In particular, the influence of economic incentives such as prize money on doping violations has been examined. Research shows that the absolute amount of prize money explains a significant proportion (36%) of the variance in the doping affinity in the observed sports disciplines (Frenger & Pitsch, 2012). Amongst the reasons for deviant behaviour including doping are commercial reasons such as making profit and fear of losing one's livelihood (Breuer & Hallmann, 2013). However, financial factors and external pressure are only two factors among others such as intrinsic rewards (e.g. fame or reputation; Mugford, Mugford, & Donnelly, 1999).

As described above, the commercialization of sport can be seen as a catalyst for doping. On the one hand there are sporting, social, and health issues of doping; on the other hand economic consequences related to sponsorship, TV rights, and employment issues must be considered. Companies typically try to avoid being linked with athletes or a sport that is regularly associated with performance-enhancing drugs. For example, cycling had been suffering several doping scandals in the 1990s and the last decade. As a consequence, several networks and sponsors cut ties with athletes, teams, or the entire sport. For example, in 2008, the German public TV stations ZDF and ARD pulled out of the Tour de France coverage, arguing that the sporting value of the Tour de France has been reduced by the accumulation of failed drug tests. Similarly, in 2012, the Dutch bank Rabobank pulled out of cycling sponsorship after 17 years (Wilson, 2013).

Third, the commercialization of sport may lead to corruption or so-called match fixing. Match fixing can be defined as follows:

> The manipulation of sports results covers the arrangement on an irregular alteration of the course or the result of a sporting competition or any of its particular events (e.g. matches, races…) in order to obtain financial advantage, for oneself or for other, and remove all or part of the uncertainty normally associated with the results of a competition. (KEA European Affairs, 2012, p. 9)

Certainly commercialization is not the only catalyst for corruption in sport since the first documented case of match fixing goes back to the Olympic Games of 388BC, when the boxer Eupolos of Thessaly bribed competitors to allow him to win a gold medal. Match fixing motivations can refer to obtaining direct or indirect economic benefits. On the one hand, cases of betting-motivated match fixing involve fixing competitions with the primary aim of achieving an economic gain indirectly from sport through betting activity. Sport appears to be a fertile breeding ground for corruption and other illicit actions given the increased financial resources (including sport betting) involved (KEA European Affairs, 2012). On the other hand, cases of sports-motivated match fixing involve fixing a competition with the primary aim of achieving a sporting advantage directly from its result. However, it is clear that this type of match fixing results in economic benefits in a second step.

In recent years, an increasing number of match fixing cases could be detected. While certain sports such as cricket, football, and tennis seem to be affected particularly often by match fixing (KEA European Affairs, 2012), other sports including snooker, basketball, sumo, or rugby were also subject to match fixing (Carpenter, 2012). Typically, individual sports such as tennis are considered easiest to manipulate because bribing can be targeted at one single athlete (Forrest, McHale, & McAuley, 2008).

A closer look at one of the biggest match fixing scandals of European football in 2009 illustrates the international and economic dimensions of match fixing: a total of 323 suspicious matches across Europe were investigated; 347 match officials, club officials, players, and serious criminals were suspected of being involved in attempts to fix matches; and approximately €2 million were paid to referees, players, coaches, and officials of sports federations in order to influence the results.

Case study 4.1: The Klitschkos

Despite the reoccurring scandals associated with professional sports, companies continue to invest in athletes as brand endorsers. Athletes are transformed into commodities when they are considered as investments and returns on investments are calculated. Several studies measured the impact of celebrity endorsements on stock returns or sales numbers. However, the results have been inconsistent: while some studies provided evidence of a positive effect of celebrity endorsements on stock returns and sales numbers (Agrawal & Kamakura, 1995; Elberse & Verleun, 2012; Farrell et al., 2000), others did not find any evidence (Ding, Molchanov, & Stork, 2011; Fizel, McNeil, & Smaby, 2008).

Yet the question is why do some athletes appear attractive for companies and are able to earn money through endorsement contracts? To help select a celebrity endorser, many companies and their advertising agencies rely on certain selection criteria. These formal selection criteria help to evaluate endorsement deals and find the right celebrity to market the respective product. One common tool for evaluating celebrity endorsements is the so-called FREDD principle developed by the Young and Rubicam advertising agency and extended by Miciak and Shanklin (1994). The FREDD principle defines five criteria used to evaluate the quality of the celebrity endorsement. An overview of the criteria is provided in Table 4.1.

Table 4.1 The FREDD model for brand endorser evaluation

Characteristic	Description
Familiarity	The person should be easy to recognize and inoffensive to the target market.
Relevance	The person should 'fit' the product in the perceptions of the target market.
Esteem	The person should have value within the target audience. This is usually accomplished by success, winning, or heroism.
Differentiation	The person should be distinct enough from other advertising to catch the eye of the target market.
Decorum	The person's past behavior should indicate that he/she would be an ongoing asset to the product campaign.

Source: Swerdlow & Swerdlow, 2003: 20

(Continued)

(Continued)

First, the ultimate goal of companies deploying sport celebrities as brand endorsers is to raise awareness for their products. Therefore, in order to be successful the chosen celebrity needs to be recognizable, likable, and friendly. The general population does not necessarily have to be *familiar* with the respective celebrity, but definitely the main target audience. Second, the athlete should have a certain reputation or image which creates a certain level of credibility when endorsing a brand, product, or service. Consequently, athletes are usually prominent brand endorsers for sport-related products or services. Similarly, conformity between the endorser and the targeted customers helps to demonstrate the *relevance* of the product or service. Third, the athlete should be considered reputable by the target audience. Following Miciak and Shanklin (1994), the sporting success of athletes is a major determinant of their *esteem*. Fourth, the endorsing athlete should be clearly *differentiable* from the average person. Moreover, the athlete should ideally also stand out from other brand testimonials including other athletes. Lastly, the considered athlete must have shown flawless *decorum* in his past professional and personal life. Involvement of brand endorsers in undesirable behaviour can be threatening to a company's brand image and consequently profits (Louie, Kulik, & Jacobson, 2001).

The presented case serves as an example to illustrate the impact of commercialization on modern athletes' lives in particular rather than on the industry as a whole. Therefore, the careers of two exceptional sporting personalities, Wladimir and Vitali Klitschko, will be examined considering the ongoing commercialization of sports. Further, the FREDD principle will be applied to evaluate the appropriateness of the Klitschko brothers as brand endorsers. The Klitschkos are not just the most successful boxers of their generation, they have also proved to be smart businessmen. Their careers have had highs and lows, while their omnipresence in the media and the public has remained constant.

The Klitschkos were born in the Ukraine, but lived in Germany during their almost entire professional boxing career. They became the most successful heavyweight boxers of their generation: together they held several world heavyweight belts over years. With an 87.23% knockout percentage rate, the retired Vitali holds the second best knockout-to-fight ratio of any champion in heavyweight boxing history. His brother Wladimir is the second longest reigning heavyweight champion of all times. Their professional record is impressive with 108 wins from 113 fights (Klitschko, 2015).

However, not only their sporting careers have been remarkable, they are also smart businessmen. Both were awarded a PhD in sports science from the University of Kiev and speak four languages. In 2007, the Klitschko brothers jointly founded the Klitschko Management Group GmbH (KMG). The KMG is responsible for the Klitschko brand and handles all their marketing activities. It also organized the World Championship fights of the Klitschkos, which means that the revenues generated through these events went directly back to the Klitschkos, thus circumventing middlemen and promoters (KMG, 2015). A single championship fight generated approximately €10 million (Pusch, 2012). Fights often took place in sold-out football arenas and were staged like spectacles comparable to entertainment show events. The first event in such an arena set a record, with 61,000 spectators attending the fight between Wladimir Klitschko and Uzbek boxer Ruslan Chagaev in the Veltins-Arena in Gelsenkirchen, Germany (home to the Football Bundesliga club Schalke 04). In addition, 11.5 million Germans watched the fight live on television which was broadcasted in over 150 countries.

As consultants the Klitschkos and their Management Group also offer their expertise to other professional athletes, entrepreneurs, and personalities from the entertainment and culture industry. They aim to establish a Klitschko Academy to make their strategy for success available to a broader audience. The younger brother is already involved in a university course at the University of St. Gallen in Switzerland. In 2015, Wladimir presented his first fitness programme: with 'Klitschko Body Performance' he aims to enter the German fitness market (KMG, 2015).

The athletic dominance of the Klitschkos is matched by their large marketing appeal which made both brothers omnipresent brands. The combination of the Klitschkos' persona – tall, muscular, good looking, intelligent, and likeable – appears to be perfect for commercial purposes of business companies and the media. The brothers serve as testimonials for several companies such as Telekom (telecommunication), Mercedes (car manufacturer), and Warsteiner (brewery). Since 2008, they have the faces of the McFit fitness chain.

Besides classic celebrity endorsement they are involved in several other businesses. For instance, in 2012 they were co-producers of the musical 'Rocky – Fight from the Heart', they were the leading roles in a documentary about their lives, and various sports gear is branded with their names. The Klitschkos are Unesco Ambassadors and founders of the 'Klitschko Brothers Fund', a charity organization to help under-privileged children (Klitschko, 2015). They regularly appear on German TV shows and have a huge fan base which is not solely interested in their sporting careers. More than 1.6 million Facebook, 190,000 Twitter, and more than 2 million Google+ users follow them online (status: March 2015).

In 2014, Wladimir Klitschko was ranked 25th in 'The World's Highest-Paid Athletes' list by Forbes. According to Forbes his overall revenue in 2014 from sporting performance has been $24 million (approximately €22 million) plus an additional $4 million (approximately €3.7 million) from endorsement contracts (Forbes, 2014). Vitali Klitschko stepped down from boxing in 2013. He has been focusing on his political career since and was elected Mayor of Kiev in 2014 (Klitschko, 2015). The example of the Klitschkos illustrates how the life of athletes nowadays goes beyond the mere sporting career and how revenues are generated through all sorts of business endeavors besides the actual sporting profession. In order to have a more detailed look at the career of the Klitschkos, the next few paragraphs apply the FREDD framework to evaluate the Klitschkos as brand endorsers:

Familiarity. The Klitschkos are likeable, friendly, and easy to recognize. Besides their masculine, attractive appearance they come across as personable men. Initially, their popularity was limited to boxing fans. However, as their fame and sporting success grew, they were more and more present at non-sports related events and TV shows, hence becoming popular and familiar across a broad audience (Hüetlin, 2003). This increased audience made it possible to endorse not only sport related products, but also for example confectioneries or beer.

Relevance. Besides the distinct familiarity of the Klitschkos there is a natural fit between all kinds of sport products and companies such as McFit and the two brothers. They have the image and reputation of healthy, high performance athletes, who go to fitness studios in their

(Continued)

(Continued)

everyday life. Additionally, a fit between the Klitschkos as celebrities and the target audience can be observed, since individuals who frequently watch sports also tend to be interested in actively participating in sports. This relevance is clearly not given for every brand the Klitschkos are standing for (like beer or confectioneries). However, in those cases other FREDD criteria outweigh the lack of relevance.

Esteem. The Klitschkos are highly respected among many population groups for both their amazing athletic talents and for their non-scandalous lifestyle. Combined with their smartness (both speak four languages and have a PhD) this respect makes them one of the most popular athlete endorsers in Germany. As athlete endorsers their ongoing success in sports contributes most to their esteem. The fact that they are smart and successful individuals increased their credibility not just among sport fans, but also within the average population.

Differentiation. One of the main reasons why companies use celebrity endorsers is to stand out in the massive advertising clutter. The Klitschkos are definitely distinctive from other sports celebrities and fulfil this criterion. They perfectly unite physical strength with intelligence and enjoy a brilliant reputation in a sport that is often afflicted with the image of rudeness, rawness, and crime. Additionally, their impressive body constitution and the fact that they are brothers further contribute to their distinctness.

Decorum. For years, the Klitschko brothers have been a prime example of success and reputable lifestyle. They did not show any erratic behaviour in public which would damage their personal or their businesses' brand value. So far the Klitschkos have not been linked to the three potential negative areas of commercialization described earlier, i.e exploitation, doping, or match fixing: at an early stage of their career they established themselves in the sporting top tier with a status minimizing the risk of physiological or psychological exploitation. Additionally, there is no link between match fixing or corruption and the Klitschkos. Accordingly, the topic of doping rarely appears in conjunction with the Klitschkos, also because both are openly opposed to drug use in sports.

However, prior to the 1996 Olympics in Atlanta, Vitali Klitschko was tested positive for steroids and consequently not allowed to take part in the Games (Neumayer, 2014). From time to time critical voices appear since the Klitschkos did not have to fear out-of-competition doping tests (Eder, 2014). Obviously any doping violation would have harmed not only their sporting careers, it would have also questioned their integrity as endorsers and private businessmen. Corruption and match fixing would of course have similar negative effects. Scandalous behaviour by celebrity endorsers is a very big risk for companies. The corporate image and product image can become associated with a celebrity endorser's misbehaviour, which then damages the company's or products' reputation.

In contrast to many other professional athletes, the Klitschkos seem to have prepared well for the time after their professional sporting careers. Vitali is quite successfully focusing on his political career and Wladimir is involved in several business endeavours. Furthermore, both are still owners of the KMG. Those achievements would have been nearly impossible if they had focused only on their sporting career. Through smart steps they established themselves as person brands and businessmen beyond their sporting career. Therefore, the popular appeal of the Klitschkos will withstand their retirement from professional sports. The above case illustrates how athletes are able to commercialize their life through their sporting profession and earn substantial income from activities outside their actual profession. Certainly, the Klitschko brothers have to be regarded as a specific case since they unite several unique characteristics that are not simply transferrable to other athletes in other sports.

Conclusion

This chapter highlighted the ongoing process of commercialization in sports and its implications for elite athletes. The particular case of the Klitschko brothers, Vitali and Wladimir, demonstrates the vast opportunities commercialization brings for athletes to gain income beyond their primary occupation. In order to partly explain their success as businessmen and brand endorsers for several well-known companies inside and outside of the sports industry, the FREDD selection criteria were applied to demonstrate their suitability as athlete endorsers and person brands. It became apparent that both brothers fit exceptionally well with most criteria, and therefore represent attractive celebrity endorsers for business companies.

Besides the positive effects that the commercialization of sports has on individuals such as the Klitschkos, potential threats such as the physical and psychological exploitation of athletes, doping, and match fixing should not be neglected. The ongoing commercialization and huge sums of money in the business do not only attract legitimate businesses. Illicit behaviour such as doping, match fixing (corruption), and exploitation is also associated with the ongoing process of commercialization. As the financial rewards for popularity increase athletes are willing to take higher risks, even when they might be associated with bending or even breaking the law.

Recommended further reading

Gratton, C., Liu, D., Ramchandani, G., & Wilson, D. (2012). *The global economics of sport*. London: Routledge.

Redmond, S., & Holmes, S. (Eds). (2007). *Stardom and celebrity: A reader*. London: SAGE Publications Ltd.

Slack, T. (2004). *The commercialisation of sport*. London: Routledge.

Smart, B. (2005). *The sport star: Modern sport and the cultural economy of sporting celebrity*. London: Sage.

Wenner, L. A. (2013). *Fallen sports heroes, media, and celebrity culture*. New York: P. Lang.

References

Abbruzzese, J. (2013). *A sporting chance of shedding celebrity endorsement problems*. Retrieved 12 March 2015 from http://www.ft.com/cms/s/0/ece33fda-ff90-11e2-a244-00144feab7de.html

Agrawal, J., & Kamakura, W. A. (1995). The economic worth of celebrity endorsers: an event study analysis. *Journal of Marketing, 59*, 56–62.

Arnaut, J. L. (2006). *Independent European sport review*. Nyon: UEFA.

Billings, A. C. (2007). *Olympic media: Behind the scenes at the biggest show on television*. London: Routledge.

Boudreau, F., & Konzak, B. (1991). Ben Johnson and the use of steroids in sport – sociological and ethical considerations. *Canadian Journal of Sport Sciences – Revue Canadienne des Sciences du Sport, 16*(2), 88–98.

Breuer, C., & Hallmann, K. (2013). *Dysfunktionen des Spitzensports: Doping, Match-Fixing und Gesundheitsgefährdungen aus Sicht von Bevölkerung und Athleten [Dysfunctions of elite sports: doping, match fixing, and health issues from the population's and athletes' perspective]*. Bonn: Bundesinstitut für Sportwissenschaft.

Carpenter, K. (2012). Match-fixing – the biggest threat to sport in the 21st century? *International Sports Law Review, 2*, 13–23.

Connor, J. (2009). The athlete as widget: how exploitation explains elite sport. *Sport in Society, 12*(10), 1369–1377.

Creswell, J. (2008). *Nothing sells like celebrity*. Retrieved 12 March 2015 from http://www.nytimes.com/2008/06/22/business/media/22celeb.html?pagewanted=all&_r=0

Der Spiegel (1963). *Geld im Schuh*. Retrieved 24 March 2015 from http://www.spiegel.de/spiegel/print/d-46171821.html

Die Welt (2008). *Wie das Geld zum Fußball kam*. Retrieved 24 March 2015 from http://www.welt.de/wams_print/article2078861/Wie-das-Geld-zum-Fussball-kam.html

Ding, H., Molchanov, A. E., & Stork, P. A. (2011). The value of celebrity endorsements: A stock market perspective. *Marketing Letters, 22*(2), 147–163.

Eder, M. (2014). *Außer Kontrolle – Klitschko und die Doping-Tests*. Retrieved 19 April 2015 from http://www.faz.net/aktuell/sport/sportpolitik/doping/boxen-ausser-kontrolle-klitschko-und-die-doping-tests-13266500.html

Elberse, A., & Verleun, J. (2012). The economic value of celebrity endorsements. *Journal of Advertising Research, 52*(2), 149.

Farrell, K. A., Karels, G. V., Montfort, K. W., & McClatchey, C. A. (2000). Celebrity performance and endorsement value: the case of Tiger Woods. *Managerial Finance, 26*(7), 1–15.

Fizel, J., McNeil, C. R., & Smaby, T. (2008). Athlete endorsement contracts: the impact of conventional stars. *International Advances in Economic Research, 14*(2), 247–256.

Forbes (2014). *The world's highest-paid athletes*. Retrieved 23 March 2015 from http://www.forbes.com/profile/wladimir-klitschko/

Forrest, D., McHale, I., & McAuley, K. (2008). 'Say it ain't so': betting-related malpractice in sport. *International Journal of Sport Finance, 3*(3), 156–166.

Frenger, M., & Pitsch, W. (2012). Erfolg(+)reich und verdorben? Eine empirische Überprüfung verbreiteter Vorurteile zur Kommerzialisierung im Sport. *Sportwissenschaft, 42*(3), 188–201.

Frick, B. (2007). The football players' labor market: empirical evidence from the major European leagues. *Scottish Journal of Political Economy, 54*(3), 422–446.

Harris, H.A. (1964). *Greek athletes and athletics*. London: Hutchinson.

Hoberman, J. (2007). History and prevalence of doping in the marathon. *Sports Medicine, 37*(4–5), 386–388.

Homewood, B. (2013). *Trafficking of young African players still rampant.* Retrieved 12 March 2015 from http://www.reuters.com/article/2013/11/08/us-soccer-africa-trafficking-idUSBRE9A70FQ20131108

Hüetlin, T. (2003). *Der Erfinder der Klitschkos.* Retrieved 19 April 2015 from http://www.spiegel.de/spiegel/print/d-28415159.html

KEA European Affairs (2012). *Match-fixing in sport: A mapping of criminal law provisions in EU 27.* Retrieved 9 June 2015 from http://ec.europa.eu/sport/library/studies/study-sports-fraud-final-version_en.pdf

Kellner, D. (1996). Sports, media culture, and race – Some reflections on Michael Jordan. *Sociology of Sport Journal, 13,* 458–467.

King, A. (2003). *The European Ritual.* Aldershot: Ashgate.

Klitschko (2015). *The official website of Vitali & Wladimir Klitschko.* Retrieved 23 March 2015 from http://www.klitschko.com/en/home/

KMG (2015). *Klitschko Management Group.* Retrieved 23 March 2015 from http://k-mg.de/en/home/

Louie, T. A., Kulik, R. L., & Jacobson, R. (2001). When bad things happen to the endorsers of good products. *Marketing Letters, 12*(1), 13–23.

Mandle, W. F. (1972). The professional cricketer in England in the nineteenth century. *Labour History,* 1–16.

McCracken, G. (1989). Who is the celebrity endorser? Cultural foundations of the endorsement process. *Journal of Consumer Research, 16,* 310–321.

Miciak, A. R., & Shanklin, W. L. (1994). Choosing celebrity endorsers. *Marketing Management, 3,* 50–59.

Mugford, S., Mugford, J., & Donnelly, D. (1999). *Social research project: athletes' motivations for using or not using performance enhancing drugs.* Canberra: Australian Sports Drug Agency.

Neumayer, I. (2014). *Die Klitschkos.* Retrieved 19 April 2015 from http://www.planet-wissen.de/sport_freizeit/kampfsport/boxen/klitschkos.jsp

Olympic Movement (2014). *Revenue sources and distribution.* Retrieved 19 April 2015 from http://www.olympic.org/ioc-financing-revenue-sources-distribution?tab=sources

Pierce, C. (2006). *Moving the chains: Tom Brady and the pursuit of everything.* New York: Farrar, Straus and Giroux.

Pusch, H. (2012). *Die Zehn-Millionen-Euro-Boxer.* Retrieved 23 March 2015 from http://www.zeit.de/sport/2012-03/klitschko-rtl-boxen-geschaeft-mormeck

Rahman, M., & Lockwood, S. (2011). How to 'use your Olympian': the paradox of athletic authenticity and commercialization in the contemporary Olympic Games. *Sociology, 45*(5), 815–829.

Roche, M. (2000). *Mega-Events and modernity: Olympics and Expos in the growth of global culture.* London: Routledge.

Sandomir, R. (2014). *NBC Extends Olympic Deal Into Unknown.* Retrieved 27 February 2015 from http://www.nytimes.com/2014/05/08/sports/olympics/nbc-extends-olympic-tv-deal-through-2032.html

Slater, D., & Tonkiss, F. (2001). *Market Society.* Cambridge: Polity Press.

Stewart, B., & Smith, A. C. (2008). Drug use in sport implications for public policy. *Journal of Sport & Social Issues, 32*(3), 278–298.

Stokvis, R. (2000). Globalization, commercialization and individualization: Conflicts and changes in elite athletics. *Culture, Sport, Society, 3*(1), 22–34.

Süddeutsche (2010). *Die Legende des Bum.* Retrieved 24 March 2015 from http://www.sueddeutsche.de/sport/gerd-mueller-die-legende-des-bum-1.780096-2

Swerdlow, R. A., & Swerdlow, M. R. (2003). Celebrity endorsers: spokesperson selection criteria and case examples of FREDD. *Academy of Marketing Studies Journal, 7*(2), 13–26.

UEFA (2014). *Distribution to clubs 2013/14.* Retrieved 12 March 2015 from http://www.uefa. org/MultimediaFiles/Download/OfficialDocument/uefaorg/Finance/02/11/95/44/2119544_ DOWNLOAD.pdf

Vincent, J., Hill, J. S., & Lee, J. W. (2009). The multiple brand personalities of David Beckham: A case study of the Beckham brand. *Sport Marketing Quarterly, 18*(3), 173–180.

Wicker, P., Breuer, C., & von Hanau, T. (2012). Understanding the income determinants of German elite athletes in non-professionalised sports. *International Journal of Sport Management and Marketing, 11*(1/2), 26–43.

Williams, C. C. (2005). *A commodified world? Mapping the limits of capitalism.* London: Zed Books.

Wilson, B. (2013). *Doping in sport: Counting the cost.* Retrieved 12 March 2015 from http://www.bbc.com/ news/business-21782447

THE BUSINESS OF RUNNING

KOEN BREEDVELD AND JEROEN SCHEERDER

Introduction: Historical and recent developments

A focus on amateurship has always been one of the pillars of the sport system of the 20th century (Bottenburg, 2001; Breuer et al., 2015; Hallmann & Petry, 2013; Scheerder, Willem, et al., 2015). Sport was practiced in non-profit clubs managed by volunteers and organized under the umbrella of federations that were in turn governed by boards of volunteers. This model holds true even for the biggest sport organizations in the world, among which is the International Olympic Committee (see Case Study 5.1 on pages 66–7).

Thus, non-profit organizations like federations and clubs play a central role in the organization of today's grassroots sports. Funding for grassroots sports comes to a great extent from national governments and local municipalities. Through subsidies to clubs, the building of sport facilities like swimming pools and football fields, and the integration of physical education in the school system, governments have stimulated sport participation and built a so-called Sport for All framework. This model holds true for almost any European country, though admittedly the role of federations and clubs in grassroots sports is less developed in some countries, especially in the South and the East of Europe. In these countries either public authorities or private enterprises act as the main providers for sports.

Needless to say there is much more to learn about this European not-for-profit model for sports. A brief glance over today's sport pages tells us that money is all-enveloping with regard to sports nowadays (Gratton & Taylor, 2000; Smith & Westerbeek, 2004 – see also Case study 5.1). From football to tennis and cycling, commercial interests shape sports' calendars and events.

Non-profit organizations like FIFA, UEFA or Wimbledon still organize the main competitions within their sports. Yet even within these non-profit competitions, commercial interests have gained ground.

This rise in commercial interests has not been limited to elite sports. On the contrary, in grassroots sports as well sport is not solely about volunteering anymore. Today, sport federations and sport clubs rely on professionals to govern their organizations and undertake activities. Outside or alongside the club system, there has been a sharp increase in commercial organizations providing opportunities has been take part in sports. From swimming pools to golf clubs, fitness centers, climbing halls and bowling alleys, sport facilities are increasingly being run by private companies. Their primary objective is to earn money and generate financial profits (Gratton & Taylor, 2000; Smith & Westerbeek, 2004). Judging by the growth of many of these commercially operated sports, they seem quite capable of striking a chord with the general sporting population. While traditional sports like basketball, swimming or gymnastics are struggling to reach out to new practitioners, commercially organized sports like fitness and golf have grown considerably during the past decades. Major sport producers like Adidas, Asics and Nike now make multi-billion turnovers selling clothing, footwear and sporting attributes (tennis rackets, heart rate monitors, etc.), using their marketing power to convince people of the merits of sports in general and their products in particular.

Challenges and critiques

What does it imply for the sport system when commercial organizations and interests gain in importance; when governments may invest in Sport for All campaigns, but see their money and efforts fade away against the marketing budgets of multi-national sponsors and sport producers, and when sport clubs may well hold their general assemblies and discuss the difficulties of opening up to new communities, while simultaneously fitness centers go out in the streets and draw people in by offering interesting discounts and appealing new concepts like Zumba or a bootcamp? How do these changes affect our Sport for All policies and the social significance of sports, which derives to a great deal from its orientation towards volunteering, non-profit organizations and a 'civil society context'?[1]

In an attempt to answer these questions, in this chapter we will highlight a sport that has its roots in the traditional sports system, but has recently undergone a tremendous amount of change away from that system: long-distance running. Over the past decades, long-distance running has transformed from an Olympic discipline dominated by a small number of elite athletes, into one of the most practiced grassroots sports attracting huge masses of runners and joggers. Running seems to have undergone this transition not because of the actions of clubs, federations and municipalities. The driving force behind today's running wave, or rather running tsunami, appears to be the actions of commercial agents – organizers of running events, sport producers, and social-media companies running apps and digital platforms (like Endomundo and Runkeeper). What can be learnt from these developments, and more importantly, what effects do they have on the future of sports and its social meaning?

The material for this chapter stems from previous research projects by both authors as well as from a project that was undertaken in 2013 and 2014 by the MEASURE network,[2] and that resulted in the book *Running Across Europe* (Scheerder & Breedveld, 2015).

Case studies: Running

The rise in running

The marathon has been part and parcel of the Olympic Games as of its start in 1896 – though women were not allowed to take part until the 1984 Games in Los Angeles. The name dates back to 490BC, referring to the Greek soldier Pheidippides who supposedly ran from Marathon to Athens to report the victory of the Greek army over the Persian army. For decades, the marathon, or more generally long-distance running, was a much appreciated discipline in the broader track-and-field family of disciplines. However, outside the scope of competitive sports, running never did seem to raise much interest in the general public: when in 1953 Statistics Netherlands ran one of its first surveys on sport participation, football and swimming and even volleyball and tennis were named as possible sports-to-do, but not running (or golf or fitness, for that matter) (Breedveld, 2014).

This changed for the good when in the 1960s governments started to focus on Sport for All as part of their welfare and health policies (see Bottenburg et al., 2006, 2010; Scheerder & Breedveld, 2015). During this first 'wave of running', the sport was taken out of its elite sport context, and introduced to the general public as a *recreational sport*. Governments teamed up with federations and health-promoting organizations to build programs for people to take up running (see Case study 5.2). Sport became a social right and a merit good, a form of serious leisure (Stebbins, 2007) that was considered worthy of spending the newly gained free time and spending power on (and to fight the accompanying welfare diseases such as cancer, diabetes and obesity).

During the economic depression of the 1980s, public interest in grassroots sports faded somewhat and so did the interest in long-distance running. In the 1990s however, and especially after the turn of the century, the growth in running accelerated again, giving rise to what is now often referred to as the 'second wave of running'. Over two decades, the number of marathons worldwide exploded to some 3,900 marathon events per year, and the number of finishers to some 1.6 million (see Figure 5.1 and Case study 5.2 on pages 67–8). Needless to say marathon running represents the high-end of long-distance road-running. Further down the chain, many runners pride themselves on realizing more modest goals, like half marathons, 10K and 5K runs, or kids' runs (often 2.5K). Running quickly attracted new markets, e.g. busy businessmen, mid-thirty singles of both sexes and young mothers eager to get back in shape again. Running fitted in nicely in an individualized society, where looking fit and in shape mattered at the workplace as well as at the busy market for relationships, and in which governments faced rising health costs. A whole new branch of the leisure economy emerged: running event organizers, producers of running shoes and shirts, publishers of websites, and magazines with a focus on running. Seeing people run in the streets and occasionally gather by the thousands at a mass running event became a familiar sight.

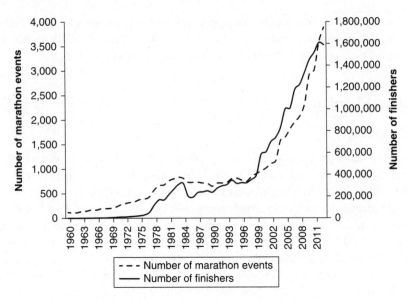

Figure 5.1 Evolution of the number of marathon events and marathon finishers worldwide, 1960–2013

Source: Scheerder, Breedveld & Borgers, 2015: 9

In recent years, a professionalization of the running industry has taken place. Companies are probing the market with new events such as 'color runs', 'mud runs' and 'lady runs'. In this so-called 'third wave', running has become a product that is actively marketed (see Case study 5.2). New concepts and segments are being defined and explored, drawing running closer into the 'experience economy' (Pine & Gilmore, 1999). Smaller running events are taken over by marketing companies that manage more than one event, in more than one sport. Event organizers from outside running introduce theatre-like elements (music, lighting). Social media allow for companies to gather data on the running market, and then sell those data to shoe manufacturers for example. In this new running world, some runners are still very much concerned over their achievement. For many others, however, striving for new personal bests is not their main goal. For them, experiencing the event is what it is all about, feeling part of a community of people that share a concern over their health and their looks, and a desire to use running as a way to do something about it (see Breedveld et al., 2015).

All in all, however, running has over the past decades developed as a very popular way of being physically active for a great number of people. In countries like Denmark and Germany, the percentage of runners is well over 20% of the population (see Figure 5.2). On average, it is estimated that 12% of the EU 15+ population is engaged in running somehow, representing 50 million runners (Breedveld et al., 2015). This equals the number of people that are estimated to be engaged in fitness.[3] Currently, running ranks as the number one sport in Belgium (Flanders) and Denmark, second in Germany, third in Hungary, fourth in the Netherlands and the UK, fifth in Spain and eighth in Finland. The biggest influx in running seems to have come from women. In several countries (e.g. Belgium (Flanders), Denmark, Germany and Hungary), participation in running is now more common among women than among men.

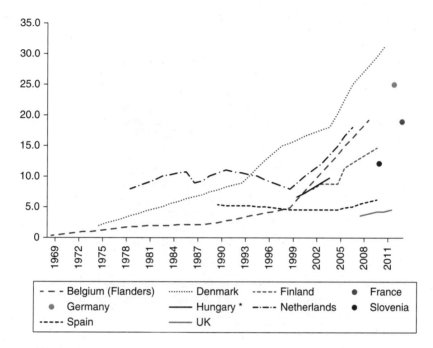

Figure 5.2   Participation in running in ten EU countries, percentages of the population

*Hungary: 15–29 year olds

Source: Scheerder & Breedveld, 2015

Explaining the rise in running

Why has running become so popular? A number of factors can be pointed at to explain how these waves of running have turned into a 'running tsunami'.

First, today's society is a time-pressured one, as well as a society that values health and looking good (meaning: not obese) (Pilgaard, 2012). Generally, there is great support for taking up sports or engaging in some form of physical activity (European Commission, 2014). Running offers an opportunity to stay healthy in a time-effective manner that is easy to fit into busy schedules. In addition, running refrains from the competitiveness and emphasis on winning and defeating (the 'agonal' aspects of sports) that is more common with for example ball games (like football). For many of today's sportsmen and sportswomen, who are drawn to sports more from an instrumental perspective (to look and feel good) than from a goal perspective (love of the game), this is considered an asset rather than a drawback.

Second is the social organization of running. Typically, the vast majority of runners are not members of a sports club (Figure 5.3). Largely, they exercise on their own or with friends, in informal networks or with colleagues. These contexts are often referred to as 'light running communities' (Bottenburg et al., 2010) as opposed to the 'greedier' setting of a sport club (with its training schedules and duties to be performed).

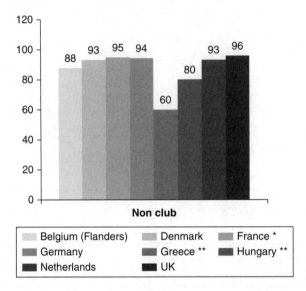

Figure 5.3   Non-membership of formal running clubs in eight EU countries (percentage of runners)

* % of participants who participate in a training session at a club

** % of participants in running events; all other come from date of population surveys

Source: Scheerder & Breedveld, 2015

Clearly, athletic clubs have only to a limited degree profited by and contributed to the growth of running.[4] In countries like Belgium (Flanders) and the Netherlands, the number of members of athletic clubs has remained fairly stable over the past years (Borgers et al., 2015; Hover et al., 2015). At the same time, the amount of runners increased considerably, and so did the number of organizers of running events (see Case study 5.2).

The reasons why running events have been so important in the growth of running are threefold:

1. First, they allow for runners to set themselves goals, to work up towards a purpose. Setting goals is one of the most powerful ways of promoting adherence in physical activity (Baart de la Faille-Deutekom et al., 2012). Participating in running events helps runners maintain their regimes. This is especially called for in running, as this misses out on other motivational aspects of sports, e.g. practicing a certain skill (aiming, catching). And as most

people run 'alone' outside the regime of a training group, they lack the kind of structure that people experience once they submit themselves to a social structure. Having a goal to work towards acts as a structuring element and a motivator.

2. Secondly, running events allow for runners to share their passion. Many runners register for events together with other runners, or meet other runners at the event. Running events, with their 'festive atmosphere', allow participants to experience their sport together and to feel part of a larger running community.

3. Thirdly, running events allow runners to put their love for running 'on display'. Running events are often organized in public areas, like city centers or (football) stadiums. This grants runners an opportunity to participate in a form of 'conspicuous jogging', visible to family, friends and the local community, expressing their identity as runners and thereby deepening their psychological commitment to running.

Larger running events and those with longer running distances (Borgers et al., 2015: 38; Petridis, 2015: 147) seem to have especially profited from the growing interest in running. Often, these larger events are being run professionally and operated by commercial or semi-commercial agents (see Case study 5.2). Their experience is as much in organizing large-scale events (with the help of local municipalities) and handling large-crowds, as it is in building experiences and drawing in sponsors and participants ('selling the event'). As they organize several larger events during a year, often in different sports, this allows them to learn from their experiences and invest in new tools and techniques (registration, time-tracking, automatic photo and film coverage). They possess the financial and creative resources, as well as the mindset, to invest in marketing campaigns and new concepts.

The fact that the business world takes an active interest in running and jogging should not come as a surprise. While a t-shirt, some shorts and a pair of running shoes may not sound like much of a business, expenditures by runners in Europe are today estimated at €9.6 billion a year (Breedveld et al., 2015). Of these expenses, roughly 40% is spent on shoes, 30% on clothes and 30% on sundry expenses (like admission fees to events, literature, nutrition and medical treatment). In the Netherlands, it is estimated that the €360 million expenditure by runners on shoes and clothing makes up 40% of the total market for sport shoes and sport clothes (Breedveld, 2015). Clearly, today's grassroots sport is not the sole terrain any more of municipalities building football pitches and sport clubs that are being run by volunteers. Today's grassroots sport is very much a matter also of the business sector. In running, event organizers, sport producers, retailers and social media companies together shape the running market. Outside running we can see comparable developments in markets like fitness, allegedly a €26.8 billion market in Europe (Europe Active and Deloitte, 2014), skiing or golf.

The role of running clubs

The running industry, and running events in particular, have been important in stimulating running. Does all of this imply that clubs and federations have no role to play, or have played no role so far, in the rise of the running market? Even though clubs and federations appear to have missed the boat somewhat (Bottenburg et al., 2010), it would be a mistake to suggest that athletic clubs and federations have not been important for running. In many countries, clubs have been at the origin of many of today's running events (see for example Finland), and even though many of these larger events now have commercial or semi-commercial origins, in some countries (e.g. Denmark and Germany) clubs and their federations[5] still play an important role in organizing running events.

Typically, in any country several hundreds to thousands of running events are organized on a yearly basis. The largest of those have become too big for clubs to be organized. But these make up only the upper segment. Below that, the majority of events are still organized by clubs, drawing on the social capital that they generate through their volunteers. In addition, while adults may often run on their own, youngsters get acquainted with running through club sports. And it is also by means of these clubs that talented young athletes develop themselves into the elite athletes that perform at World Championships and Olympic Games and draw our attention in the media. Therefore, sports clubs still play a key role in building and maintaining today's running communities, from their foundation of both recreational running and youth sports to the very top of elite performances.

The marketing powers of the sport business

If commercial players have a bigger hold on the sport sector, not just in elite sports but also in grassroots sports, how should one judge these developments? From a welfare policies perspective, in which access to sports is considered a social right, one is inclined to think critically of commercial agents' increasing influence over the sport sector. Can commercial interests be realigned with welfare ideals and government expenditures? Is not the language of marketing in contradiction with the values that guide civil society and voluntary organizations?

Judging by the socio-economic profiles of runners, one is inclined to remain critical of the increasing influence of commercial parties in the running industry (Gratton & Taylor, 2000). In running, as well as in fitness, more or less to the same degree, higher SES groups are overrepresented (Scheerder & Breedveld, 2015). It is also true that the interest of the commercial sector is oriented most towards those markets that yield the biggest opportunities for making profits. It should hardly come as a surprise that running and fitness, with their wealthy practitioners and their relatively low investments, are markets that are of interest to sport companies – much more than football, gymnastics or volleyball for example. It is also true that commercial agents tend to raise prices and that their interest is primarily in social groups that can afford those prices, and not for example in the unemployed or those that live off welfare checks. At the end of the day, the goal of a company is to make profit, not to make society sustainable or to grant access for marginal groups.

This being said, it is important to keep in mind that it has been because of the activities of commercial agents that sports like running and fitness have experienced such tremendous growth. With their marketing experience and techniques and their drive for generating revenues, commercial organizations seem to have succeeded where local governments and clubs often fail, namely in reaching out to new markets and target groups (Smith & Westerbeek, 2004).

If the essence of a company is to make a profit, the essence of a club is to be of service to its members. A sport club's interest lies with its members, not with non-members (Breuer et al., 2015). A sport club may be on the look-out for new members, but it will always judge the value of bringing in new members by how that may serve the interests of the present members. When membership is low and new members are needed to raise budgets, or to raise the level of play within a club, clubs may actively seek new members. At other occasions however, e.g. when the maximum playing capacity is reached or when newcomers are feared to bring along customs that are not appreciated, the influx of new members may be restricted or even actively discouraged.

In addition, the experience and expertise to cater for new markets and target groups are much more limited within clubs than within commercial organizations. Within the latter, the free market urges entrepreneurs to renew and innovate and to develop new concepts for new groups of sport consumer. In these days of abundance of leisure supply and shortage in time, it is essential for any service to keep renewing itself and remain top-of-mind with consumers. This is a message that is well understood by the business sector, but largely ignored by the traditional sport sector. The outwards-reaching approach of commercial organizations has meant that great numbers of people who previously were not active or interested in sport have somehow been seduced to take up sport. As such, commercial agents are in large part responsible for the growth in sport participation over the last decades. Admittedly, sports like fitness suffer from low adherence figures (Baart de la Faille, 2012). Newcomers easily get bored or disappointed, and drop out even after weeks or months. This should not come as a great surprise though. It is much easier to make a small number of intrinsically motivated sportsmen and sportswomen stick, than it is to draw in and keep a much bigger number of extrinsically interested people. That is what the sport business deserves credit for.

The social significance of the sport business

There is a second issue here, one that has to do with the social relationships that are being built whilst running. Sport clubs are valued for the opportunity they offer for members to interact, to connect with people they might never have met otherwise. At a sport club, one meets and gets acquainted with different sorts of people, whether that is the chairman, the referee or opponents in a competition. These new contacts bring social capital to individuals, and allow them to turn for help or social support from these so-called 'weak ties' (Granovetter, 1973). In addition, the democratic structure of the club system provides members with an opportunity to be part of the decision-making process for their favorite sports. Volunteering allows people to be actively engaged in society and to use and develop their talents (Breuer et al., 2015).

Athletic clubs share these features as much as any sport club. So, for any runner who belongs to a track-and-field club, these merits are there to grasp and take advantage of. However, as we have seen, most runners do not join clubs. Apparently, ties to the club are not always merely 'weak', but can also be compelling and demanding. Most runners prefer to run by themselves, with friends or relatives, or maybe in a small running group. Every now and then, they will take part in a running event.

The fact that most runners do not join a club, does not mean that running does not offer them social interaction. As Petridis rightfully says (2015), 'the fact that runners run alone, does not mean that they feel alone'. Many runners are connected to other runners merely because of their co-presence at an event, because they meet fellow runners in the streets, or because they share information on running through social media. Runners even connect socially while reading running magazines or ads. Media messages help runners remind themselves of the challenges, the pain and the effort they have put in running, and help them feel part of a larger and even global running community. Needless to say these ties are extremely weak. They may cause a smile of recognition on one's face or perhaps start a friendship, but most often they will not provide the same kind of social support that a fellow club member might offer.

Often runners run with friends, colleagues, family members or other relatives who are close to them. In these cases running helps to re-establish existing bonds (and/or helps to create new ones). A mutual interest in running helps to share experiences, brings memories back to life and acts as a conversation topic. In this sense, the 'bonding' force of running is stronger than the 'bridging' force of running.[6] As participants in running events generally do not have a say on what is going on inside the event, or play a role in organizing the event, running outside a club misses out on much of the democratic and educational potential that a club system has to offer. Apparently however, as most runners do not join clubs, these are not values that are sought by today's runners (Hurenkamp, 2009). Most value the opportunity to stay healthy ánd remain the master of their agenda, to find some peace of mind amidst a day that is packed with deadlines and appointments, or simply to mingle with those one already knows. For the broader society that attitude may have its disadvantages. However, for individual runners it appears to realign well with their values and day-to-day concerns over their health and looks.

Case study 5.1: Amateurism and commercial influences in sports

As of its start in 1896, participation in the Olympic Games was only open to amateur sportsmen (and since 1990 to women too). The amateur status of sport was considered to best reflect the values that the IOC embraced and strived for, and that are still reflected today in the Olympic charter (see http://www.olympic.org/olympic-charter/documents-reports-studies-publications). Until this day, the IOC is ruled by officials who are not paid salaries, and merely receive a reimbursement for their costs (which of course, can be quite considerable). The same goes, inter alia, for the many national and international sport federations that are the governing bodies and spokespeople for their sports nationally and internationally, and that hold the monopoly on their competitions. Thus, for example, both FIFA and UEFA, ITF (International Tennis Federation) and Tennis Europe, and their many national counterparts, are non-profit organizations that are governed by boards which consist of 'volunteers'.

The background of sport in volunteerism and amateurship is quite complicated, and has as much to do with very honorable notions like egalitarianism and keeping sports 'pure', as with very personal interests like noble men trying to keep strong and well-trained farmers and industrial laborers away from their competitions (see Bottenburg, 2001).

Today, commercial influences are seen all over sports. Most professional football clubs, like Manchester United or Chelsea, are owned by private companies or investors. The IOC has big contracts with sponsors like Coca-Cola and McDonald's. Competitions are being altered (games shortened, finals played late at night) to ensure greater audience and hence bigger incomes from television rights. In the 2009–2012 period, the IOC generated revenues of US$8.046 million from marketing and broadcasting campaigns (US$2,630 million in 1993–1996; see IOC, 2015).

This shift towards commercialism has not out of the blue. In its striving to set the stage for the best athletes to meet and compete, the IOC abandoned its dedication to the amateur ideal in the early 1980s. Since the Los Angeles Olympic Games of 1984, professionals have been allowed to take part in the Olympics. In football, amateurism was abandoned earlier, though in some countries it took until the 1950s to switch to professional football.

Yet it would be misleading if we were to state that sport has its origins in volunteerism and amateurship alone. Commercial influences have always been closely linked to sports. For example, the world's main cycling competition, the Tour de France, started off in 1903 as an initiative of the company that published the sport journal L'Auto-Velo. Today, the Tour de France is owned and organized by the French company ASO (Amaury Sport Organisation). ASO is part of the Amaury group of companies that also publishes the sport newspaper L'Équipe and the newspaper Le Parisien. In addition to organizing the Tour de France, ASO 'owns' the Paris-Dakar car rally, as well as several of the most important one-day cycling races in both France and Belgium, and the Spanish three-week racing course La Vuelta (www.aso.fr). Likewise, the Fédération Internationale de l'Automobile's FIA Formula One car racing competition is operated by the Formula One Group, a group of companies owned largely by the CVC Capital Partners together with JP Morgan (the bank/investment company) and led by Bernie Ecclestone (https://en.wikipedia.org/wiki/Formula_One_Group).

Case study 5.2: Three waves of running events

The first wave in running originated from the Sport for All policies that hit Europe in the late 1960s (Scheerder & Breedveld, 2015). Easy to organize, requiring little technical expertise or expensive facilities, running soon found itself at the core of Sport for All. In the Netherlands, campaigns to stimulate running were initiated in 1968 ('Trim Actie'). In Germany a similar campaign ('Trimm Dich') started in 1970 and in Hungary, the 'Run for your Health' campaign started off in 1972. In a few years' time, seeing people in shorts running across the streets became a familiar sight in European cities, with marathon events originating in Athens (1972), Berlin (1974), Amsterdam (1975), Paris (1976), Madrid (1978), Stockholm (1979), Warsaw (1979), Barcelona (1980), Dublin (1980), Frankfurt (1981), Helsinki (1981), London (1981), Rotterdam (1981), Budapest (1984), Reykjavik (1984), Vienna (1984), Lisbon (1986) etc.

(Continued)

(Continued)

Over the past ten to fifteen years, a second wave of running has fueled a further increase in the number of running events. The Association of Road Racing Statisticians (ARRS) documented some 3,900 marathons in 2013 worldwide, against less than 1,000 at the start of the century (see Figure 5.1). In Belgium (Flanders), the amount of running events is estimated to have increased from some 100 in 1985 to over 600 nowadays (Borgers et al., 2015). In Denmark, the number of events rose from some 500 in 2008 to around 900 in 2013, but with fewer participants per event (Forsberg, 2015). In Germany, the number of events skyrocketed from 646 in 1977 to 3,551 in 1999 (Hallmann et al., 2015). In Greece, there was growth from 63 events in 2006 to 2,014 events in 2012 (Petridis, 2015), in Hungary from 50 in 2000 to 240 in 2012 (Perenyi, 2015), in Slovenia from 328 in 2007 to 665 in 2012 (Topic & Rauter 2015), and in Finland from 200 in the 1970s to approximately 600 in 2012 (Vehmas and Lahti, 2015).

Whilst running events in the 1970s were mainly organized by cities and athletic clubs, running events in the 21st century are often organized by commercial agents, e.g. Golazo (http://www.golazo.com/), the Color Run brand (https://thecolorrun.com/about/) or by foundations that operate on the edge of profit/not-for-profit like the Dutch Le Champion (http://www.lechampion.nl/). Many of today's running events are named after the main sponsor, like the Argenta Running Tour in Belgium (http://www.sport.be/runningtour/?v=15102014) and the Nationale Nederlanden Marathon Rotterdam (http://www.nnmarathonrotterdam.nl/) (both Argenta and NN are insurance companies). Retailers like Run2Day or Running World may sponsor the events, team up with the organizers and offer discounts on racing days. Sport producers may adopt an event and come up with a dedicated product (like New Balance does with the NN Rotterdam Marathon shoe). Alternatively, they may develop their own events, like the Nike's Women Races, N+TC tour or We Own The Night (WOTN – http://www.run2day.nl/nike-we-own-the-night), or start their own running clubs (http://www.nike.com/nl/nl_nl/c/cities/amsterdam). For those interested, social-media platforms like Endomondo, Runkeeper, Strava or Start-to-Run offer services such as contact with other runners, virtual competitions and (personalized) training advice and guidance (see http://www.start-to-run.be/).

Conclusion

During most of the 20th century leisure-time running was practiced mainly on a track-and-field arena as an athletic event. Today, millions of people partake in road and city runs. The success of running can be attributed to the cultural, fitness and experience (r)evolutions of the 1960s, 1990s and 2010s respectively. So far, this has resulted in three so-called running waves. The first running boom was characterized by the cultural revolution of the 1960s, including a shift from the track to the street. During the 1990s the fitness revolution ended in a second boom of running, encompassing a process of democratization in terms of age and sex. The third running wave only started recently and focuses on the experiential and sensorial value of running, leading to the rise of fun and adventure runs such as color runs, light runs, electric runs, mud runs, obstacle runs, urban trail runs, etc.

Today, mass running has grown into a gigantic economic market, in Europe being worth a tidy €9.6 billion. Although the majority of running expenditures is on running clothes and shoes, more and more runners also spend their money on 'new' services (registration fees for running events, subscriptions for running magazines, running exercise testing, etc.) and 'new' goods and accessories (heart rate monitors, GPS running watches, running apps, etc.). Amateur runners contribute highly to the economics of running. Thus the popularization and commercialization of running go hand in hand.

Generally, the growth of this market has come from powers outside the world of federations and sport clubs (European Commission, 2014; Gratton & Taylor, 2000; Scheerder et al., 2011). Most runners nowadays are not members of a sport club. Memberships of sport clubs have not kept up with the 'running tsunami' that flooded the sport system during these last decades. The rise in running has mainly come about through the actions of running events, social media companies and the running industry. These commercial powers both benefited from and contributed to the growth in running. As a result, the social capital that stems from running has changed. Today, running is more about maintaining bonds with a smaller circle of close relatives, and staying loosely in touch with the running community, than it is about joining the social democratic structures of voluntary sports organizations.

This is not to say that public and non-profit organizations have not played and do not play a significant role in supporting and promoting running as a leisure-time physical activity. Local governments invest in running by providing facilities such as running tracks. An increasing share of cities and municipalities have discovered the economic and social value of events as part of their marketing policy, and stage running events or act as the partners of private companies that organize these events.

For the traditional sport sector, with its clubs and federations, it is important to keep a weather eye on these developments, and to not miss the boat of the current running boom (Bottenburg et al., 2010). Given the fact that running has much to offer in terms of social and physical capital, in the years to come different social groups – not only athletes, but also runners and joggers, as well as elderly, less well-off people, foreigners, etc. – will knock at the door of federations and clubs. Track and field federations and clubs are still regarded as the rightful spokespeople for their 'industry': they act as natural partners for governments, both nationally and locally; they provide the necessary infrastructure for talented youngsters to develop into true athletes; and they offer a social and agogic context for anyone interested in practicing their sport.

However, both clubs and federations need to realize that other powerful parties now give a shape to the running landscape. Some of these are better equipped to cater to the needs of large groups of runners than are athletic clubs and federations. Clubs and federations need to learn to open up and work with those parties rather than against them (Smith & Westerbeek, 2004). They also need to take into account the contemporary needs and wants of new groups of (potential) sports participants and learn to differentiate their supply. But they especially need to recognize which role suits them best, alongside the powerful commercial powers that are now part and parcel of the running industry.

Recommended further reading

The best suggestion for further reading is:

Running across Europe: The rise and size of one of the largest sport markets (Scheerder & Breedveld, Eds, 2015).

Running across Europe consists of different chapters on ten different countries, put together by local experts, and accompanied by an introduction and a concluding chapter by the editors.
    In addition, we point to several books on sport participation and sport policies:

Breedveld, K., Gratton, C., Hoekman, R., Scheerder, J., Stege, J., Stubbe, J. & Vos, S. (2013). *Study on a possible future sport monitoring function in the EU.* Brussels: European Commission/Directorate-General for Education & Culture/Sport Unit.
Hallmann, K. & Petry, K. (Eds). (2013). *Comparative sport development: Systems, participation and public policy* (Sports Economics, Management & Policy 8). New York, NY: Springer Science.
Scheerder, J., Vandermeerschen, H., Van Tuyckom, C., Hoekman, R., Breedveld, K. & Vos, S. (2011). *Understanding the game: Sport participation in Europe. Facts, reflections and recommendations* (Sport Policy & Management 10). Leuven: University of Leuven/Research Unit of Social Kinesiology & Sport Management.
Scheerder, J., Willem, A., Claes, E. & Billiet, S. (2015). *International study on the organisation of sport in twelve countries and their policy towards sport federations: Country profiles* (Volume 2). Leuven/Ghent: University of Leuven – Policy in Sports & Physical Activity Research Group/Ghent University – Team Sports Management.

On the development of sport clubs in different EU countries:

Breuer, C., Hoekman, R., Nagel, S. & van der Werff, H. (Eds) (2015). *Sport clubs in Europe.* New York: Springer.

On sport business:

Gratton, C. & Taylor, P. (2000). *Economics of sport and recreation.* London: Spon.
Smith, A. & Westerbeek, H. (2004). *The sportbusiness future.* Basingstoke: Palgrave Macmillan.

Notes

1   In the UK often referred to as 'Big Society', after the UK's Conservative Party election campaign of 2010.
2   As part of the broader European Association for the Sociology of Sport EASS network (http://www.eass-sportsociology.eu/), in 2010 a smaller network of researchers on sport participation was formed, called MEASURE. MEASURE (Meeting for European Sport Participation and Sport Cultures Research) consists of sport sociologists and sport statisticians who share knowledge on how sport participation is developing over time, on the differences in sport participation between social groups, and on research methods for studying sport participation See www.measuresport.eu/news

3   See http://www.europeactive.eu/blog/europeactive-and-deloitte-publish-new-official-european-health-fitness-market-report
4   Much like gymnastics did not benefit much from the increasing popularity of aerobics and fitness, which in many aspects are not that different from gymnastics.
5   Sometimes also, clubs develop outside a 'traditional' sport federation, and form an adjacent structure. For examples see the case of 'health runner clubs' in Greece, but also those in Denmark (with 'DGI' operating next to 'DIF') and Hungary.
6   'Bonding' generally refers to the connections people maintain with people they were already familiar with; 'bridging' refers to building connections with people one did not know beforehand (Putnam 2000).

References

Baart de la Faille-Deutekom, M., Middelkamp, J. & Steenbergen, J. (2012). *The state of research in the global fitness industry.* English edition. Deventer: ...da M uitgeverij.

Borgers, J., Vos, S. & Scheerder, J. (2015). Belgium (Flanders): Trends and governance in running. In J. Scheerder & K. Breedveld (Eds), *Running across Europe* (pp. 28–58). Houndmills, Basingstoke, Hampshire/New York: Palgrave Macmillan.

Bottenburg, M. van (2001). *Global Games.* Urbana/Chicago: University of Illinois Press.

Bottenburg, M. van, Kalmthout, J. van & Meulen, R. van der (2006). *The second running wave: On the growth and size of the running market and how the KNAU can further develop its market share.* 's-Hertogenbosch: W.J.H. Mulierinstituut.

Bottenburg, M. van, Scheerder, J. & Hover, P. (2010). Don't miss the next boat: Europe's opportunities and challenges in the second wave of running. *New Studies in Athletics,* 25(3/4), 125–143.

Breedveld, K. (2014). *Sportparticipatie. Uitdagingen voor wetenschap en beleid.* Nijmegen: Radboud Universiteit Nijmegen.

Breedveld, K. (2015). BV Sportland. In *Sport & Strategie,* 8–2: 35.

Breedveld, K., Scheerder, J. & Borgers, J. (2015). Running across Europe: The way forward. In J. Scheerder & K. Breedveld (Eds), *Running across Europe* (pp. 241–264). Houndmills, Basingstoke, Hampshire/New York: Palgrave Macmillan.

Breuer, C., Hoekman, R., Nagel, S. & van der Werff, H. (Eds) (2015). *Sport clubs in Europe.* New York: Springer.

Europe Active and Deloitte (2014). *The European health and fitness market report.* Brussels: Europe Active.

European Commission (2014). *Special Eurobarometer 412: Sport and physical activity.* Report. Brussels: European Commission.

Forsberg, P. (2015). Denmark: Running for the sake of running? In J. Scheerder & K. Breedveld (Eds), *Running across Europe* (pp. 59–80). Houndmills, Basingstoke, Hampshire/New York: Palgrave Macmillan.

Granovetter, M. (1973). The strength of weak ties. *American Journal of Sociology,* 6, 1360–1380.

Gratton, C., & Taylor, P. (2000). *Economics of sport and recreation.* London: Spon.

Hallmann, K., Breuer, C. & Dallmeyer, S. (2015). Germany: Running participation, motivation and images. In J. Scheerder & K. Breedveld (Eds), *Running across Europe* (pp. 121–139). Houndmills, Basingstoke, Hampshire/New York: Palgrave Macmillan.

Hallmann, K. & Petry, K. (2013). *Comparative sport development: Systems, participation and public policy.* New York: Springer Science+Business Media.

Hover, P., Werff, H. van der & Breedveld, K. (2015). The Netherlands: Rising participation rates, shifting segments. In J. Scheerder & K. Breedveld (Eds), *Running across Europe* (pp. 187–207). Houndmills, Basingstoke, Hampshire/New York: Palgrave Macmillan.

Hurenkamp, M. (2009). Organize liberal, think conservative: Citizenship in light communities. In J.W. Duyvendak, F. Hendriks & M. van Niekerk (Eds), *City in sight: Dutch dealings with urban change* (pp. 141–158). Amsterdam: Amsterdam University Press.

IOC (2015). *Olympic marketing factfile 2015*. DOI on 5 December, from www.olympic.org/Documents/IOC_Marketing/olympic_marketing_fact_file_v3_2015.pdf).

Perenyi, S. (2015). Hungary: The popularisation and expansion of amateur running culture. In J. Scheerder & K. Breedveld (Eds), *Running across Europe* (pp. 140–162). Houndmills, Basingstoke, Hampshire/New York: Palgrave Macmillan.

Petridis, L. (2015). Greece: Mass running: A new trend for ancient times? In J. Scheerder & K. Breedveld (Eds), *Running across Europe* (pp. 163–187). Houndmills, Basingstoke, Hampshire/New York: Palgrave Macmillan.

Pilgaard, M. (2012). *Flexible sports participation in late-modern everyday life* (PhD thesis). Odense: University of Southern Denmark.

Pine, J., & Gilmore, J. (1999). *The experience economy*. Boston, MA: Harvard Business Review.

Putnam, R.D. (2000). *Bowling alone: The collapse and revival of American community*. New York: Touchstone, Simon & Schuster.

Scheerder, J. & Breedveld, K. (Eds) (2015). *Running across Europe: The rise and size of one of the largest sport markets*. Houndmills, Basingstoke, Hampshire/New York: Palgrave Macmillan.

Scheerder, J., Breedveld, K. & Borgers, J. (2015). Who is doing a run with the running boom? In J. Scheerder & K. Breedveld (Eds), *Running across Europe* (pp. 1–27). Houndmills, Basingstoke, Hampshire/New York: Palgrave Macmillan.

Scheerder, J., Vandermeerschen, H., Tuyckom, C. van, Hoekman, R., Breedveld, K. & Vos, S. (2011). *Understanding the game: Sport participation in Europe. Facts, reflections and recommendations*. Leuven: KU Leuven.

Scheerder, J., Willem, A., Claes, E. & Billiet, S. (2015). *International study on the organisation of sport in twelve countries and their policy towards sport federations: Country profiles (volume 2)*. Leuven/Ghent: University of Leuven – Policy in Sports & Physical Activity Research Group/Ghent University – Team Sports Management.

Smith, A. & Westerbeek, H. (2004). *The sportbusiness future*. Basingstoke: Palgrave Macmillan.

Stebbins, R. (2007). *Serious leisure: A perspective for our time*. New Brunswick, NJ: Transaction.

Topic, M. & Rauter, S. (2015). Slovenia: A study of Ljubljana marathon participants. In J. Scheerder & K. Breedveld (Eds), *Running across Europe* (pp. 208–224). Houndmills, Basingstoke, Hampshire/New York: Palgrave Macmillan.

Vehmas, H. & Lahti, J. (2015). Finland: From elite running to mass running events. In J. Scheerder & K. Breedveld (Eds), *Running across Europe* (pp. 105–120). Houndmills, Basingstoke, Hampshire/New York: Palgrave Macmillan.

MADE IN
EUROPE

SECTION B

**SPORT
MARKETING
AND MEDIA**

THE COMMERCIAL GROWTH OF SPONSORSHIP

THORSTEN DUM AND ULRIK WAGNER

Introduction

Sponsorship is a conspicuous example of the interconnectedness of sport and business. As the professionalisation of sponsoring as well as spending on sponsorships have increased rapidly in recent years, this marketing instrument has come to be viewed as a legitimate element in the promotional and communicational mix that has been justified as a business expense (Amis & Cornwell 2005; Cornwell 2014). A 'sponsorship' can be any sort of licensing deal in which a sponsored property ('sponsee') is usually paid money to leverage various forms of objectives for the benefit of the sponsoring party ('sponsor'). According to Cornwell's definition 'sponsorship-linked marketing is the orchestration and implementation of marketing activities for the purpose of building and communicating an association to a sponsorship' (Cornwell 1995, p. 15).

The sponsorship market has grown into a billion euro business and has thus become serious competition for traditional advertising. The share of expenditure on sponsorship of the entire communication budget of sponsoring companies has increased significantly in recent years, with sport and football in particular the most significant sponsorship fields (IEG 2015). In contrast to other communication tools, where spending has stagnated, investments in sports sponsorships continue to rise (Sportfive 2009). The average spending of sponsoring companies accounts for almost 20 percent of their communications budgets (Pleon 2010; Pilot Checkpoint 2012).

At the 2014 FIFA World Cup football tournament in Brazil, FIFA's revenues from commercial rights, including all sponsorships, accounted for US$1.35 billion of the total turnover of US$4 billion, indicating that sponsorships are a necessary component for financing the tournament (Forbes 2014). FIFA partners and official sponsors such as Adidas, Emirates, Sony, Visa, Hyundai and Coca-Cola are obsessively eager to throw money at the World Cup because this high-profile sporting event is followed passionately throughout most of the world. Globally, the 2015 spending on sponsorships was forecasted to rise by 4.1 percent to US$57.5 billion (IEG 2015). Spending by European companies was projected to grow by 3.3 percent in 2015 and reach US$15.3 billion (ibid.).

The range of sponsorship deals has grown steadily in recent years. More and more individuals, groups of individuals, organisations such as associations and federations or organisers of events offer potential partners, and most notably commercial corporations, a collaboration in the form of sponsorship requests and proposals. These increasing sponsorship portfolios have intensified competition among sponsored entities and led to a progressive over-commercialisation and professionalisation of the business of sponsoring (Chadwick & Thwaites 2004). As a consequence, billionaires such as Roman Abramovich (FC Chelsea), Sheikh Mansour bin Zayed Al Nayhan of Abu Dhabi (Manchester City) and Dietmar Hopp (TSG 1899 Hoffenheim) among others have either purchased or invested in football clubs; and likewise professional cycling is currently – despite doping accusations – attracting growing interest from commercial stakeholders like SKY or billionaires like Oleg Tinkoff. At the same time, some sport disciplines still suffer from scant commercial interest.

The popularity of sponsorship can be explained by the fact that sponsoring companies are able to reach multiple objectives. These include not only marketing and communication but also – and increasingly – economic goals such as an increase in sales and revenue. For example, sponsoring companies tend to create tailor-made 'event moments' and build communities by means of involvement or experiential marketing, with the aim of creating a sense of belonging leading to consumer loyalty. Integrated activation programmes including public viewing and digital media are increasingly used to encourage fans to become a part or a piece of the sponsored property. Furthermore, sponsoring corporations also focus heavily on internal audiences (Farrelly et al. 2012) and/or CSR activities aiming to achieve responsible sponsorships (Lacey et al. 2010; Plewa & Quester 2011; Seok Sohn et al. 2012).

Below we will provide some examples of the contemporary use of sponsorships which are followed by a typology. We will briefly highlight some of the challenges, capabilities and critiques, well aware that more issues can be added. Finally, before concluding the chapter, we will provide two examples of sponsorships that focus on human resource management and corporate social responsibility, thus transcending classical marketing approaches to sponsoring.

Broadening the sponsorship scope: Marketing and beyond

Co-branding through strategic partnerships

In recent years the worlds of sport and business have converged dramatically, with branding at the centre of that development. Sports brands now range from traditional commercial companies which make sports products, such as Adidas, to sponsors like Emirates, organisations, events, clubs and players. As a consequence, commercial goals, such as media (e.g. TV) and commercial (e.g. sponsorship) returns, have clearly gained in importance in the sports industry. Sports managers are beginning to view their teams, leagues and properties as 'brands' to be managed. Given its highly competitive nature, branding can play an important role by influencing fan preferences and perceptions regarding the club and differentiating it from competing clubs and other leisure activities. Today, being a brand is one of the most important assets for a sports team (Richelieu et al. 2008; Bouchet et al. 2013). Sponsorship, therefore, has evolved as a strategic instrument of brand management for many sponsors (Gwinner & Eaton 1999; Cornwell & Roy 2001; Smith 2004), more specifically as a 'co-branding' tool, aimed at establishing a symmetrical brand alliance between two or more brands for mutual benefit. For example, the sponsor's name is associated with a high-profile sporting event tournament (such as the FIFA World Cup, the UEFA EURO, the Olympics, etc.). Co-branding is considered to be another way of gaining benefit from intangible assets and a brand leverage strategy (e.g. Blackett & Boad 1999).

Conversion of implicit targets to explicit performance indicators

In the early days of sponsorship management, companies sought implicit targets (image, brand awareness, etc.) as one of the exclusive means of sponsorship engagements to attract external audiences. Nowadays many sponsors pursue explicit targets (e.g. new customer and revenue targets) by fostering sales and creating 'co-marketing alliances' with the sponsored entities and/ or channel members (Farrelly & Quester 2005). Channel members are specialist organisations which can be classified into two broad categories: 1. Resellers generally purchase or take ownership of products from the company intending to sell them to others (resellers may include – but are not limited to – sub-categories such as retailers, wholesalers and industrial distributors); 2. Professional service firms (PSF) are organisations that provide additional services but generally do not purchase products (PSFs may include – but are not limited to – agents, brokers and distribution service firms).

Sponsoring corporations and a wide range of their channel members create value for their company by helping the consumer to understand sponsorship-specific information and to differentiate their brand from those of competitors, which subsequently induces the consumer to purchase the sponsor's product and thus creates revenue (Aaker 1996). Besides, sponsorship can intensify the corporation's brand and create awareness of its business and products in the minds of a new set of customers (Muniz Jr & O'Guinn 2001).

Digitisation, technologisation and connectivity

Due to technological progress sponsors are now able to reach a variety of audiences and target groups by means of digital media (such as social media, etc.), which they address and activate in a personalised manner with the aim of achieving enhanced contact quantity and quality. Although interest in watching events on television remains high, the usage patterns of audiences have changed, essentially due to increased online and mobile media consumption. In addition to the traditional media such as TV and radio, mobile media are increasingly gaining in importance, especially in the field of gathering information in sports. Younger viewers in particular have transformed into 'moving picture consumers' using modern audiovisual platforms and devices (Deissenberger 2014).

Sponsoring platforms to build theme parks, business and customer care

Well-defined and targeted sponsorships try to create an authentic and credible representation of the performance of businesses and thus allow valuable product experiences and the demonstration of their own brand and product performance. Therefore, sponsors increasingly attempt to present the potential of their products and services under the best conditions. In modern football stadiums as well as at mega events 'hospitality zones' are increasingly being set up to give the sponsoring company a platform for Business to Business (B2B) (Farrelly & Quester 2003). A case study on sports sponsorship alliances at such an event indicates that both formal and informal governance play a crucial role in underpinning relationships among sponsors (Morgan et al. 2014). In their paper outlining the development of sponsorship, Ryan and Fahy (2012) emphasise that the ability of sponsorships to create relations and networks is a significant development and one which has been witnessed since the early 2000s.

Sponsorship as a human resource management device (see Case study 6.1)

There has been a strong focus on internal audiences in recent sponsorship management. Sponsoring companies are increasingly looking for sponsoring platforms with creative content and emotions for their sponsorship commitment with which they can activate internal stakeholders. It is therefore not surprising that more and more companies now offer their employees health-management programmes including work-life balance activities. Sports sponsorship can contribute in these important areas by providing appropriate programmes that are designed and implemented within the framework of sponsorships for internal audiences.

The growing relevance of this trend has been reinforced by its inclusion in the academic discourse. Sports sponsorship has a positive impact on the enthusiasm, motivation and identification of employees (Hickman et al. 2005; Garry et al. 2008). Furthermore, perceptions of pride are considered to be another key mechanism through which sport sponsorship and employee support for this will foster an increase in employee identification and discretionary effort, which has been described as the 'Olympic Effect' (Edwards 2015). According to a conceptual work by Farrelly, Greyser and Rogan (2012) consideration of the sponsorship-specific activation of internal stakeholders can be subsumed under the term 'Sponsorship-Linked Internal Marketing' (Farrelly et al. 2012). As part of SLIM activities, employees are assumed to display higher levels of motivation as well as loyalty towards colleagues and their company. At the team level, the actors should identify with the performance level of the sponsored object. At the cultural level, sponsorships are assumed to contribute towards increased identification. All SLIM elements should be aligned and coordinated in such a way as to contribute towards an increase in the company's success (e.g. increased identification, motivation and productivity of employees).

The link between Corporate Social Responsibility (CSR) and sponsorship (see Case study 6.2)

Many companies use their sponsorship commitment to demonstrate Corporate Social Responsibility (CSR). With regard to the ethical and legal behaviour of organisations in the workplace and within the wider community, the issue of CSR has clearly gained importance (Plewa & Quester 2011). For years businesses have tended to spend their CSR budgets on supporting environmental or arts-based causes, but sport is increasingly being seen as a way to meet social and community obligations. These include fair play shown to everyone involved, including employees and suppliers; transparency and opportunities for all to succeed; and good community relations. CSR programmes are increasingly using sports sponsorship as a vehicle to deliver a wide range of objectives for many reasons. First and foremost, sport can really modify people's attitudes and behaviour as they engage with sport in such a manner that it can make a huge difference to their health and/or their lifestyle. Secondly, sport – and especially football – has a huge impact as it plays a crucial role in society (e.g. the FIFA World Cup or the Olympic Games). Companies are also transforming their communication on sponsorship as part of their CSR strategies by shifting parts of their sponsorship to their CSR-budgets (Pleon 2010).

Addressing target groups, setting objectives and planning the strategic sponsorship process

Primarily, sponsoring organisations use sponsorship opportunities to achieve commercial targets such as sales, awareness, image, brand attitudes and many others. However, with growing awareness of the importance of demonstrating corporate social responsibility or managing human resources the scope of sponsorship broadens. Management objectives concerning sponsorship may now often be either commercial or relational in nature (such as the establishment of commitment, goodwill and improved community relations) (see Table 6.1). In his seminal article Meenaghan set out to examine a taxonomy of sponsorship objectives, ranging from broad corporate objectives (e.g. medium for community involvement, increase public awareness, etc.) to product, sales, media, guest hospitality and personal objectives (1983, p. 17). For many years a distinction in sponsorship objectives has been made between corporate-related and product/brand-related objectives (Irwin & Sutton 1994, p. 95) or – according to the degree of complexity – short-term basic objectives (e.g. corporate/brand image enhancement) and long-term sophisticated objectives (e.g. build brand equity) (Cornwell 2014, p. 29). Recently, a further perspective has been developed on sports sponsorship focusing on the strategic intent of sponsorship. In their conceptual framework for the strategic management of sports sponsorship, Demir and Söderman (2015) have identified three basic strategies: 1. sponsoring as an investment strategy; 2. sponsoring as a relational strategy; and 3. sponsoring as an animation strategy.

Generally, the power of sponsorship is to achieve returns for a broad variety of objectives (raising awareness, demonstrating community involvement, etc.), and therefore one integral component is to focus clearly on target groups (consumers, channel members, etc.). In more recent works some evidence of the linkage of target groups and sponsorship objectives can be found (Thompson & Speed 2007) (see Table 6.1). Based on a conceptual framework with targets and objectives as the dimensions of classification, a sponsorship typology consists of different types such as:

- consumer-targeted sponsorships
- channel member-targeted sponsorships
- employee- and management-targeted sponsorships
- community- and government-targeted sponsorships
- competitor-targeted sponsorships

Table 6.1   Sponsorship targets and objectives

Target	Objective (Selection)	Means (= Activation of Sponsorship Rights) (Selection)	Measurability	Theoretical Lens
Consumers	Raise awareness, impact brand attitudes and perceptions, stimulate trial and sales	Perimeter advertising, sweepstakes, prize draws, testimonial advertising, on-site product-demonstration, and many more	Implicit (e.g. branding and image dimensions) and explicit (e.g. on-site sales, press awareness)	Resource-based view, marketing (branding), psychology (effects)
Channel members	Raise awareness, impact brand attitudes and perceptions, garner distribution commitment, develop trade relationships	Hospitality zones	Implicit (e.g. branding and image dimensions) and explicit (e.g. on-site deals)	Resource-based view, marketing, branding, relationship marketing, B2B marketing, networks and alliances
Employees and management	Impact brand attitude, motivation, improved internal relationships	Storytelling, active participation, tickets, etc.	Implicit	Human resource management, organisational culture
Community and government	Raise awareness, impact brand attitude and perceptions, demonstrate involvement in community, enhance relationships	Storytelling of 'good will'	Implicit	Resource-based view, marketing, branding, relationship marketing, B2B marketing, networks and alliances
Competitors	Exclude from opportunity	High-profile sporting events	Implicit	Strategic management (competitive advantage)

Source: modified from Thompson and Speed, 2007

Depending on the strategic benefits of sponsorships, not only might different audiences be addressed but also various sponsorship objectives can be pursued. The sponsoring companies typically purchase a package of rights (= sponsorship) with which they associate themselves with the sponsored entity.

For the sponsored entity, consumer-targeted sponsorships comprise a wide range of activation components such as classic perimeter advertising, sweepstakes, contests and product presentations among many others. Hospitality zones are often used for channel member-targeted sponsorships in order to intensify Business 2 Business (B2B) in the sport-related environment (arena, stadium, event, etc.). As part of employee- and management-targeted sponsorships employees are rewarded by tickets for special merit with the objective of increasing motivation and identification with the sponsor. Community- and government-targeted sponsorships are often used to demonstrate corporate social responsibility by means of good-will activities. Finally, sponsors aiming at competitor-targeted sponsorships make use of their sponsorship's brand exclusivity to prevent competitors from being official sponsors (of, for example, high-profile sporting events such as the FIFA World Cup).

Due to the variety of objectives and the multiple uses of sponsorships, sponsoring as a research area has been studied within different scientific disciplines for several years. Coming from the classic marketing discipline, sponsoring has evolved as a versatile instrument that is examined under the lens of a variety of disciplines such as relationship marketing, corporate social responsibility, organisational theory and, more recently, human resource management. Furthermore, the key to measuring returns from a sponsorship is primarily focused on what the sponsor is trying to achieve, be it implicit (e.g. good-will) or explicit (e.g. sales) objectives or a combination of both.

In recent years, sponsorship management has increasingly followed a professional sponsorship planning process, especially when it comes to global sporting event sponsorship (cf. the FIFA World Cup, Super Bowl, or the Olympics) (see also Figure 6.1) (Masterman 2014). The planning process progressively plays a central role in the sponsorship because the sponsor's sponsoring managers determine which sponsorship-specific target groups and objectives are defined as well as how to select and activate sponsorship opportunities.

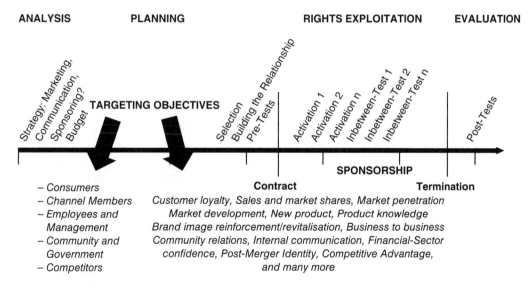

Figure 6.1   Strategic process in sporting event sponsorship

Source: Authors, adapted from Thompson and Speed 2007 and Masterman 2014: 339

Targeting and setting sponsorship objectives are crucial elements in analysing sponsorships designed to match the sponsor's strategy (with regard to marketing strategy in general, and corporate communications and sponsoring strategies in particular) and the further activation of additional marketing instruments (see also Table 6.1). The selection of the sponsored entity and the structure of the relationship follows a solid planning process and introduces the phase of activation ('Rights Exploitation') which is heralded by the sponsorship contract. The sponsorship will be particularly set to run over a given period at major events. Usually, pre-, in-between and post-tests are conducted to keep track of its effectiveness (e.g. media coverage).

Present and future challenges, capabilities and criticisms

The professionalisation of sponsorship management

Being an instrument of integrated marketing communications, sponsoring can be characterised as having a high degree of intra- and inter-organisational coordination (Olkkonen et al. 2000; Thjømøe et al. 2002). Thus, a synergistic enhancement of the overall effect is only achieved when internal coordination and networking between the sponsoring decision makers with other departments (for example, press, marketing and procurement) are given.

In the course of the professionalisation of sponsorship, sponsoring decision makers have commonly felt compelled to introduce methods of controlling to ensure the quasi-effectiveness and -efficiency of sponsorship investments at the behest of higher authorities or budget decision makers. Prejudging sponsoring as a modern marketing instrument, the budget decision maker is often more concerned about numbers and figures – and thus the return on investment (ROI) – rather than the brand or a greater return on objective (ROO). Consequently, sponsorship managers as brand custodians understand the value of sponsorship and want to use it as a brand building tool, but might be undermined by the purse-string holders who think that their brand is healthy. Hence, the challenge to sponsorship managers is how to convince the purse-string holders to invest in the brand through tools such as sponsorship, where the impact on the bottom line is not always direct or immediate (see next section). In order to gain accountability and legitimacy within the organisation, sponsorship-specific scorecards are typically developed, especially among big event sponsors, to justify the acquisition, selection and evaluation of a specific sponsorship to intra-organisational stakeholders (cf. Hertle 2012).

To design the planning, implementation and evaluation of sponsorship-specific communication, different external partners and suppliers are usually required depending on the size of the sponsorship. In particular, professional service firms (PSF), having the appropriate 'know-how', are becoming more common as advisory, intermediation or execution agencies. Their expertise is broadly used to achieve the desired strategic and/or communications policy objectives. Cooperation usually ranges from the creation, testing or selection of sponsorship proposals (submitted, for example, by event agencies on implementing communications activities) by consulting firms such as IMG, Octagon, Kogag, Sportfive, ESB Marketing Network, etc. to the evaluation of sponsoring effects by, for example, market research institutes such as IPSOS

GmbH, Pilot Group, Sport & Markt AG, TNS Infratest GmbH, etc. Moreover, there is great interest in the continuous assimilation of market-related information through, for example, attendance at relevant conferences and meetings. It might be criticised, however, that these professional service firms can play a counter-productive role since their own existence relies on the success of sponsorships, which may lead to over-selling the commercial capacity of sponsorships.

Sponsorship evaluation – nice to have or irrational to do?

Despite its economic growth, high acceptance and widespread use, as well as the fact that sponsors invest vast sums of money to activate and leverage their investments (Pleon 2010; Pilot Checkpoint 2012), sponsors need to pay more attention to planning sponsorship strategically, on leveraging their investments and measuring sponsorship effectiveness. However, most sponsors treat their sponsorship investments differently in terms of evaluation (Meenaghan 2005), with nearly 75 percent of sponsors showing very limited interest in measuring effectiveness (Crompton 2004). There is a lack of publicly available metrics and only a few sponsorship measurement tools are used; however, their precise applicability still remains problematic (Cornwell 2008). While the inclusion of certain measures is critical for future research, the evaluation of sponsorship must determine its effectiveness in achieving sponsors' objectives, as well as its relative effectiveness (O'Reilly & Madill 2007). The fact that sponsors rarely pursue a single sponsoring objective presents further difficulties when determining its value.

Performance indicators in sponsorship can usually be divided into business-related indicators (e.g. corporate image) and sponsorship-specific indicators (e.g. the media coverage of events), which can further be divided into three central action levels: the cognitive effects (e.g. recall), the affective impact (e.g. sympathy, emotional impact) and intentional/behavioural action (e.g. purchase intention) (Breuer et al. 2013; Cornwell 2014).

Despite this development, there is little ground-breaking innovation in terms of impact assessment. To date, the overall ROI of a sponsored property cannot be calculated reliably. In terms of measurability, there are only a few and hardly valid tools that attempt to describe the effects of sponsorship activities. Some procedures are based primarily on explicit effects using quantitative indicators (e.g. media coverage). Aided or unaided recall surveys, for example, or television ratings are more like temporary and one-dimensional aids, and therefore do not provide adequate answers for sponsors. Numerous solutions and commissioned research, including those of sponsor associations such as Germany's 'S20', have not changed anything significantly yet. Qualitative criteria and implicit effects, such as the emotional appeal of the brand in association with the sponsored property, cannot be measured reliably. Thus, many companies have difficulty when it comes to pricing, evaluating sponsorship alternatives and measuring effectiveness (O'Reilly & Madill 2009). Measuring sponsorship effectiveness is difficult since the sponsor's brand and the sponsorship's context have different mechanisms of action that cannot be modelled with each other (Kuske 2013). In the global sponsorship market no standard of sponsorship impact measurement has established itself so far although there have been various attempts at unification (Felten 2007). These include, for example, a number of methods for collecting media data. While eye-tracking and neuromarketing methods have

brought some new insights (Breuer et al. 2013), their precise applicability still remains problematic (Kuske 2013). Neuromarketing is a field of marketing research that studies consumers'
sensorimotor reactions to marketing stimuli by using state-of-the-art technology (for example
functional magnetic resonance imaging). In summary, it must be stated that in the past sponsorship effectiveness research focused primarily on explicit impact dimensions while implicit
dimensions were mostly neglected; however, evidence and approaches can be found in more
recent studies of such factors as the emotional appeal of the sponsor brand (Schmidt et al.
2013) and the enhancement of employees' identification with and loyalty to their company
(Farrelly et al. 2012).

Sport disciplines without media exposure

Being an attractive sponsorship property is nearly always related to mass-media exposure
(Cornwell 2014). Despite the rapid growth of new forms of mass media such as Facebook and
Twitter and, before that, the emergence of the internet, television remains a core media platform for exposure. Mega-events like the Olympic Games contain a multiplicity of disciplines;
nonetheless, few sport disciplines dominate in Europe (for instance football, tennis and pro
cycling) while minor disciplines like rowing, floorball and curling receive scant media promotion. Such disciplines are often highly valued from a political perspective because of their
contribution of medals that are counted as part of national prestige, but they suffer nonetheless
from reduced commercial attractiveness (Wagner & Nissen 2015). Accordingly, one major challenge for these disciplines is to become attractive to sponsors despite low (or no) mass-media
exposure. Players or athletes in some sport disciplines find themselves in the peculiar situation
of belonging to the world elite and exercising like professionals yet financially they are amateurs. Thus, a key question is to decide to what extent these athletes or their sports organisations
are willing to promote themselves in order to become attractive as sponsorship properties and
simultaneously maintain their sporting integrity – and not just becoming a business asset subjected to short-term commercial interests.

Case study 6.1: Topdanmark – using a sports sponsorship as an HRM instrument

Topdanmark is the second largest Danish insurance company with a long history rooted in the agri-
cultural industry. During the 2000s the company was engaged in sponsoring the female handball
team, Viborg HK. Handball was at that time one of the most popular and media-exposed sport disciplines in Denmark. The Danish national team won Olympic gold in 1996, 2000 and 2004, and the
professional Danish league was considered a world leader, attracting players from all over the world.
Both Viborg HK and Slagelse Dream Team managed to win the European Champions League, so
sponsoring one of these teams could be conceived as a good match – a successful team that enables

---

mass-media exposure. After the company had ended its sponsorship and waited some years before engaging with sport again, in late 2010 it signed a sponsorship agreement with the Golden Four (G4, consisting of four male lightweight rowers), the most successful Olympic rowing boat in recent Danish history.

Unlike handball, rowing hardly attracts any media exposure besides the few weeks during the Olympic Games; thus, from a marketing perspective this commitment seems less obvious. In an early interview conducted in the summer of 2011 with the marketing director of the company the rationale for this decision was explained: 'Topdanmark has chosen a marketing strategy where we actually proclaim that we are visible enough already [...] In reality we have said goodbye to mass communication.' Accordingly, increased visibility was not the objective as, according to Topdanmark's top management, potential customers were already aware of the company and its products. Digging deeper into the set-up revealed that this sponsorship was signed with the sole purpose of attracting an internal corporate audience, and therefore this case can be seen as Sponsorship Linked Internal Marketing (Farrelly et al. 2012). It was targeted towards service-centre employees, i.e. those employees who work daily at the company's call centre. This meant that the management of the sponsorship, typically carried out by the marketing department, overlaped with the responsibilities of the HRM department. According to the HRM Director:

> Based on some strategic considerations about how important it is that we create publicity, we withdrew from it [handball, authors] [...] the next sponsorship [...] was G4, which in reality is a bit of a different sponsorship as it is much more internally directed ... and because we could see G4 as someone who could lift the company where we wanted it to go.

The company designed a campaign using the sponsorship to improve its customer services. The main objective was to decrease the percentage of dissatisfied customers and increase the number of customers who were willing to recommend the company, thus gaining a positive word-of-mouth effect. Most customers will sooner or later get in contact with service centre employees, and therefore this specific sector was chosen by the top management as an intervention target. G4 was used because the boat represented some characteristics the managers wanted to transfer to a working-day situation, such as peak performance, team work, high performance under pressure and feedback mechanisms among team members.

As part of the sponsorship agreement the rowers gave speeches, made short YouTube-like videos, participated in small corporate events and even signed Christmas cards for the employees. As an original and unconventional way of designing and engaging in a sponsorship, this set-up brought along with it a time-consuming commitment. Finding a balance between sport and business also implied cooperation from the Sports Director of the Danish Rowing Federation. On the one hand, the agreement had to be fulfilled and value added to the company; on the other, however, the rowers had to be protected against hyper-commitment, which could potentially lead to a poor sporting performance. Interviewed after the 2012 Olympic Games, where G4 won a bronze medal, the sports director explained his tasks as being both a salesman (selling the property rights), a mediator (being the link between the company and G4) and a guardian (protecting the amateur values of rowing).

(Continued)

(Continued)

The multiplicity of tasks associated with this kind of sponsorship management illustrates clearly the complexity that arises when sport meets business. In October 2012 two of the rowers were interviewed. They both emphasised that the deal contained more than just a photo-shoot session and that they actually had to deliver a lot; however, the positive effect on the company's employees also filled them with joy and pride. According to the rowers '...we had to pick out resources because this means that both the energy we add to it and the recharging we spend on it we had to take from our own weekdays'.

Case study 6.2: BASF and Sportclub 2020 – demonstrating CSR through regional sports sponsorships

The numbers are impressive: a turnover of more than €74 billion, a net profit of almost €5.5 billion and more than 113,000 employees. Chemical company BASF is not only the largest employer in Germany's 'Südpfalz' [Southern Palatinate] region and one of the largest DAX (Deutscher Aktienindex) companies but also the world leader in chemical and plastics products. However, unlike many other DAX companies [German stock index], the chemical company is spending only a fraction on sports sponsorship per year.

Out of a total of €45.4 million which BASF pays out annually for donations, sponsoring and its own projects, only €2.9 million was generated into sports. By comparison, BASF invests about €23 million yearly in coaching, development and training.

Why is such a large corporation, making billions of euros of profit year after year, only investing around €3 million in sports sponsorship? And what are the strategic motives behind the actions of the global industrial player from Ludwigshafen?

At BASF three principles are linked to sports sponsorship: mobilising people; bringing together social groups and networking; and raising social awareness of health. Thus, marketing objectives play no crucial role at BASF. Instead of placing their own company or the brand at the forefront, BASF strives to present itself as an attractive employer by fostering corporate social responsibility (CSR). As a result of constantly supporting CSR for many years, BASF was nominated for the annual CSR award by the Federal Ministry of Labour and Social Affairs [Bundesministerium für Arbeit und Soziale, BMAS] in 2013 and 2014.

In 2014, the chemical company launched the CSR project 'Sportverein 2020' [Sport Club 2020], focusing on sports development, to prepare sports clubs of the Rhine-Neckar region for demographic trends, to train volunteer workers in the field and to encourage them in their strategic development. Supported by professional service firms responsible for conceptual support and the implementation of the project, BASF acts as a concept initiator and supports the project with a high six-figure euro amount as a premium partner. Other partners of the project are SAP and Südzucker, both big companies in the region. Participation is free for the clubs, but they must belong to one of the sports federations or sports circles Baden-Nord [North Baden], Rheinhessen [Rhine-Hesse], Pfalz [Palatinate] or Bergstraße ['Mountain Road']. The project is structured into four phases/modules:

1. *Online Diagnostic Tool (2014)*

    In the first phase clubs will fill out an online diagnostic tool with 30–40 questions and will then receive a detailed evaluation of the demographic challenges of their club. These include changes in membership structures and creating an attractive club programme to attract and retain members of all age groups, the development of a formative and effective club management and the development of strategies for maintaining their own infrastructures, as well as the introduction of a volunteering management. The measured values are compared with the reference values of similar clubs in Germany.

2. *Club Coaching (2015/2016)*

    In the second step professional coaching workshops with individual solutions are designed for selected clubs to make them competitive for the future. The ultimate goal of this module is to create solution-oriented, best-practice examples of different club types, which then form the basis of the third block, the 'Best Practice Conference'. Currently, 28 sports clubs are receiving professional club coaching.

3. *Conference (2016)*

    Accompanied by experts from sports, science, politics and business, a congress is to take place in which the results of the club coaching workshops and best practices are presented.

4. *Implementation (2017–2020)*

    Further and expanded consulting and training opportunities are available for the clubs to implement their strategies successfully.

Instead of agreeing multiple and expensive sponsorships with municipal sports clubs, BASF is aiming at regional sport development under the umbrella of CSR because it boasts values that socially-responsible businesses are striving for. In this sense, sports development is an effective and rational weapon to demonstrate good will within the regional community which also aims at increasing employees' identification and motivation.

Conclusion: Rationalising sponsorship opportunities through the lens of social trends?

The growing importance of sponsorship as a multi-functional instrument and the consequential development of the sponsorship market demonstrate that sponsoring corporations must increasingly react to contemporary societal issues to ensure legitimacy (cf. Meyer & Rowan 1977). These might include – but are not limited to – increasing experience orientation, individualisation tendencies and the need to invest in corporate social responsibility activities as companies are increasingly turning to the issue of CSR as part of their performance in (sports) sponsorship (Sheth & Babiak 2010; Plewa & Quester 2011). CSR is becoming an ever more important instrument in enhancing corporate reputation, improving employee morale and playing a wider role within society.

While in the past sponsoring corporations primarily relied on marketing objectives (awareness, image transfer, etc.), corporations today are trying to meet societal demands by the use of tailor-made sponsoring activities and their communicative accompaniment. In essence, sponsorship has become a reliable vehicle with which sponsoring corporations can ensure legitimacy towards their many stakeholder groups, be it external (e.g. demonstrating good will to communities) [see Case study 6.2] or internal (e.g. increasing employee morale) [see Case study 6.1]. Therefore, it might be assumed that sponsoring businesses would continue to seek an ideal in which they wish to appear socially responsible, both ethically and corporately. One may also assume that sponsors will select potential partners in accordance with their own CSR orientation in the future. As CSR is currently *en vogue*, a further rise in the linkage between CSR and sponsorship investments might be expected. However, research into sports sponsorship in CSR is surprisingly rare and only in its infancy (cf. Sheth & Babiak 2010; Plewa & Quester 2011).

The aforementioned developments might help to explain why sponsorship volumes are steadily rising and more and more companies are leveraging their sponsorship investments. However, sponsoring as an interdisciplinary marketing tool does not usually lie in their core areas; its direct profitability (ROI) cannot be calculated holistically; many sponsorship decisions are based on a personal interest in the sponsored property; and, finally, negative effects might actually lead to a decline in sponsorship investments. Negative effects might include – but are not limited to – ambush marketing and compliance. For example, numerous corporations act as 'ambush marketers', appearing as quasi-sponsors by associating themselves with a sponsored property (e.g. the FIFA World Cup) without having acquired any official marketing rights. Sponsorship has also been suspected of 'infidelity' and 'corruption' in recent years and subjected to government investigations, leading to considerable uncertainty in the sponsorship business worldwide. The main reason for this is because a 'third advantage' might be granted to third parties when donating sponsorship endowments.

Against the backdrop of social phenomena such as the 'war for talent', 'Generation Y' and a shortage of skilled labour, sponsorship is also progressively being used as a means to achieve an increase in employee morale and in the attractiveness of the sponsoring employer, which has holistically been described as sponsorship-linked internal marketing (SLIM). In summary, SLIM is a thought-provoking label for a frequently studied phenomenon in the past called 'internal marketing'. There are many studies available on internal marketing; these, however, are neither labelled SLIM nor undertaken in a sporting context. Although there is growing importance in the academic debate, empirical evidence describing the effects of SLIM remains rare (cf. Dum 2015). Future empirical studies are necessary to investigate all this.

Recommended further reading

The recently published book by T. Bettina Cornwell (2014), *Sponsorship in Marketing*, offers a comprehensive overview by the leading scientist of sponsorship. The article by Farrelly et al. (2012) offers a useful model for investigating sponsorships that have a distinct internal employee approach. The article 'Evolving priorities in sponsorship: From media management to network management' (Ryan & Fahy 2012) outlines the development of sponsorships towards networking potentials.

References

Aaker, D. A. (1996). *Building strong brands*, New York, The Free Press.

Amis, J. and T. B. Cornwell (2005). *Global sport sponsorship*, Oxford, Berg Publishers.

Blackett, T. and M. R. W. Boad (1999). *Co-branding: The science of alliance*, Basingstoke, Palgrave Macmillan.

Bouchet, P., D. Hillairet and G. Bodet (2013). *Sport Brands*, Milton Park, Routledge.

Breuer, C., C. Rumpf and S. Kurz (2013). 'Ein Bewertungsmodell zur Analyse von Sponsoring-Alternativen.' *Marketing Review St. Gallen* **1**(2013): 72–81.

Chadwick, S. and D. Thwaites (2004). 'Advances in the management of sport sponsorship: fact or fiction? Evidence from English professional soccer.' *Journal of General Management* **30**(1): 39–60.

Cornwell, T. B. (1995). 'Sponsorship-linked marketing development.' *Sport Marketing Quarterly* **4**(4): 13–24.

Cornwell, T. B. (2008). 'State of the art and science in sponsorship-linked marketing.' *Journal of Advertising* **37**(3): 41–55.

Cornwell, T. B. (2014). *Sponsorship in Marketing – Effective communication through sports, arts and events*, London, Routledge.

Cornwell, T. B. and D. P. Roy (2001). 'Exploring managers' perceptions of the impact of sponsorship on brand equity.' *Journal of Advertising* **30**(2): 41–51.

Crompton, J. L. (2004). 'Conceptualization and alternate operationalizations of the measurement of sponsorship effectiveness in sport.' *Leisure Studies* **23**(3): 267–281.

Deissenberger, T. (2014). Sport 4.0: Mobile und Internet werden für Sportrezeption immer wichtiger. In: P. Strahlendorf (Ed.). *Jahrbuch Sponsoring 2014*. Hamburg, New Business Verlag GmbH & Co. KG:18–22.

Demir, R. and S. Söderman (2015). 'Strategic sponsoring in professional sport: a review and conceptualization.' *European Sport Management Quarterly* **15**(3): 271–300.

Dum, T. (2015). 'Perspektivenwechsel im Sponsoringmanagement.' *Marketing Review St. Gallen* **32**(1): 90–100.

Edwards, M. (2015). 'The Olympic Effect: employee reactions to their employer's sponsorship of a high-profile global sporting event.' *Human Resource Management*, DOI: 10.1002/hrm.21702.

Farrelly, F. and P. Quester (2003). 'The effect of market orientation on trust and commitment: The case of the sponsorship business-to-business relationship.' *European Journal of Marketing* **37**(3/4): 530–553.

Farrelly, F. and P. Quester (2005). 'Investigating large-scale sponsorship relationships as co-marketing alliances.' *Business Horizons* **2005**(48): 55–62.

Farrelly, F., S. Greyser and M. Rogan (2012). 'Sponsorship linked internal marketing (SLIM): A strategic platform for employee engagement and business performance.' *Journal of Sport Management* **26**(6): 506–520.

Felten, J.-B. (2007). 'Defining industry standards for sponsorship performance: A German perspective.' *Journal of Sponsorship* **1**(1): 62–66.

Forbes (2014). 'World Cup Brazil Will Generate $4 Billion for FIFA, 66% More Than 2010 Tournament.' 2015, available at: http://www.forbes.com/sites/mikeozanian/2014/06/05/the-billion-dollar-business-of-the-world-cup/ [Accessed 15 May 2015].

Garry, T., A. J. Broderick and K. Lahiffe (2008). 'Tribal motivation in sponsorship and its influence on sponsor relationship development and corporate identity.' *Journal of Marketing Management* **24**(9/10): 959–977.

Gwinner, K. and J. Eaton (1999). 'Building brand image through event sponsorship: The role of image transfer.' *Journal of Advertising* **28**(4): 47–57.

Hertle, K. (2012). *Die Sponsorship-Scorecard: Ein strategisches Marketinginstrument für das Sponsoringcontrolling*, Saarbrücken, AV Akademikerverlag.

Hickman, T. M., K. E. Lawrence and J. C. Ward (2005). 'A social identities perspective on the effects of corporate sport sponsorship on employees.' *Sport Marketing Quarterly* **14**(3): 148–157.

IEG (2015). 'Sponsorship Spending Report – Where the Dollars are going and Trends for 2015.' L. International Events Group.

Irwin, R. L. and W. A. Sutton (1994). 'Sport sponsorship objectives: An analysis of their relative importance for major corporate sponsors.' *European Journal for Sport Management* **1**(2): 93–101.

Kuske, T. (2013). 'Und was bringt's? – Wo die Branche bei der Frage zur Werbewirkung steht.' *Sponsors*, Vol. 2013, Issue 7, Sponsors Verlags GmbH, Hamburg, pp. 42–45.

Lacey, R., A. G. Close and R. Z. Finney (2010). 'The pivotal roles of product knowledge and corporate social responsibility in event sponsorship effectiveness.' *Journal of Business Research* **63**(11): 1222–1228.

Masterman, G. (2014). *Strategic Sports Event Management*. 3rd edn, London and New York, Routledge.

Meenaghan, J. A. (1983). 'Commercial Sponsorship.' *European Journal of Marketing* **17**(7): 5–73.

Meenaghan, T. (2005). Evaluating sponsorship effects. In: J. Amis and T. B. Cornwell (Eds.). *Global sport sponsorship*, Berg Publishers, Oxford and New York, pp. 243–264.

Meyer, J. W. and B. Rowan (1977). 'Institutionalized organizations: Formal structure as myth and ceremony.' *American Journal of Sociology* **83**(2): 340–363.

Morgan, A., D. Adair, T. Taylor and A. Hermens (2014). 'Sport sponsorship alliances: Relationship management for shared value.' *Sport, Business and Management: An International Journal* **4**(4): 270–283.

Muniz Jr, A. M. and T. C. O'Guinn (2001). 'Brand community.' *Journal of Consumer Research* **27**(4): 412–432.

O'Reilly, N. J. and J. J. Madill (2007). 'Evaluating social marketing elements in sponsorship.' *Social Marketing Quarterly* **13**(4): 1–25.

O'Reilly, N. and J. Madill (2009). 'Methods and metrics in sponsorship evaluation.' *Journal of Sponsorship* **2**(3): 215–230.

Olkkonen, R., H. Tikkanen and K. Alajoutsijärvi (2000). 'Sponsorship as relationships and networks: implications for research.' *Corporate Communications: An International Journal* **5**(1): 12–19.

Pilot Checkpoint (2012). 'Sponsor Visions 2012.' Pilot Checkpoint GmbH, Hamburg.

Pleon (2010). 'Sponsoring Trends 2010.' Pleon Event & Sponsoring GmbH, Bonn.

Plewa, C. and P. G. Quester (2011). 'Sponsorship and CSR: Is there a link? A conceptual framework.' *International Journal of Sports Marketing & Sponsorship* **12**(4): 301.

Richelieu, A., S. Lopez and M. Desbordes (2008). 'The internationalization of a sports team brand: the case of european soccer teams.' *International Journal of Sports Marketing & Sponsorship* **9**(4): 29–44.

Ryan, A. and J. Fahy (2012). 'Evolving priorities in sponsorship: From media management to network management.' *Journal of Marketing Management* **28**(9–10): 1132–1158.

Schmidt, S., N. Hennigs, S. Langner and M. Limbach (2013). 'The explicit and implicit impact of sport sponsorship.' *Marketing Review St. Gallen* **1**(2013): 58–70.

Seok Sohn, Y., J. K. Han and S.-H. Lee (2012). 'Communication strategies for enhancing perceived fit in the CSR sponsorship context.' *International Journal of Advertising* **31**(1): 133–146.

Sheth, H. and K. Babiak (2010). 'Beyond the Game: Perceptions and Practices of Corporate Social Responsibility in the Professional Sport Industry.' *Journal of Business Ethics* **91**(3): 433–450.

Smith, G. (2004). 'Brand image transfer through sponsorship: A consumer learning perspective.' *Journal of Marketing Management* **20**(3–4): 457–474.

Sportfive (2009). 'Sponsorship in Europe – A Comparison of Key Marketing Tools.' Hamburg: Sportfive GmbH & Co. KG.

Thjømøe, H. M., E. L. Olson and P. S. Brønn (2002). 'Decision-making processes surrounding sponsorship activities.' *Journal of Advertising Research* **42**(6): 6–15.

Thompson, P. and R. Speed (2007). A Typology of Sponsorship Activity. In: M. M. Parent and T. Slack (Eds.). *International Perspectives on the Management of Sport*, Elsevier, London, pp. 247–267.

Wagner, U. and R. Nissen (2015) 'Enacted ambiguity and risk perceptions: Making sense of national elite sport sponsorships.' *Sport in Society: Cultures, Commerce, Media, Politics* 18: 1179–1198.

THE BATTLE FOR MEDIA RIGHTS IN EUROPEAN CLUB FOOTBALL

HARRY ARNE SOLBERG

Introduction

The revenues in elite football have increased significantly since the 1990s. The main reason for this is the strong growth in media rights. In 2014, the total global media rights were estimated at $36.8 billion, of which $13.1 billion (36%) was related to football (TV Sports Markets, 2014). Media rights have become the major source of revenue for those at the top of the financial ladder. During the 1997/98 season, the big-five European leagues (England, Italy, Spain, Germany and France) brought in a total of US$894 million. Fifteen years later, the amount had increased to US$4.7 billion (Baskerville Communication, 1997; *TV Sports Markets*, 2013).

In recent years, these leagues have also earned substantial revenues from exporting TV football, also to other continents. From the season starting in 2016, the clubs in the Spanish LaLiga can even bring in more from the export markets than from the domestic market. The richest clubs also bring in substantial revenues from the UEFA's Champions League, with media rights being the main source.

This chapter will analyse the media rights in club football, giving special attention to the big five European leagues. First, it will focus on the forces behind the growth in rights fees, both in the domestic and external markets. Second it will analyse the factors that influence the distribution of the revenues, both between clubs within the same leagues and between the leagues in different nations. The chapter also includes a case study that is based on an article from *TV Sports Markets*, and which focuses on the Spanish LaLiga's sale of their international rights.

Historical and recent development

BSkyB's acquisition of the English Premier League in 1992 was a milestone in European club football. On this occasion, the rights were sold for €55 million per season, which was four times the value of the former deal (Ofcom, 2007). Twenty-five years later, the figure had increased to €2.46 billion. A similar development, with strong price increases, has occurred elsewhere in Europe, although none of the other leagues have been as successful as the Premier League in monetary terms. This development is illustrated in several tables in this chapter. The figures in Table 7.1 illustrate how the media rights have become the major source of revenue for the leagues at the top of the financial ladder. Those that are further down the financial ladder, however, still earn most of their revenues from other sources. While the Italian Serie A clubs have earned 60% of the total revenues of the sale of media rights, they only accounted for 16% and 11% of the revenues of the Swedish and Norwegian Clubs (including both the top two divisions) during the 2014 season.

European football clubs, and particularly the top clubs, have also benefited from a massive growth in revenues from UEFA's club tournaments, and particularly from the Champions League, of where media rights accounted for the largest proportion. Real Madrid earned at total of US$15 million in price-money from winning the tournament in 1997/98 (Baskerville Communication, 1999). When they copied the achievement in 2013/14, the amount had increased to US$78.4 million (UEFA.com). From the 2015/16 season, UEFA will earn $1.644 billion from the Champions League rights, of which 28% will come from other continents (TV Sports Markets, 2015a). UEFA distribute more than 75% of

Table 7.1 Total revenues/media rights proportion – Elite leagues 2013/14 season

	Total revenues (€ million)	Media rights: percentage of total
English Premier League	3,898	54
Germany Bundesliga	2,275	32
Spanish LaLiga	1,933	49
Italien Serie A	1,699	59
France Ligue 1	1,498	40
Netherlands Eresdivisie	439	18%
Belgium Jupiler League	284	29
Denmark Super League	149	18
Scottish Premier League	147	31
Sweden Allsvenskan*	133	16
Norway Tippeliga**	173	11

Source: Deloitte – Annual Review of Football Finance 2013/14, June 2015

* 2013 season

** Both figures includes also the second-tier division

these revenues to the clubs. Indeed, this is so much that UEFA is running a deficit in three of the four years over the four year cycle, which ends with the UEFA Euro. This pattern stands in contrast to UEFA Euro (The European Championship for national teams) where the local organising committee only receives 10%.

There are several reasons behind the strong growth in rights fees. First, the technology innovations in the media industry have increased the transmission capacity. Different from some years ago, TV companies no longer meet any shortage in frequencies. Furthermore, TV signals can also be accomodated on other outlets such as computers, touchpads and mobile telephones. This has made football fans more flexible with regard to when and where they can watch matches. Hence, the demand for TV football is no longer restricted to taking place in front of a traditional TV. This development has triggered the competition for content, and from an increasing number of media companies. Football has also turned out to be the most successful sport on pay TV. With some few exceptions, live matches in the domestic leagues are only shown on pay TV. This corresponds with empirical research, which has documented that football fans are more willing to pay to watch their favourite sport than fans of other sports (Hammervold & Solberg, 2006).

The production of TV football allows several opportunities to enjoy *economies of scale advantages*. The average costs decline with the greater number of markets and viewers being reached. A large proportion of the programming costs are sunk costs. This means they are independent of the number of both viewers and markets in which the matches are shown. The programming costs of a TV match, say from the English Premier League, are the same, no matter if the match is shown only in England or worldwide. The exception is the costs of commentators if the programmes are exported to foreign markets. The variable costs of transmitting the programmes to other markets are low. Therefore, most of the additional revenue from attracting more viewers is net profit.

All these characteristics provide incentives to extend the market and recruit more viewers, from both internal and external markets. They are partly a consequence of the fact that TV signals are *impure public goods*. This means they are non-rivalling, but can be made exclusive in consumption. See Gratton and Solberg (2007) for a fuller discussion of this matter.

Table 7.2 illustrates the growth in media rights for the elite leagues in the big five European football nations in recent years. Note that the periods are not 100% identical. The figures also show that a growing proportion has come from export. The English Premier League has been in the driving seat in the external markets. During all periods their revenues from external markets have exceeded the collective revenues of the other members of the big five.

In subsequent years, the Spanish LaLiga will see strong revenue growth. The case study at the end of this chapter presents detailed information about the sale process. The rights increased from €235 million to €650 million, which was a rise of 177%. This made LaLiga the second most valuable league outside their own market, only surpassed by the English Premier League. With some few exceptions, the rights increased in about every market.

However, the Premier League is expected to increase their revenues significantly when signing a new deal at the end of 2015 (*TV Sports Markets*, 2015b and 2015c). In Norway and

Table 7.2   Media rights – big five European leagues: Domestic market/International markets(€ million)

	Period 1	Period 2	Period 3	Period 4
England	800 / 311 (72% / 28%)	796 / 591 (57% / 43%)	1299 / 908 (59% / 41%)	2211 / (1500*). –
Spain	435 / 65 (85% / 15%)	471 / 123 (74% / 26%)	532 / 235 (75% / 31%)	n.c. / 650 –
Italy	793 / 70 (91% / 9%)	817 / 91 (89% / 11%)	858 / 117 (88% / 12%)	1150 / 215 (84% / 16%)
France	642 / 8 (99% /1%)	668 / 17 (97% / 3%)	607 / 33 (95% / 5%)	727[1] / 80[2] (91%/ 9%)
Germany	320 / 18 (94 % / 6%)	322 / 53 (85% / 14%)	470 / 71 (83% / 13%)	534 / 175 (75% / 25%)

[1]Period: 2016/17–2019/20
[2]Period: 2018/19–2023/24

Source: TV Sports Markets: The Football Media Money League, November 2013; TVSM: Vol. 18(7); 18(11); 18(22); 19(10); 19(14); 19(15) and 19(16). The periods are somewhat different and therefore not 100% comparable. England periods: 2007/08–09/10; 2010/11–12/13; 2013/14–15/16; 2016/17–1018/19. France periods: 2005/06–2007/08, 2008/09–2011/12; 2012/13–2015/16. Italy periods: 2009/10; 2010/11–11/12, 2012/13–14/15; 2015/16–2017/18. Spain periods: 2006/07–08/09, 2009/10–2012/13; 2013/14–2014/15; 2015/16–2019/20. Germany periods: 2006/07–2008/09, 2009/10–2011/12, 2012/13–2014/15; 2015/16–2016/17)

*Predictions by October 2015

Sweden, the Premier League deals commencing from 2016 will have increased by 143% and 130% from the former deals, and by 100% in the US and Hong Kong (TV Sports Markets, 2015d). By October 2015, all deals had not been completed, but media predictions indicated an increase in value of about 60%.

The growth in export revenues is also the result of a promotion strategy. Many football fans have a strong psychological relationship with their favourite clubs. For those who identify strongest, the connection is an important part of their identity. It is documented that supporters with a high degree of club identification consume more sport (directly and indirectly), pay more for tickets, spend more on club equipment, and are more loyal in periods when the club is struggling (Melnick & Wann, 2004; Wann et al., 2001). This explains why many clubs are willing to put substantial effort into recruiting supporters outside their core market.

Identification usually involves a geographical dimension, since people in general have preferences for local clubs. However, technological innovations in the media have improved their ability to reach supporters. Many clubs have therefore extended their fanbase outside the core markets. That sports programmes, such as football matches, have a low *cultural discount* represents a major advantage in that respect (Gaustad, 2000). The cultural discount reflects the reduction in value on media products when they are shown beyond the home market. In general, this reduction is lower for sports programmes than for many other media products, since viewers often have preferences for local content. Domestic news programmes, as an example, attract little interest outside the core market.

Live football matches are fresh commodities. Yesterday's matches will attract no interest. Differences in times zones can therefore make it inconvenient for foreign viewers to follow live matches. To some degree, clubs can compensate for this by rescheduling matches forwards or backwards in time. Such a strategy, however, must be balanced to avoid conflicting interests with the home markets. In recent years, the English Premier League and the Spanish LaLiga have both rescheduled kick-off times on some matches to better suit audiences in Asia and the Americas in particular (*TV Sports Markets*, 2015c).

The internet has improved the ability of the clubs to promote themselves more efficiently worldwide. Similar to TV signals, the internet also has the characteristics of *impure public goods*. The information that is published online can be downloaded by everyone that has access, independent of where they are living. The cost structure of producing information on the internet has the same economies of scale advantages as the production of TV programmes. A large proportion is made up of sunk costs. Therefore, the costs of publishing information on the internet are independent of how many people read and watch it. In summary, all these characteristics make it effective for clubs to promote themselves. The big clubs have also translated their websites into several languages. Additionally, many do both pre-season and post-season tours outside their core market, both to recruit fans and cultivate relations with existing fans.

Another promotion instrument has been the investments in multinational squads. Indeed, contained some of the big five European leagues have had more foreigners than domestic players during some seasons. Many players have been recruited because of their skills as football players. However, while there have never been any doubts raised that Latin-American players were recruited because of their skills, this has not necessarily been the case for Asian players. Indeed, in some cases, clubs have been accused of more taking into account commercial concerns rather than emphasising a player's skills (Gratton, 2003).

Everton was the first English club that intentionally promoted themselves in China, which involved the recruitment of two Chinese players. In addition, the club was pioneering in going on promotion tours to China and also set up a website in Mandarin. This strategy gave beneficial results. By the start of the 2002/03 season, they had surpassed Liverpool and Manchester United as the most popular Premier League club in China. Manchester City also recruited a Chinese player in the same season. As an illustration of its effectiveness, the highest viewed TV-match from the Premier League was the match between these two clubs on 1 January in the

Table 7.3 Percentage of foreign players – big-five leagues

	2008/09	2010/11	2012/13
England	57	58	61
Italy	39	46	52
Germany	55	43	44
Spain	37	40	38
France	31	30	26

Source: http://www.football-observatory.com/-Publications,18, downloaded 7 May 2014

2002/03 season. The match was estimated to have attracted about 365 million Chinese viewers, which was 200 times the number of viewers that such a match normally would have attracted. The main reason for this was that both teams had one Chinese player in their starting line-up (Gratton, 2003). Such promotion efforts have also paid off in other markets. In 2005, the English Premier League was the most watched sport on TV in Malaysia, Thailand and Singapore, as well as in China (Solberg & Turner, 2010).

Contemporary and future challenges

A part of what attracts people to football matches is the *uncertainty of outcome*. This is based on the philosophy that spectators in general prefer contests between clubs or individuals that are even. The phenomenon is well known in the sport economics literature (Rottenberg, 1956). In team sports, uncertainty of outcome reflects the *competitive balance* of teams participating in a tournament. Where many teams have a similar probability of winning, the league has a high degree of competitive balance. In contrast, there is a low degree of competitive balance when only a small number of teams have a high probability of winning. Competitive balance depends primarily on the distribution of playing talent across teams, which in turn depends on the relative economic revenues of the teams (Gerrard, 2000).

The uncertainty of outcome dimension represents a two-edged sword for teams and their sup-porters. Although both of them prefer to win, many find it boring if one or a few teams become too dominant. Hence, clubs (and leagues) are facing a permanent challenge to find a balance between the desire to win and at the same time upholding a sufficient degree of *competitive balance* to make the league attractive for the general audience. Unlike any conventional industry, the clubs have an interest in upholding the economic health of their rivals. It is in all the teams' own interest to ensure that none of them becomes too dominant. Therefore, leagues use a variety of mechanisms to protect the collective interest in upholding uncertainty of outcome/competitive balance. This includes various forms of cross-subsidisation of the smaller clubs by the larger clubs. The importance of upholding the competitive balance has allowed sports clubs to establish co-operations that would be in violation of *anti-trust policy* in other industries.

In European club football, media rights have become the major instrument to uphold the competitive balance (Gratton & Solberg, 2007). By 2015, the majority of European football leagues sell the rights collectively, with Spain and Portugal being the exceptions after the clubs in Greece and Italy went over from individual to collective sale in 2009. From the 2016/17 season, the Spanish LaLiga clubs will also sell the rights collectively. Table 7.4 provides an overview of the distribution models in the big five leagues.

The most common instrument to measure the distribution of revenues and wealth is the Gini-coefficient. This coefficient, which can take values from 0 to 1, was developed by the Italian statistician and sociologist Corrado Gini and published in his 1912 paper 'Variability and Mutability' (Gini, 1912). The lower the coefficient, the more equal is the distribution. If the revenues are 100% equally shared, the coefficient will be 0. On the other hand, if one club earns all the revenues alone, it takes the value 1. See Atkinson (1975) for a more extensive explanation and discussion of the Gini Index.

Table 7.4   Distribution of media revenues in the big five European leagues

England:	50% is distributed equally, 25% on basis of performance and 25% on basis of TV matches. International rights are distributed equally.
France:	50% is distributed equally, 30% on basis of performance and 20% on basis of TV matches.
Germany:	50% is distributed equally, the rest on basis of performances in the last three years and this year. The best team is limited to 50% of the total, while the bottom club will receive at least 2.9%.
Italy:	The rights have been sold collectively since the 2010/11 season. By 2015, 40% is distributed equally, 30% on basis of performance, and 30% on basis of the number of supporters. The clubs sold the rights individually. Until the 2009 season, 19% were paid into a common fund, which in turn was equally distributed.
Spain:	The clubs in LaLiga have sold the rights individually since 1996. Since 2003, a group of the smallest clubs and the majority of the clubs in SecundaLigahas sold the rights collectively. The clubs have agreed to sell the rights collectively from the 2016/17 season.

Source: *TV Sports Markets* Vol. 16, no. 11; Størseth & Åsmul, 2007

Table 7.5   Gini-indexes 2001/12 season

	Total revenues	Media rights — domestic leagues	Media rights including UEFA tournaments
England	0.307	0.074	0.225
France	0.302	0.202	0.272
Germany	0.334	0.126	0.273
Italy	0.395	0.242	0.396
Spain	n.a.	0.422	0.478

Source: Editions of *TV Sports Markets*; UEFA.com
n.a. = not available

As seen from Table 7.5, the Gini-coefficients of the media revenues for domestic leagues are lower than the coefficients of the total revenues. This confirms that the redistribution of media rights has reduced the financial distance within the leagues, and hence improved the competitive balance. However, the coefficients increase when including the media rights from the UEFA tournaments, i.e. the Champions League and the Europe League. Hence, the media rights from the two sources work in opposite directions.

The table also confirms that the distribution is more equal in the leagues that sell the rights collectively (England, France and Germany) than in those that sell them individually (Spain and Italy). The English Premier League has gone furthest on this road, a pattern that has become stronger over the years. The reason for this is the strong growth in the international rights, which so far have been 100% equally shared between the clubs.

In the Premier League, the strong growth in values combined with the equal distribution have strengthened the position of clubs other than those at the top of the financial ladder. During the 2011/12 season, the media revenues of Wolverhampton who finished at the bottom of the Premier League exceeded the media revenues of each club in Germany, Italy and Spain (except for Barcelona and Real Madrid). On the other hand, the two top Spanish clubs earned significantly more than those at the top of the ladder in the Premier league. While Barcelona and Real Madrid each earned €125 million, the two Manchester clubs that were the best clubs in the Premier League earned respectively €75 million and €74 million (Solberg & Kringstad, 2014). This policy of equalisation not only contributes to upholding the competitive balance, it also improves the ability of all the clubs in the Premier League to recruit players from other nations, and not just the top clubs. In that way, it strengthens the league as a unit towards rival leagues. For the bottom clubs in the Premier League, the media revenues account for about 80% of their total revenues.

The average clubs in other European leagues earn only a small fraction of the average clubs in England and Germany (Table 7.6). For the 2013/14 season, the media revenues of the average Premier League club amounted to €105,2 million. This was 35% more than the total media revenues of all the 18 Dutch elite clubs. The media revenues of the bottom club in the Premier League, Cardiff City, was 67% of the media revenues of all the Dutch elite clubs (Deloitte, 2015).

Table 7.6 Revenues of average clubs in specific football nations as a percentage of the revenues of the average clubs in the English Premier League and German Bundesliga

2013/14 season	English Premier League	German Bundesliga
Netherlands	12%	19%
Belgium	9%	14%
Austria	8%	13%
Denmark	6%	10%
Scotland	6%	10%
Sweden	4%	6%

Calculated on basis of information from Deloitte (2015)

The Gini coefficients in Table 7.5 confirm that the UEFA tournaments and particularly the Champions League have widened the financial gaps between rich football nations and others. Firstly, the big football nations can have more teams than the smaller nations. Secondly, a substantial portion of the revenues ('Market Pool') correlates with the commercial revenues in the specific markets. In principle, these are independent of the sporting performance. To illustrate how this works, we compare the prize money for Juventus from Italy and FC Victoria Plzen from the Czech Republic who participated in the tournament in the 2013/14 season. The clubs performed 100% equally with the same number of wins, draws and losses, and both finished third in their respective groups. Despite the equality in performances, Juventus nevertheless earned €32 million more than the Czech club did. While Juventus earned €32 million from the 'Market Pool' and a total of €43.1 million, FC Victoria Plzen only earned €1.5 million from the 'Market Pool' and €11.1 million in total.

However, the Champions League also benefits top clubs in the smaller football nations, despite the fact that they earn less than the clubs from the top nations. When clubs from the Nordic countries have participated, the Champions League revenues have accounted for more than 50% of the total revenues in the respective seasons (Solberg & Gratton, 2004). Hence, the Champions League has widened the financial gap between the top and bottom, both within and between the leagues.

The major reason for strong growth in the Champions League revenues is the power of the top clubs in European football. On two occasions they have been invited to join a European Super League (Baskerville, 1999). This would have given them significantly higher revenues than what they earned from the domestic and international tournaments they participated in at that time. The national football federations and UEFA were of course not happy with the idea. UEFA's countermove was to restructure the former European Cup for league winners and establish the Champions League in a way that benefited the top clubs. Firstly, the big football nations were allowed to have more teams. Secondly, the tournament was extended with more teams and matches. While the European Cup for league winners was organised as a knock-out tournament, the Champions League has many more matches. During one period, it had two group stages. At this stage, the finalists had to play 17 matches. Since then, the second group stage has been replaced by a knock-out procedure. By 2015, the finalists had to play 13 matches. For more details on the historical development, see Solberg and Gratton (2004).

The export of TV football from the top nations can also displace domestic club football in the importing nations. Table 7.7 shows how much TV channels in specific markets spent on the media rights from the big five European leagues as a percentage of what they have spent on their own domestic league. The figures for the non-European markets also include the UEFA Champions League and Europe League. TV channels in Malaysia, India and Thailand spend many times more on European football than on their respective domestic leagues. This is in contrast to the respective big five nations, which all spend very moderately on foreign media rights relative to their own domestic league. This illustrates the financial leakage from the football nations somewhere down the financial ladder towards the wealthiest football nations.

It is not only in Asia that the European top-five leagues cost more than the domestic leagues. Since Table 7.7 was constructed, new contracts have been signed in Norway, both for the Premier League and the Norwegian Tippeliga (named after its main sponsor). While the Premier League rights increased by 143%, the Tippeliga had growth of 7%. Because of this, the Premier League will bring in 50% more than the Norwegian elite league when the new deals commence from the season commencing in 2017.

One reason for this pattern is that the demand for football, as for goods in general, is affected by a quality dimension (Wann et. al., 2001). All things being equal, football fans prefer to watch the best clubs and the best players. Europe has been the leading football continent in the last decades in terms of revenues. Every year in this century, the Football Money League (the list of the 20 richest clubs in the world) has only included clubs from the big five European nations (Deloitte, 2015). The export of TV football has strengthened their financial superiority, which in turn also has enabled them to recruit talented players from the rest of Europe as well as from other continents. The innovations in the media industry, which have improved their abilities to reach fans all over the world, have worked in the same direction.

Table 7.7   Media rights for club football tournaments from the big five European leagues as percentage of domestic leagues (2014/15 season). The non-European markets also include UEFA's Champions League and Europa League.

Asian markets	
Malaysia	900%
India	800%
Thailand	700%
Korea	300%
Japan	100%
South America	
Latin America	21%
Top 5 European markets	
France	16%
Italy	2.,7%
Germany	1,3%
Spain	1.3%
UK	1.2%
Other European markets	
Nordics	77%
Holland	70%
Greece	39%
Belgium	22%
Turkey	5%

Source: SportBusiness Intelligence. European top club competitions include the UEFA Champions League and Europa League, English Premier League, Spanish Liga, German Bundesliga, Italian Serie A and French Ligue 1. European markets compare only the domestic league spending with the other top four European leagues, so exclude the UEFA Champions league and Europa League. Latin America includes the domestic leagues of Brazil, Argentina, Chile, Ecuador, Paraguay, Uruguay, Columbia, Venezuela and Peru.

Case study 7.1: The sale of the international media rights of the Spanish LaLiga for the period from 2016/17 to 2019/20

The following case study resumes the main points from an article in *TV Sports Markets*, 28 August 2015, which is about the sale of the international media rights for the Spanish LaLiga. When the article was written, the LaLiga clubs had already reached their revenue target of €650 million ($720 million) per season, but despite that the sale had not been completed in all markets. This was a rise of 177% from the former deal, which covered 2012/13 to 2014/15. In addition to presenting data, it

(Continued)

(Continued)

also highlights six reasons behind the growth. These reasons correspond with some of the theoretical perspectives discussed above.

First, was the rescheduling of kick-off times, which has taken place since the rights were last sold. Kick-off slots have been moved to better suit audiences in Asia and the Americas in particular.

Second, the league has held many meetings with potential broadcasting partners since the last cycle in order to build direct relationships. These meetings, and the establishment of a direct link between the two, have translated into higher rights fees.

Third, the depreciation of the euro against the dollar, and also the pound, means deals in euros are more affordable for broadcasters that operate in these currencies.

Fourth, by selling worldwide at the same time, the rights have taken on greater importance for wealthy multi-territory broadcasters like beIN Media Group, ESPN and Fox International Channels. The league also benefited from selling its rights ahead of the English Premier League, which has just begun its own international sales cycle.

Fifth, the league includes two of the best teams in the world in Barcelona and Real Madrid, as well as the two best players, Lionel Messi and Cristiano Ronaldo.

Sixth, in 2014 LaLiga had a strategy where teams participated in tournaments on other continents with the purpose of promoting the international image of the Spanish league. The league has spent about €10 million over the past two years on accommodation, flights, event hosting and other costs.

Below are some examples from markets.

Middle East and Africa

In the Middle East and North Africa, beIN renewed its deal at an 80% uplift. The fee increased from about $50 million per season to close on $90 million per season.

LaLiga's value in sub-Saharan Africa is thought to have more than doubled to about €40 million per season. This has been driven by a big increase from pay-television broadcaster SuperSport, which will pay about €20 million per season for English-language rights across the region, up from about €8 million per season.

The remaining €20 million per season derives from a French-language deal across the region with pay-television broadcaster Canal Plus Afrique, a Portuguese-language deal with satellite operator Zap in Angola and Mozambique, and a deal with pay-television operator Azam TV in Tanzania. All deals in the region are for three seasons, from 2015/16 to 2017/18.

Americas

BeIN paid a huge increase to retain rights in the US and Canada. The fee rose to $120 million per season from $32 million per season. The deal is for five seasons, 2015/16 to 2019/20.

Rights fees also soared by more than 360% in Latin America, reaching about $105 million per season across the region in three separate deals. The previous deal was worth $22.7 million.

Pay-television broadcaster Sky Mexico was awarded rights in Mexico and Central America for about $30 million per season. Pay-television broadcaster ESPN bought rights in Brazil for about

$45 million per season, and in the rest of South America for about $30 million per season. All new deals are for five seasons, from 2015/16 to 2019/20.

Asia

BeIN also acquired rights in six Southeast Asian territories for about €50 million per season. These rights cover Thailand, Laos and Cambodia, as well as Indonesia, Malaysia and Singapore.

In Japan, the MP & Silva agency was awarded the rights in a deal worth in excess of €15 million per season. This was a slight increase on the previous value of €13.3 million per season. MP & Silva has since sold live rights to pay-television broadcaster Wowow.

In the Indian subcontinent, pay-television broadcaster MSM acquired rights in a three-season deal, from 2015/16 to 2017/18, worth close to €9 million per season. It beat an offer of just over €5 million per season from pay-television rival Neo Sports. The previous deal was worth €2 million per season.

In China, online streaming platform PPTV bought exclusive rights in a five-season deal, from 2015/16 to 2019/20, worth about €50 million per season.

Europe

Rights fees across Europe increased in most territories, but fell in the Nordics. Deals across the region were for three seasons, from 2015/16 to 2017/18.

MP & Silva bought rights in Denmark, Finland, Norway and Sweden for about €13.3 million per season – a 26% decrease on the €18 million per season paid by the TV4 Group in the last cycle.

MP & Silva also bought rights in the Balkans for about €7 million per season, double the €3.5 million per season paid by pay-television broadcaster Sportklub in the last cycle. Additionally, they also picked up rights in Albania for about €2 million per season.

France is the most valuable territory in the region in the new cycle, with beIN doubling its fee from about €20 million per season to close to €40 million per season.

In the UK and Ireland, pay-television broadcaster Sky will pay about €30 million per season, about double the value of its previous deal, which was worth between €14 million and €15 million per season. The fee was forced up by competition from rival BT.

In Germany, Austria and Switzerland, the Perform Group was a surprise winner of the rights, paying about €9 million per season – an 80% increase on the €5 million per season paid in the last cycle.

Belgium provided an increase of about 180%, as Andrea Radrizzani's Eleven Sports Network ousted the incumbent rights-holder, pay-television broadcaster Belgacom. The deal was worth about €7 million per season, up from €2.5 million per season.

In Romania, pay-television broadcaster RCS-RDS picked up the rights for about €6 million per season. The former deal was worth between €4 million and €4.5 million per season.

The Saran Media agency was awarded rights in the Czech Republic and Slovakia in a deal worth about €3.5 million per season, while the Pragosport agency retained rights in Hungary for about €2.3 million per season. Pragosport had held rights across all three territories in the last cycle in a deal worth about €2.5 million per season.

Conclusion

This chapter has illustrated how the revenues in elite football have increased significantly in recent years. Media rights have become the most important source for those at the top of the financial ladder. One reason for this is the technology innovation in the media industry, which has removed the scarcity of transmission frequencies. This has improved the ability of clubs to distribute TV matches to fans, also outside the core markets. While a stadium has capacity constraints, such limits do not exist for TV matches. In principle, football fans all over the world can tune in to the same live matches from wherever they are. Additionally, the Internet has made it easier for clubs to promote themselves globally. These factors have added fuel to the competition for content, which in turn has increased the value of media rights.

This development has benefited many stakeholders within the global football family. However, in club football, the advantages have particularly benefited those that have the products of best quality, which in club football are the leagues in the big five European football nations. They have earned the highest revenues from their domestic markets. In recent years, they have also benefited from exporting TV matches to external markets. In summary, this has created financial advantages that have allowed them to recruit the best players. This, in turn, also enables them offer the best matches.

Never before have football fans in smaller football nations had better opportunities to watch TV football from the top football nations. This may have displaced domestic football clubs in their respective nations, and hence widened the financial gap between those at the top of the financial ladder and others. The strength and direction of such effects depend on whether the imported TV matches are considered to complement or offer alternatives to domestic football. If the import promotes football in general, this can attract more spectators and higher TV audiences at domestic matches. However, if fans spend too much time and money on foreign TV football, this reduces what they can spend on domestic football. The large number of TV matches can also make fans supersaturated with football. In addition to the big five European leagues, fans can also watch the UEFA Champions League and Europe League, as well as cup matches. A large proportion of matches are shown exclusively on pay TV channels. Some fans cannot afford to purchase both European club football and their own domestic league. All things being equal, football fans prefer the products of best quality if they are offered alternatives. The more important the quality dimension is, the more likely they are to spend time and money on club football from the big five in Europe.

Principally, the market forces have distributed the revenues in club football. The only exception is the internal redistribution resulting from the collective sale procedures. This has given the bottom clubs a higher proportion of the revenues than if the rights had been sold individually by the clubs. The purpose of such procedures is to uphold the competitive balance and hence make the league more popular as a unit. However, since it also strengthens the purchasing power of the bottom clubs, it allows more clubs to recruit players from special interest markets. In that way, the redistribution of revenues can strengthen these leagues as a unit, both towards leagues that sell the media revenues individually and leagues in the respective importing nations.

Despite market forces having worked in favour of the clubs at the top of the financial ladder, this has not saved them from financial problems. Indeed, many have struggled severely. The major reason for this has been the fierce competition for talent. Agents have orchestrated bidding wars between clubs, which in turn have increased salaries as well as the amounts necessary to release players from their current contracts (Haugen & Solberg, 2010). According to the literature, European clubs operate as win maximisers. Consequently, they spend more on recruiting talents than North-American clubs, which operate more as profit maximisers (Késenne, 1996). This also makes European clubs more vulnerable in case unforeseen negative shifts in demand reduce their revenues. These problems are the reason why UEFA implemented the Financial Fairplay Regulation, the purpose of which has been to enable the clubs to better control their costs.

These circumstances have 'captured' many clubs in a prisoner's dilemma situation. To climb up the financial ladder, they have no choice but to behave as aggressively as their rivals do when recruiting players. This competition has grown extremely fierce, and there are no indications of any change in the near future. Therefore the clubs and leagues at the top of the hierarchy are likely to use whatever efforts are deemed necessary to uphold their position. The innovations in the media industry have improved the abilities of those that have the best products to reap financial rewards from external markets. Therefore the development described in this chapter, with a growing proportion of the revenues of the clubs in the big five leagues coming from external markets, is likely to continue. Have in mind that, by 2015, the UK population only accounted for 4.5% of the Chinese population. Although the clubs in the Chinese Super League outspent the Premier League on international transfers in the first transfer window in 2016, it is too early to conclude whether this was the start of a U-turn of the pattern described in this chapter. The Chinese clubs will meet several challenges before they can take over the hegemony in international club football. One of the challenges will be to increase the commercial revenues from external markets. By 2016, they have a long way to go before they can surpass the English Premier League and the Spanish La Liga.

Recommended further reading

Gaustad, T. (2000). The economics of sports programming, *Nordicom Review*, 21(2), 101–113.

This article focuses on the characteristics of sports programmes as commodities, and which are essential to analyse the market behaviour of the media companies involved in sport broadcasting. It presents a useful starting point for readers who want to understand more about sport broadcasting, and it is accessible without any background in economics.

Gratton, C. & Solberg, H. A. (2007). *The Economics of Sport Broadcasting*. London: Routledge.

This book analyses factors that influence both the demand and supply of TV sport. Special attention is paid to the stakeholders who operate at the supply side, and to their behaviour. This involves not only different kinds of TV stations, but also transmission companies such as satellite operators, cable companies and terrestrial distribution. The cost structure of the producers and the consequences they can have are also analysed. The book also analyses the sale of media rights by means of game theory and auction theory. Finally, it focuses on regulations of TV sport, such as the Listed Events regulation and the rationale behind it.

Jeanrenaud, C. & Késenne, S. (2006). *The Economics of Sport and the Media*. Cheltenham UK/Northampton, UK: Eward Elgar Publishing Limited.

This volume contains a set of original essays, written by eminent European and North American sports economists. It is accessible to readers without an economics background. It will be of interest to students of sport and the media and those interested in the commercialisation of sport in general. It presents research results on the sports–media relationship and analyses developments, prospects and key policy concerns related to this issue.

References

Atkinson, A. B. (1975). *The Economics of Inequality*. London, UK: Oxford Unity Press.

Baskerville Communication Corporation (1997). *Global TV Sports Rights*. Thousand Oaks, CA: BCC.

Baskerville Communications Corporation (1999). *Global TV: Sports Rights* (2nd edition). London: BCC.

Deloitte (2015). *Football Money League*. Manchester, UK: Sport Business Group.

Gaustad, T. (2000). The economics of sports programming, *Nordicom Review*, 21(2), 101–113.

Gerrard, B. (2000). Media ownership of pro sports teams: who are the winners and losers? *Sports Marketing & Sponsorship*, 2, 199–218.

Gini, C. (1912). Italian: *Variabilità e mutabilità* [Variability and Mutability], C. Cuppini, Bologna, 156 pages. Reprinted in *Memorie di metodologica statistica* (Ed. Pizetti, E. & Salvemini, T.). Rome: Libreria Eredi Virgilio Veschi (1955).

Gratton, C. (2003). Everton football club and china: sport in the global marketplace. In Trenberth, L. (Ed.), *Managing the Business of Sport*. Palmerston North: Dunmore Press.

Gratton, C. & Solberg, H. A. (2007). *The Economics of Sport Broadcasting*. London: Routledge.

Hammervold, R. & Solberg, H. A. (2006). TV sports programmes – who is willing to pay to watch? *Journal of Media Economics*, 19, 147–162

Haugen, K. & Solberg, H. A. (2010). The financial crisis in European football – a game theoretic approach. *European Sport Management Quarterly*, 10(5), 553–567.

Késenne, S. (1996). League Management in professional team sport with win maximizing clubs. *European Journal for Sport Management*, 2(2), 14–22

Melnick, M. J. & Wann, D. L. (2004). Sport fandom influences, interests, and behaviours among Norwegian university students. *International Sports Journal*, 8, 1–13.

Office of communication (2007). Summary of UK sports rights. Annex 10 to pay TV marketinvestigation consultation. Retrieved 26.04.2016 from: http://stakeholders.ofcom.org.uk/binaries/consultations/market_invest_paytv/annexes/annex_10.pdf

Rottenberg, S. (1956). The Baseball Players' Labor Market. *Journal of Political Economy*, 64, 242–258.

Solberg, H. A. & Gratton C. (2004). Would European soccer clubs benefit from playing in a super league? *Soccer and Society*, 5, 61–81.

Solberg, H. A. & Kringstad, M. (2014). *Europeisk klubbfotball – kampen om tilskuerne og inntektene i de store fotballnasjonene*. Samfunnsøkonomen, 12 (6), 40–49.

Solberg, H. A. & Turner, P. (2010). Exporting sports rights to overseas markets – the case of European football. *Sport in Society*, 13(2), 354–366.

Størseth, C. H. & Åsmul, H. O. G (2007). Salg av TV-rettigheter til fotball (Sale of TV rights football). Master's thesis. Trondheim, Norway: Trondheim Business School.

TV Sports Markets (2013). *The Football Media Money League,* November 2013. Sport Business Group.

TV Sports Markets (2014). *TVSM Global Report 2015.* London: Sport Business Group.

TV Sports Markets (2015a). Vol. 19, No. 16.

TV Sports Markets (2015b). Vol. 19, No. 14.

TV Sports Markets (2015c). Vol. 19, No. 15.

TV Sports Markets (2015d). Vol. 19, No. 18.

Wann, D. L., Melnick, M. J., Russel, G. W. & Pease, D. G. (2001). *Sports Fans: The Psychology and Social Impact of Spectators.* London: Routledge.

AMBUSH MARKETING IN SPORT

SIMON CHADWICK, NICHOLAS BURTON AND CHERI BRADISH

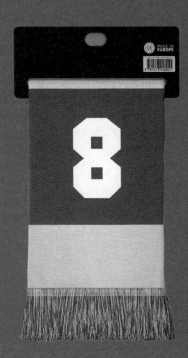

Introduction

Few industries or marketing communications activities mark out sport as a unique and specialized business as effectively and significantly as sponsorship. Today a defining component of integrated sport marketing communications, sponsorship has evolved over the past thirty years growing in value, sophistication, and strategy, and has become established as a major source or revenues for sport organizations and an important vehicle for marketers around the world. However, in line with this progressive development as a strategic sport marketing tool, competition to official sponsorship in the form of ambush marketing has also emerged and evolved, offering brands the opportunity to go above and beyond the legal and contractual rights of official partnerships in an effort to leverage against the ever-increasing value of sport in marketing. The presence and proliferation of ambush marketing have presented sponsors, commercial rights holders, event organizers and consumers alike with a number of important challenges, and today represent a fundamental consideration for sponsorship management, marketing, and sport business.

Historical and recent development

The 1984 Los Angeles Summer Olympic Games have long been considered one of the most successful and progressive events in modern Olympic history; born of political and economic turmoil which threatened the long-term viability of financial sustainability of the Olympic

Movement, the 1984 Los Angeles Games introduced a new era of commercialization and managerial sophistication to Olympic broadcasting, merchandising, and sponsorship. Whereas prior to 1984 Olympic sponsorship was delivered on an open, unrestricted basis – allowing interested organizations to associate with the Games for a nominal fee – the 1984 Games pioneered the development of category exclusivity and rights bundling, along with the 1982 FIFA World Cup. By limiting the number of official international partners for the Games, selecting one official sponsor per product or market category (e.g., credit cards, restaurants, sportswear and apparel, non-alcoholic beverages, beer, etc.), the Los Angeles Games created an auction between rival corporations for the right to sponsor the event, driving the cost of sponsorship, and ensuring exclusivity and prestige for the successful brand. The bundling of rights offered sponsors comprehensive marketing inventory, and granted official sponsors extensive activation opportunities and added value for their investment.

These structural changes ushered in a period of progressive growth in sponsorship expenditure – and subsequent managerial sophistication. The reforms enacted by the Los Angeles organizing committee made the 1984 Games the most successful in Olympic history to that point, earning a $250 million surplus (LaRocco, 2004), and inspiring changes throughout the sport sponsorship industry. Prior to 1984, individual marketing media or opportunities were negotiated independently, resulting in a reported 628 official partners at the 1976 Montréal Olympics (Gratton et al., 2012). Following the re-structured sponsorship programme implemented by Ueberroth and the 1984 organizers, the number of brands officially partnered with the Games was reduced to only 43. The IOC created the TOP (The Olympic Programme, since renamed The Olympic Partners) sponsorship platform, combining category exclusivity, rights bundling, and a multi-tiered sponsorship framework in order to further grow sponsorship revenues and build upon the success of the Los Angeles Games. These moves ushered in a period of astronomic growth in international sponsorship spending, growing from approximately $2 billion in 1984 (Meenaghan, 1991) to an estimated $55.3 billion in 2014 (International Events Group, 2014).

Despite these advances, however, the effects of the IOC's sponsorship reforms have not all been positive. In response to the restrictions placed on official partnerships available to would-be sponsors, and the increased costs incurred to interested organizations, many major corporations with Olympic marketing ambitions were left out in the cold and forced to identify new opportunities to align their brands with the Olympic Games. As a result, a new form of sport marketing – labeled 'ambush marketing' – emerged at the 1984 Los Angeles Games, providing non-sponsors with a means of leveraging against the rising marketing value of the Olympic Games. Defined as *the marketing communications activities of a brand seeking to capitalize on the attention, awareness, fan equity, and goodwill generated by having an association with an event or property, beyond the official or authorized rights of association delivered by that event or property*, ambush marketing has since emerged as a significant and growing threat to major event sponsorship and sport marketing.

The earliest examples of ambush marketing were marked out by incidents of direct competition between market rivals, in light of the product category exclusivity newly implemented in 1984. Kodak, for example, had long been associated with the Olympic Games as an official partner prior to Los Angeles; however, Fuji were able to secure the official international sponsorship rights for the 1984 Games, effectively terminating Kodak's long-term Olympic affiliation. Kodak responded by agreeing to partner the United States Track and Field team, ensuring that their brand was visible at and around the Games, and attempting to weaken Fuji's official IOC sponsorship agreement. Four years later, Kodak were able to return to the Olympic sponsor family for the 1988 Seoul Summer Olympic Games at Fuji's expense, leading Fuji to sponsor the United States Olympic Swimming team in an aggressive counter-sponsorship ambush. Likewise, the 1992 Barcelona Summer Olympic Games and 1992 Albertville and 1994 Lillehammer Winter Olympic Games saw credit card company American Express famously ambush rivals Visa's official Olympic partnership – and exclusive vendor rights mandating only Visa cards could be used to buy Olympic tickets or merchandise – noting that fans 'don't need a visa' to travel to the host countries.

These initial examples of ambushing inspired its name, with emphasis placed on a parasitic or attack-minded intent on the part of the non-sponsor. The earliest scholarly research into ambushing (e.g., Sandler & Shani, 1989; McKelvey, 1992, 1994; Meenaghan, 1996) reinforced this view as an aggressive marketing tactic, and suggested that the ultimate aim of ambushers was 'to weaken, or "ambush", a competitor's official association with a sports organization … Most often, an ambush marketing campaign is designed to intentionally confuse the buying public as to which company is in fact the official sponsor or a certain sports organization' (McKelvey, 1994, p. 20). Subsequent events, including the 1996 Atlanta Summer Olympic Games, the 1998 FIFA World Cup Finals in France, and the 2000 UEFA European Championships in Belgium and the Netherlands, saw ambush marketing grow throughout Europe and across the world, and become an established and evolving source of competition for official sponsors.

Nike, for example, earned international attention and plaudits for their ambush of the 1998 FIFA World Cup in France by leveraging their sponsorship of the Brazilian national team. Nike constructed a 7,800m^2 Nike Park on the site of Paris's La Défense and created an expansive television commercial featuring the Brazilian team en route to France playing football in London's Heathrow Airport. Pepsi, too, emerged as a prominent ambush marketer, signaling their intentions in 1996 at the ICC Cricket World Cup through billboard advertisements boasting 'Nothing Official About It', in response to Coca-Cola's official event sponsorship. Likewise Guinness, in an effort to ambush the 1999 Heineken Cup final in Ireland, flew a branded blimp over Lansdowne Road stadium during the final, drawing the attention of those fans in attendance and earning national headlines for their creativity.

Such efforts became commonplace around events and emerged as integral parts of the event marketing environment surrounding mega sporting events. However, more importantly, the creativity and innovation of non-sponsoring brands in identifying and exploiting potential ambush opportunities evidenced a progressive shift in ambush strategy away from predominantly aggressive or attack-minded campaigns and towards more opportunistic and inventive attempts. Specifically targeted campaigns against official sponsors such as were common in the 1980s and early 1990s, like American Express's ambush of Visa in Barcelona and Lillehammer, were replaced by highly suggestive and subversive marketing efforts which made use of associative imagery or terminology, and incorporated participant athletes or countries, in order to craft more innovative and associative ambush campaigns.

Table 8.1 Selected notable examples of ambush marketing

Year	Event	Famous alleged ambush marketing cases
2010	FIFA World Cup: South Africa	*Heineken*, following on their Euro 2004, 2008, and FIFA World Cup 2006 ambush campaigns, created a vuvuzela-themed hat to give away to Netherlands supporters traveling to South Africa. The hat, called a Pletterpet, featured South African and Dutch imagery, and the popular football chant 'Hup Holland Hup!' The Pletterpet was part of a broader ambush strategy by Heineken, including an international advertising campaign targeting Dutch football supporters and awareness around the FIFA World Cup.
2007	Rugby World Cup: France	Tongan rugby player Epi Taione legally changed his name to *Paddy Power*, after the Irish bookmaking agency, prior to the tournament as part of a promotion of Paddy Power's sponsorship of the Tongan national team. Event organizers banned the player from competing under his new name, forcing him to revert to Taione in order to participate in their World Cup.
2006	FIFA World Cup: Germany	Dutch brewery *Bavaria* gave away thousands of pairs of branded orange lederhosen, called Leeuwenhose, to Dutch fans on their way to the World Cup in Germany. An advertising campaign for the giveaway launched the promotion, showing fans wearing the lederhosen in a football stadium, cheering on the Dutch side. Stadium officials reportedly forced fans to remove the offending merchandise prior to entering the stadium, sparking international controversy over fans allegedly being forced to watch the World Cup in their underpants.
1996	Summer Olympics: Atlanta, Georgia	Linford Christie, a *Puma* sponsored athlete, appeared at a press conference ahead of the men's 100m sprint finals wearing contact lenses embossed with the Puma logo, a move which was in breach of Olympics rules prohibiting the wearing of non-official sponsor materials.
1984	Summer Olympics: Los Angeles, CA	*Nike* painted murals near Olympic sites around Los Angeles featuring Nike-sponsored track athletes, visible even from within the Los Angeles Olympic Coliseum, resulting in 42% of American consumers surveyed confusing Nike as the official sponsor of the 1984 Summer Olympic Games.

This evolution in ambush marketing methods ultimately necessitated a response on the part of sponsors and rights holders in order to better manage and protect their partnerships, and saw the rise of a progressive interventionism in sponsorship relations internationally. The earliest forms of counter-ambush activities relied upon predominantly reactive, defensive tactics focused on ambush marketing's alleged illegality or immorality. 'Name and shame' public relations activities, for example, emerged as one of the most common counter-ambush measures, as rights holders sought to identify and condemn alleged ambush marketers in the media in an effort to influence public opinion against ambushers. Media releases such as Reebok's response to Nike's ambush of the 1996 Atlanta Summer Olympics – including the erection of a temporary store neighbouring the Olympic village – reproved ambush marketers' efforts, stating: 'Shame on them. They're undercutting people and companies and products and services that will go to make the ultimate success of their own athletes…' (Myerson, 1996). These calls of support on ethical or moral grounds ultimately proved ineffective and largely counter-productive, however, as the coverage afforded to ambushers became a source of added value for the ambushing brand, and consumers evidenced little sympathy for sponsors and rights holders in their plight.

Concurrent to the rise of public relations-focused counter-ambush marketing efforts on the part of sponsors and rights holders was the emergence of a progressive use of legal protection governing intellectual property rights and the illegal usage of trademarked and copyrighted materials. This enforcement of legal rights has proven largely effective in combatting the myriad cases of rights infringements sporting events experience every year, ranging from the illegal use of the Olympic Rings in marketing, to the erroneous use of protected terminology such as 'football World Cup'. Major sporting events rights holders like the International Olympic Committee or FIFA face hundreds of ambush marketing campaigns during the course of each major event, but the majority of those reported and investigated are local businesses unknowingly or unwittingly using protected words or symbols in promotions. In many such cases, polite requests to remove the offending marks or logos have proven successful; in instances requiring more aggressive protection, legal teams at and around major events have sent cease and desist letters or will seek court-ordered injunctive relief in an effort to terminate the alleged infringements.

Unfortunately, the value of legal protection in prohibiting larger-scale ambush marketing has been negligible. These legal tactics have offered little reprieve against international- or national-level ambush marketing campaigns, whose potential impact on sponsorship value or returns is of greater concern than smaller, local infringements. Larger-scale ambush marketers have historically been more careful in avoiding intellectual property rights infringements, and resorted to more creative, innovative, and subversive methods in suggesting a link to the ambushed property, or in attempting to capitalize on the attention surrounding the event. The use of suggestive imagery or terminology, for example, or the timing of campaigns strategically around event broadcasts or positioning advertising media in proximity to host facilities, has allowed ambushing brands the opportunity to align with sporting events in clever, legal ways and to avoid potential litigation. The more subversive, intelligent approach taken by major ambush marketers has instead led to rights holders and local organizing committees pursuing legal remediation on the grounds of 'passing-off' or 'misappropriation', legal protection designed to prevent organizations from implying or misrepresenting an association with another brand or product in an attempt to mislead or confuse consumers. Unfortunately, as with more direct or explicit cases of intellectual property rights infringements, the legal precedence internationally for ambush marketing as passing-off is underdeveloped and offers little protection for event sponsorship. As a result, little in the way of jurisprudence exists at the upper echelons of ambushing: most cases to be pursued have been settled confidentially out of court, or more significantly, have been found in favor of the ambush marketer, giving further encouragement to ambushers and reinforcing the need for greater protective measures on the part of events and organizers.

Contemporary and future challenges

Nevertheless, the enforcement of intellectual property rights has remained a consistent component of commercial rights protection for major events and rights holders, and has informed much of the contemporary practices employed by sporting events to limit or protect against ambush marketers. Initiatives such as increased contractual sophistication regarding the use and resale of tickets, and more restrictive regulations governing supporters' rights and responsibilities within event arenas and marketing protected areas, have limited direct access for ambush marketers to fans in attendance and in the immediate vicinity of events. Likewise, organizers and broadcast partners have accepted greater responsibility in mitigating potential ambush marketing opportunities, and have ensured in many countries that television advertising time be incorporated into sponsorship agreements. In the aftermath of the 1996 Atlanta Summer Olympic Games and the 1998 FIFA World Cup, major commercial rights owners including the International Olympic Committee and UEFA implemented new protocols for the sale and distribution of advertising rights during the televised broadcasts of their events. These counter-ambush measures, intended to restrict immediate access to international television audiences for potential ambushers, have succeeded in many instances in 'blocking-out' ambush marketers from the events – limiting the media and marketing opportunities available to ambush marketers in and around events.

This has been an important evolution not only in the prevention of ambush marketing, but also in the managerial sophistication and contractual complexity of sponsorship agreements. Today's partnership contracts are significantly more advanced in the rights and responsibilities established for both parties – sponsor and sponsee – and establish clearly the counter-ambush measures expected of commercial rights holders in protecting their sponsors, and the marketing media corporate partners are expected to utilize and maximize in activating their sponsorships.

Perhaps most influential in contemporary rights interventionism and sponsorship protection has been the creation and maintenance of clean marketing venues and restricted radii for advertising media surrounding event host facilities. In response to the overwhelming and highly-visibly ambush marketing efforts around the 1996 Atlanta Summer Olympic Games and the 1998 FIFA World Cup in France, UEFA and their marketing consultancy International Sports and Leisure (ISL) established marketing exclusion zones around host stadia for the 2000 UEFA European Championships in the Netherlands and Belgium. This initiative saw UEFA and ISL secure all outdoor advertising media around their games to a radius of three kilometers; the billboards and public transport signage were then offered to UEFA's official sponsors as additional marketing inventory to encourage the sponsors to further leverage their associations, or left blank in order to prevent competition for attention from non-sponsoring brands. Similarly, the IOC have long held their events in 'clean stadia' – removing all visible branding and advertising from their host arenas, including those of official sponsors, in order to maintain Olympic amateur sport ideals whilst simultaneously prohibiting potential ambush marketing opportunities or confusion.

The size and scale of such marketing exclusion areas have grown rapidly in the wake of the 2000 European Championships, including a 30 kilometer protected radius established around host sites for the 2008 Beijing Summer Olympic Games. Unfortunately for sponsors and commercial rights holders, however, these new, more marketing-focused counter-ambush measures have seemingly encouraged the creativity and ingenuity of ambush marketers, and have led to a number of new methods, media, and strategies designed to circumvent the regulations in place. In 2008, for example, Pepsi created a marketing campaign featuring Chinese basketball star Yao Ming in order to capitalize on the Beijing Summer Olympic Games. Whilst Beijing was protected and marketing media throughout the city were owned by the Beijing organizing committee and the IOC, Pepsi were able to target other domestic markets throughout China, including Shanghai, and successfully ambushed the event in the largest cities.

Also in 2008, sportswear manufacturer K-Swiss successfully ambushed the ATP/WTA French Open in Paris, creating a highly visible and unique guerrilla promotion on a main commuter and pedestrian route outside the event's protected property. The American shoe brand parked a car on a public street outside the stadium, crushed by a giant, oversized, branded purple tennis ball; on the opposite side of the street, a promotional van staging a giveaway met with visitors. Combined, the marketing stunt earned K-Swiss headlines across Europe and became a main tourist stop for visitors to and from Roland Garros. Similar efforts have become commonplace around events targeting supporters en route to competitions, including along train lines or in rail stations, on public transit in host cities, and in and around major airports.

This creativity on the part of ambush marketers, and ability to circumvent the regulatory frameworks created around events and sponsors, have ultimately led to an increased reliance on the part of major sporting events on event-specific legislation designed to restrict the marketing activities of non-sponsors and local businesses. First emergent in Australia in 1996 as protection for the upcoming 2000 Sydney Summer Olympic Games, ambush marketing legislative protection represents an integral component of contemporary sponsorship interventionism; the *Sydney 2000 Games (Indicia and Images) Protection Act* provided a template for future events in reinforcing the existing intellectual property rights owned and protected by major events. Traditionally, all countries have granted the IOC and the national Olympic committee or sporting governing body exclusive rights to the Olympic name, logo, and associated imagery. However, the legislation enacted by the Australian government strengthened the legal rights owned by the Olympics for the duration of the Games preparation and competition, including historically fair-usage words and phrases which when used in combination could be utilized by an ambush marketer to suggest an affiliation with the Games. So, for example, where previously the words 'gold' and 'Sydney' were both exempt from trademark or copyright protection as fair usage words, a combination of those in a marketing campaign – such as 'bring home the gold in Sydney' – would be in contravention of the new legislation, and thus grounds for legal action.

The *Sydney 2000 Games (Indicia and Images) Protection Act* ultimately proved successful in the eyes of Olympic organizers and the IOC, and has since become a required component of any city's bid to host the Olympic Games. Countries throughout Europe and around the world have thus been forced to enact ambush marketing legislation granting commercial rights holders increasingly stringent protection against potential ambush marketing, including notably draconian legislative acts in the likes of the United Kingdom and South Africa. The scope and scale of Olympic legislation have expanded progressively over time, affording organizers near-monopolistic marketing rights around their events. The 2012 London Summer Olympic Games, for example, received special legislative exemptions covering marketing activities including the use of similar or suggestive sporting imagery, in an effort to curtail ambush marketing efforts.

Nonetheless, ambush marketing has continued to grow and evolve, as new marketing opportunities, media, and strategies are identified or created by brands seeking to capitalize on the consumer attention, awareness, and goodwill surrounding major sporting events. The creativity and innovation ambush marketers have shown that circumventing the interventionist frameworks in place has come to define ambush marketing, and has highlighted the struggle faced by event organizers and host governments in preventing ambush marketing's presence and proliferation.

Case study 8.1: Caught with their pants down?

Europe has been host to a number of important and impactful ambush marketing campaigns in recent years, with major implications for ambush marketing's development and event sponsorship's continued indemnification from competitive marketing practices. From guerrilla marketing-style ambush attempts on Wembley Way at the 1996 UEFA European Championships in England, to Nike's 'Joga Bonito' viral marketing success around the 2006 FIFA World Cup in Germany, to headphones manufacturer Beats By Dre outfitting British athletes at the 2012 London Summer Olympic Games, Europe stands out as an important battleground in the fight between ambush marketers and commercial rights holders. In response to this proliferation of ambush marketing attempts, European events have pioneered a number of counter-ambush marketing tactics, including the use of marketing exclusion zones surrounding event facilities, in-stadium regulations and clean venues, and new depth and breadth to the legislative protection granted to major events.

The 2012 UEFA European Championships in Poland and Ukraine offered arguably one of the most interesting and provocative examples of ambush marketing in recent history. On 13 June 2012, Denmark met Portugal in Group B of the opening round of the tournament in Lviv, Ukraine. Whilst Portugal emerged victorious, defeating the Danes 3–2, it was Danish striker Nicklas Bendtner who stole the headlines. After scoring his second goal of the match to level the affair at two-all, Bendtner lifted his shirt to reveal eye-catching green under-shorts, branded with the name of Irish bookmakers Paddy Power. The betting agents, whose previous ambush marketing efforts included models stalking Tiger Woods at The Open in 2010 at St Andrews and an attempted sponsorship of the Tonga national rugby team at the 2007 Rugby World Cup, earned international media attention from the stunt, successfully ambushing the European Championships. Bendtner, however, incurred severe disciplinary action from UEFA, highlighting the importance major events place on protecting their corporate partners and image, and the restrictions in place to protect against ambush marketing.

In wearing and revealing branded undergarments bearing the name of a non-sponsoring brand, Bendtner's actions were deemed to be in contravention of two significant regulations governing player behavior and non-UEFA sponsor activation. According to Law 4 of FIFA's Laws of the Game, which concern player conduct and equipment, 'Players must not reveal undershirts which contain slogans or advertising.' This restriction was put in place to discourage players from removing their shirts during goal celebrations, and from using goal celebrations as an opportunity to share or reveal a political or branded message. In 2011, for example, Italy and then-Manchester City striker Mario Balotelli famously marked a goal against rivals Manchester United by unveiling an undershirt asking 'Why Always Me?' Balotelli's celebration, and similar actions by players in removing their shirts or revealing messages or images on their base-layer clothing, have resulted in a strengthening of FIFA regulations regarding player conduct and apparel, and have typically resulted in a yellow card for the offending player.

More significantly, Article 18.18 of UEFA's own 'Regulations of UEFA European Football Championship 2010–12' dictates that 'All kit items worn during the final tournament must be free

(Continued)

(Continued)

of any sponsor advertising'. Separate from FIFA's Laws of the Game, this restriction was implemented by UEFA in order to protect their sponsors against the potential ambush marketing efforts of rival corporations or more creative or opportunistic non-sponsors. As such, the penalties for infringing upon the contracted sponsorship rights of UEFA's corporate partners, and for participating in an ambush marketing campaign during the competition, are considerably more severe than the standard outcome of FIFA's Law 4. Bendtner was fined €100,000 and banned for one match, despite pleading ignorance of the regulations prohibiting player participation in non-sponsor marketing activities and claiming that the Paddy Power-branded shorts were his lucky under-shorts.

The punishment levied against the Danish forward marked an important moment in European ambush marketing and sponsorship protection history. The fine imposed on Bendtner stood in stark contrast to UEFA's response to a number of significant incidents involving racial abuse and fan misconduct during the tournament, underpinning the severity with which events view ambush marketing and the importance placed on protecting sponsors and the European Championships' commercial value. The Spanish and Russian football associations, for example, were levied €20,000 and €30,000 fines respectively due to racist behavior and fan misconduct on the part of their supporters during the event; the Croatian federation likewise was sanctioned for racism amongst its support, earning a €80,000 penalty for its second offense.

The difference in disciplinary actions taken between Bendtner's misconduct and the infringements on civil rights by the supporters of Spain, Russia and Croatia earned UEFA wide-ranging criticism from the international press, supporters, and players alike. Belgium captain Vincent Kompany, amongst others, took to social media to decry UEFA's handling of the situation and questioned how protecting against ambush marketing could be worth more than protecting supporters or athletes from racist behavior or threats of physical violence. Former England defender Rio Ferdinand, too, spoke out against UEFA's response to Paddy Power's ambush on Twitter.

The debate surrounding Bendtner's Paddy Power shorts and UEFA's subsequent response provides an enlightening view into the wider discussion happening in sport and marketing throughout Europe and around the world as to the legitimacy and morality of ambush marketing, and equally of the severity and need for the interventionist counter-ambush marketing measures being implemented and employed by major events, commercial rights holders, host countries, and official sponsors. Important questions were asked regarding the viability and place of the increasingly draconian sponsorship protection activities enacted, such as event-specific ambush marketing legislation in Olympic host countries, or limitations placed on the clothing or apparel fans are permitted to wear in tournament stadia. Likewise, concerns over the aggressive and brazen nature of ambush marketing attempts such as that of Paddy Power which incorporate participant athletes, or like that of Bavaria at the 2006 FIFA World Cup in Germany which employed unknowing supporters as branded Bavaria ambassadors, necessitate greater consideration as to how far is too far for ambush marketers?

More broadly, UEFA's actions highlight how important business and marketing have become for sport at the highest levels, and reveal the extent to which commercial rights holders and event organizers are prepared to go in order to protect their sponsors and corporate partners. This at-times uncomfortable but necessary relationship between events and sponsors creates a number of challenges for sport managers, ranging from how to manage the expectations and needs of official sponsors, to how best to allow local business, supporters, and players to benefit commercially from the value and potential of sport. Protection against ambush marketing and outside competition is a standard component of contemporary sponsorship contracts, intended to mitigate the risks of larger, more visible ambush marketing campaigns which threaten to diminish the value of sponsorships or negatively impact the brand image and equity of sporting events. Those regulations today represent an important component of partnership agreements and necessitate that events and right holders play an active role in the defense against ambushing. However, governing bodies like the IOC and FIFA have been criticized by businesses and local communities around their events due to the restrictions in place prohibiting them from capitalizing on the presence of major events in their regions, all in the name of ambush marketing.

Conclusion

The rise and development of ambush marketing is an important issue in contemporary sport marketing research and discourse. Without fully understanding the nature, role, and evolution of ambush marketing as a marketing communications strategy, it is impossible to truly assess the impact ambush marketing has had on official event sponsorship, and what potential remedies or lines of recourse are available to rights holders and sponsors. The proliferation – and evolution – of ambush marketers, and the creativity shown by ambushers in evading the legal, managerial, and legislative sponsorship protection measures in place, have encouraged a pronounced development in the managerial and contractual sophistication of major event sponsorship. Moreover, the competition for fan attention and awareness, and the often-innovative and clever campaigns created by ambush marketers, have necessitated greater activation and sponsorship-linked marketing efforts on the part of sponsors in order to secure their partnerships and achieve their strategic objectives. Commercial rights holders and corporate partners have accepted and embraced a more collaborative, proactive approach to ambush marketing prevention, developing multi-layered and synergistic partnership agreements and marketing campaigns, in an effort to establish greater ownership of the event marketing space. This cooperation could be integral to the continued success of sport sponsorship, as ambush marketers show no signs of abating.

Ultimately, ambush marketing and its effects on sponsorship agreements and marketing is a relatively new phenomenon, and is constantly evolving. Contemporary ambush marketing is much changed from the earliest examples born of the 1984 Los Angeles Summer Olympics. Ambush marketing today reflects a much more strategic, opportunistic, inventive approach to event-associated sport marketing, than past competitive or parasitic efforts. The implications for sport marketing, management, and law, are manifest: sponsorship contracts, government legislation, in-stadium regulations, sponsorship-linked marketing have all been influenced by ambush marketers, and will continue to experience significant changes as ambush marketing grows. The true effects of ambushing, however, remain to be seen. To date, the creativity and innovation of ambush marketers has earned brands recognition and plaudits for their efforts, yet the potential costs to sponsorship should not be ignored. There is no evidence to date that sponsorship values have been negatively impacted by ambush marketing, or that an official sponsor has terminated their relationship with a property in order to become an ambush marketer. But these challenges remain for events like the Olympics or UEFA European Championships whose financial viability is contingent on the continued success and growth of corporate partnerships.

Recommended further reading

As an emerging area of study in contemporary sport business and marketing scholarship, ambush marketing represents an ever-growing field of research. A number of important contributions merit recognition and further consideration within the literature, however, helping to better define and elaborate upon the implications of and unique challenges posed by ambush marketing for sport managers:

Chadwick, S. & Burton, N. (2011). The evolving sophistication of ambush marketing: a typology of strategies. *Thunderbird International Business Review*, *53*(6), 709–719.
Crompton, J.L. (2004). Sponsorship ambushing in sport. *Managing Leisure*, *9*(1), 1–12.
McKelvey, S. & Grady, J. (2008). Sponsorship program protection strategies for special sport events: are event organizers outmanoeuvring ambush marketers? *Journal of Sport Management*, *22*(5), 550–586.
Meenaghan, T. (1994). Point of view: ambush marketing: immoral or imaginative practice? *Journal of Advertising Research*, *34*(5), 77–88.
Sandler, D.M. & Shani, D. (1989). Olympic sponsorship vs. 'ambush' marketing: who gets the gold? *Journal of Advertising Research*, *29*(4), 9–14.
Scassa, T. (2011). Ambush marketing and the right of association: clamping down on reference to that big event with all the athletes in a couple of years. *Journal of Sport Management*, *25*(4), 354–370.
Séguin, B. & O'Reilly, N. (2008). The Olympic brand, ambush marketing and clutter. *International Journal of Sports Marketing & Sponsorship*, *4*(1/2), 62–84.

Sandler and Shani (1989) and Meenaghan (1994) provide two of the earliest examinations of ambush marketing's formative stages, and also provide an initial look into the apparent threat and potential effects ambushing presents for sponsorship. These maiden studies laid the groundwork for the long-standing ethical, moral, and legal debate regarding ambush marketing's place in sport and event marketing, key concerns in ambush marketing's perceived legitimacy. Likewise, Crompton (2004) and McKelvey and Grady (2008) amongst others offer valuable perspectives into the commercial rights management and counter-ambush initiatives employed by events and sponsors in combatting the threat posed by ambushers, an integral part of ambush marketing research and contemporary sponsorship practice. Finally, recent studies by the likes of Chadwick and Burton (2011), Seguin and O'Reilly (2008), and Scassa (2011) have re-contextualized ambush marketing research, exploring the complex, diverse, and strategic methods utilized by ambush marketers today, and examining the changing perceptions and perspectives of sponsors, rights holders, and consumers regarding ambush marketing, and the efforts made by major events to prohibit ambushers.

References

Gratton, C., Liu, D., Ramchandani, G. & Wilson, D. (2012). *The Global Economics of Sport*. New York: Routledge.

International Events Group (2014). *IEG Sponsorship Report*. Chicago: IEG.

LaRocco, C. (2004). Rings of Power: Peter Ueberroth and the 1984 Los Angeles Olympic Games. *Financial History*, 10–12, 36.

McKelvey, S. (1992). NHL v. Pepsi Cola Canada Uh-Huh! Legal parameters of ambush marketing. *Entertainment and Sport Law Journal*, *10*(3), 5–18.

McKelvey, S. (1994). Atlanta '96: Olympic countdown to ambush Armageddon? *Seton Hall Journal of Sport Law*, *4*(2), 397–445.

Meenaghan, T. (1991). Sponsorship – legitimising the medium. *European Journal of Marketing*, *25*(11), 5–10.

Meenaghan, T. (1996). Ambush marketing – a threat to corporate sponsorship. *Sloan Management Review*, *38*(1), 103–113.

Myerson, A.R. (1996). Olympic Sponsors Battling to Defend Turf. *The New York Times*. Retrieved 14 August 2008, from: http://www.nytimes.com/1996/05/31/business/the-media-business-advertising-olympic-sponsors-battling-to-defend-turf.html?src=pm.

Sandler, D.M. & Shani, D. (1989). Olympic sponsorship vs. 'ambush' marketing: who gets the gold? *Journal of Advertising Research*, *29*(4), 9–14.

SPORT, SOCIAL MEDIA AND ONLINE COMMUNITIES

BASTIAN POPP AND HERBERT WORATSCHEK

Introduction: Historical and recent development

Definition of social media

The economic relevance of ongoing interactions of individuals in groups has been particularly promoted by Hagel and Armstrong (1997) who were the first to extensively study virtual communities from a business perspective and define them as a 'dispersed group of people who share interest and expertise in a specific topic' (p. 18). Due to the recent emergence of social media, the focus of managers increasingly shifted from traditional online communities to social media which are considered as 'a group of internet-based applications that builds on the ideological and technological foundations of Web 2.0, and it allows the creation and exchange of user-generated content' (Kaplan & Haenlein, 2010, p. 61). In their topical review of sport and social media research, Filo, Lock, and Karg (2015) define social media in sport as 'new media technologies facilitating interactivity and co-creation that allow for the development and sharing of user-generated content among and between organizations (e.g. teams, governing bodies, agencies and media groups) and individuals (e.g. consumers, athletes and journalists)' (p. 167). Consequently, social media in sport comprise a variety of platforms including social networking sites, blogs and micro-blogs, online communities and discussion forums. Figure 9.1 illustrates the manifold appearances of social media and their most prominent representatives.

Among the different platforms, social networks (e.g. Facebook, Twitter) have received the biggest attention in research and practice. These web-based services 'allow individuals to (1) construct a public or semi-public profile within a bounded system, (2) articulate a list of

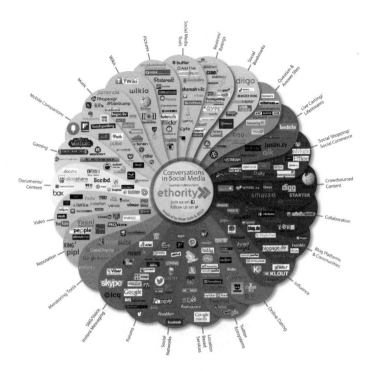

Figure 9.1 Social media prism

Source: Ethority, 2015

other users with whom they share a connection, and (3) view and traverse their list of connections and those made by others within the system' (Boyd & Ellison, 2008, p. 211): 1.44 billion monthly active users of Facebook, the world's biggest social network (Facebook, 2015), illustrate that this phenomenon makes an inevitable impact on companies and their brands.

Sport and social media

Not surprisingly, social media have also profoundly changed the delivery and the consumption of sport. Consumers and fans increasingly use social media to create, share and discuss sport-related contents. As a consequence, over 98% (99%, 85%) of the football clubs in the top five leagues in Europe run an official Facebook page (Twitter account, YouTube channel) in order to facilitate brand-related online interaction. With more than 84 million Facebook likes and 15 million followers on Twitter, FC Barcelona currently leads the way as the world's most popular sports team on social media. Currently, another ten European football clubs have more than 10 million likes. High numbers of users throughout the top five European football leagues (see Table 9.1) demonstrate the enormous relevance of social media for sport teams. Social media also affect any kind of sport brand (e.g. company, team, and athlete) or sport organization, which is revealed by many users liking their Facebook pages (e.g. Premier League > 30m, adidas > 30m, Roger Federer > 15m). Accordingly, professional teams, sport events, sport associations, manufacturers and service providers in sport and many other sport organizations invest significant time and resources to monitor social media, and to drive engagement and relationships online.

Table 9.1   'Big Five' football league clubs in social media

League	Club	Facebook Users	Twitter Followers	YouTube abonnents
English Premier League	Manchester United	65,165,423	5,314,524	(only own video service MUTV)
	FC Chelsea	42,537,135	5,728,535	437,677
	FC Arsenal	32,875,206	5,929,896	242,749
	FC Liverpool	25,566,189	4,452,996	348,408
	Manchester City	19,124,844	2,540,012	404,782
Spanish La Liga	FC Barcelona	84,902,758	15,337,990	1,845,796
	Real Madrid	82,947,774	16,254,846	1,765,493
	Atletico Madrid	11,260,615	1,644,344	77,222
	FC Valencia	2,511,962	574,371	24,526
	FC Sevilla	1,005,234	472,956	14,151
German Bundesliga	FC Bayern München	30,105,040	2,172,904	351,070
	Borussia Dortmund	12,830,914	1,656,020	112,829
	FC Schalke 04	2,574,323	296,772	50,052
	Bayer 04 Leverkusen	1,304,230	128,233	1,331
	SV Werder Bremen	838,076	182,556	28,454
Italian Serie A	AC Mailand	24,376,969	2,621,233	271,476
	Juventus Turin	18,894,550	1,950,261	358,368
	Inter Mailand	5,264,444	818,884	153,394
	AS Rom	4,608,858	731,989	112,043
	SSC Neapel	3,515,964	582,251	44,448
French Ligue 1	Paris Saint-Germain	19,615,939	2,288,263	218,504
	Olympique Marseille	4,148,859	1,502,877	39,241
	AS Monaco	2,591,090	608,990	20,693
	Olympique Lyon	2,053,471	716,440	(only own video service OLTV)
	Lille OSC	616,045	366,047	6,770

Source: Facebook, Twitter, and YouTube

Notes: As of: 22/06/2015. Ordered by country and number of Facebook fans.

Key characteristics of social media

The increasing power of social media in sport and business goes back to a number of characteristics that make social media an excellent forum for interacting both with other individuals and with sport brands or sport organizations. For instance, the ubiquity of the internet overcomes time and space restrictions and permits cost-effective communication. Moreover, the prevalent adoption of smartphones and tablet computers has finally enabled individuals to instantly share their passion or experiences of a particular sport, sports team or a sports-related interest with others. As a result, mobile technologies increasingly help to integrate online and offline contexts, so that even fans attending a game in the stadium can contribute to social media interaction.

The big relevance of social media in sport further goes back to a number of sport-specific factors that foster online interaction and community building processes. First, 'a large percentage of the world's population spend time and money to support sport' (Hickman & Ward, 2007, p. 316) which is also reflected in social media. Second, sport offers social components that facilitate sport-related interaction. Third, sport fans are highly involved, and sport plays an important role in the everyday lives of many fans (Sutton et al., 1997). Fourth, sport teams are among the most powerful brands within society, thereby constituting a particularly strong basis for interaction in social media. Fifth, sport is a particularly strong interest in terms of group cohesion on the internet (Stavros et al., 2014).

As a result, many sport fans use social media before, during and after a particular sport event. The 24/7 availability of social media has created ample opportunities to extend the fan experience beyond a game itself and even to the off-season of a league (Yoshida, Heere, & Gordon, 2015). In particular, fans use social media to discuss any kind of sport-team related topic including past and upcoming games, player transfers, and sponsorship announcements. Moreover, fan groups use social media to organize themselves and to arrange fan get-togethers and trips to away games.

Team-related Facebook pages, whether the official ones organized by the club or privately organized, regularly play a vital role for all kinds of fan interaction. They can be considered as brand communities embedded in social networks (Zaglia, 2013) and have positively influenced various objectives of the brand including identification with the brand and positive word-of-mouth. Besides communication related to their own club, fans also make use of these sites to act out their rivalry against other teams. In some cases, this rivalry or aversion to a certain sports-team brand or even its sponsors is the only reason that unites individuals on the internet in so-called anti-brand communities.

Forms and typology of social media in sport

Sport-related social media originate from the social media activities of both sport consumer and sport brands (e.g. teams, manufacturers, associations) who share posts, comments, and media on social media sites (e.g. Facebook, Twitter, YouTube). Given the manifold appearances of sport in social media, it is not surprising that there is a lack of an established typology of sport-related social media. One possible way to characterize different social media activities could focus on the ownership or administration of the platform that can be organized either by (1) private persons or organizations (e.g. athletes, fan clubs) or by sport properties (e.g. companies, sport clubs, sport organizations). Moreover, a distinction of sport-related social media can be made based on the shared interest that social media users focus their interaction on: this interest can be aligned on a continuum from a sport itself to a sports brand (e.g. team, athletes, association, and manufacturer). Figure 9.2 illustrates this proposed typology of sport-related social media.

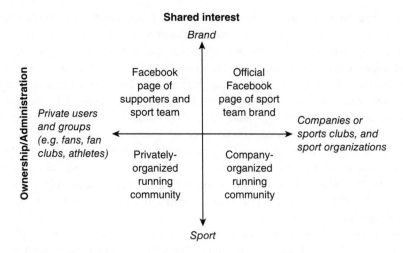

Figure 9.2 Typology of sport-related social media based on ownership/administration and shared interest

Many sport brands are particularly interested in providing official brand pages on the common social media platforms. In Europe, Facebook and Twitter are undoubtedly the most prominent forms of social media. Both platforms have the greatest numbers of members who come from all kinds of population groups. Among the long line of other social media platforms it is particularly Google+ which should be on sport marketers' checklist for platform choice. Although it currently has fewer users than Facebook and suffers with regard to user engagement, there are positive aspects of a brand presence on Google+ including better Google ranking and unique services such as Google Hangouts. Moreover, there is a vast amount of other social media platforms which often focus on more specialized services such as video sharing (e.g. YouTube), picture sharing (e.g. Pinterest, Instagram), blogging (e.g. Tumblr), and location-based check-in services (e.g. Foursquare, Yelp). Recently, livestreaming apps (e.g. Meerkat, Periscope) have enriched the social media landscape by enabling users to share any video in real-time with other users of the services and friends in their other social media platforms. Consequently, sport fans and athletes are enabled to watch live broadcast sport games or sport events, which brings along not only more interaction on the streamed event, but also new legal aspects (e.g. violation of broadcasting rights).

Besides these rather general platforms, there is a variety of social media sites that are closely linked to the field of sport. For example, athletes may track workouts with Fitness Apps such as RunKeeper and share them with friends on the community website or other social media (e.g. Facebook). Moreover, sport manufacturers such as Nike also try to engage their customers in their own community (e.g. Nike+) in order to make use of social components (e.g. challenging friends or sharing their own success with them). Equivalently, several companies for sport bets (e.g. betandwin) try to engage their customers via social interaction. Social media also brought along a number of successful online football managers (e.g. COMUNIO) which allow members to manage their own unique team and create a virtual league with their friends. Moreover, of course, there are also tons of privately organized communities and Facebook pages that deal with a particular kind of sport (e.g. basketball) where members share their interest in a sport, thereby interacting on various topics including different leagues, skills, tricks, and events. Finally, social media platforms also offer many other opportunities such as generating feedback for product or service improvements, market research, and product innovations (e.g. Nike Basketball) (Fuller, Jawecki, & Muhlbacher, 2007).

Contemporary and future challenges, capabilities and critiques

Implementing social media strategies

The pervasive phenomenon of social media affects all kinds of value co-creation processes in sport management that involve consumers. Social networks such as Facebook have become a fundamental venue for positive sport-related interaction. This ongoing revolution of interaction between sport organizations and fans as well as among fans themselves has dramatically changed the way sport organizations look at sport fans and how they try to build relationships with them. There has been a shift to recognizing consumers as active participants in value co-creation rather than passive recipients of sport marketing activities (Woratschek, Horbel, & Popp, 2014). In sport-related social media value is co-created in a collaborative process between the sport property, its customers, fans and potential consumers, the operator of the social network site and other actors. From a service-dominant logic perspective (Vargo & Lusch, 2004), these actors actively participate in the value co-creation process by integrating resources from (one or more) service providers with their personal (e.g. knowledge, competencies and skills) and other resources (Woratschek et al., 2014). Thus, sport properties can only offer a value proposition as input for potential value creation and its social media outlets represent their value proposition which enables various actors (predominantly fans of the brand) to co-create value.

Due to the various positive effects for a variety of actors within the field of sport (e.g. sport clubs, sponsors, fans, and media), sport entities increasingly consider social media as a suitable marketing strategy for building meaningful relationships. Therefore, in the dynamic environment of social media, sport clubs, sport brands and other organizations from the sport-context continuously have to derive promising social media strategies. One of the key challenges in this endeavour is to successfully build the social audience in order to profit from network effects. Therefore, clubs and sport organizations call attention to their social media channels in broadcasts, online and direct marketing, advertising, and during the game. Moreover, sport clubs particularly face the challenge to continuously provide attractive contents on their social media outlets.

First of all, this may mean the extension of all parts of communication to social network sites. Press releases, important information on the team, players or certain games should either be advertised on social media or even fully available on third-party websites such as Facebook in order to foster interaction among fans and spread coverage via viral effects. Clubs may also make use of social networks such as Twitter for covering current standings during the game and quickly providing results. Social networks easily allow fans to follow and discuss postgame interviews and press conferences.

Using social network sites makes content viral, as contents get validated to the personal network of friends when people like, share, or comment on a story, picture, or video. In particular, common standards in social media help sport organizations to successfully make use of its unique interactive network character. For example, hashtags enable readers to easily follow all Tweets regarding their favourite team, not only tweeted by the club but also by other Twitter users (e.g. #mufc for all Tweeds related to Manchester United FC). Moreover, hashtags are successfully used for identifying all interaction regarding a particular game (e.g. #UCLfinal for the Champions league final or #BVBFCB for a league game between Borussia Dortmund and FC Bayern München). Providing coverage on games or other events afterwards extends consumer experience and may increase overall satisfaction and strengthen the bond with it.

Providing sport-related social media platforms thus has a facilitative role and social media have created an empowered sport consumer in terms of access to information, instant publishing power and an active audience. The rapid onslaught of social media and mobile technologies conveys meanings and values that enable fans to develop and communicate their identity and distinguish themselves from others (Escalas & Bettman, 2005). Given that this symbolic value for some fans is much more important than the physical attributes and functions of a product or service, i.e. the game itself, it is quite obvious that fan interaction on social media plays an important role for the long-term emotional relationship with a sport brand.

In particular, social media activities of sport brands not only influence their fans' relationships with the sports club, they are also an important means through which fans can interact with other fans, including those of a rival team (Carlson, Donavan, & Cumiskey, 2009; Underwood, Bond, & Baer, 2001). Social integration on team-related websites therefore also contributes to ensuring the fans' loyalty, even in hard times without athletic success.

Finally, it is important to realize that sport brand pages on social media are embedded in a bigger network of relationships between social media users and that they are essentially becoming delocalized. Therefore, sport brand-related interaction among users is not limited to those actively liking or participating in a Facebook brand page, it also affects the brand perception of other social media users and sometimes brand-related interaction can even spill over to other media. Social media, which easily enable fans of a particular brand to unite and form more powerful, influential groups, can therefore lead to increasing consumer power (Fournier & Avery, 2011). A well-known, yet not very enduring example for the potential of group processes has been the case of MyFootballClub.co.uk, an online platform that has been initiated to allow its paid members to control an English association football club through a democratic voting process conducted over the internet. Starting with at least 50,000 members in 2007 the organization controlled Ebbsfleet United FC from 2008 to 2013. However, during these years the project suffered from decision-making problems and membership decline, finally resulting in the club's handover to an investor consortium.

Brand communities

Sport teams particularly become aware of the power of brand-related group-building processes in social media. Extensive research on brand communities, which have been defined as 'specialized, non-geographically bound communities, based on a structured set of social relationships among admirers of a brand' (Muniz & O'Guinn, 2001, p. 412), has demonstrated the bonding role of fan groups for brands. Fans derive social benefits from a community in which a commonly favoured brand creates a link between individual members, who share a consciousness of kind, shared rituals and traditions, and a sense of moral responsibility (Muniz & O'Guinn, 2001). Community participants also stand out for high levels of engagement in the community and their associated brands and sport teams (Pongsakornrungsilp & Schroeder, 2011). Empirical evidence demonstrates that many strong brand communities focus on sport brands (Pongsakornrungsilp & Schroeder, 2011) and researchers consider sport teams as being among the most powerful brand communities within society (Heere & James, 2007). Given the positive outcomes of online fan interaction, football fan communities are considered 'as platforms for value co-creation' (Pongsakornrungsilp & Schroeder, 2011). As a result, sport marketers try to make use of brand communities for strengthening their brand and creating both team identification and identification with other fans of the brand. Therefore, sport marketers build and maintain brand communities around their sport or team brand. This may mean either that clubs will organize a community on their an own website (e.g. the 'myFCB community' of FC Bayern München) or that they will use third-party hosted social network sites (e.g. Facebook) to create an official brand page for fan interaction.

Branded communities

However, not every sport brand has the potential to serve as a basis for enduring customer interaction. While sport teams regularly stir up enough emotions among their highly identified fans to drive conversation on the team brand over an extended period of time, other sport brands (e.g. manufacturers, associations) could follow other community-building strategies on the web. For instance, manufacturers may build communities that focus on a particular sport rather than the company brand, i.e. Nike established their Nike+ community which has integrated Nike products, mobile technology, and athletic communities, thereby benefiting from different kinds of value co-creation (e.g. challenges, tips, sharing success and emotions). Fussball.de, an online community relating to football operated by the German football association (DFB) and the leading German mail service provider Deutsche Post, constitutes another example for using sports-related online communities for branding purposes. Such a 'branded community' is commonly defined as a group of people 'sharing their interest and expertise in a specific topic which is sponsored or operated by a specific brand for marketing purposes' (Popp & Woratschek, 2015). The phenomenon of branded online communities illustrates that sport-related social media also bring along new opportunities for sponsorships.

Social media and sport sponsorship

Indeed, social media have also gained in importance for sponsorships (Chanavat & Desbordes, 2014). Sport clubs high in Facebook likes and Twitter followers possess a valuable platform for posts including sponsors or even posts from sponsors. Moreover, intense club-related interaction in social media constitutes an indicator of customer-based brand equity and attractiveness to sponsors. Social media obviously extended the traditional perspective of sport sponsorships beyond onsite sponsorships and traditional mass media usage, so that both sponsored clubs or athletes and sponsors need to get a more comprehensive view of sponsorship 2.0.

Athletes especially have recognized the value of social media for not only getting in touch with their fans, but also promoting their sponsors (Hambrick & Mahoney, 2011). By sharing personal sport and non-sport related information with their fans, they manage to engage them on a regular basis. In these social media activities they regularly integrate their sponsors, e.g. by using sponsor-related hashtags or reporting on sponsor-related events, challenges, or products. Notably, fans are rather broad-minded towards these activities. Therefore, athletes increasingly attempt to leverage their ties with sponsors via subtle mentions on social media in the form of pictures containing the sponsor's product, status updates, or links to online content tied to the sponsor.

Fan empowerment in social media

However, social media also come along with negative outcomes including the loss of company control, anti-brand activism, and negative effects on sponsorships. These activities may lead to value co-destruction and therefore deserve particular attention by sport managers.

Social media create new channels for effectively promoting countervailing interests (e.g. fan dissatisfaction with high ticket prices or kick-off times). Therefore, fan empowerment through social media can also have negative consequences for sport clubs in case the fans take actions against management decisions they do not agree with. Numerous examples for increasing fan power based on social media activities could be observed in European professional sport in recent years and many of these were carried on in the mass media and successfully affected management decisions. For example, in the 2014/2015 season of the German Bundesliga fans of the football club Hannover 96 used websites and social media to organize their boycott of the team's home games and the club finally had to admit to failures in its policy. Social media are thus a means that helps fans to force the club and owners to listen to them and to protect them from double exploitation that emerges because fans have dedicated personal resources such as time, money, information, and other efforts to support the club.

Another prominent example is the '12:12' in the 2012/2013 season of the German Bundesliga, in which fans deliberately refused to cheer the teams for 12 minutes at the beginning of each game in order to protest against tighter security guidelines proposed by the Deutsche Fußball Liga (Stieler, Weismann, & Germelmann, 2014). Again, social media platforms such as Facebook (e.g. https://www.facebook.com/12doppelpunkt12) or online communities (http://www.12doppelpunkt12.de) helped to form a powerful group of protestors. As a result, sport organizations and managers have to recognize that mass use of the internet has also amplified the power of fans and negative brand-related communication.

In particular, social media-based online interaction has facilitated the emergence of so-called anti-brand communities that are based on common aversions to brands (Hollenbeck & Zinkhan, 2006). Fans regularly use social media platforms such as Facebook for deliberately distancing themselves from other teams and their fans. In doing so, individuals act out their rivalry towards a team and enhance their enjoyment of sports-related activities. Social media features such as posting, commenting, and sharing messages, pictures, and videos provide a fruitful environment to provoke and disparage rival teams and fans. While this on the one hand increases the loyalty of both the anti-brand community's members and the rival teams' fans to their favorite team, anti-brand communities may also harm a rival brand and the actors affiliated to it (e.g. fans, sponsors).

Key drivers of sports team-related anti-brand communities, including oppositional brand loyalty, schadenfreude and the desire to dissociate from a specific club, unite fans of other clubs that compete against each other in the league (Popp et al., in press). In particular, dominant or strong clubs and clubs facing controversial issues such as commercialization, corruption, or contraventions in law are at risk of facing social media-based anti-brand activism. Small and large-scale Facebook groups that oppose major team sport brands such as FC Barcelona, Chelsea FC, FC Bayern München, and Inter Milan illustrate the relevance of this phenomenon for sport teams and its sponsors. Moreover, sport brands and organizations such as FIFA have been the focus of intense online anti-brand activism which for example targeted the FIFA World Cup 2014 in Brazil for corruption.

Negative posts, user-generated graphics, and comments may lead to a reinterpretation of brand meaning and the formation of what has been referred to as a doppelgänger image (Thompson, Rindfleisch, & Arsel, 2006). Anti-brand community members therefore negatively influence brand meaning and generate negative perceptions of the opposed sports team both within the community and among other Facebook users who get in contact with the negative interaction.

Given potential spillover effects from the club to its sponsors and considering the fact that anti-club communication in social media also includes sponsors of the club, sponsors are advised to be aware of anti-brand activism in social media. In particular, sponsors of a sports team may lose the members of anti-brand communities of opposing teams or suffer from a negative image transfer from a rival team to the own brand as a sponsor. Therefore, sponsors should consider the threat of anti-brand activism, as the number of fans viciously opposing a specific brand can easily exceed the number of fans who support it. This may lead to more negative than positive associations with a sponsorship.

Moreover, there are recent examples which demonstrate that social media-based anti-brand communities may directly target a sponsor and/or a sponsorship as well as investors in sport clubs. These bring particularly negative consequences for the sponsor, but also for the sponsored team (see Cases).

Social media-based anti-brand communities are forming around common aversions toward a specific brand. While in the field of sports this phenomenon has been particularly studied with a focus of a sport team as the opposed brand, there is also empirical evidence of a number of anti-brand communities which do not oppose a sport team, but its sponsor or investor. In the following, two cases are presented in order to demonstrate the nature and the consequences of these anti-sponsor communities or anti-investor communities.

Case study 9.1: Anti-RB Leipzig activism

The German association football club 'RasenBallsport Leipzig e.V.' was founded on the initiative of the Austrian energy drink company Red Bull. With the intention to develop the club into one of the leading clubs in the German Bundesliga, Red Bull purchased the licence of fifth division club SSV Markanstädt in 2009. Since the regulations of the German Football Association (DFB) did not permit the company name Red Bull to be part of the name, the club chose the unusual name RasenBallsport Leipzig, commonly and deliberately promoted as RB Leipzig. Moreover, the logo of the club draws on the Red Bull brand logo. Although the club's organization complies with the principles of the 50 + 1 rule established by the German Football League (DFL) which should protect clubs from the influence of external investors, the de facto influence of Red Bull as both investor and main (jersey) sponsor is publicly looked on skeptically. Anti-RB activism was especially stirred up after RB Leipzig had been given the licence to the Second Bundesliga after RB Leipzig won promotion to this league in 2014. Social media platforms such as Facebook and online communities have taken an essential role in organizing the various anti-RB movements (see Figure 9.3).

Figure 9.3   Logo and banner of anti-RB communities

Source: http://www.nein-zu-rb.de (Retrieved 20/06/2015). Used with permission of Nein Zu RB.

   In particular, supporters of other clubs in the Second Bundesliga created the campaign 'Nein zu RB! Für euch nur Marketing – Für uns Lebenssinn!' ['No to RB! For you it's only marketing, for us it's the meaning of our lives']. A corresponding online community (http://www.nein-zu-rb.de) and Facebook (e.g., https://www.facebook.com/GegenRedBull with over 13,000 likes) have been used to share the joint aversion of RB, organize boycotts, and put in claims against the DFL. Quick growth in the number of users of these anti-RB appearances in social media demonstrates the relevance of this phenomenon which can become a very instant challenge for investors, sponsors and the club. Moreover, these activities have also been carried on in mainstream media and sports magazines thereby also spreading the protests to a broad audience.

   Netnographic studies on these anti-Red Bull communities disclose that most users join the community to fight against Red Bull which is considered an incarnation of the ultimate commercialization of football. Users complain about the fact that Red Bull engages in football only for marketing purposes and they criticize the loss of tradition and fair competition that comes along with Red Bull's investment. Members disparage the sponsors, the club, and its fans in posts consisting of paroles or provoking graphics. Moreover, fans of opponent teams call for boycotts of RB Leipzig games or organize actions at RB Leipzig games. Activists further urge the football association to fight against the commercialization and Red Bull's actions that undercut league rules. Finally, fans of RB Leipzig visit the anti-RB Leipzig communities and try to defend their team, thereby contributing to the interaction as well as rivalry among fans. Hence, the case of RB Leipzig also shows that the perception of the investment of RB into the club differs between the fans depending on their attachment to the sponsored team. While anti-RB activism is largely driven by fans of opponent teams, the fans of RB Leipzig and residents of Leipzig seem to think much more positively and open-mindedly about Red Bull's function as investor and sponsor of the club.

Case study 9.2: Anti-Wiesenhof activism

Social media-driven anti-brand activism may also target a particular sponsorship. An anti-sponsor community that illustrates this phenomenon originated from the rejection of the poultry producer Wiesenhof as the jersey sponsor of the German Bundesliga club Werder Bremen. After Werder Bremen announced the sponsorship in August 2012, more than 13,000 supporters quickly joined the Facebook page 'Wiesenhof als Werder-Sponsor? NEIN Danke' [Wiesenhof as sponsor of Werder? NO thanks] (https://www.facebook.com/Allez.Werder.Fans.Gegen.Wiesenhof). By raising a unified voice against the sponsorship, the anti-Wiesenhof activists created a very instant challenge for sponsor and club. Members shared comments and graphics that called for a boycott against Wiesenhof as a sponsor of Werder Bremen. Moreover, users organized concerted spam attacks in which they posted negative comments on the club's website in order to be heard by the club. While there are some parallels here to the anti-RB Leipzig community (e.g. a battle against the commercialization of football), a detailed look at the main motivation to join the anti-Wiesenhof community reveals a more differentiated picture of its members. Almost half of the members stated that to be a fan of Werder Bremen meant trying to protect the club against a bad reputation spilling over from the sponsor. They complained about a bad fit between Wiesenhof and their club and they indicated that Wiesenhof as a sponsor negatively affected their relationship with the club. As a result, they intended to boycott merchandising articles incorporating the sponsor brand and even home games of Werder Bremen. In contrast, most of the other members of the anti-Wiesenhof community joined the community to engage with animal rights and harm the sponsor. Their posts and comments particularly complained about poor standards in poultry farming and they accused Werder Bremen of supporting these problems.

Mass media including TV and newspapers reported about the anti-sponsor community and its activities thereby reinforcing the activists' protests. Subsequent actions that have been taken by Wiesenhof and Werder Bremen illustrate a dilemma for sponsees and opposed sponsors: while public media appreciated reactions from the sponsor and the club such as discussion sessions with fans and player visits to Wiesenhof, these had the opposite effect on the anti-sponsor community and initially rather stimulated the negative debate. However, interaction within the anti-sponsor community

(Continued)

(Continued)

steadily decreased over time and the announcement of the prolongation of the sponsorship agreement in 2014 only briefly stirred up anti-Wiesenhof activism in the community.

Both cases provide insights into the problems of 'when sport meets business'. While possible image transfers from sport entities to companies have been extensively studied and are highly valued by sport athletes or organizations and their commercial partners, the reverse negative effects of sponsorships are still under-investigated.

The multifaceted negative effects anti-brand communities opposing sponsors or investors exert on different actors (e.g., club, sponsor, investor, and association) suggest that this phenomenon has to be considered and monitored. The strong dynamics of social networks and propagation of anti-sponsor or anti-investor communities by other media to a broad mass of individuals corroborate this finding. Moreover, sport entities have to be aware that social media-based anti-brand activism is not limited to the virtual space, but also leads to offline activities. Finally, the imbalance of fan attachment to a team and its investor or sponsor can lead to negative changes in fans' attitudes towards the team. Therefore, teams and brand managers are advised to identify the (varying) motivations of members in order to find suitable strategies for coping with anti-sponsor and anti-investor activism.

However, both cases presented in this chapter offer a number of relevant unanswered questions: for example, it is unclear which strategy to choose against anti-brand activism. In particular, there seems to be no general answer to the question to what degree sport managers should consider their fans' voice that often is split up between several groups of fans. Given the strong competition within European professional sport teams and their dependency on financial assets, teams (and athletes) should weigh up the chances and risks regarding a specific sponsorship.

Conclusion

Social media are a powerful phenomenon that affects the way value is created in and through sports in various ways – both to the good and to the bad. Sport organizations have to engage the audience with a lot of balance, authenticity, and attention.

One of the key questions here is the selection of social media platforms which should be used. Regularly, teams will focus on the most prominent platforms with the greatest number of members, i.e. Facebook and Twitter (almost all clubs from the big five European football leagues operate official accounts on both platforms). However, social media platforms have been shown to be very dynamic (new ones are introduced nearly every day, others get acquired and merged, and others have to close down), so that sport companies are advised to constantly follow this market and rethink their activities on a regular basis. Moreover, it is important to be aware that social media platforms differ regarding their diffusion in different countries or regions. Whereas the platforms presented in this chapter are very well established in European countries (and America), other platforms such as Weiboo and Tencent dominate the Chinese market. Therefore, sports properties have to think of different ways to activate certain markets.

While many existing third-party social media platforms (e.g. Facebook, Twitter, and YouTube) provide access to a huge network of members, they also may come along with shortcomings that limit their use for sport entities. Limitations for example may relate to the layout, the contents and aspects of usability. Moreover, social media platforms hosted by third-party companies are commonly rather limited in terms of a sport brand's participation in revenues from online advertisements, and do not allow for charging users for subscription fees or one-off payments. Because of these limitations, sport clubs may (additionally) establish their own solutions for operating a brand community and sharing videos and other contents (e.g. MUTV of Manchester United, myFCB of FC Bayern München).

Finally, after having chosen the platforms used, sport brands, athletes, and organizations have to ensure consistency not only in their social media activities on different platforms, but also across all media (e.g. TV, press releases, website, and email). Managers in the field of sport are advised to make use of the particular strengths of all platforms.

Managing multiple social media platforms is a complex task for sport properties. They have to find a solution for an integrated communication that takes care of all stakeholders. Contents have to be adapted to specific platforms and all of the relevant platforms have to be monitored. Sport organizations therefore have to align their functional organization to achieve these challenges. Moreover, sport properties may use the help of the growing industry of consultancies and providers that specialize on social media management. These service providers provide guidance and carry out tasks in all aspects related to social media including publishing, content scheduling, and analytics application development.

Besides pro-active strategies to foster consumer-brand engagement, sport brands particularly have to monitor and listen to social media. Interaction among consumers provides real-time feedback on brand perception and possibilities for making the own product or service better. Sport organizations are therefore advised to use netnographic analyses, i.e. the qualitative analysis of relevant social media channels and interaction to identify relevant information. Moreover, a multitude of quantitative tools organizing and aggregating fan and follower sentiment may help to derive implications for sport management. These activities may also be useful for optimizing social media activities (e.g., the time and content of posts) and the effective integration of third-party (e.g., sponsor) posts on their own social media page.

However, using social media for increasing fan interaction seems to be a narrow pathway. Whereas many NBA and NFL teams have become very aggressive in promoting their social media activities in the stadium and successfully encourage fans to interact via social media during the game, the situation seems to be somewhat different for traditional sports in Europe. Like a recent protest by PSV Eindhoven supporters against the introduction of Wi-Fi in their stadium shows, (at least some) supporters' groups are skeptical about the interference of digital media as they believe that the introduction of this technology is just the latest decision in attempting to gentrify fans at games (*The Guardian*, 2014).

Sport managers also have to recognize that they only have limited control over their brand as the power of both fans of the brand and rival fans increases. While most of the own fan interaction on social media is aimed at strengthening the sport brand, it also may cause management problems in the case of unfavorable fanaticism. Moreover, Facebook algorithms decide which posts are shown to a particular user. As a result, sport entities are unable to control the spread of their communication, and instead they rely on the host of the social network who also determines which other posts and advertisements are shown to the users (e.g. from competing sport brands or sponsors).

Another challenging task for European sport properties seems to be the privacy concerns of social media users and data protection. Individuals exhibit rather strong privacy concerns that may hinder the use of a particular social media platform. For example, there have been intense discussions about privacy protection and the terms of use of Facebook in Germany in 2014 which have sparked a debate on the role of trust in those companies which operate social media for the brand's social media success (Pentina, Zhang, & Basmanova, 2013). Moreover, strict European legislation for online services might negatively affect the potential of value co-creation in social media.

Recommended further reading

Sport management should consider sport-related social media as platforms for value co-creation in which members are both beneficiaries and providers in the value co-creation process. As a result, marketers are advised to support the development and maintenance of this cost-effective and powerful tool. A recent meta-analysis by Filo, Lock and Karg (2015) who reviewed 70 journal articles published in English-language sport management journals may be a good starting point for getting a general overview of academic literature on the use and effects of social media in sport.

From a theoretical perspective, Pongsakornrungsilp and Schroeder (2011) especially make a noteworthy contribution to understanding value co-creation in a co-consuming online football community. Thereby, they illustrate the potential double exploitation within the co-consuming group which occurs when companies interfere with the social media users' perspective on brand culture. Practitioners in sport management may find helpful insights into the issues facing sport organizations when developing their social media strategy gained from a multiple case study on UK football clubs (McCarthy et al., 2014).

Finally, those who want to gain an impression of online tools for social media analytics and monitoring are encouraged to have a look at commercial online services (e.g. http://www.fanpage karma.com, http://www.talkwalker.com) that help to engage fans better in the social networks.

References

Boyd, D. M., & Ellison, N. B. (2008). Social network sites: Definition, history, and scholarship. *Journal of Computer-Mediated Communication*, *13*(1), 210–230.

Carlson, B. D., Donavan, D. T., & Cumiskey, K. J. (2009). Consumer–Brand relationships in sport: Brand personality and identification. *International Journal of Retail & Distribution Management*, *37*(4), 370–384.

Chanavat, N., & Desbordes, M. (2014). Towards the regulation and restriction of ambush marketing? The first truly social and digital mega sports event: Olympic Games, London 2012. *International Journal of Sports Marketing and Sponsorship, 15*(3), 151–160.

Escalas, J. E., & Bettman, J. R. (2005). Self-construal, reference groups, and brand meaning. *Journal of Consumer Research, 32*(3), 378–389.

Ethority (2015). Social Media Prism. Retrieved 20/06/2015 from http://ethority.net/social-media-prisma/

Facebook (2015). Company Info. Retrieved 06/06/2015 from http://newsroom.fb.com/company-info/

Filo, K., Lock, D., & Karg, A. (2015). Sport and social media research: A review. *Sport Management Review, 18*(2), 166–181.

Fournier, S., & Avery, J. (2011). The uninvited brand. *Business Horizons, 54*(3), 193–207.

Fuller, J., Jawecki, G., & Muhlbacher, H. (2007). Innovation creation by online basketball communities. *Journal of Business Research, 60*(1), 60–71.

Hagel, J., & Armstrong, A. G. (1997). *Net gain: expanding markets through virtual communities.* Boston, Mass.: Harvard Business School Press.

Hambrick, M. E., & Mahoney, T. Q. (2011). 'It's incredible – trust me': Exploring the role of celebrity athletes as marketers in online social networks. *International Journal of Sport Management and Marketing, 10*(3), 161–179.

Heere, B., & James, J. D. (2007). Sports teams and their communities: Examining the influence of external group identities on team identity. *Journal of Sport Management, 21*(3), 319–337.

Hickman, T. M., & Ward, J. (2007). The dark side of brand community: Inter-group stereotyping, trash talk, and schadenfreude. *Advances in Consumer Research, 34*, 314–319.

Hollenbeck, C. R., & Zinkhan, G. M. (2006). Consumer Activism on the Internet: The Role of Anti-brand Communities. In C. Pechmann & L. L. Price (Eds), *Advances in Consumer Research, Vol. 33* (pp. 1–7). Duluth, MN: Association for Consumer Research.

Kaplan, A. M., & Haenlein, M. (2010). Users of the world, unite! The challenges and opportunities of Social Media. *Business Horizons, 53*(1), 59–68.

McCarthy, J., Rowley, J., Jane Ashworth, C., & Pioch, E. (2014). Managing brand presence through social media: The case of UK football clubs. *Internet Research, 24*(2), 181–204.

Muniz, A. M., & O'Guinn, T. C. (2001). Brand community. *Journal of Consumer Research, 27*(4), 412–432.

Pentina, I., Zhang, L., & Basmanova, O. (2013). Antecedents and consequences of trust in a social media brand: A cross-cultural study of Twitter. *Computers in Human Behavior, 29*(4), 1546–1555.

Pongsakornrungsilp, S., & Schroeder, J. E. (2011). Understanding value co-creation in a co-consuming brand community. *Marketing Theory, 11*(3), 303–324.

Popp, B., Germelmann, C. C., & Jung, B. (in press). We love to hate them! Social media-based anti-brand communities in professional football. *International Journal of Sports Marketing and Sponsorship.*

Popp, B., & Woratschek, H. (2016). Introducing branded communities in sport for building strong brand relations in social media. *Sport Management Review, 19*(2), 183–197.

Stavros, C., Meng, M. D., Westberg, K., & Farrelly, F. (2014). Understanding fan motivation for interacting on social media. *Sport Management Review, 17*(4), 455–469.

Stieler, M., Weismann, F., & Germelmann, C. C. (2014). Co-destruction of value by spectators: The case of silent protests. *European Sport Management Quarterly, 14*(1), 72–86.

Sutton, W. A., McDonald, M. A., Milne, G. R., & Cimperman, J. (1997).Creating and fostering fan identification in professional sports. *Sport Marketing Quarterly, 6*(1), 15–22.

The Guardian (2014). PSV Eindhoven fans protest against introduction of Wi-Fi at stadium. Retrieved 22/06/2015 from http://www.theguardian.com/football/2014/aug/18/psv-fans-protest-against-wifi-access

Thompson, C. J., Rindfleisch, A., & Arsel, Z. (2006). Emotional branding and the strategic value of the doppelgänger brand image. *Journal of Marketing, 70*(1), 50–64.

Underwood, R., Bond, E., & Baer, R. (2001). Building service brands via social identity: Lessons from the sports marketplace. *Journal of Marketing Theory and Practice, 9*(1), 1–13.

Vargo, S. L., & Lusch, R. F. (2004). Evolving to a new dominant logic for marketing. *Journal of Marketing, 68*(1), 1–17.

Woratschek, H., Horbel, C., & Popp, B. (2014). The sport value framework – a new fundamental logic for analyses in sport management. *European Sport Management Quarterly, 14*(1), 6–24.

Yoshida, M., Heere, B., & Gordon, B. (2015). Predicting behavioral loyalty through community: Why other fans are more important than our own intentions, our satisfaction, and the team itself. *Journal of Sport Management, 29*(3), 318–333.

Zaglia, M. E. (2013). Brand communities embedded in social networks. *Journal of Business Research, 66*(2), 216–223.

CORPORATE SOCIAL RESPONSIBILITY IN SPORT

MATHIEU DJABALLAH

Introduction

Since the beginning of the last decade, sport organizations' social and environmental behaviors have been under increasing public attention. According to an investigation conducted by the *Guardian* in 2014, more than 900 migrant workers had already died building the infrastructure to host the 2022 World Cup in Qatar (Gibson & Pattisson, 2014). In Brazil, anti-World Cup public demonstrations gathered over 1 million people, who protested against the spending of billions of reais of public money on stadiums rather than on social welfare (Winter & Teixeira, 2014). In Europe, the 2014 Olympic Games in Sochi were described as an ecological disaster by residents as well as by various NGOs (Grove, 2014). In the same timeframe, sport organizations have taken various actions, notably in Europe. Professional clubs engage in community development, through initiatives like the 'Everton Free School' – an alternative learning program run by Everton FC for disenfranchised youth – or Dartford FC's 'living roof' – which covers the club's stadium with renewable timber beams and green sedum in order to encourage bird and insect life. National sport associations create specific positions like the French Tennis Federation's 'CSR officer' or the British Judo Federation's 'club welfare officer'. Sport sponsors also follow this trend, becoming 'sustainability partners' like EDF (an electric utility company), BMW or Cisco (a telecommunication equipment company) during the 2012 Olympic Games in London.

All these examples point to two important observations: (1) sport is no exception to the renewal of business ethics engendered by corporate social responsibility (CSR), and (2) CSR takes very particular forms in the sports field. In this chapter, we therefore examine the specificities of CSR in sport. A brief description of general CSR issues and debates is provided, before addressing sport-CSR. We then draw on the case of a national sport organization, which allows readers to envision the range of CSR activities as well as the different rationales behind those activities. Since CSR concerns various sport organizations, the chapter also includes several other examples. To conclude, we offer a critical perspective on these practices, which can sometimes be used only as instruments to pursue brand image or reputation objectives, without achieving genuine social benefits.

CSR and sport, a relationship of both proximity and distance

The roots of corporate social responsibility

Given the success of CSR since the middle of the 1980s, in terms of both academic works and corporate practices, this notion could be seen as fairly recent. But that is not the case. The first author who formulated a genuine definition was Howard Bowen in his book *Social Responsibilities of the Businessman*, published in 1953. According to Bowen, corporate social responsibility 'refers to the obligations of businessmen to pursue those policies, to make those decisions, or to follow those lines of action which are desirable in terms of the objectives and values of our society' (1953, p.6). It has to be noted that while this definition has been largely recognized, Bowen's book was not originally intended for use by corporations, but was actually ordered by the Federal Council of Churches. Furthermore, CSR did not come to the fore in the immediate aftermath of Bowen's work, notably in Europe where post-war economic growth and the development of the welfare state relieved corporations of the social duties that some had fulfilled through corporate paternalism (Matten & Moon, 2008). As a matter of fact, Bowen was not the first author to reflect on the role of corporations in society. Since antiquity, economic activities have always generated tensions within human societies, as pointed out by several authors.

Hence, it was only from the beginning of a long-lasting economic slowdown in the 1980s that CSR gained importance, helped by several corporate scandals liked the *Exxon Valdez* oil spill in 1989 or the Enron collapse in 2001. Besides this important lapse of time between the first definition of CSR and its actual awareness by public opinion, it is also possible to distinguish between its American and European roots. Matten and Moon (2008) defined CSR in the United States as liberal and based on a tradition of business philanthropy, whereas European CSR was largely reframed through the principles of sustainable development, which emerged in the 1960s and became part of European Union policies. These differences partly explain why there is not a unique definition of CSR today, and why this notion is the subject of several debates.

The conflicting views of CSR

Despite its success, CSR has never achieved a real consensus among researchers. It seems, on the contrary, that it has initiated more controversies than it has solved. Two of the most critical authors of CSR are Theodore Levitt and Milton Friedman. In his article *The Dangers of Social Responsibility* (1958), Levitt posits that corporations should not be given a general interest mission, due to the fact that their owners and managers are not elected by universal suffrage. General interest should therefore only be devolved to the State. Unlike Levitt, Friedman's critique is based on a Liberal view of economy. As the founder of the Chicago school and one of the most influential economists of the 20th century, he strongly opposed CSR principles, stating that 'the social responsibility of business is to increase its profits' (1970, p.122). According to him, managers who allocate resources for CSR arbitrarily impose a tax either on shareholders (by siphoning off their profit), customers (by raising prices), or employees (by lowering wages if neither profit nor prices are affected). While these first opponents could not prevent CSR from spreading throughout the corporate world, three major issues have still not been answered – What are corporations responsible for? Towards whom are they responsible? And to what extent are they responsible?

The first question relates to the scope of CSR, as most authors agree that this notion goes beyond purely economic and legal considerations. In order to identify the various responsibilities of corporations, Carroll (1991) proposes a pyramid structured around four levels. The first level, at the base of the pyramid, encompasses economic responsibilities, in as much as corporations have first to ensure their survival by being profitable. At the second level are legal responsibilities, namely the laws and regulations which corporations have to comply with. Hence, Bowen's definition of CSR actually starts with the third level, called 'ethical responsibilities', through which managers have to follow society's implicit norms and values, when faced with situations which are not covered by the law. Carroll specifies that even if ethical responsibilities are not mandatory, corporations which ignore them might face economic sanctions like strikes or consumer boycotts. The fourth level consists of philanthropic responsibilities, in other words discretionary social actions not specifically prescribed by society, which Carroll calls the 'icing on the cake' (1991, p.42). Examples of philanthropy include contributions to education, the arts or humanitarian causes. While the logic of this pyramid is that corporations take on these levels one after the other, some only do philanthropy without fulfilling the ethical standards of their core activities. This form of CSR is often called whitewashing (or greenwashing for the environmental aspects), and was notably illustrated by Nike when the company was accused of launching various charities while remaining silent about the labor conditions in its workshops in Asia (Kahle, Boush, & Phelps, 2000).

The second question is also a major stumbling block in CSR literature, as it still cannot determine once and for all the groups – otherwise called stakeholders – towards whom corporations are responsible. While some authors like Clarkson (1995) recognize as stakeholders only the groups which engage in economic transactions with a company (shareholders, customers, suppliers, and employees), other authors like Freeman (1984) define stakeholders as 'any group or individual who can affect or is affected by the achievement of the organization's objectives' (p.46) including, for example, corporations' nearby residents or even future generations. For this reason, so-called stakeholder theory is actually a constellation of contradictory approaches, from instrumental views according to which the management of stakeholders is only a means for achieving economic objectives, to moral views through which every legitimate stakeholder should be taken into account, regardless of the strategic value. This central confusion leads to many others, among which is the fact that individuals can belong to several stakeholder categories (for example an individual can be employee, consumer and nearby resident at the same time).

The third question refers to the debate between voluntary and mandatory CSR. Although Carroll's pyramid envisions ethical responsibilities as voluntary by definition, some of these tend to be required under country legislation. This is the case for environmental practices, with the development of carbon taxes in Finland, Denmark and France. Besides these examples, international institutions, among which is the European Union via its 2001 green book *Promoting a European framework for corporate social responsibility*, have endorsed the voluntary character of CSR. For most business representatives, CSR is precisely intended to avoid new regulatory constraints (Gond, Kang, & Moon, 2011). Thus, if CSR has expanded to nearly all kinds of corporations, nowhere does it mean the same thing, whether because of cultural or sectorial differences. And sport is a very peculiar sector for CSR, due to the ethical, economic and organizational factors which we next delineate.

CSR and sport: Cooperation or competition between two ethics?

Sport is a symbolic universe, an ever-increasing source of stories in which individuals, groups and organizations draw an inspiration that is mobilized in various situations. From a critical standpoint, one could argue that sport inherited the role of maintaining a form of popular religiosity (Giulianotti, 2005). A central pillar of this role is sport ethics. Although this ethics has largely evolved since ancient times, its formal establishment through the Olympic Charter gave it a quite homogeneous base throughout the 20th century, which can be summarized as 'a philosophy of life, exalting and combining in a balanced whole the qualities of body, will and mind' (p.11). Mass (2007) identifies six ethical principles within the charter: non-discrimination, humanism, universalism, solidarity, culture and education. The Olympic movement constantly emphasizes these principles, which have also been integrated by most non-Olympic sports (Elias & Dunning, 1986). Sports ethics has led the sports movement to support the idea that social responsibility – which was integrated into the charter in the early 2000s as well as sustainability – is in the genetic code of sport organizations (Bayle et al., 2011). This could explain why sport-CSR has grown rapidly in the last decade. However, this idea can be partly deconstructed. The first and simplest argument is that all sport organizations do not necessarily behave in an ethical manner. But more fundamentally, it appears that sports ethics is very different from business ethics – of which CSR comes from – for intrinsic reasons. Indeed, sports ethics is an ethics of conviction, structured around the belief that sport is essentially good for society, due to its prominent role in promoting social integration and cohesion. On the other hand, business ethics is an ethics of responsibility, which is based on the potential negative effects of business on society (Van Marrewijk, 2003). Hence both ethics lead to two opposed rationales. Sports ethics aims to spread the positive effects of sport, while business ethics aims to reduce the negative externalities of corporations. For this reason, both ethics may be juxtaposed but cannot be merged. Still, the success of sport-CSR is undeniable, and implies other factors.

Sport organizations' economic and organizational CSR drivers

Sport management researchers have accordingly taken a growing interest in CSR in the sport context. First contributions put forward the philanthropic power of sport (Kott, 2005). Several authors then provided explanations regarding these particular aspects. Sport organizations appear to be influenced by two sets of determinants (Babiak & Wolfe, 2009), namely unique internal resources and strong external pressures.

Internal resources have different origins. Firstly, sport as a whole has some features that make it an effective vector for CSR: youth appeal, positive health impacts, social interaction, sustainability awareness or cultural integration (Smith & Westerbeek, 2007). Alongside sport's inherent values, other resources pertain to sport organizations themselves. Professional teams and athletes, national sport associations, and even some sport facilities have key assets which can be summarized in three notions, namely admiration, passion and identification (Babiak & Wolfe, 2009). Regarding sport events, their celebratory nature makes them all the more able to foster social values (Chalip, 2006) since they are condensed in time and thereby particularly adapted to spectacular actions – like the 2006 Superbowl's tree planting initiative (Babiak & Wolfe, 2006).

On the other hand, sport organizations face strong external pressures that compel them to act in a more responsible way. Babiak and Wolfe (2009) identify various types of external determinants. The first is their specific economic structure, namely the fact that they often rely on public subsidies or infrastructures, and are consequently expected to give back to the community. The second is the transparency of their activities, as their external performances as well as their internal life arouse the curiosity of media and fans. Another CSR factor is sport organizations' strong interconnectedness, which can lead them to share social and environmental good practices, especially given the integration of these matters by the IOC and most international federations. It is also to be noted that CSR has consequences on sponsorship deals, in the sense that most sponsors face their own CSR issues as corporations, thereby intending to use sport organizations as a vehicle for their responsible communication (Walters, 2009). Finally, external pressures also come from growing criticism towards some of these organizations, as is for example the case with Federation Internationale de Football Association's (FIFA) 2015 corruption scandal.

Contemporary and future questions of sport-CSR

Sport organizations have a growing understanding of CSR. Although their view is not necessarily strategic, CSR actions can serve to 'attract fans, secure corporate sponsors, generate goodwill among various stakeholders, and have effective dealings with local and state governments' (Babiak & Wolfe, 2006, p.215). However, they do not share an equal footing. Above-mentioned sport values, as widespread as they may be, do not fit all kinds of sports. For example, environmental awareness may fit motor sports less than nature sports, and cycling may not be relevant for expressing positive health impacts given the doping scandals which have tarnished its image. There may also be limits due to the somehow hypertrophied 'business aspects' of some sports – among which are high salaries, the purchase of professional clubs by billionaire businessmen, or the economic weight of sports betting – leading public opinion to a form of distrust. Hence, for instance, it can be difficult to express the values of grassroots soccer in a professional soccer context.Concerning sport events, and more particularly mega-events like the Olympic Games or the FIFA World Cup, researchers showed that these often cost more than they benefit the host communities (Preuss, 2004). Beyond economic considerations, they can generate other adverse effects – crowding and traffic congestion, noise pollution in stadiums, violence and security issues, environmental impacts (Leopkey & Parent, 2009) – which then limit their CSR abilities. Lastly, sport-CSR often relies on the celebrity and role model status of individual athletes, whose potential unethical behaviors present risks, as illustrated by the Lance Armstrong doping case which greatly harmed his cancer foundation, leading its directors to end their collaboration with the professional cyclist.

Another specific challenge of sport-CSR is that it does not only come from sport organizations themselves. Since sport ethics can be exploited by public and private partners to fulfill their own social responsibility issues, there appears to be a complex coexistence of distinct sets of CSR rationales, whether these pertain to sport organizations, sponsors, public authorities, or NGOs. Given the heterogeneity of sport-CSR practices, one could wonder whose CSR is at stake. Some stakeholders may actually not feel concerned about sport organizations' core CSR as long as they are provided with a communication space for their own CSR. Consequently, many sport-CSR practices may refer to the philanthropic level of Carroll's (1991) pyramid and not to its ethical level. This raises the question of sport-CSR authenticity: what are the role and place of sport inherent CSR issues in sport-CSR practices? Should sport organizations serve as stakeholders' CSR delivery agencies without tackling their own social responsibilities? Should they accept to be associated with stakeholders, more particularly corporations, which intend to use them as white- or greenwashers? Without seeking to be judgmental, this chapter provides insights into the semantic richness of sport-CSR, which oscillates between branding and genuine ethical concerns. For this purpose we draw on the case study of a sport organization – namely the French Tennis Federation. In the following sections, we present the context of this case and provide a detailed analysis of the federation's CSR strategy.

Case study 10.1: French Tennis Federation – A 'genuinely strategic' CSR

Case context

The French Tennis Federation (or Fédération Française de Tennis – FFT) is one of the oldest French sport associations. It was created in 1888, and was renamed as it is today in 1920. It is also the second French sport association in terms of both budget and members behind the French Football Federation (Table 10.1). Although a non-profit organization, the FFT is regarded as one of the most business-oriented national associations. This is notably because it is the owner of a hallmark

Table 10.1   FFT in key figures

Members	Budget	Other key figures and elements
1.1 million (first individual sport in France) • 30% of them women • 52% of them aged under 18	€ 200 million (2014)	• 2.2 million matches per year • 12,500 tournaments per year • 32,000 tennis courts • 27,800 jobs, 18,000 full-time equivalent • Owner of the French Open

event, namely the French Open at Roland Garros, which generates a large part of its revenues (€50 million in 2014).

The FFT is also one of the most active national sport associations regarding CSR. This can be explained by the fact that its board has a strategic view of social responsibility, as compared to other sport federations, which either merely started communicating on the social (and more rarely, environmental) actions, or complied with the ethical requirements of the sports movement as well as the French government, seeing it more as a duty than an opportunity.

The FFT initiated a sustainable development policy in 2008 by signing a charter with the French Olympic Federation and the French ministries of sport and ecology. The charter had nine objectives: (1) integrate sustainable development at both national and local levels, (2) diffuse its values to the society, (3) use tennis as a sport for all, (4) use tennis to foster equal opportunities and well-being, (5) ensure job satisfaction for employees, (6) integrate stakeholders to its actions, (7) ensure responsible sourcing and production, (8) optimize energy use and waste recovering, (9) reduce its environmental footprint. In order to implement this charter, the FFT established a specific division and recruited skilled staff. Rapidly, the federation decided to refer to 'CSR' rather than 'sustainable development', which marked the actual starting point of their strategic approach, as explained by the CSR officer (interviewed by the author in July 2013): 'clearly we found that CSR was more appropriate, firstly because sustainable development is too oriented towards the environmental aspects, and secondly because it refers to politics, whereas we wanted to address our corporate partners'. From this point, FFT established a real business case for CSR.

CSR strategy

A first observation is that the FFT's CSR is widely publicized. The global approach 'La FFT s'engage' (which can be translated as 'The FFT is committed') has its own name and logo. Flagship actions have also been specifically branded in order to be highlighted. An example is the 'Yellow Ball campaign', a nationwide collection and recycling of used tennis balls. For the 6th edition (in 2014), 1.6 million balls were collected from the 31 participating regional leagues, and ground down to produce 40 tons of rubber granules, which are then used to create sports surfaces for hospitals, schools and social institutions. This innovative action is communicated through various mediums, insisting on its 'triple bottom line' dimension, namely environmental, social and economic (as it helps maintain the industrial branch of complex waste recycling in France).

(Continued)

(Continued)

The FFT's CSR also involves the use of Roland Garros as a major communication means. It makes it the model of its CSR approach, by addressing a broad spectrum of issues. On the environmental front, the federation set up a car pooling website in order to reduce carbon emissions due to spectator transport. It also offers responsible catering products and promotes awareness of its actions by deploying a 'green team', which advises the public on the site's waste sorting system. At social level, one of the main actions is 'Kids Day', during which various activities dedicated to children take place, including exhibition matches, autograph sessions and music shows. The French Open also improved disabled accessibility, from the vocalization of web pages for deaf persons to the enlargement of wheelchair places, echoing the federation's 'sport for all' objective. All these actions allowed the tournament (in 2014) to be the second international sport event to achieve the ISO 20121 event sustainability certification, after the 2012 Olympic Games in London.

The FFT made the strategic choice of integrating its stakeholders into the CSR policy, which led to important strategic implications (Table 10.2). The most apparent concerns corporate sponsors. The federation positioned itself as a CSR platform, using CSR partnerships as brand content in order to promote sponsors' image and at the same time to fulfill its own CSR program. Hence these partnerships are based on a form of storytelling, by which sponsors are presented as helping the FFT in its social and environmental efforts. For example Peugeot, which is a longtime partner of Roland Garros, lends electric cars and bikes both to players and the organizing team, which allows a reduction in the FFT's environmental footprint, and displays the automotive company's model ranges and its environmental commitment. The same principle applies to business to business partners like IBM, for which the event constitutes a stage to showcase its sustainable information technology (IT) system. Other examples include the promotion of gender equality with the gas company GDF Suez, initiatives for children with the banking company BNP Paribas, and the recycling of Perrier bottles and Nespresso capsules with their mother brand Nestlé during the French Open.

The FFT's CSR partnerships are not limited to corporate sponsors. The federation works in close collaboration with the French ministry of sport, whose annual subsidy (more than €1 million) partly depends on social and environmental achievements. The ministry created a platform for the exchange of good practices, and holds regular meetings with national sport associations: as the CSR officer explains, 'originally the ministry set up a "carbon club" involving the five major sport federations. The aim was to carry out a carbon audit [...] but our relationships have evolved towards many other issues, now we are among the most implicated actors and the ministry sees us as a laboratory of new ideas and proposals'. The FFT is also helped by the French Olympic Association, which formalized a voluntary action plan with regard to sustainable development (called Agenda 21) in 2003, since assuming a consulting role, particularly by offering training to federations' staff. Other CSR partnerships notably include charities, which are intermediaries towards the beneficiaries of CSR actions, and which at the same time represent a legitimacy enabler. The two main partnered charities are 'Fête le Mur', founded by the former player Yannick Noah to help deprived children, and 'Tennis en Liberté', which uses tennis to promotes equality of opportunity.

A last key CSR input for FFT is its internal communication, since there are over 8,000 tennis clubs in France which represent an important lever for action. Hence, the federation launched a call for

Table 10.2   The FFT's CSR partnership strategy

Type of partner	FFT's objectives	Partner's objectives
Private sponsors	• Finance CSR actions • Transfer CSR competencies related to sponsor's sector of activity	• Enhance image through CSR communication • Other marketing objectives – increase sales/market share, build trade relations, enhance employee relations – depending on sponsors' target audience
Public authorities	• Finance CSR actions • Benefit from CSR tools and expertise related to public authorities' social and environmental policies	• Incentivize national sport associations to take part in the sustainable development policy • Use sport as an example of social and environmental innovations
Sport movement	• Share CSR good practices • Receive institutional support	• Institutionalize CSR within sport organizations • Use CSR to renew sport ethics and generate stakeholder value
Charities	• Legitimize CSR actions	• Finance charitable actions • Increase the visibility and awareness of charitable causes • Recruit new volunteers

social responsibility projects, starting in 2010. Not only does this initiative enhance the impact and geographic scope of its CSR policy, it also revitalizes the relationship between the national decision-making center and the locally-based member associations. It also establishes a two-way communication stream through which local initiatives enrich a central database, allowing for the sharing of good practices. To date, more than 200 clubs carried out various projects in the fields of education, solidarity, physical and mental disability, reaching out to more than 6,000 beneficiaries (including more than 4,000 children). In order to further help clubs improve their community involvement and local stakeholder relations, the FFT trained and appointed CSR local officers in each of the 29 regional leagues.

Case discussion

In summary, the FFT's CSR strategy is structured around three key elements – namely CSR external communication, CSR partnerships and CSR internal communication – which are summarized in Figure 10.1.

This strategy is all the more remarkable as there is not necessarily a natural link between the inherent values of tennis and social or environmental concerns. Indeed, this sport has often not only been regarded as one of the most polluting, given the annual use of millions of tennis balls, but in addition, as an upper classes' sport, thus also not intended to promote social integration. The FFT has hence attained quite delicate objectives. Furthermore, while sport organizations' CSR can sometimes be invaded by their stakeholders' CSR goals and targets, thereby reducing it to a diluted and off-ground set of actions, the federation managed to keep control of its action scheme, using its partners' resources in order to fulfill it. The philanthropic responsibilities of Carroll's (1991) pyramid are therefore

(Continued)

(Continued)

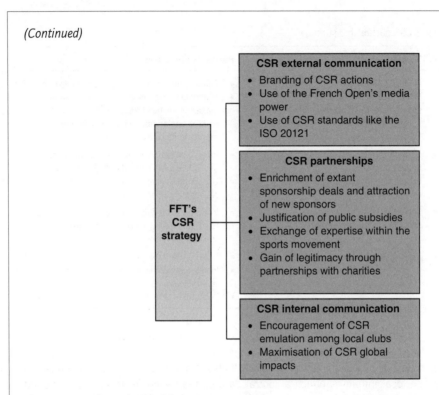

Figure 10.1 The FFT's CSR global strategy

counterbalanced with ethical responsibilities, namely actions related to core sport-CSR issues, including illegal betting, match fixing and doping, which are for example mentioned in the annual CSR report within an 'ethics' section.

Nonetheless, several flaws and limits can be identified. The first pitfall is a certain difference between the FFT's real CSR performance and a form of CSR symbolic management. This can however be credited, from a strategic and somehow amoral perspective, to the success of its communication. Indeed, one could say that the federation's CSR achievements come more from the valorization of its initiatives than from their actual results. In terms of environmental impacts, and contrary to what one might think, the French Open still releases four times more tons of carbon than events like the Dakar Rally, which are still far more often criticized. Besides, despite the usefulness of the 'Yellow Ball' campaign, it must be noted that only 50% of tennis balls can actually be recycled (the other 50% are made of synthetic rubber, which is non-recyclable). Concerning social aspects, the financial support granted by the FFT to local clubs through the call for social responsibility projects amounts in total of €80,000 (FFT, 2014). This seems little compared to the French Open's prize money, namely €1.8 million for the winner, €900,000 for the runner-up, €450,000 euros for semi-finalists and €250,000 euros for each quarter finalist.

Another major limit to the FFT's CSR has been the renovation of the Roland Garros site, which has been validated by the French government during the 2015 tournament after five years of debate (FranceTV Info, 2015). The expansion, estimated at over €350 million, will increase the Roland Garros ground from 21 acres to about 34 acres. Although the federation referred to the national public debate commission, no public debate was held, as the commission instead recommended a conciliation under the aegis of a guarantor. The project validation appears even more surprising given that the French Ministry of Ecology issued a negative instead in February 2015. Local residents and wildlife associations are fiercely opposed to this expansion, notably because it will cut off a nearby botanical site classified as heritage site. The FFT's attitude, namely strong lobbying and repeated threats to relocate the tournament outside of Paris, particularly reflects the conflict between CSR and business considerations and confers a certain degree of relativity to our conclusions.

Conclusion

Throughout this chapter, we intended to show that CSR represents both opportunities and threats for sport organizations. Opportunities come from the symbolic power of sport ethics. The Olympic philosophy erected by Pierre de Coubertin keeps enlightening these organizations with a genetic CSR, based on the positive use of sport to address various societal concerns, and hence providing them with a presumption of honesty and exemplary role. However, this advantage, which is essentially related to philanthropy, tends to diminish as CSR and sustainability principles spread through the economy. By shifting the focus from their broad social leverage capacity to their often unresolved core issues, this trend raises the risk of damaging sport ethics' credibility. Consequently, the sport movement faces increasing legitimacy challenges.

Perhaps the most daunting of these relates to their sponsors, which they financially depend on. One of the main objectives of sponsorship is the image transfer from the positive image of the sport entity to sponsors' own brand image (Gwinner & Eaton, 1999). Since CSR has also become, for most corporations, a central issue for brand image (Smith, 2003), some sport properties may have a diminishing range of sponsorship opportunities due to a lack of commitment towards their own CSR issues. This observation evidently calls for nuance, as many sponsors do not base their sport sponsorship on CSR values. Quite the contrary, some use sports to enhance specific dimensions of their brand personality like excitement or ruggedness (Lee & Cho, 2009) and consequently partner with sport properties that can be criticized over ethical aspects, as illustrated by the deal between Reebok and the Ultimate Fighting Championship (UFC) (UFC staff report, 2014), whose professional fights are still banned in several countries because of their alleged violence. Still, there are a growing number of instances where sponsors have actively called for a better integration of CSR from sport partners, among which the sponsors of the Tour de France that launched a charter for cleaning cycling from doping. Fortunately, it appears that sponsors are interested in helping sport organizations in their CSR efforts. This may lead to a converse pattern of image transfer, based on sport properties' bad CSR image in order to display sponsors' contribution to resolve sport-CSR issues. An example of such strategies is the FFT's partnerships with Peugeot and IBM.

Yet another challenge relates to the gap between spectacular sport-CSR actions and their daily CSR management, which has the drawback of being less eye-catching. The risk is that sport organizations base their CSR initiatives on the momentum presented by sport events, thereby engendering a one-off form of responsibility. But rather than suspecting them of green-washing intentions, one should question the real significance of CSR when applied to such hybrid organizations. For example, in most countries national sport associations have always had general interest missions like youth education or health promotion. Are these missions part of their social responsibility, or do they constitute their very nature? Furthermore, can CSR be applied to the entire sport sector, given that issues like doping or corruption are not under the direct control of sport organizations themselves, but engage the responsibility of outside actors such as partners, providers and the media?

At a more fundamental level, sport-CSR may be envisioned as an illustration of one of CSR's most radical criticisms, namely its logic of privatizing general interest. Indeed, some authors view CSR as a victory of capitalism since it dispossesses public authorities of their power of regulation (Gond, Kang, & Moon, 2011). In parallel, sport has often been described as an outpost of capitalism (Bray, 1983). Brought together, these two analyses spark the question of sport as a justification for a capitalist view of CSR. More specifically, sport organizations have the particular capacity of enabling relationships between corporations and various social and charitable actors, which often have opposite goals. This reflects a vicious circle, whereby the narrowing of the public sphere, encouraged by the corporate world, increases the role of charities, and at the same time leads them to accept corporations' financial support. Within this global scheme, sport organizations serve to activate corporation–charity links through sport-CSR. For example Secours Populaire, one of the largest French associations combating child poverty, has carried out several social initiatives with the chocolate and confectionery manufacturer Ferrero, through their mutual partnership with the French Basketball Federation. One could wonder about the ethical appropriateness of these CSR actions since Ferrero, through its brands Kinder and Nutella, has been pointed out multiple times for child obesity issues.

To summarize, sport managers dealing with CSR should not base their strategy on the sole showpiece effect of sport ethics. As numerous previous mentioned examples show, stakeholders and public opinion can no longer be content with philanthropic initiatives simply using the virtues of sport to play the Good Samaritan. Sport organizations' CSR has to be centered on specific issues. This rationale should particularly apply to CSR partnerships, for two reasons: (1) sport organizations cannot solve issues like doping, corruption, hooliganism or environmental costs without the help of their stakeholders and (2), this help is a very interesting means of content creation, as it appears more genuine and subtle, knowing that subtlety is the key advantage of sponsorship over other forms of communication because it faces less consumer skepticism (Plewa & Quester, 2011). A good example is the partnership between the British Olympic Association and 33 of the largest companies listed on the London Stock Exchange during the preparation phase of the 2012 Olympic Games, through which these companies supported various British sport associations in the areas of governance, human resources or environmental management (Dowling, Robinson, & Washington, 2013).

A last aspect is the use of CSR standards by sport organizations. The most prevalent in the sport field is the ISO 20121 standard, which was formalized during the 2012 Olympic Games in order to specify requirements for an event sustainability management system for any type of event or event-related activity. While this kind of standard may provide several benefits like enhancing stakeholder relations or improving image, it also presents the risk of reducing – through its formal character – innovation and storytelling opportunities, thereby losing its appeal to sponsors, which are one of the main financers of sport-CSR. Hence, ISO 20121 was deemed 'too general' by FIFA to be implemented during the 2014 World Cup (FIFA, 2014).

Recommended further reading

For those who want to know more, see also:

Bradish, C. L., & Cronin, J. J. (2009). Special Issue: Corporate social responsibility in sport. *Journal of Sport Management*, 23(6), 691–794.
Hemsley, S. (2009).Corporate social responsibility and sports sponsorship. *International Marketing Reports* (IMR).
Salcines, J. L. P., Babiak, K., & Walters, G. (2013). *Routledge handbook of sport and corporate social responsibility*. London: Routledge.

References

Babiak, K., & Wolfe, R. (2006). More than just a game? Corporate social responsibility and Super Bowl XL. *Sport Marketing Quarterly*, 15(4): 214–222.
Babiak, K., & Wolfe, R. (2009). Determinants of corporate social responsibility in professional sport: internal and external factors. *Journal of Sport Management*, 23(6), 717–742.
Bayle, E., Chappelet, J.-L., François, A., & Maltèse, L. (2011). *Sport et RSE. Vers un management responsable ?* Bruxelles: De Boeck Editions.
Bowen, H.R. (1953). *Social Responsibilities of the Businessman*. New York: Harper & Row.
Bray, C. (1983). Sport, capitalism, and patriarchy. *Canadian Woman Studies*, 4(3).
Carroll, A.B. (1991). The pyramid of corporate social responsibility: Toward the moral management of organizational stakeholders. *Business Horizons*, 34(4), 39–48.
Chalip, L. (2006). Towards social leverage of sport events. *Journal of Sport & Tourism*, 11(2), 1–19.
Clarkson, M.B.E. (1995). A stakeholder framework for analyzing and evaluating corporate social performance. *Academy of Management Review*, 20, 92–117.
Dowling, M., Robinson, L., & Washington, M. (2013). Taking advantage of the London 2012 Olympic Games: corporate social responsibility through sport partnerships. *European Sport Management Quarterly*, 13(3), 269–292.
Elias, N., & Dunning, E. (1986). *Quest for excitement: Sport and leisure in the civilizing process* (Vol. 288). Oxford: Blackwell.
Fédération Française de Tennis (2014). Bilan Appel à projets 2014, retrieved from: http://www.fft.fr/sites/default/files/pdf/bilan_appel_a_projets_2014.pdf

Fédération Internationale de Football Association (2014). Summary of the 2014 FIFA World Cup Brazil Carbon Footprint, retrieved from: http://www.mgminnova.com/web/summaryofthe2014fwccarbon footprint_neutral.pdf

FranceTV Info (2015, 4 June). Le gouvernement donne son feu vert à l'extension de Roland-Garros, retrieved from: http://www.francetvinfo.fr/sports/tennis/roland-garros/le-gouvernement-donne-son-feu-vert-a-l-extension-de-roland-garros_935651.html

Freeman, R.E. (1984). *Strategic management: A stakeholder approach*. Boston: Pitman.

Friedman, M. (1970). The social responsibility of business is to increase its profits. *New York Times Magazine* (13 September), 122–126.

Gibson, O., & Pattisson, P. (2014, 23 December). Death toll among Qatar's 2022 World Cup workers revealed. *The Guardian*, retrieved from: http://www.theguardian.com/world/2014/dec/23/qatar-nepal-workers-world-cup-2022-death-toll-doha

Giulianotti, R. (2005). *Sport: A critical sociology*. Polity.

Gond, J.P., Kang, N., & Moon, J. (2011). The government of self-regulation: On the comparative dynamics of corporate social responsibility. *Economy and Society*, 40(4), 640–671.

Grove, T. (2014, 17 January). OLYMPICS – Sochi residents blame Games for ecological damage, *Reuters*, retrieved from: http://www.reuters.com/article/2014/01/17/olympics-russia-environment-idUSL5N0IY04720140117

Gwinner, K.P., & Eaton, J. (1999). Building brand image through event sponsorship: the role of image transfer. *Journal of advertising*, 28(4), 47–57.

Kahle, L.R., Boush, D.M., & Phelps, M. (2000). Good morning, Vietnam: an ethical analysis of Nike activities in Southeast Asia. *Sport Marketing Quarterly*, 9(1), 43–52.

Kott, A. (2005). The philanthropic power of sport. *Foundation News and Commentary*, 20–25.

Lee, H.S., & Cho, C.H. (2009). The matching effect of brand and sporting event personality: Sponsorship implications. *Journal of Sport Management*, 23(1), 41–64.

Leopkey, B., & Parent, M.M. (2009). Risk management issues in large-scale sporting events: A stakeholder perspective. *European Sport Management Quarterly*, 9(2), 187–208.

Levitt, T. (1958). The dangers of social responsibility. *Harvard Business Review*, 36(5), 41–50.

Maass, S. (2007). The Olympic Values. *Olympic Review*, 63, 28–33

Matten, D., & Moon, J. (2008). 'Implicit' and 'explicit' CSR: A conceptual framework for a comparative understanding of corporate social responsibility. *Academy of Management Review*, 33(2), 404–424.

Plewa, C., & Quester, P.G. (2011). Sponsorship and CSR: Is there a link? A conceptual framework. *International Journal of Sports Marketing & Sponsorship*, 12(4), 301.

Preuss, H. (2004). *The economics of staging the Olympics: A comparison of the Games 1972–2008*. Cheltenham: Edward Elgar.

Smith, A.C.T., & Westerbeek, H.M. (2007). Sport as a vehicle for deploying Corporate Social Responsibility. *Journal of Corporate Citizenship*, 25, 43–54.

Smith, N.C. (2003). Corporate social responsibility: Whether or how? *California Management Review*, 45(4), 52–76.

UFC staff report (2014, 1 December). Reebok, UFC announce landmark apparel deal, retrieved from: http://www.ufc.com/news/reebok-ufc-announce-landmark-apparel-deal

Van Marrewijk, M. (2003). Concepts and definitions of CSR and corporate sustainability: Between agency and communion. *Journal of Business Ethics*, 44(2–3), 95–105.

Walters, G. (2009). Corporate social responsibility through sport: the community sports trust model as a CSR delivery agency. *Journal of Corporate Citizenship*, 35, 81–94.

Winter, B., & Teixeira, M. (2014, 12 June). Brazil police, protesters clash as World Cup begins, *Reuters*, retrieved from: http://www.reuters.com/article/2014/06/12/us-brazil-worldcup-protests-idUSKBN0EN 1DD20140612

ISBN-13: 978-1-473-94805-1

9 781473 948051

SECTION C

SPORT AND FINANCE

PROFITS, CHAMPIONSHIPS AND BUDGET CONSTRAINTS IN EUROPEAN PROFESSIONAL SPORT

KLAUS NIELSEN AND RASMUS K. STORM

Introduction

The business of professional team sports is not an ordinary business. The competitive environment and the character of the product are indeed peculiar, which explains why consumers and producers behave differently from economic actors in other industries. In a ground-breaking article, Neale (1964) identified the need for uncertainty regarding the outcome of sporting contests as the reason for the many peculiarities of North American professional team sports, which takes place in closed leagues organized by monopolies. However, the peculiarities of team sport business in North America compared to the normal business enterprise are not related to different motivations and different underlying goals. The owners of team sport franchises are profit maximizers as other enterprises.

In Europe, the business of professional team sports is equally peculiar when measured by the yardstick of the typical business enterprise. However, it is radically different from North American team sport businesses in terms of competition and regulation. In at least one respect, the European context is even more peculiar than its North American equivalent in the sense that profit maximization does not appear to be the ultimate motive of enterprise behaviour. Rather, the pursuit of 'win maximization' seems to determine the decision making of the professional European team sports enterprise. The pursuit of the best possible sporting results is superior to any other motives in all team sports clubs independent of whether it is a non-profit voluntary organization or a for-profit business enterprise. The professional team sports club in Europe is perceived to maximize its wins under a break-even constraint. As long as costs do not exceed revenues, clubs are doing whatever they can to be as successful as possible in their respective leagues.

There is much empirical evidence in support of this view. European team sport clubs do not seem to be motivated by profit. They normally do not earn profits and they definitely do not maximize profits. They instead seem to do what is seen as required for sporting success independent of profit implications. However, does that mean that they maximize wins under a break-even or zero deficit constraint? This is often not the case. Many professional team sport clubs seem to pursue sporting success without bothering about any budget constraints. Their accounts show persistent deficits and growing debts. Despite these problems, the clubs have an abnormally high survival rate. When in financial trouble, the vast majority are bailed out, saved by rich individuals ('sugar daddies') or the government or its private creditors.

The expectation of being saved in case of financial problems affects the behaviour of professional team sports clubs. They behave as if there is no need to balance the books. They act as if it is not a threat to the survival of the company to operate financial losses. In other words, their budget constraints are soft. They do not seem to care about profits but maximize sporting success within budget constraints, which are soft in the sense that they expect that expenditures in excess of revenues can be covered in various ways *ex post*.

The phenomenon of soft budget constraints exists at all levels of professional team sports. However, paradoxically, this phenomenon prevails more often when clubs are rich. Often, the higher the revenue streams that clubs earn, the higher the deficits. This is particularly evident in top-level European professional football. The richest leagues operate the largest accumulated losses. This chapter mainly refers to football but the phenomenon of soft budget constraints also exists in other professional team sports in Europe, such as basketball, ice hockey, handball and rugby.

Why are the budget constraints of professional team sport businesses often soft? Why is the degree of 'softness' different in different contexts? What are the mechanisms that explain the phenomenon of soft budget constraints? Why do saviours save loss-making sport clubs from financial collapse? How prevalent is the phenomenon?

This chapter attempts to answer these questions, and is structured as follows. The first section outlines the background for the prevailing win optimization theory. The second section presents evidence, which indicates that something different from win optimization under a break-even constraint is at play. The third section is a general presentation of the syndrome of soft budget constraints, which is followed by a discussion of the institutional preconditions and the social and emotional attachment in European professional team sports. The next section provides examples of six different forms of 'softness', which are followed by two case studies and a concluding section.

Win optimization rather than profit maximization

For-profit business enterprises normally not only try to survive but also attempt to earn a profit. In case of no profits or lower profits compared to alternative uses of capital, the investor is expected to withdraw from the firm in favour of investing in another. This means that in order to survive the firm will have to maximize profits, and in economic theory businesses are assumed to behave in such a way that their profits are maximized. Real-life business enterprises do not always follow this behavioural rule. They may instead prioritize growth of market share, or they may 'satisfice' rather than optimize (Simon, 1979), which means that they do not pursue optimal but rather satisfactory solutions. They may be non-profit social enterprises who primarily pursue social aims and invest surpluses back into the business itself. They may also aim for shared value, i.e. a combination of profit maximization and the creation of societal value beyond what the effects on the company's balance sheet are (Porter & Kramer, 2011).

Increasingly, European professional team sport clubs have become business enterprises with capital injections by owners and sometimes flotations on stock markets. Arguably, this has caused major changes in the functioning of the clubs. They have become commercialized in practice and in rhetoric (Horne, 2006; Storm, 2010). Focus has shifted to give priority to the maximization of revenue streams such as sponsorships, media rights, merchandise, luxury seating, branding and diversified services. Professional management and labour markets have emerged, and corporate governance has become a hot topic. Further, new economic and managerial discourses of club management linked to commercialization have emerged. However, profits are seldom and in any case insignificant. Increasing revenues lead to similar or even larger increases in expenditures. If maximization of profits is what motivates and guides the owners of professional team sport clubs they are not very successful and it is difficult to understand why anyone would want to invest in such an unrewarding line of business.

These phenomena have puzzled sport economists. Some advocate a direct application of mainstream economic theory including an assumption of profit maximizing club owners (Dobson & Goddard, 2001; Sandy, Sloane, & Rosentraub, 2004). However, others conclude that 'owners are just as likely to be win-maximizing sportsmen' (Vrooman, 2007, 353). Indeed, a consensus seems to have emerged that clubs behave according to a win optimizing motive (Garcia-del Barrio & Szymanski, 2009). Club owners are assumed to disregard a return on capital and instead give priority to doing whatever is needed to become as successful in the relevant sporting contests as possible. If that means zero profits so be it. However, it is assumed that club owners do not want to lose the invested capital so win optimization with a zero deficit constraint is seen as prevalent.

Fort (2000) disagrees with the argument. He maintains that European professional football clubs are in fact profit maximizers. However, there is ample evidence that win optimization rather than profit maximization characterizes European professional team sports (Garcia-del Barrio & Szymanski, 2009).

Comparisons with North American major leagues have contributed to this emphasis on the European peculiarities (Andreff, 2011). The North American leagues are closed with no relegation and promotion whereas European leagues are open. The North American leagues are local monopolies with strong entry barriers. They impose limits to player mobility and have measures designed to level out the competitive strength of individual clubs such as a reverse-order-of-finish draft. They redistribute income by pooling a TV rights sale at the league level. The leagues are cartels exempted from the American anti-trust regulation. These conditions are favourable for profit maximization whereas the competitive structure of open leagues in Europe encourages win-optimizing behaviour.

There are obvious historical reasons for this contrast. Whereas major leagues in North America were pure market phenomena from the start, the European context is radically different. Professional team sport originates from voluntary organizations in civil society which have maintained an influence on league structures. The contemporary structures have emerged gradually and still reflect the influence of their emergence, the overall competitive structure is still heavily influenced by its past and the major European leagues are still more or less linked to the inherited civil society organizations.

Persistent losses but a high survival rate[1]

Arguably, the assumption of win optimization is highly valuable in attempts to understand the business of professional team sports and explain the behaviour of club owners in Europe. It explains why increasing revenues result in equivalent increasing costs. Or, as Tottenham Hotspur's former owner Alan Sugar famously expressed it when commenting on a new windfall Premier League TV rights deal, 'It is like prune juice. It will go in one end and out the other'.[2]

However, it does not explain why win optimization behaviour often persists without any break-even constraint. In their pursuit of sporting success, owners often accept deficits leading to debt and loss of capital. This is reflected in persistent losses in professional European team sport clubs.

According to UEFA's club licensing benchmarking report (UEFA, 2010), more than 50% of all top division clubs in Europe have operating losses. In 28% of the clubs salaries alone constitute more than 120% of revenues.

The situation is much worse in the major European leagues. The English Premier League is the richest and most popular league in Europe. It has experienced phenomenal revenue growth rates following the unilateral decision of clubs in the prevision first division in 1992 to break away from the Football League. The Premier League has since taken advantage of increasingly lucrative television rights deals and experienced a growth in revenues of more than 900% in the period between 1992 and 2007. Even so, the business has not been profitable (Hamil & Walters, 2010). All of this increased revenue, and still more, has been used on players' salaries or transfers, leaving no profits. In fact, there has in this period not been one single year in which the Premier League has generated an aggregate pre-tax profit for the Premier League clubs (Hamil & Walters, 2010).

There are similar trends in other European countries, for example in Italy (Morrow, 2006; Szymanski & Zimbalist, 2006). There have been persistent and increasing operating losses in all Serie A clubs. From 1996/97 to 2006/07 the accumulated losses of Italian Serie A clubs amounted to a total of €1.4 billion, even before transfer deficits were taken into account (Hamil et al., 2010). The players' salaries increased more than 700% in the top six clubs from 1996 to 2002 alone (Baroncelli & Lago, 2006).

Spanish football also holds persistent deficits (Garcia & Rodriquez, 2003; Boscá et al., 2008). The first tier league has experienced rapidly growing revenues similar to the English Premier

League. However, the clubs are spending even larger amounts on player salaries and transfers, resulting in rising levels of debt. In spite of the booming revenues, several Spanish clubs have been threatened with closure due to overspending. Almost half of the clubs in the first and second divisions are in serious trouble when measured on factors such as indebtedness, capacity to refinance debts, and expenditure on players seen in relation to operating revenues (Barajas & Rodríguez, 2010). For instance, in 2008, the aggregate losses in the two top-tier leagues were a staggering €2.8 million (Andreff, 2007): 90% of the clubs operated with an aggregate loss, with nine clubs being technically insolvent. Total salaries were 99% of revenues in the top tier and 98% in the second tier (Barajas & Rodríguez, 2010). This situation is not a novel phenomenon. In Spain, accumulated operating results have always been negative, and more than half of the clubs are operating in the red each and every year (Boscá et al., 2008).

The situation in France is less serious although aggregate operating losses also characterize French football (Andreff, 2007). In the period 1997–2007, the aggregate losses in the top-tier French football league were €298 million.

Germany is the exception. The Bundesliga is clearly the most profitable of the major European football leagues and players' salaries constitute a much lower share of revenues than in the other major leagues (Deloitte, 2011). This is no doubt to do with the specific ownership structure in German football. Apart from a few exceptions where companies own the clubs (VfL Wolfsburg, Bayer Leverkusen and TSG 1899 Hoffenheim), all German top clubs have 51% member ownership.

However, despite the economic hardships outlined above, the history of European football is also a history of extremely high survival rates. Szymanski (2009) compared with business firms in general. Despite the chronic deficits, there have been only three cases of tier one–four insolvency in English football since 1985 (Beech et al., 2008). In 1923, the Football League consisted of 88 teams organized into four divisions: 97% of these still existed in the 2007/08 season, and 54% were in the same division as they were in 1923 (Kuper & Szymanski, 2009). In comparison, only 20 of the top 100 English companies in 1912 remained in the top 100 in 1995 (Szymanski, 2009).

The survival rate of Italian football clubs is also extremely high. Of the 60 clubs playing in the top Italian League from its inauguration in 1929 until 2010, 58 clubs are still in existence. It is remarkable that 20 of the 36 top two-tier league teams in 1929 are still playing in the two best tiers. In recent years, some Italian top clubs have been relegated due to financial collapse. However, almost all of them have reemerged after being restructured.

Spanish football clubs have also had high rates of survival, although not as high as in the English and Italian leagues. In total, 13 of 20 clubs (65%) playing in the best or second best tier in 1929 were playing in one of these tiers in 2009 which arguably indicates a high rate of survival.

Why is the survival rate so extraordinarily high among professional European football clubs, who almost always operate with operating losses and accumulated debt? As pointed out in Storm and Nielsen (2012), we believe that the paradox can be fruitfully understood though the lens of Kornai's (1980) soft budget constraint approach. This argument is developed in the following sections. First, we give a brief introduction to the ideas. Second, the prevalence of soft budget constraints is illustrated and followed by a discussion of the conditions that lead to soft budgets in the European professional team sports clubs.

Soft budget constraints – theory and practical relevance

What is a soft budget constraint? The concept was originally developed by the Hungarian economist Kornai in order to understand the phenomena of widespread shortage and inefficiency in socialist economic systems, and, in particular, the failure of attempts to reform the system (Kornai, 1980; Kornai, Maskin, & Rolland, 2003). Later, Kornai applied the approach in efforts to understand the post-socialist transition economies (Kornai, 2001), and the concepts have been used to explain a multitude of phenomena in capitalist economies as well (Kornai, Maskin, & Rolland, 2003). The soft budget constraint phenomenon describes a situation in which firms survive even when they repeatedly run a deficit from their operations. Environmental economic actors more or less systematically bail them out.

However, it is not the phenomenon of bailouts in itself that constitutes the syndrome of soft budget constraints. The *ex post* act of saving a firm from collapse is often sensible when seen in isolation and this does not in itself constitute a problem unless it has *ex ante* behavioural implications. The phenomenon of soft budget constraints constitutes a syndrome if firms expect that they can rely on external financial support if they run into financial trouble.

If this is the case, they will not bother much about profits or even about balancing the books. They will pay less attention to efficiency, and hoard scarce resources as it will practically be costless to accumulate too much, and focus on strengthening the relationship with the supporting organizations rather than properly manage the resources of the firm. In the classic socialist system, managerial incentives to be efficient or create innovative products were heavily distorted due to institutionalized *ex ante* expectations of *ex post* support if the firm in question failed to meet its planned financial goals.

In contrast to socialist societies, Kornai (1986) argues that, in general, the capitalist economies are dominated by hard budget constraints, in the sense that firms operating in a free market environment cannot generally rely on survival through bailouts from external supporters. Instead, they will face bankruptcy if they do not ensure efficient and optimized operations and do not curb spending in case of deficits. In other words, capitalist firms can only survive in the long term if they seriously master the relationship between their sales and costs and pay utmost attention to efficiency.

In an ideal sense, hard budget constraints ensure the creative destruction of inefficient organizations and a high level of innovation and high quality of products.

Kornai (1980; also Kornai et al., 2003) outlines five main criteria for assessing whether firms face hard or soft budget constraints. Firms are facing hard budget constraints when the following conditions are met: (H1) the firm is a price-taker for both inputs and outputs; (H2) the firm cannot influence the tax rules and no individual exemption can be given concerning the volume of tax or dates of collection; (H3) the firm cannot receive any free state or other grants to cover current expenses or as contributions to finance investment; (H4) no credit from other firms or banks can be obtained (all transactions are made in cash); and (H5) no external financial investment is possible, i.e. investments are dependent on retained profits.

If all of these conditions are fulfilled, the firm in question is constrained on its budget in a hard way. However, this extreme situation only exists in exceptional circumstances. Generally,

H4 and H5 are not fulfilled in monetary economies with developed financial systems. Further, H1 presupposes an absence of firms with market power, i.e. a capacity to influence the market price. There are many exceptions to H1 in capitalist economies. In practice, the efficiency driving budget hardness in capitalist economies is seen as linked to hardness in relation to H2 and H3. In general, firms are unable to influence their tax payments and will not be able to extract negotiated subsidies from the state contrary to powerful state-owned companies in socialist economies. Paradoxically, an extreme case of ideal-type hardness existed in the former socialist economies where the household sector experienced hardness in relation to all five criteria with an absence of consumer credit in addition to hardness with respect to the other criteria.

In fact, there are numerous examples from capitalist economies of firms facing relaxations on several of the conditions of hardness listed above including H2 and H3, thus showing that the soft budget constraint syndrome is not a phenomenon found exclusively in socialist or post-socialist economies. In capitalist economies, large-scale (usually public) organizations such as the military, public transport, hospitals, and also the banking sector, are shown to be facing significant relaxations of hardness. Generally, if an organization is seen as 'too big to fall' by its stakeholders there is a strong motive to save it in case of trouble and the behaviour of the organization then reflects an expectation of bailouts.

Soft budget constraints in European professional football

Even though some European clubs behave as win maximizers subject to a break-even constraint, many are facing environmental conditions that effectively result in a high survival rate despite continuous financial problems (Storm & Nielsen, 2012, 2015). Bankruptcies are seldom and only seem to occur for clubs in the second or lower divisions. Normally, state bailouts and sugar daddies come to the rescue and/or creditors accept debt arrears and non-payment of debt.

Using Kornai's (1986) framework, we distinguish between six types of softness. Soft pricing (S1), soft taxation (S2), soft subsidies (S3), soft credit (S4) and soft investment finance (S5) represent relaxations of each of Kornai's five conditions of hardness. We would add another category: soft accounting (S6). In the following paragraphs, we will present a range of examples that illustrate the different mechanisms of softness in European professional football.

Soft pricing (S1) takes place when a public stadium and/or training facility is made available to football clubs at below market fees and when governments or city councils buy naming rights to stadia at above market prices (see Case study 11.2 below). This has happened in many countries, including Spain, Italy and Denmark.

Soft taxation (S2) takes the form of tax exemptions and non-payment of taxes, non-enforcement or amnesty of tax debt. There are numerous examples of soft taxation in Spain (Barajas & Rodríguez, 2010) and Italy (Foot, 2006). For instance, Lazio was saved from collapse in a major rescue operation in 2005 by means of a relaxation of its tax obligations. The club reached an agreement with the Italian tax authorities of paying a €140 million tax liability over an extended period of 23 years to prevent the club from closure (Foot, 2006; Storm & Nielsen, 2012).

Soft subsidies (S3) come in either open or hidden forms provided by governments or rich 'glory seekers' to reduce deficits and pay off debts to keep clubs running in situations of severe financial problems. This has happened often in English (Grant, 2007) and French football (Andreff, 2007), but there are also numerous examples in other parts of Europe. Other subsidies take the form of access to guaranteed income-generating schemes such as football pools, inflated sponsorship deals and other indirect subsidies.

Soft credits (S4) are reflected in the acceptance of overdrafts, unpaid bills and non-enforcement of repayment arrangements with routine postponement and rescheduling of debt. Often the most prominent clubs enjoy very soft forms of credit (Ascari & Gagnepain, 2006).

Soft investments (S5) exist, for instance, when the government or other sponsors pay for a part, or perhaps all, of the costs when clubs build new stadia or other revenue-boosting infrastructure – without getting any substantial direct or indirect economic gain in return.

Finally, **soft accounting (S6)** takes the form of discretionary, and even illegal, praxis, with the purpose of bypassing rules and creative fulfillment of legal conditions and credit criteria to fool the creditors. This is often accepted or even, at least in Italian cases, encouraged by the government which has also in some cases changed legislation to facilitate softer accounting (Foot, 2006). A recent study shows that the introduction of the UEFA Financial Fair Play rules has been followed by a reduction in the quality of financial statements of European football clubs (Dimitropoulos, 2015); the employment of earnings management, conditional accounting conservatism and auditor switching are used as indicators for accounting quality, and a study of 84 clubs for a four-year period (2009–12) showed a decline in accounting quality in all three dimensions. Massaging of accounting is seemingly applied as a means to avoid FFP-induced penalties without changing behaviour and actual financial outcome.

According to Kornai, the soft budget constraints syndrome is an effect of vertical relationships between the state and economic micro-organizations. This reflects his primary focus on socialist and post-socialist economies. As a broader interpretation, a soft budget phenomenon can be said to reflect a relationship between an organization and its environment (Kornai et al., 2003).

In the application of the soft budget constraint concept in the context of this chapter, the perspective is widened. The focus on vertical relations characteristic of a classical supporter–supported relationship is stretched to grasp a more complex situation where many types of stakeholders – not only public supporters, but also private investors, creditors or alike – in a firm are perceived by the firm as potential supporters, whereby expectations of *ex post* support can grow even though a vertical supporter–supported relationship does not exist *ex ante* in a formal sense (see Storm & Nielsen, 2012).

In the classical case, the organization experiencing soft budget constraints has an important societal role that serves or affects a large number of people. This has the effect that the supporter considers the organization as 'too big to fail', which translates into expectations of *ex post* support. Many European professional team sport clubs are similarly seen as 'too big to fail' by their stakeholders.

By taking such an approach, it becomes possible to understand the paradox of European football. Several stakeholders, private and public, play from time to time a role as supporters of their respective clubs, thus establishing the conditions for development of the SBC syndrome in a sector normally perceived as capitalist and embedded in a horizontal environment but instead functioning as a supported firm in a vertically organized sector.

Storm and Nielsen (2012) argue that the emergence and institutionalization of the soft budget constraints syndrome in European football are due to two main factors: 1) the institutional mechanism of the European football market, and 2) the specific emotional logic of sport focused on winning. We will touch upon these two in turn below.

Institutions and social and emotional attachments

The institutional framework regarding competitions is part of the reason for the existence of soft budget constraints in European professional football. The severe financial problems are at least partly due to the ruining conditions of competition in the European league structures enforced by: a) the open league structure; b) the unequal distribution of the league revenue; c) growing inequality between the first and second divisions in the domestic leagues; and d) an additional exogenous prize (e.g. participation in international competitions) awarded to the winner of the domestic championship (Dietl, Franck & Lang, 2008).

The problem of open leagues is well recognized in the sports economic literature. It represents a threat that pushes the (lower performing) clubs to invest in player talent in order to avoid relegation, which in turn exclude the clubs from the high revenues in the best league(s). For clubs at the higher end of the sporting ladder, the challenge of staying in the top positions often induces investment in players. This is in order to remain competitive in relation to lower level performing clubs. In addition, the existence of an exogenous prize – for example in the form of participation in the Champions League with promises of a significant hike in income – provides further incentives for investment by the top-level clubs.

According to Dietl et al. (2008), polarization between the clubs within and between leagues increases clubs' willingness to gamble on success. A 'bidding to bankrupt', 'zombie'[3] sporting arms race on players is the result, thus increasing the risk of deficits among the majority. In expectation of *ex post* support, weak performances – or a threat of relegation – are not met with reduced costs, but the opposite.

Such institutional mechanisms for the football market certainly create problems for the clubs. However, without the existence of significant softness this could not continue. It would break down the entire sector.

The soft budget constraints approach helps to explain how the sector prevails despite growing debt and deficits. Or put differently, if the clubs in general were facing hard budget constraints – with the consequences of failure when gambling on success in the sporting arms race – they would very likely curb their expenses, thus finding their position in the league hierarchy with (at least) a break-even budget constraint. Their persistent overspending indicates the softening of budget constraints.

A second main factor contributing to the syndrome is social and emotional attachments to sport. Football clubs are often markers of identity in their respective localities, not only for hardcore fans but also for citizens, in general, and politicians. The effects are often significant, because the clubs serve as a common flagship of reference and branding in the local context. This provides clubs with enough resources to counter the threat of collapse, which is significant due to the ruining conditions of competition in the sector.

The prestige attached to being part of European football also contributes to explaining the high survival rate of clubs. Some investors are attracted to the sector because they see a professional team sports club as a kind of consumer good or because it puts them in the spotlight of one the most media exposed popular sports. This constitutes another type of identity making, which in turn softens budget constraints for the clubs.

Case study 11.1: Soft budget constraints and rescue operations in Spain

This soft budget constraint syndrome is more entrenched among football clubs in Spain than in any other European country. In Spain, the popularity of football has seen many instances of rescue operations aimed at assisting clubs that are close to collapse.

For example, in 1985 public authorities poured in public subsidies in order to help Spanish League clubs, which had debts then exceeding €124 million. A few years later, in 1992, when Spanish clubs once again had stacked up debt, a sum of €192 million owed to the government was cancelled (Barajas & Rodríguez, 2010).

In addition, local Spanish governments frequently help to remove the link between profits and survival, which according to the soft budget constraints approach is a prime indicator of softness. According to Barajas and Rodríguez (2010), regional authorities sponsor the local clubs or buy their stocks to help them. Furthermore, there are examples of local city councils that have bought stadiums from clubs at above market prices. In addition, it is not uncommon to see local government renting their stadiums out at subsidized prices.

In total, the willingness to support the Spanish football clubs, either by state cancellation of debts or by local govermental support, adds to the impression that Spanish clubs are more or less able to survive even the greatest losses. Should the clubs be unable to make it on their own, external stakeholder organizations step in with the needed *ex ante* financial support.

In response to a question asked in the Spanish parliament in July 2013, the government was obliged to disclose the amount of unpaid tax owed by professional football clubs in the country's top two divisions. The sum was a staggering €663 million (*The Independent*, 2013). This should be seen in the context of the benefits from a European Union bailout potentially worth as much as €100 billion and a government plan the year before for an amnesty on football club debt to the state, which was blocked by Germany (EU Observer, 2012).

The amount of unpaid tax did not include the tax debts of four clubs that were exempt because they were not obliged to reconstitute themselves as public limited companies and could continue to be owned by their members. Those four clubs were Real Madrid and Barcelona, who also take around 50% of La Liga's total television revenue for themselves, as well as Athletic Bilbao and Osasuna.

However, the privileged status of the four exempted clubs is under threat from a European Commission investigation. The European Commission has opened three distinct in-depth investigations to verify whether various public support measures in favour of seven Spanish clubs, including Real Madrid and Barcelona, are in line with European Union state aid rules (European Commission, 2013).

Case study 11.2: Soft pricing and subsidies in Denmark – The case of Viborg F.F.

The evidence presented above indicates that softness mainly prevails in the largest European Leagues. However, smaller European football nations also face softness of budget constraints. The case of Viborg F.F., a Danish professional football club currently playing in the best Danish league, shows how subsidies through soft pricing (S1) can be used to soften the budget constraints of football clubs.

In 2008, Viborg F.F. was relegated to the second tier of Danish football and found itself in financial difficulties shortly after. In 2010, the club was close to collapse. The football club is located in a municipality that prides itself on the achievements of its football and handball teams. The clubs play an important role as a marker of local identity. In addition, in the part of Denmark where Viborg is located, there is an intense competition among second tier cities to prevail in the Superliga, i.e. the top division of Danish football.

Relegation and subsequent deficits implied the threat of a decisive setback in this respect in case of reduced investment in player talent in order to reduce the deficit. In 2010, the football club needed an injection of a significant amount of cash (around 2.5 million DKKr) to balance the books.

Local politicians were eager to find a way to help the club. The dynamic mayor was instrumental in developing and implementing a solution. This happened in a way which was by Danish standards sophisticated. It took the form of indirect subsidies following two interconnected steps:

- Viborg municipality sold the naming rights of the municipal stadium to Viborg F.F. for a period of five years at a price of 50,000 DKKr/year.
- Viborg F.F. then resold the naming rights to the municipal energy company, Energy Viborg (owned 100% by Viborg municipality) for 3 million DKKr for a period of three years.

The transactions did the trick and Viborg F.F. received the support it needed. This happened through an indirect transfer of taxpayer money. Energy Viborg also subsequently suffered from the costly acquisition of the sponsorship.

No doubt, the mayor and his political allies would have preferred a lack of publicity regarding the transactions but this did not happen. Political opponents in the municipal council and among the board of directors of Energy Viborg exposed the deal in the media and sought clarification of its legality. In 2014, the Danish state administration concluded that the deal was a conscious attempt to subsidize a private business by illegal means.

Conclusion and further perspectives

European professional team sports suffer from soft budget constraint syndrome. The Financial Fair Play (FFP) initiative of UEFA reflects a political awareness of the negative impacts on the management of clubs and the unfair effect on the terms of competition between clubs.

The FFP is designed to institutionalize a break-even constraint, which will make it harder, and in the long run impossible, to operate with deficits and soft budget constraints (Franck, 2013; Pieper, this volume). Initial data showing the effects on the clubs in the English Premier League indicate that FFP has the desired effect (Cohen, 2015). Perhaps soft budget constraints are a thing of the past or at least a phenomenon of declining importance.

There are many reasons why this is hardly the case. UEFA has experienced significant opposition and has diluted some of its regulation in response. Further, the long-term effects are uncertain. In addition, human imagination is borderless and successful attempts to counteract the intended effects of regulation will no doubt dampen the effects.

As far as the prevalence of soft budgets, a comparison with the North American major leagues may be useful. Storm and Nielsen (2015) identify similarities between European and North American professional team sports when seen through the prism of the soft budget constraint theory.

The study shows that expectations of rescue in case of financial trouble and the associated effects on firm level efficiency do not prevail in the USA and Canada. However, American major leagues experience softness of budgets in ways that are remarkably similar to the European experience and with a similar distortion of resource allocation. North American leagues receive *ex ante* support which is in many ways similar to the *ex post* support representing the six types of softness.

Recommended further reading

The following contributions are essential for understanding the soft budget constraint approach and how it can be applied in order to understand professional team sports:

Andreff, W. (2015). Governance of professional team sports clubs: agency problem and soft budget constraint. In W. Andreff (Ed.), *Disequilibrium Sport Economics: Competitive Imbalance and Budget Constraints*. Cheltenham: Edward Elgar.

Franck, E. (2013). Financial Fair Play in European Club Football: What is it all about? *International Journal of Sport Finance*, 9 (3), 193–217.

Storm, R. K., & Nielsen, K. (2015). Soft budget constraints in European and US leagues – similarities and differences. In W. Andreff (Ed.), *Disequilibrium Sport Economics: Competitive Imbalance and Budget Constraints*, 151–171. Cheltenham: Edward Elgar.

Notes

1   This section is an elaboration of (smaller parts of) Storm and Nielsen (2012).
2   http://www.bbc.co.uk/sport/football/31391778
3   See Franck (2013).

References

Andreff, W. (2007). French football: A financial crisis rooted in weak governance. *Journal of Sports Economics*, 8 (6), 652–661.

Andreff, W. (2011). Some comparative economics of the organization of sports: Competition and regulation in North American vs. European professional team sports leagues. *European Journal of Comparative Economics*, 8 (1), 3–27.

Ascari, G. & Gagnepain, P. (2006). Spanish football. *Journal of Sports Economics*, 7, 76–89.

Barajas, A. & Rodríguez, P. (2010). Spanish football clubs' finances: Crisis and player salaries. *International Journal of Sport Finance*, 5, 52–66.

Baroncelli, A. & Lago, U. (2006). Italian football. *Journal of Sports Economics*, 7, 13–28.

Beech, J., Horsman, S., & Magraw, J. (2008). *The circumstances in which English clubs become insolvent.* Coventry: Coventry University.

Boscá, J. E., Liern, V., Martínez, A., & Sala, R. (2008). The Spanish football crisis. *European Sport Management Quarterly*, 8, 165–177.

Buraimo, B., Simmons, R., & Szymanski, S. (2006). English football. *Journal of Sports Economics*, 7, 29–46.

Cohen D. (2015). Premier League clubs turn loss into profit as fair play rules kick in. *The Guardian*, 30 April. http://www.theguardian.com/football/2015/apr/29/premier-league-clubs-profit-fair-play

Deloitte (2011). *Annual Review of Football Finance: National Interest.* Manchester: Sport Business Group at Deloitte.

Dietl, H. M., Franck, E., & Lang, M. (2008). Overinvestment in team sports leagues: A contest theory model. *Scottish Journal of Political Economy*, 55, 353–368.

Dimitropoulos, P. (2015). The New UEFA Club Licensing Regulations and the Quality of Financial Information: Evidence from European Football Clubs, *Research Paper*, University of the Peloponese.

Dobson, S. & Goddard, J. (2001). *The economics of football.* Cambridge: Cambridge University Press.

EU Observer (2012). Spain's football clubs cause stir in Germany. 16 March. https://euobserver.com/economic/115620

European Commission (2013). State aid: Commission opens in-depth investigation into public funding of certain Spanish professional football clubs. *Press release*, 18 December, available at http://europa.eu/rapid/press-release_IP-13-1287_en.htm.

Foot, J. (2006). *Calcio: A History of Italian Football.* London: Fourth Estate.

Fort, R. (2000). European and North American sports differences (?). *Scottish Journal of Political Economy*, 47, 431–455.

Franck, E. (2013). Financial Fair Play in European club football: What is it all about?, *International Journal of Sport Finance*, 9 (3), 193–217.

Garcia, J. & Rodriguez, P. (2003). From sports clubs to stock companies: The financial structure of football in Spain, 1992–2001. *European Sport Management Quarterly*, 3, 253–269.

Grant, W. (2007). An analytical framework for a political economy of football. *British Politics*, 2, 69–90.

Garcia-del Barrio, P. & Szymanski, S. (2009). Goal! Profit maximization and win maximization in football leagues. *Review of Industrial Organization*, 34, 45–68.

Hamil, S., Morrow, S., Idle, C., Rossi, G., & Faccendini, S. (2010). The governance and regulation of Italian Football. *Soccer & Society*, 11, 373–413.

Hamil, S. & Walters, G. (2010). Financial performance in English professional football: 'an inconvenient truth'. *Soccer & Society*, 11, 354–372.

Horne, J. (2006). *Sport in Consumer Culture.* New York: Palgrave Macmillan.

Kornai, J. (1980). *Economics of Shortage: Volume A.* Amsterdam: North Holland.

Kornai, J. (1986). The soft budget constraint. *KYKLOS*, 39, 3–30.

Kornai, J. (2001). Hardening the budget constraint: The experience of the post-socialist countries. *European Economic Review*, 45, 1573–1599.

Kornai, J., Maskin, E., & Roland, G. (2003). Understanding the soft budget constraint. *Journal of Economic Literature*, 41, 1095–1136.

Kuper, S. & Szymanski, S. (2009). *Soccernomics: Why England Loses, Why Germany and Brazil Win, and Why the US, Japan, Australia, Turkey – and Even Iraq – are Destined to Become the Kings of the World's Most Popular Sport*. New York: Nation Books.

Lago, U., Simmons, R., & Szymanski, S. (2006). The financial crisis in European football: An introduction. *Journal of Sports Economics*, 7, 3–12.

Morrow, S. (2006). Impression management in football club financial reporting. *International Journal of Sport Finance*, 1, 96–108.

Neale, W. C. (1964). The peculiar economics of professional sports. *Quarterly Journal of Economics*, 78, 1–14.

Porter, M. E. & Karmer, M. R. (2011). Creating shared value. *Harvard Business Review*, January/February, 89 (1/2), 62–77.

Sandy, R., Sloane, P. J., & Rosentraub, M. S. (2004). *The economics of sport: An international perspective*. Hampshire: Palgrave Macmillan.

Sloane, P. J. (1980). *Sport in the Market?: The Economic Causes and Consequences of the 'Packer Revolution'*. London: The Institute of Economic Affairs, Paisley College of Technology.

Simon, H. A. (1979). Rational decision making in business organizations. *The American Economic Review*, 69 (4), 493–513.

Storm, R. K. (2010). Professional team sports clubs and profits: An irreconcilable combination? In U.Wagner, R. K. Storm, & J. Hoberman (Eds.), *Observing Sport: Modern System Theoretical Approaches*, 103–130. Schorndorf: Hofmann Verlag.

Storm, R. K. and Nielsen, K. (2012). Soft budget constraints in professional football, *European Sport Management Quarterly*, 12 (2), 183–201.

Storm, R. K., & Nielsen, K. (2015). Soft budget constraints in European and US leagues – similarities and differences. In W. Andreff (Ed.), *Disequilibrium Sport Economics: Competitive Imbalance and Budget Constraints*, 151–171. Cheltenham: Edward Elgar.

Szymanski, S. (2009). The reassuring stability of football capitalism. Retrieved from http://www.play thegame.org/uploads/media/Stefan_Szymanski-The_Reassuring_stability_of_Football_Capitalism.pdf

Szymanski, S. & Kuypers, T. (2000). *Winners and losers: The Business Strategy of Professional Football*. London: Penguin Books.

Szymanski, S. & Smith, R. (1997). The English football industry: Profit, performance and industrial structure. *International Review of Applied Economics*, 11, 135–153.

Szymanski, S. & Zimbalist, A. S. (2006). *National Pastime: How Americans Play Baseball and the Rest of the World Plays Soccer*. Washington D.C.: Brookings Instition Press.

The Independent (2013). How tax break gives Real Madrid and Barcelona an unfair edge. http://www.independent.co.uk/sport/football/european/how-tax-break-gives-real-madrid-and-barcelona-an-unfair-edge-8749146.html

UEFA (2010). 'European Club Football Landscape'. Club Licensing Benchmarking Report.UEFA.

Vrooman, J. (2000). The economics of American sport leagues. *Scottish Journal of Political Economy*, 47 (4), 364–398.

FINANCIAL FAIR PLAY IN EUROPEAN FOOTBALL

JAN PIEPER

The need for regulation in European Club Football

According to the UEFA Benchmarking Report for the financial year 2011, the revenues of 700+ European top division clubs had grown by an average yearly rate of 5.6% in the preceding five years to a record total of €13.2bn. The 26 European top divisions with the biggest aggregate revenues had grown by 42% in five years (UEFA, 2013). While club revenues fluctuate more in the 27 mid and smaller top divisions, their aggregate revenues still increased by 29% in the same period, 2007 to 2011. The football industry was booming everywhere in Europe despite the challenging economic climate.

In the same period, the same clubs' aggregate net losses had almost tripled from €0.6bn to €1.7bn: 38% of clubs reported negative net equity facing a situation with debts larger than reported assets in the financial year 2011 and 45 of the 53 European top divisions reported aggregate net losses (UEFA, 2013).

The reason for this genuine paradox of exploding losses despite exploding revenues in football is that clubs spent more than they could reasonably afford on players. The clubs' cost base increased at an even faster rate than their revenues, with employee and net transfer costs growing particularly fast. Wages alone increased by 38% from €6.2bn to almost €8.6bn between 2007 and 2011. The key ratio impacting the clubs' bottom-line results, the combined employee and net transfer costs to revenue ratio, increased from 62% to 71%. As the revenue increase did not cover the increase in combined employee and transfer costs, clubs accumulated losses.

The shared perception of club representatives, players, leagues and national associations, that these developments posed an increasing threat to the financial stability and long-term viability of the entire European football system, led UEFA to introduce the UEFA Club Licensing and Financial Fair Play Regulations (FFP regulations) in 2011.

What the FFP regulations are about

The FFP regulations are an enhancement of the Club Licensing System introduced at the start of the 2004/05 season. To be admitted to the UEFA club competitions (Champions League and Europa League) each club has to meet a series of defined sporting, infrastructural, personnel, legal and financial quality standards. The new FFP regulations cover additional financial requirements with the key goal to enforce more financial discipline in club football and to contain the clubs' inflationary spending on salaries and transfer fees.

The main pillar of the FFP regulations is the 'break-even requirement'.[1] By and large, this new rule requires clubs to live within their own financial means. More specifically, clubs comply with the break-even requirement if their 'relevant expenses'[2] do not exceed their 'relevant income'[3] to by more than the 'acceptable deviation'[4] of €5mn in one so-called 'monitoring period' covering initially two and later three consecutive reporting periods combined.[5] Clubs which break their budget in the one reporting period carry over a break-even deficit to the next reporting period(s), when the total result for the monitoring period is not allowed to exceed the 'acceptable deviation'. On top of the €5mn, the 'acceptable deviation' can currently[6] go up to a level of €45mn, provided that equity participants are willing to inject the respective funds. To monitor and enforce the FFP regulations, UEFA has installed a new body of independent legal and financial experts, the Club Financial Control Body (CFCB). The severest sanction is exclusion from the UEFA club competitions. Other sanctions include fines, the withholding of prize money, and player transfer bans.

The definitions of relevant income and relevant expenses imply that clubs have to operate with a cap on payroll injections under the new FFP regulations. Both public and private benefactors are no longer able to rescue a club for licensing purposes if the club overinvested in salaries and transfers with the result that relevant expenses exceed relevant income by more than the 'total acceptable deviation'. To promote investments in stadia, youth academies and community projects, such expenditures do not count as relevant expenses and are therefore excluded from the break-even calculation.

Why clubs overinvest in playing strength

Two basic factors shape the clubs' incentives to excessively invest in playing strength.[7] First, the tendency to overinvest is immanent in the contest structure of interlinked national and international club football competitions. Second, many clubs operate with what Kornai (1980a, 1980b, 1986) termed soft budget constraints, that is, they can chronically overspend without the same threat of dissolution as firms in other industries.

The contest structure of football competitions

Clubs' tendency to invest in playing strength beyond the point where marginal investment costs equal marginal investment returns is immanent in the rank-ordered contests of all professional team sports leagues (Alchian and Demsetz, 1972). If, for example, club *A* moves up in rank by developing and hiring additional playing skills, all overtaken clubs inevitably move down in rank *ceteris paribus*. The now higher ranked club *A* will likely increase its revenues *ceteris paribus* because club revenues (i.e., prize money, broadcasting, sponsoring, gate attendance and merchandise) are largely rank-dependent. At the same time, club *A* induces a negative externality on the overtaken clubs as they now generate less revenue. Thus, rank-ordered contests are essentially zero-sum games, in which each club hopes to improve its rank by means of additional investments in playing strength. However, even if 'money scores goals' and 'goals generate revenue' *ceteris paribus*, the clubs' individual winning probabilities do not change if all clubs invest more.

In a similar vein, Akerlof (1976) speaks of rat races in which many participants, the rats, compete for a fixed price, the cheese. The faster each rat is running, the higher are its chances of winning the cheese and the more calories it will burn, that is, the more it will invest. As only the fastest rats will win the cheese, all other rats will not be able to recuperate their investments (calories). In the rat race of football, even profit-maximizing clubs tend to dissipate resources by systematically overinvesting in playing strength.[8] Win-maximizing clubs, as most European football clubs are best described as, are even more likely to over-invest.[9] In an environment where clubs tend to spend as much as possible on playing strength to be as successful as possible on the pitch, spending power is the key driver of competitive advantage.[10] Any profit requirement is in fact a handicap in this specific spending power game because profits limit the maximum amount of funds to be channeled into playing strength.

Both increased commercialization and various regulatory changes leading to the current format of competition in European football have intensified the clubs' incentives to overinvest in playing strength.[11] The practices of seeding and group stages in the Champions League, for example, have reduced the importance of coincidence. Investment incentives become more high-powered if money buys success with a higher probability, *ceteris paribus*. The strong growth of revenues in the UEFA Champions League and the applied distribution scheme strongly favoring sportive success increase revenue differentials between positions in the national championship races and create genuine jackpots for the winners of the qualification slots. Player market deregulations like the Bosman ruling of 1995 made by the European Court of Justice have also contributed to the overinvestment problem as one obvious effect is again a stronger relationship between payrolls and sportive success.

In conclusion, the tendency in European club football to overinvest is, to some extent, 'normal'. While even rational and profit-maximizing clubs tend to overinvest, win-maximizing clubs are even more likely to engage in such dissipation of revenues. The theoretical arguments, however, are insufficient to explain the extreme level of overinvestment that has brought many clubs into a situation of technical bankruptcy.

Soft budget constraints and their inefficient side-effects

To better explain the mechanisms that led to the alarming dimension of club losses in European football, several authors (Andreff, 2007, 2011; Storm, 2012; Storm & Nielsen, 2012; Franck, 2014) have applied the concept of soft budget constraints (Kornai, 1980a, 1980b, 1986; Kornai, Maskin, & Roland 2003). Hungarian economist János Kornai originally developed the concept as a means to understand the chronic inefficiency of loss-making firms in socialist economies which were repeatedly bailed out by public authorities.

Very briefly, the economic logic of soft budget constraints in football can be stated as follows. In a case where a club faces a deficit very often some form of 'supporting organization' (Kornai et al., 2003, p. 5) – either the state or a private benefactor – steps in with a sufficiently high probability and relieves the club of the pressure to 'cover its expenditures out of its initial endowment and revenue' (Kornai et al., 2003, p. 4). As a consequence, clubs with soft budget constraints can chronically overspend without the same threat of dissolution as firms in other industries.[12]

It surely makes a difference whether the state (and thus ultimately the taxpayers) or private benefactors (i.e., individual equity participants and/or related parties) are 'funding footballers' Porsches' (Kuper, 2009). Unlike the state, private benefactors are unlikely to make uninvolved citizens liable for their football investments. Intuitively, one might think that private benefactors should therefore be free to spend their money as they please. As long as 'the show goes on'[13] and as long as the money injected does not originate from illegal activities, everything should be fine. The real problem, however, is that soft budget constraints and the resulting expectation to be bailed out *ex post* create several seriously distorted incentives for decision-makers in football clubs, regardless of whether both public and private money are spent.[14]

Runaway demand for talent and escalating player costs

If clubs operate with soft budget constraints, their demand for talented players becomes price-inelastic. Clubs with very soft budget constraints are willing to pay basically any price for the best players in their pursuit to outperform their rivals on the pitch. For example, in their first 14 months as new club owners, Roman Abramovich spent €283.6mn at Chelsea, Sheikh Mansour spent €234.3mn at Manchester City and the Qatar Investment Authority spent €212.6mn at Paris Saint-Germain (Bairner, 2012). These figures clearly indicate very soft budget constraints.

While demand increases, the supply of talented players is limited because the very definition of talent is the capacity of a player to be better than most others (Frank and Bernanke, 2004). Demand for talented players increasingly exceeds the limited supply of talented players as soft budget constraints spread throughout the football industry. As a consequence, the wages and transfer fees of a limited number of talented players reach levels that are totally unsustainable without systematic new money injections.

Risk escalation and managerial negligence

Another consequence of the declining price-elasticity of football clubs operating with soft budget constraints is risk-escalation. Instead of responsible investment decisions to balance accounts, club managers are tempted to take excessive risks and gamble on success. The emergence of such managerial moral hazard behaviour in environments with soft budget constraints is a standard result that has been studied in different contexts. A prominent example is the 'too big to fail' problem in the finance sector, where managers are inclined to take excessive risks because they can reliably expect to be bailed out *ex post* (e.g. Stern & Feldman, 2004). Franck and Lang (2014) have formally shown that, as soon as the option to be bailed out with a certain probability is introduced, football club managers take significantly more risk in their investment decisions.

Moreover, the absence of a 'dead-serious' budget constraint can lead to managerial negligence. As the existence of the club is not at stake, decision-makers do not invest enough of their own time and energy to sort out bad projects and develop good projects. 'Money coming like manna' (Kornai, 1986, p. 12) tends to trigger waste and undermine the club managers' sense of business responsibility.

Rent-seeking instead of 'real' business development

Managers of clubs with soft budget constraints face strong incentives to win and maintain the favour of their benefactor. As such rent-seeking behaviour is systematically rewarded in organizations with soft budget constraints, their managers invest less effort in building a sustainable competitive advantage by 'improving quality, cutting costs, introducing new products or new processes' (Kornai, 1986, p.10). To the extent that such efforts of 'real' business development are more 'painful' for a club manager than asking for new money injections to compensate for unfavourable developments, clubs with soft budget constraints are likely to be less innovative and their managers less entrepreneurial – at least in the long-run.

Crowding out clubs with hard budget constraints

Clubs operating with hard budget constraints are negatively affected by the spread of soft budget constraints in the football industry. If a few clubs with soft budget constraints inflate player market prices, all other clubs need to increase their expenditures just to maintain a given level of playing strength. To a certain limited extent, clubs with hard budget constraints may be able to compensate for their lack of spending power by 'better club management'. Eventually, however, they will be less competitive than their rivals with soft budget constraints and almost unlimited spending power.

As a consequence, clubs with hard budget constraints face only two options: either they accept sportive decline or they change sides and start gambling on success, hoping to be rescued by external money injections if the gamble goes wrong. Taking into account that sportive decline generates substantial disutility both for decision-makers and fans of the clubs, the soft budget constraints of some clubs are likely to be contagious in the sense that they intensify the incentives of all other clubs to overspend as well. Thus, soft budget constraints tend to crowd out business models which are based on more sustainable and forward-looking management attitudes.

The state's incentives to soften the budget constraints of football clubs and the effects of the FFP Regulations

Rescue measures taken by the state which soften the budget constraints of football clubs usually consist of the toleration or write-off of tax debts and overdue payables, the extension of credit lines through state controlled banks, the provision of public infrastructure below cost, inflated sponsorship deals with state controlled or state dependent firms etc.[15]

The case of Spain provides a prominent example of professional clubs operating with very soft budget constraints due to the constant failure of the state to enforce its tax laws. As of September 2012, Spanish professional football clubs owed €750mn in taxes and €600mn in social security to the Spanish state and therefore ultimately to the Spanish taxpayer (Van Rompuy, 2012).

Franck (2014) argues that one motive for a state to bail out overspending clubs is to avoid the loss of previous public investments in those clubs. The problem is that each bailout reduces the credibility of the state's commitment not to bail out overspending clubs in the future.

Each further bailout cultivates a mentality among clubs to carelessly overspend. Van Rompuy (2012) gives an example to illustrate this mentality among Spanish clubs:

> The Scottish club Rangers was forced into administration after running up £9 million in unpaid taxes. In Spain, the enormous tax debt of €155 million proved no barrier to Atlético Madrid to buy the top striker Falcao for a club record deal of €40 million in August 2011. (p. 2)

As discussed by Franck (2014), there is a related motive for the state to bail out overspending clubs. A rational political decision-maker must weigh the total bailout costs against the collateral damage to the local economy if the club was actually shut down. In case of a shut-down, many supporters would be frustrated if they lost their joint object of identification. Employees of the club would lose their jobs. Suppliers would have to write off the club's due payables, which might cause further bankruptcies. The image of the city would deteriorate and potentially discourage investors etc.

Considering that past bailouts cultivate a mentality of careless overspending among the clubs, the total bailout costs are likely to grow geometrically year after year in expectation. In comparison to these 'endless' bailout costs, the one-time collateral damage of a club's shut-down should not be too hard to accept. Elected politicians, however, tend to ignore future bailout costs because their primary motivation is to keep their voters happy as long as they are in office. Future politicians are unlikely to stand up to the 'old' commitments of their predecessors. The consequence of comparing the costs of an isolated bailout with collateral damage instead of anticipating the entire progression of future bailout packages is straightforward: too many clubs are rescued too often by the state.

In the case of state-funded bailouts, EU state aid law applies.[16] State aid law operates to restrict government manipulation of markets, limiting the extent to which public resources may be used to assist specific businesses or specific economic activities. This should mean that rival clubs, such as Real Madrid and Arsenal, which operate against each other on a variety of markets, as well as on the pitch, compete without illegitimate government help.

Despite the football industry's economic and international significance and repeated indications of pervasive abuse of public funds, the European Commission had delayed any real enforcement action until late 2013 when the Commission launched state aid investigations into high-profile football clubs in Spain, including Real Madrid and FC Barcelona. Although no final conclusions can be drawn so far, such a contentious, resource intensive and public step is clearly a negative signal for the clubs involved.

EU state aid law is largely compatible with the objectives of the FFP regulations: a club's financially sustainable business model under the FFP regulations would make bailouts with public funding redundant. Likewise, the FFP break-even requirement would be seriously undermined by lax state aid compliance. Thus, it is no surprise that the Commission and UEFA have publicly stated to act in close collaboration (European Commission, 2012). Both the Commission and UEFA emphasize their intention to put in place stronger market incentives, with government support not looked upon as a reliable safety net and route around FFP spending restrictions.

The Commission's reluctance to act decisively before 2013 indicates the uncomfortable nature of the investigations, which may not only be in conflict with Member State spending autonomy. Football is powerful, economically and culturally, in Member States and the EU, intensifying the political sensitivity. The link between communities and football is so deeply embedded in European society that the Commission seemingly lacked the willingness and strength to tackle the problem head on. In addition, in times of a challenging economic climate in Europe, the Commission was probably wary not to upset the commercial growth of professional football.

Regardless of how well state aid law and FFP regulations are complementarily enforceable, the FFP regulations certainly imply that a club's funding undergoes intense scrutiny, including from the media. An increased public awareness for state-funded club bailouts alone will reduce the tolerance level of taxpayers as well as clubs complying with the FFP regulations, especially if the state-supported clubs are renowned for excessive spending on star players. On top of enforceable sanctions, public pressure is likely to push the regime towards less state-funded bailouts and thus more financial discipline among the clubs.

The incentives of private benefactors to soften the budget constraints of football clubs and the effects of the FFP Regulations

Private benefactors who cover the losses and liquidity shortfalls of their clubs year after year and thereby create soft budget constraints are a common phenomenon in European club football. According to the UEFA benchmarking report, the 700+ European top division clubs reported net financing cash inflows of €1.5bn from club owners and related parties in the financial year 2012.

Prominent examples of such benefactors are Roman Abramovich (see Case study 12.2) and Sheikh Mansour, who had already spent around the same amount in the four years up to 2012 at Manchester City (Conn, 2012b), winner of the Premier League Championship in 2011/2012. In Italy, Massimo Moratti had spent around €1bn by 2012 paying the open bills of Inter Milan year after year, while Silvio Berlusconi had injected around half of this sum at AC Milan (Iaria, 2012).

Losing money in football can be rational for a private benefactor (or a related party) once and even on a repeated basis if the bailout costs are outweighed by certain rewards to the private benefactor. To better understand the specific incentives of private benefactors to inject money in a football club, Franck (2015) suggests a distinction between two paradigmatic types of private benefactors is helpful. There are 'true investors' who are looking for a competitive financial return and there are 'pure success-seekers' who are willing to pay for success *per se*. Both types differ systematically not only with regard to their incentives but also with regard to how they are affected by the new FFP regulations.

Before going into detail, it is important to note that for both types, true investors and pure success-seekers, the governance structure of 'their' club plays a crucial role. The club governance structure largely determines how well the intended rewards can be managed and captured.[17] Clubs governed as privately owned firms are clearly superior in attracting private benefactors in comparison to clubs governed as members' associations as well as clubs governed as stock corporations with dispersed public ownership.[18] The key explanation is that ownership automatically allocates residual control to the owner. Residual control rights are not only important to make and enforce internal decisions but also to be associated with those decisions and resultant sportive success in the public perception.[19] Thus, private benefactors have a strong incentive to also be club owners.

The incentives of true investors to soften the budget constraints of football clubs and the effects of the FFP Regulations

True investors are looking for a competitive financial return on their investment in a football club.[20] A football club and the public attention that comes with its sportive success may be an attractive platform from which to manage and capture positive financial spillovers to other businesses. Probably the most common form of such spillovers is sponsoring. A sponsor pays for clearly specified sponsoring rights and services such as the right to name the stadium, the right to place their logos on player shirts, the right of using players for promotion events etc. In return, a club's media exposure draws attention to the sponsor.[21]

Besides exposure, the sponsor also gains access to certain positive image attributes associated with the club.[22] The received 'units of exposure' and 'units of transferred image' constitute what the sponsor 'walks away with' when entering into a sponsorship agreement with a club. Of course, sponsorship agreements include also direct consumption opportunities for the sponsor, such as privileged access to the games etc. Such add-on benefits, however, can also be bought directly without any sponsorship agreement. Accordingly, there is no reason why a knowledgeable and well-informed sponsor should pay more for what he 'walks away with' in a particular football sponsorship than in any other deal offering comparable exposure and image transfer elsewhere in the market. Sponsorship contracts between a true investor and a club will be at 'fair market value'.[23]

The incentives of pure success-seekers to soften the budget constraints of football clubs and the effects of the FFP Regulations

Pure success-seekers do not care whether their investment in a football club pays off financially. Quite the opposite, they are willing to lose money.[24] To understand the motives of pure success-seekers at a very basic level, it suffices to assume that some people have a willingness to pay for success *per se*. A very wealthy individual dreaming of winning the Champions League with his football club more than anything else will be willing to spend a part of his wealth on the pursuit of this dream.

Rosen (1981) provides a possible additional motive for pure success-seekers to lose money in a football club. He argues that the utility derived from certain consumptive activities tends to increase more than proportionally with the quality of the consumed good or service. One important attribute of perceived quality is exclusivity. In professional sports, club ownership as a consumptive activity which only a few wealthy sportsmen can afford has a long tradition. The economic growth of the football industry in recent years has made club ownership an extremely exclusive object of consumption which ever fewer people can afford.

The phenomenon of positional competition/consumption (e.g. Frank, 2005) may provide another, related motive. Accordingly, the actual and potential benefactors of football clubs belong to certain peer groups, for example sheikhs from the Middle East, Russian oligarchs, political leaders of developing countries etc. Besides possible success-induced paybacks to their countries, enterprises etc., such individuals may derive additional personal utility from comparisons within their own peer group. Winning the Champions League (or the bid for the World Cup, the bid for the Olympics etc.) may become much more valuable precisely because the other members of the respective peer group (i.e., other sheiks, oligarchs or leaders of developing countries) have been outpaced.

As a rapid accumulation of the individual wealth necessary to buy a 'big' football club is only possible in economic environments with systematic market failures and regulatory deficits, huge wealth is often linked to social and political legitimacy deficits. Ownership of a football club and the public attention and admiration that come with its sportive success may produce exactly the kind of social and political legitimacy a (potential) club owner with a dubious background needs.

Under the new FFP regulations, fair market value contracts can, of course, be contingent on the sportive success of a club. If a club advances through the rounds of the Champions League, for example, its sponsors receive valuable additional 'units of public exposure' and additional 'units of transferred image'. The success-dependent remuneration scheme just has to be agreed upon *ex ante* as part of a fair market value contract. Pure success-seekers are not allowed any more, however, to inject money into a club's payroll in excess of the fair market value of the goods and services transacted with the club. All payments that contribute to a club's success without creating a fair market reward for the benefactor (or the related party) will be capped under the FFP regulations.

Expenditures in stadia, youth academies and community projects, on the contrary, are not subject to any regulatory limit. Such expenditures are explicitly excluded from break-even calculations.

A popular point of critique in this context is that the FFP payroll cap would 'freeze' the European club hierarchy and reduce the suspense of the club competitions because even the richest club benefactors are no longer able to challenge the dominant clubs by simply spending more money on players (e.g. Vöpel, 2011; Sass, 2012).

At first sight, it is a matter of perspective whether unlimited money injections of success-seeking benefactors actually contribute to more suspense in European football competitions. At the top of the European club hierarchy, FFP critics have a point: Chelsea and other clubs like Paris Saint-Germain (PSG) and Manchester City, backed by owners with very deep pockets, have increased the competitive pressures for the incumbent clubs like FC Barcelona, Real Madrid and Bayern Munich in recent years. However, in the case of PSG, for example, formerly close rivals from Lyon, Marseille or Bordeaux would certainly reject the argument that PSG's benefactor, Qatar Investment Authority, has contributed to more suspense in the French championship race. At the national level, PSG has become literally unbeatable.

Thus, there is anecdotal evidence both for and against the critics' claim that the FFP regulations 'freeze' the European club hierarchy. On closer examination, however, it is clear that the critics' claim is unfounded.[25] In the spending power game of football, small market clubs are very unlikely to systematically attract more funding than big market clubs and thereby increase their relative spending power to seriously challenge big market clubs. Generally and regardless of their true underlying motives, pure success-seekers will strictly prefer to inject money into those clubs with the highest winning probabilities available.

Without external money injections, a club's winning probability is determined by its market potential, that is, the exogenous upper bound to what 'good club management' and 'good luck' can mobilize. It is not important whether a club's market potential is constant over longer periods of time. The crucial point is that the local, regional, national and league-specific determinants of market potential cannot be changed by the club. Accordingly, 'big market clubs' beat 'small market clubs' in expectation. There is simply no compelling reason to assume that small market clubs are systematically better managed and luckier than big market clubs. Pure success-seekers will pick the biggest club available, making them even more dominant and thus reducing the suspense of the competitions.

Under the new FFP regulations, the income generated through money injections of true investors at fair market value are a component of the club's market potential and therefore allowed. Payroll injections by pure success-seekers, however, clearly increase a club's spending power on top of its market potential. By capping the payroll injections of pure success-seekers, the FFP regulations constrain this immanent 'money comes to money' mechanism.

Thus, although it is not even a declared objective, the new hard budget constraints actually prevent a further 'freezing' of the European club hierarchy. The FFP regulations contribute to more (not less) suspense. Still, competitive pressures for all clubs to open their doors for private benefactors and change their governance structures if necessary and possible are likely to remain strong.[26]

Do the FFP regulations bite?

Of course, any evaluation of the FFP regulations is bound to be preliminary at the moment. To date, data are available on the first two FFP monitoring periods.Of all clubs applying for a licence to participate in the UEFA club competitions in the 2013/14 season (i.e., the first FFP monitoring period covering the initial two reporting periods 2012 and 2013), 18 clubs were in danger of not complying with the FFP break-even requirement and therefore investigated by the CFCB. All nine clubs allegedly in breach of the break-even requirements eventually agreed to settlements with the CFCB.[27] Sanctions ranged from payroll restrictions to squad size limits in UEFA club competitions and fines. The highest fines were those for PSG and Manchester City. Both clubs agreed to pay €60mn each (€40mn of which are subject to the clubs' fulfilment of several conditions imposed by the CFCB).

In the 2014/15 season (i.e., the second FFP monitoring period covering the three reporting periods 2012, 2013 and 2014), the CFCB reached settlement agreements with 14 clubs allegedly in breach of the break-even requirement. Sanctions again ranged from payroll restrictions to squad size limits in the UEFA club competitions and fines. The two highest fines were those imposed on FC Internazionale (€20mn, €14mn of which is conditional) and AS Monaco (€13mn, €10mn of which is conditional).

To some observers these sanctions may appear too soft to fundamentally change clubs' spending behavior, especially when bearing in mind the enormous wealth of many clubs' private benefactors. However, the development of the annual growth rates in wages and revenues of the 700+ European top division clubs from 2008 to 2013 clearly indicates that the FFP regulations and the sanctions that follow non-compliance influence clubs' spending behavior as intended (see Table 12.1). Annual wage growth had slowed down from 14.0% in 2008 to 4.3% in 2013. For the first time in recent years, revenues increased by a faster rate (6.7%) than wages (4.3%) in 2013.

Moreover, in 2013 clubs reported positive aggregate operating results[28] for the first time since 2008 (see Figure 12.1). Since 2012, a clear downward trend in the aggregate losses has been apparent. Of course, it remains to be seen if the data for the following years will confirm this development.

Table 12.1   Annual growth rates for the 700+ top division clubs

Year	Wages	Revenues
2008	14.0%	7.3%
2009	6.0%	3.2%
2010	9.1%	9.0%
2011	5.2%	3.2%
2012	6.9%	6.7%
2013	4.3%	6.7%

Source: Franck (2015)

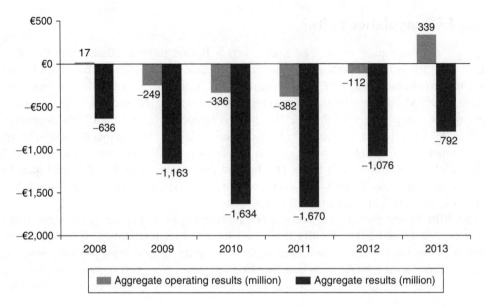

Figure 12.1   Aggregate operating results

Source: Franck (2015)

Case study 12.1: Bayer AG as a true investor at Bayer 04 Leverkusen

Bayer 04 Leverkusen, a German Bundesliga club, can be interpreted as a provider of public exposure and transferred image to the various businesses of its 100% owner, Bayer AG, a German chemical and pharmaceutical conglomerate. To comply with the new FFP break-even requirement, Bayer AG must not pay more to its subsidiary club in a sponsoring agreement than a comparable amount of public exposure and transferred image would cost in the free market.

This may have also been the case in the past. Yet, under the new FFP break-even requirement, Bayer AG will have to write a sponsoring contract *ex ante*, clearly specifying all transacted rights before paying money to the club. As long as the contract qualifies to be at fair market value, the sponsoring income is not in conflict with the break-even requirement.

Only money injections in excess of the fair market value will be capped by the FFP regulations. Thus, the FFP regulations do not handicap true investors who aim to earn (and not to lose) money with a football club. In other words, the FFP regulations protect the shareholders of Bayer AG, who are looking for a competitive financial return, from Bayer 04 Leverkusen's spending on players at their expense. Money from true investors will continue to flow into clubs' payrolls because fair market value represents the upper bound to their willingness to pay by definition.

The same fair market value logic applies to all kind of transactions with all kinds of true investors under the FFP regulations. True investors are not affected by the FFP regulations.

Case study 12.2: Roman Abramovich as a pure success-seeker at Chelsea FC

One of the most prominent examples of a private benefactor is Roman Abramovich. In June 2003 the Russian multi-billionaire became the owner of the companies that control Chelsea Football Club in West London. By 2012, he had injected around £1bn into the football club (Conn, 2012a).

To some extent, Abramovich may be a true investor, using the club as a vehicle to promote his other businesses. Yet, even without detailed information about the structures of his businesses, Abramovich seems unlikely to be a true investor who looks for a competitive financial return on his investment in Chelsea FC. Rather, the club seems to provide substantial non-financial rewards to its owner which exceed his financial contributions. Otherwise Abramovich would withdraw from his football venture. Thus, the description as a pure success-seeker who is willing to pay for success *per se* seems more accurate than the description as a true investor.

As the owner, Abramovich certainly enjoys basking in the reflected glory of the club's sporting success. Who would not? Similarly, the ownership of Chelsea FC represents an extremely prestigious and thus effective means of social distinction which Abramovich will not be indifferent to.

But in Abramovich's case, pragmatism may be more important than sportsmanship and vanity. More specifically, his club ownership and the public attention and admiration that come with its sportive success can produce exactly the kind of social and political legitimacy many former Russian oligarchs seek. The fate of Mikhail Khodorkovsky, another Russian oligarch, imprisoned in 2003 and sent to a Siberian jail in 2005, may have made Abramovich aware of his fragile personal situation in Russia. In this context, it is also no wonder that he chose to support Chelsea FC, a club playing in the biggest football league worldwide and situated in one of the biggest, most affluent agglomerations worldwide. When Abramovich became the club owner, Chelsea was probably the biggest club available in the market for corporate control. Clubs with possibly even more market potential (and thus even more winning potential), such as Real Madrid, FC Barcelona or Bayern Munich, have not been available for benefactor-owners because these clubs are governed as members' associations.

Of course, Abramovich's true motives – as those of any club owner – are complex and varying over time. However, after more than a decade of money injections in Chelsea FC and several trophies won, Abramovich is a well-known personality in Western Europe and beyond. His close association with the club's successes seems to confirm the calculus he explained at the very beginning of his club ownership: 'I have no Napoleonic dream. I am just hard-working and pragmatic'.

The new FFP regulations constrain Abramovich's willingness to pay for success *per se*. To increase his chances of winning a second Champions League title with Chelsea FC under the new FFP regulations, he could build a better stadium, invest more heavily in promising young talents and take measures to increase the club's fan base. Expenditures on stadia, youth academies and community projects are not subject to any regulatory limit. Such expenditures are explicitly excluded from break-even calculations. However, he cannot inflate the club's payroll by covering a break-even deficit *ex post* any more.

Conclusion

The main objective of the FFP regulation is to preserve the long-term financial stability of European club football. In this respect, the FFP break-even requirement creates important incentives for club managers to compete with a team based on payrolls that allow them to stay within the hard limit drawn by their football income and the 'acceptable deviation'. By introducing hard budget constraints, the FFP break-even requirement terminates the 'too popular to fail' problem in the football industry and corrects the contagious mentality among club managers to excessively gamble on success.

The FFP regulations restore the incentives for 'good club management' in an industry that has degenerated into a 'zombie race' with an ever-increasing number of technically bankrupt participants.[29] A poorly managed club can no longer trump a well-managed club with similar market potential by winning and maintaining the favor of a solvent benefactor.

As a positive (yet not officially intended) side-effect, the FFP regulations contribute to a more competitive balance in European club competitions.[30] In the absence of payroll caps (i.e., before the introduction of the FFP regulations), the success-seeking benefactors with the deepest pockets were systematically allocated to the clubs with the largest market potential and the highest winning probabilities. Their money injections on top of the clubs' superior market potential made those clubs even more dominant. Against this background, the FFP regulations reduce the gap between underdogs and favorites by forcing the latter to operate within their given market potential instead of allowing them to increase their spending power with money from benefactors chasing after sportive success.

Major stakeholders in European club football, including the European Club Association (ECA),[31] have repeatedly assured their support of the FFP regulations (e.g. UEFA, 2014). There may still be loopholes to keep a club's budget constraint soft (e.g. by means of inventive fair market value calculations and inflated sponsorship deals), but these loopholes are likely to shrink as UEFA gains experience and updates its FFP regulations accordingly.

The settlement procedure is a key element in the current implementation process of the FFP regulations. Settlement agreements between the CFCB and overspending clubs are, in contrast to exclusions from competitions, likely to be in the interests of both parties. By agreeing to CFCB's terms, the involved clubs can secure their participation in the UEFA competitions – in many cases one of the clubs' main revenue sources. A club's appeal in front of the Court of Arbitration for Sport (CAS) would be expensive and time consuming and its outcome would be uncertain. To UEFA, a settlement is a guarantee that the case ends there. The FFP regulations do not get challenged in front of the CAS, and UEFA can save the cost of long and costly legal battles. Moreover, the settlement procedure provides the flexibility needed for a case-by-case approach to the sanctions. The balance between over-regulation that would make it difficult for clubs to invest and take risks, and under-regulation that would render the FFP toothless, is indeed very difficult to find. Settlement practice seems to be a sensitive way to walk this thin line.

Recommended further reading

Franck, E. (2014). Financial fair play in European club football – What is it all about? *International Journal of Sport Finance*, 9, 193–217.

Kornai, J., Maskin, E., & Roland, G. (2003). Understanding the soft budget constraint. *Journal of Economic Literature*, 41, 1095–1136.

Storm, R. K., & Nielsen, K. (2012). Soft budget constraints in professional football. *European Sport Management Quarterly*, 12, 183–201.

Notes

1 The break-even requirement is defined in Articles 58–63 (see UEFA, 2012).

2 Relevant expenses are defined in Article 58(2) of the UEFA Club Licensing and Financial Fair Play Regulations.

3 Relevant income is defined in Article 58(1) of the UEFA Club Licensing and Financial Fair Play Regulations.

4 Acceptable deviations are defined in Article 61 of the UEFA Club Licensing and Financial Fair Play Regulation.

5 The initial monitoring period assessed for the 2013/14 licence season covers the reporting period ending 2013 and the reporting period ending 2012.

6 Article 61(2) of the UEFA Club Licensing and Financial Fair Play Regulation explains that the total acceptable deviation will then go down to €30mn for the monitoring period assessed in the licence seasons 2015/16, 2016/17 and 2017/18.

7 The following section largely draws on Franck's (2014) discussion of why football clubs systematically overinvest.

8 See e.g. Dietl, Franck, and Lang (2008) and Müller, Lammert, and Hovemann (2012) for a detailed analysis and discussion of overinvestment phenomena in sports leagues.

9 See e.g. Késenne (1996, 2000) for formal analyses or Garcia-del-Barro and Szymanski (2009) for empirical evidence for Spain and England.

10 See Franck (2014) for a detailed discussion of the importance of spending power in club football.

11 See Dietl, Franck, and Lang (2008) for a formal analysis and Franck (2010) for a detailed discussion.

12 See Storm and Nielsen (2012) and Franck (2014) for more detailed discussions.

13 See Szymanski (2010) for a range of arguments why football clubs almost always manage to remain viable despite situations of financial distress.

14 The following discussion of the various inefficiencies induced by soft budget constraints largely corresponds to Franck's (2014) more detailed discussion.

15 See Kornai (1986, pp. 5–6) for a more detailed account of the possible measures of state intervention.

16 This section largely draws in Craven's (2014) more detailed discussion of the operation of EU state aid law in professional club football.

17   See Franck (2010) for a detailed discussion of the influence of club governance structure on the capability to tap funding from private benefactors.

18   The majority of the 700+ clubs in the national top division of the 53 UEFA national associations are governed as members' associations (42%). Alternative club governance structures are incorporated companies (38%), and in some cases stock exchange listed (4%), state owned (3%) or specifically defined sporting incorporated companies (13%) (UEFA, 2012).

19   In clubs governed as members' associations the principle of direct democracy does not allow any private benefactor to gain the residual rights of control necessary to actively manage and capture paybacks that would justify losing money in football. In the public perception, sportive success would be attributed less to the private benefactor than it would be attributed to a private benefactor who also owns the club. The dispersed anonymous shareholders of clubs governed as stock corporations have no residual rights of control at all and would hardly be associated with the club's sportive success (see Franck (2010) for a detailed discussion).

20   This section largely draws on Franck's (2015) discussion of the incentives of true investors and how they are affected by the FFP regulations.

21   The advertising equivalency method is commonly applied to evaluate the alleged value of various public relation activities. The method seeks to determine the value of a sponsorship by calculating the cost of achieving a comparable amount of exposure by using classical advertising formats (see e.g. Jeffries-Fox, 2003).

22   Companies specialized in sponsorship valuation typically capture the more intangible components of positive image transfers by applying multiplicators to the tangible value calculated by using the advertising equivalency method.

23   Fair market value estimates the (highest) price at which a willing seller and a willing buyer who are informed, prudent and knowledgeable and act independently of each other transact a property in an open and unrestricted market. The concept is of utmost importance in tax law and in accounting.

24   This section largely draws on Franck's (2015) discussion of the incentives of pure success-seekers and how they are affected by the FFP regulations.

25   See Franck (2014) for a detailed discussion.

26   In the case of clubs in the German Bundesliga, to open their doors completely for private benefactors would even require regulatory adjustments at the league level. The uniquely German '50% plus one vote' rule guarantees residual control of the soccer team to the parent members' association. At Bayern Munich, for example, 49% of the shares could be sold to an investor if the club members agree. Currently the members' association still owns 82% of the shares of the football team after selling 18% to Adidas and Audi in order to partially finance the club's new stadium. There are only two exceptions from the '50% plus one vote' rule. First, the professional football team Bayer Leverkusen was transformed from a members' association into a GmbH, a limited liability company, in 1999, and Bayer AG has been granted the exception to take over 100% of the shares in the GmbH. Second,

the professional team of VfL Wolfsburg was transformed from a members' association into a GmbH in 2001 and Volkswagen AG, a German car manufacturer, has been granted the exception to hold 90% of the shares in the GmbH.

27 See UEFA (2015) for detailed information on all cases in which the CFCB sanctioned clubs for breaching the FFP break-even requirement.

28 Operating results refer to losses/profits after wages and all operating costs but before transfer activity, financing and investment/divestment.

29 See also Franck (2014, 2015) for a consistent line of argument.

30 See also Franck (2014, 2015) for a consistent line of argument.

31 The ECA is a body representing the interests of association football clubs in UEFA. It is the sole such body recognized by UEFA, and has member clubs in each UEFA member association. It was formed in 2008 to replace the G-14, which comprised a small number of elite clubs and was unrecognized by UEFA.

References

Akerlof, G. (1976). The economics of caste and of the rat race and other woeful tales. *The Quarterly Journal of Economics*, 90, 599–617.

Alchian, A. A., & Demsetz, H. (1972). Production, information costs, and economic organization. *American Economic Review*, 62, 777–795.

Andreff, W. (2007). French Football: A financial crisis rooted in weak governance. *Journal of Sports Economics*, 8, 652–661.

Andreff, W. (2011). Some comparative economics of the organization of sports: Competition and regulation in North American vs. European professional team sports leagues. *European Journal of Comparative Economics*, 8, 3–27.

Bairner, R. (2012, 19 June). PSG turned into a European giant after being taken over by QIA in May 2011, but how has their spending compared to the first 14 months of City and Chelsea's opulent ownerships? Retrieved from http://www.goal.com/en/news/1717/editorial/2012/07/19/3248341/how-psgs-200m-spending-spree-compares-to-abramovichs-chelsea-abu-

Conn, D. (2012a, 31 August). Chelsea wanted to break even but they are breaking the bank first. Retrieved from http://www.theguardian.com/football/david-conn-inside-sport-blog/2012/aug/31/chelsea-breaking-bank-transfer-deadline

Conn, D. (2012b, 18 May). Manchester City: a tale of love and money. Retrieved from http://www.guardian.co.uk/football/2012/may/18/fall-and-rise-manchester-city

Craven, R. (2014). Football and State aid: too important to fail? *International Sports Law Journal*, 14, 205–217.

Dietl, H., Franck, E., & Lang, M. (2008). Overinvestment in team sports leagues: A contest theory model. *Scottish Journal of Political Economy*, 55, 353–368.

European Commission (2012, 21 March). Joint statement by Vice-President Joaquin Almunia and President Michel Platini. Retrieved from http://ec.europa.eu/competition/sectors/sports/joint_statement_en.pdf

Franck, E. (2010). Private firm, public corporation or member's association – governance structures in European football. *International Journal of Sport Finance*, 5, 108–127.

Franck, E. (2014). Financial fair play in European club football – What is it all about? *International Journal of Sport Finance*, 9, 193–217.

Franck, E. (2015). Regulation in leagues with clubs' soft budget constraints: the effect of the new UEFA Club Licensing and Financial Fair Play Regulations on managerial incentives and suspense. In: W. Andreff (Ed.), *Disequilibrium Sports Economics* (pp. 241–265). Herndon, VA: Edward Elgar.

Franck, E., & Lang, M. (2014). Theoretical analysis of the influence of money injections on risk taking in football-clubs. *Scottish Journal of Political Economy*, 61, 430–454.

Frank, R. H. (2005). Positional externalities cause large and preventable welfare losses. *American Economic Review*, 95, 137–141.

Frank, R. H., & Bernanke, B. S. (2004). *Principles of microeconomics* (2nd edn). Boston, MA: McGraw-Hill.

Garcia-del-Barro, P., & Szymanski, S. (2009). Goal! Profit maximization versus win maximization in soccer. *Review of Industrial Organization*, 34, 45–68.

Iaria, M. (2012). How to spend € 2.5 billion and be happy and dissatisfied. Retrieved from http://english. gazzetta.it/Football/15-10-2012/how-to-spend-e25-billion-and-be-happy-and-dissatisfied-912915713057.shtml

Jeffries-Fox, B. (2003). A discussion of advertising value equivalency. The Institute of Public Relations Commission on PR Measurement and Evaluation. Retrieved from http://www.instituteforpr.org/wp-content/uploads/2003_AVE1.pdf

Késenne, S. (1996). League management in professional team sports with win maximizing clubs. *European Journal for Sport Management*, 2, 14–22.

Késenne, S. (2000). Revenue sharing and competitive balance in professional team sports. *Journal of Sports Economics*, 1, 56–65.

Kornai, J. (1980a). *Economics of shortage*. Amsterdam: North-Holland.

Kornai, J. (1980b). Hard and soft budget constraint. *Acta Oeconomica*, 25, 231–245.

Kornai, J. (1986). The soft budget constraint. *Kyklos*, 39, 3–30.

Kornai, J., Maskin, E., & Roland, G. (2003). Understanding the soft budget constraint. *Journal of Economic Literature*, 41, 1095–1136.

Kuper, S. (2009). Football abandons the fantasy that it is a business. Retrieved from http://www.ft.com/intl/cms/s/2/fd77a01c-aa07-11de-3ce00144feabdc0.html#axzz2GRMmCmGD

Müller, J.C., Lammert, J., & Hovemann, G. (2012). The financial fair play regulations of UEFA: An adequate concept to ensure the long-term viability and sustainability of European club football? *International Journal of Sports Finance*, 7, 117–140.

Rosen, S. (1981). The economics of superstars. *American Economic Review*, 71, 845–858

Sass, M. (2012). Long-term competitive balance under UEFA financial fair play regulations. Working Paper No. 5/2012, Otto von Guericke University Magdeburg.

Stern, G. H., & Feldman, R. J. (2004). *Too Big to Fail: The Bazards of Bank Bailouts*. Washington, DC: Brookings Institution Press.

Storm, R. K. (2012). The need for regulating professional soccer in Europe: A soft budget constraint argument. *Sport, Business and Management: An International Journal*, 2, 21–38.

Storm, R. K., & Nielsen, K. (2012). Soft budget constraints in professional football. *European Sport Management Quarterly*, 12, 183–201.

Szymanski, S. (2010). The financial crisis and English football: The dog that will not bark. *International Journal of Sport Finance*, 5, 28–40.

UEFA (2012). UEFA Club Licensing and Financial Fair Play Regulations, Edition 2012. Retrieved from http://www.uefa.com/MultimediaFiles/Download/Tech/uefaorg/General/01/80/54/10/1805410_DOWNLOAD.pdf

UEFA (2013). The European Club Licensing Benchmarking Report Financial Year 2011. Retrieved from http://www.uefa.com/MultimediaFiles/Download/Tech/uefaorg/General/ 01/91/61/84/1916184_DOWNLOAD.pdf

UEFA (2014, 13 October). European football stakeholders restate support for UEFA Financial Fair Play Regulations. Retrieved from http://www.uefa.org/protecting-the-game/club-licensing-and-financial-fair-play/news/newsid=2164620.html

UEFA (2015).Club Financial Control Body Cases. Retrieved from http://www.uefa.org/protecting-the-game/club-licensing-and-financial-fair-play/news/newsid=2164620.html

Van Rompuy, B. (2012). Plan to relieve the Spanish football club tax debts. Retrieved from http://football perspectives.org/plan-relieve-spanish-football-club-tax-debts (last visited 24 May 24 2015)

Vöpel, H. (2011). Do we really need financial fair play in European club football? An economic analysis. CESIfo DICE Report, 3/2011. Retrieved from http://hwwi-rohindex.de/fileadmin/hwwi/Publikationen/Externe_PDFs/1210201.pdf

CORRUPTION AND THE GOVERNANCE OF SPORT

ARNOUT GEERAERT

Introduction

An alarming number of ethical scandals involving international sport federations (ISFs) have surfaced in recent years, involving different forms of corruption such as bribe taking, vote rigging, racketeering, wire fraud, and money laundering. The litany of corruption-related indictments surrounding *Fédération Internationale de Football Association* (FIFA) has unquestionably been the most glaring. Recently, two reports issued by the World Anti-Doping Agency (WADA) found extortion, fraud and bribery practices at the highest levels of the International Association of Athletics Federations (IAAF) (WADA Independent Commission, 2015, 2016). Perhaps lesser known is that a number of smaller ISFs, including the International Volleyball Federation (FIVB), the International Weightlifting Federation (IWF), and the International Handball Federation (IHF), have been enveloped in similar corruption accusations (Hoy, 2005; Ahl, 2013; Hartmann, 2013). As the number and severity of ISF corruption accusations are brought to light, there is an increasingly vociferous call by public institutions at different levels for more ethical governance of the world's sports governing bodies. National parliaments and governments, the European Parliament and the Parliamentary Assembly of the Council of Europe called for change (Randall and Brady, 2011; UK Parliament, 2011; Parliamentary assembly of the Council of Europe, 2012; European Parliament, 2013, 2015). Before change can be achieved, however, we need a sophisticated understanding of the factors that lead to corruption in an increasing number of ISFs (Gorta, 2006). Is corruption the case of a few 'bad apples'; a small number of individuals lacking moral character, as is often argued? Or can we identify specific variables that increase the likelihood of corruption in ISFs?

This chapter explores the factors that may lend ISFs to corruption. Importantly, it does not advocate that ISFs have a general tendency to become corrupted. It has been shown, however, that both systemic and organisational factors increase the likelihood of ISF corruption because they provide both motive and opportunity for ISF officials to behave unethically. Firstly, the commercialisation of sport and the instrumentalisation of sport by politics provide a *motive* for corruption. Secondly, corruption cultures and bad governance provide an *opportunity* for corruption. ISFs need to implement better governance – robust organisational structures and rules – in order to decrease corruption risks. However, change towards better governance is often very difficult and necessitates sufficient outside pressure for reforms.

Systemic trends that provide motive for corruption

As organised sport transformed from a parochial and amateur activity to a global phenomenon governed by a complex transnational network involving public and private (business) interests, ISFs have increasingly become exposed to corruption risks. Two systemic trends, which partly overlap, increase the *motives* for a wide and diverse group to engage in bribery and fraud, two practices that potentially envelop ISFs in corruption. Going back to the origins of international sports governance, this sections explores both these trends, namely the commercialisation of sport and the instrumentalisation of sport by politics.

The commercialisation of sport

At the turn of the twentieth century, the first ISFs arose from a need to centralise the organisation of sport and to unify rules due to increased international competition. Because they could provide an answer to the need for consistent rules, ISFs were able to consolidate their monopolies as global regulating bodies for their respective sports. The governance system that soon emerged can generally be described as a hierarchical pyramid in which, for a single sport, an international sport federation stands at the apex of a vertical chain of command, running from the global to continental, national, and local levels (Geeraert, 2016b). The success of the modern Olympic Games further consolidated this system (Chappelet & Kübler-Mabbott, 2008, p. 64). Because public actors did not demonstrate much appetite for intervening in the field of sport, the sporting pyramid has remained largely private in nature. One of the most important reasons is that the public sector has long regarded sport a cultural and, above all, amateur activity. Indeed, the commercialisation of sport did not occur until the 1970s and 1980s.[1]

The roots of the commercialisation of sport, however, are found in the period after World War II, when more individual leisure time not only augmented opportunities to practise (organised) sport, but also to *consume* sport (Andreff, 2008). The development of radio and television broadcasting enabled sport's growing (global) reach, providing the means for remote consumption of sport events. The technological innovations regarding cable, satellite, and digital television in the 1990s and the breakup of public broadcasting monopolies in Europe further boosted the demand for sports broadcasting (Andreff & Staudohar, 2000; Andreff & Bourg, 2006). The emergence of the internet furthermore enables the instant transmission (and consumption) of large sporting events (Andreff, 2008). Benefiting from more lucrative broadcasting deals for sporting events, the largest ISFs have increasingly realised the business potential of their sporting events. Since the mid-1980s, they have marketed their events more effectively and sold exclusive marketing rights for enormous sums of money (Tomlinson, 2005; Chappelet & Kübler-Mabott, 2008).

The increasing global economic significance and popularity of sport generate increasing money flows to and from ISFs. This creates two particular catalysts for corruption. First, ISF's accumulation of wealth and power provides a motive for senior officials to either use money to obtain power, or to use power to obtain money (Huntington, 2002; Blaug, 2014). Second, as sport transitioned from an amateur activity to a more commercialised and professional setting, governance challenges became more complex. In order to keep control over their respective sports, ISFs increasingly adopted more (diverse) tasks on behalf of a larger and more diverse set of actors (Geeraert, 2016a). Put simply, the body of rules and decisions issued by ISFs has grown exponentially in order to cope with the growing number of tasks and they affect an increasingly large group. This has made corruption beneficial for an increasing number of actors, who seek to influence ISFs' rules and decisions that affect them (Tanzi, 1998, p. 563). Moreover, any regulatory action ISFs undertake may hurt some group, rendering this group a potential source of corruption (MacMullan, 1961, p. 196; Geeraert, 2016a).

The instrumentalisation of sport by politics

Besides the commercialisation of sport, the instrumentalisation of sport by politics provides increased motives for corruption. Modern sport's construction is, in essence, rooted in the concept of freedom of association (Szymanski, 2006). Autonomy from formal regulatory public interference is therefore not only a deeply ingrained, but also a cherished principle in the sports world. It has even become an obsession for ISFs, which seek to keep the governance of (international) sport strictly private (Geeraert, Mrkonjic & Chappelet, 2015). The sports world's official discourse on sport-politics has aptly been summarised by Jackson and Haigh as 'a naive moral/philosophical perspective that stipulates that sport and politics do not, and should not, mix' (Jackson & Haigh, 2008, p. 349). Remarkably, however, the sports world has never formulated a clear definition or justification of the autonomy of sport. In a document submitted to the European Union by the IOC on behalf of the Olympic and sports movement, *autonomy* is said to mean 'preserving the values of sport and the existing structures through which it has developed in Europe and in the world'. Regarding justification, the text mentions that 'the responsibility sport has in society, and the autonomy with which it regulates itself, have led to its credibility and legitimacy' (IOC, 2008, p. 1). This strange circular argument indicates that the sports world realises that a strict definition and justification of sporting autonomy would delineate the concept and open the door to a restricted use. Autonomy, consequently, is a vague concept that is often used as a passe-partout to justify self-governance.

At the same time, however, ISFs' claims for autonomy often ring hollow when considering that many of them have been rather open to (informal forms of) political pressure. According to Jackson and Haigh, 'within the context of an increasingly interconnected world there is little doubt that the global spectacle, commodity and cultural phenomenon that is modern sport influences, and is influenced by, politics and foreign policy' (Jackson & Haigh, 2008, p. 349). This symbiosis has become particularly visible in recent years as states increasingly regard sport as a political resource. By instrumentalising sport, states try to increase their international prestige, which gives them more influence in the international political arena (Nye, 2008; Geeraert, 2017). There are two ways in which sport can augment states' international prestige. First, many (large) countries invest in sporting success at international sporting events like the Olympics. If a country or its athletes perform well, this increases its international prestige (Levermore, 2004, pp. 8–9). Second, an increasing number of states seek to host large sporting events (Nye, 2008; Cornelissen, 2010; Brannagan & Guilianotti, 2014; Persson & Petersson, 2014). This has become particularly visible in the politics and policies of countries like Russia, China, Brazil and India, but also Azerbaijan and Qatar, which tend to see sport mega-events as 'proxies for integration and influence' (Cornelissen, 2010, p. 3015).

The increased instrumentalisation of sport by politics has often led to corrosion of the ethical character of international sport because of undue political pressure. First, states and their leaders have exerted pressure on ISFs to overlook performance-enhancing drug use or other violations of ISF policies. States' struggle for medals in international sports events can put severe pressure on athletes, coaches, clubs and federations. This may encourage doping abuse and even induce institutionalised practices or state-sponsored doping, a phenomenon mentioned mostly in relation to the Soviet Union (Voy & Deeter, 1991). However, the recent revelations by two reports issued by WADA demonstrate that such practices continue to emerge, detailing institutionalised practices of performance enhancing drug use by Russian athletes (WADA Independent Commission, 2015, 2016). Countries have a high incentive to prevent such practices from being discovered since revelations of systemic doping may tarnish a countries' image and this may induce improper political influence. Second, countries' attempts to secure the hosting of major sporting events are also rife with corrupt behaviours. A country can never be sure that other countries do not engage in unethical practices (such as vote buying) in order to increase their chances. When countries begin to pay bribes, they put pressure on their competitors to do the same because the cost of not doing so is losing the bid (cf. Tanzi, 1998, p. 563).

Organisational variables that provide opportunity for corruption

The previous section outlined the systemic trends that increase the motives for a wide and diverse group to engage in corrupt behaviours. While these trends increase corruption risks, they do not automatically envelop ISFs in corruption. This section explores the organisational variables that provide an opportunity for corruption enveloping ISFs. Corruption thrives where opportunities exist for it to fester. The literature provides two different perspectives on factors that lead to organisational corruption, which are operationalised through differential epistemologies: a cultural and a structural perspective (Geeraert, 2017). The former perspective assumes ideational bases for action and focuses on cultural factors; the latter perspective emphasises structural factors as the main determinant of behaviour.

Corrupt Culture

Culture links to corruption in that intrinsic motivations for corruption can be culturally determined (Barr & Serra, 2010). People acquire intrinsic motivations to act in a certain way through the internalisation of social norms existing in a society through interaction, a process known as socialisation. Within a culture, norms are shared and deviation from these norms results in social disapproval and even feelings of shame and guilt when the norm is internalised (Elster, 1989; Barr & Serra, 2010, p. 862). In corrupt cultures, individuals do not have anti-corruption norms internalised; instead, 'the impact of intrinsic motivations on their decision to engage in or abstain from corruption is weak' (Barr & Serra, 2010, p. 862). Offering bribes to public officials, for instance, is considered 'normal' in some cultures. Corrupt cultures exist and persist not only in countries, but also in organisations. Through daily socialisation, employees indeed develop values consistent with an organisation's culture (DeBacker, Heim & Tran, 2015). An organisation's culture can even lead to personality change among employees (Lejeune & Vas, 2008). Moreover, employees are more likely to behave according to what is considered normal in their organisational context than what they perceive as normal outside their organisation.

The existence of weak anti-corruption norms can explain why internal reactions against the blatant corruption in FIFA and the IAAF or in other ISFs, such as the FIVB, IHF and IWF, have remained largely absent. In corrupt cultures, corruption is not considered illegal or immoral. In the absence of internalised anti-corruption norms, corrupt behaviour does not result in social disapproval or feelings of shame and guilt. Such cultures thus provide individuals with plenty of opportunity to behave unethically. Moreover, they are persistent because people's norms tend to change very slowly (Sandholtz & Taagepera, 2005) and corrupt organisations appear to attract corrupt people (DeBacker, Heim & Tran, 2015, p. 124).

What causes cultures of corruption in ISFs? There is no easy answer to this question. Numerous social and structural factors shape intrinsic motivations to engage in corruption. In relation to ISFs, several factors are palpable (Geeraert, 2017). Most importantly, corrupt cultures thrive in a climate of impunity (Luis & Stewart, 2014). The Swiss authorities' lax approach to corrupt ISFs fostered an environment conducive to corrupt practices, an approach that was only recently reversed. Moreover, ISFs operate in the absence of effective internal accountability lines. Structural factors lie at the heart of this problem.

Bad governance

This brings us to the structural perspective on organisational corruption. Individuals are more likely to engage in corruption if they do not think corrupt behaviour will be discovered and punished, or if they think the punishment will be light (Tanzi, 1998). According to the structural corruption perspective, organisations' internal rules and structures influence the credible occurrence of (significant) punishment of officials' deviant behaviour. When such rules and structures are not in place, individuals have plenty of opportunity to engage in corruption. The term 'good governance' is often used as a normative benchmark to evaluate the internal rules and structures of different forms of organisations (Woods, 1999). Consequently, an absence of robust internal organisational structures is associated with 'bad governance', a term often used in relation to ISFs.

In the absence of effective lines of external accountability, ISFs have been able to carry out their activities with large degrees of autonomy (Geeraert, 2016a, 2016b). Most importantly, because they operate on a global playing field, ISFs can pick a favourable regulatory environment as the home base for their international activities. Many ISFs, by choosing a strategic location for their headquarters, benefit from a quasi-unregulated system. The Swiss Civil Code, for instance, lists very basic minimum requirements for associations, while the overall Swiss legal framework allows for large degrees of both fiscal and organisational autonomy and limited prosecution of private corruption. Moreover, ISFs are generally outside the scope of other countries' laws and policies. This absence of external control has allowed ISFs to develop serious governance deficits (Geeraert, 2015).

Many ISFs were established in an era when sport was an amateur activity. ISFs' initial amateurish structures did not keep pace with the rapid commercialisation and professionalisation of sport. To some extent, ISFs' failure to implement robust organisational structures can be explained by the lack of a generally accepted, homogeneous and practical set of core principles for good governance in ISFs. In recent years, important progress has been achieved in this regard. Especially noteworthy is the work by Chappelet and Mrkonjic (2013) and the Action for Good Governance in International Sport organisations (AGGIS) group (AGGIS group, 2013). Chappelet and Mrkonjic suggest the Basic Indicators for Better Governance in International sport (BIBGIS), which are organised along seven broad dimensions: organisational transparency, reporting transparency, stakeholders' representation, democratic process, control mechanisms, sport integrity, and solidarity. The AGGIS group defined 44 variables of good governance across four dimensions, namely transparency; democratic processes; checks and balances; and solidarity.

Geeraert (2015) further refined the AGGIS group variables into 36 governance variables and quantified each of these by means of a scoring system. These indicators were applied to survey the governance of the 35 Olympic ISFs. His work demonstrates that the majority of these federations have governance deficits. Of particular concern with regard to corruption are deficits relating to transparency, democracy and checks and balances. When such deficits occur, corruption is less likely to be discovered and punished.

- First, transparency is defined as the 'degree of openness in conveying information' (Ball, 2009, p. 297). Transparency allows external actors to monitor the workings of an organisation and therefore decrease the likelihood of corruption (Kiewiet & McCubbins, 1991).

In measuring *transparency* in ISFs, Geeraert (2015) shows that the majority of the federations do not report internal activities to the general public. Most notably, only eight federations publish the agenda and minutes of their general assembly, four federations publish governing body decisions, six federations publish comprehensive annual general activity reports, none of the federations publishes reports on remuneration of its senior officials, and 23 federations do not publish externally audited financial reports on their website.

- Second, democratic processes concern rules and norms inherent to a democratic conduct. Democratic processes increase the accountability of organisations because they increase stakeholder scrutiny by involving affected parties in policy processes (Calvert, McCubbins & Weingast, 1989; Fearon, 1999; Klijn & Koppenjan, 2004). Geeraert (2015) demonstrates that a large majority of ISFs have not implemented robust *democratic processes*. In general, athletes are not represented adequately – in only eight federations, athletes elect the chairman/chairwoman of the athletes' commission. Furthermore, the general assemblies of about half of the federations meet less than once a year, and the allocation of major events – a high risk area in relation to corruption – does not take place according to a transparent and objectively reproducible process. A large majority of federations moreover, 31 to be precise, do not screen candidates standing for election on professional and integrity criteria. Of particular concern is the lack of adequate term limits in all of the federations – 11 federations have some form of limitation in place – which leads to a concentration and abuse of power.

- Third, checks and balances or mutual control procedures ensure that no senior official or department has absolute control over decisions (Bovens, 2007). Such checks hinge on the fact that an institution is established and charged with monitoring the activities of those that hold decision-making power (Kiewiet & McCubbins, 1991, pp. 33–34). Institutional checks, such as (internal and external) audits and ethics committees, are usually employed in order to prevent embezzlements, insider trading, corruption, and abuse and concentration of power. According to Geeraert (2015), checks and balances is ISFs' most problematical governance area. Gaps are most pronounced in the quality of the internal audit, and the presence and quality of codes of ethics and conflict of interest rules and the enforcement of these principles. Only six federations have an internal audit committee that has a clearly defined role and the authority to oversee the internal audit and assesses the quality of the internal control system, seven federations do not make any reference to a code of ethics in their governing documents or on their websites, only six federations have clear conflict of interest rules in place, and in only five federations the ethics committee is independent from the governing body and has the power to initiate proceedings on its own initiative.

Case examples: FIFA scandals and other cases of ISF corruption

In order to demonstrate how the factors laid out above contribute to corruption, this section discusses the most serious allegations of ISF corruption. Focusing in particular on explaining the multiple episodes of bribery and fraud in FIFA, it also discusses allegations of corruption levelled against the IAAF and a number of smaller ISFs.

Bribe taking, vote rigging, racketeering, wire fraud, and money laundering seem to have been rampant in FIFA since the 1970s. This should not come as a surprise. FIFA is subject to particularly high corruption risks because it operates in an extremely commercialised and politicised setting. FIFA operates in an immensely commercialised setting. Football is a commercial product with worldwide appeal and the football World Cup attracts one of the largest broadcasting audiences. The World Cup has been dubbed FIFA's cash cow since TV and marketing rights relating to the event are FIFA's major source of income (Tomlinson, 2014). The organisation generated €2,156 billion through the sale of the 2014 football World Cup media rights and €1,403 billion via the sale of marketing rights (FIFA, 2014). FIFA currently has mutually dependent partnerships with powerful and highly successful multinational companies such as Coca-Cola, Visa, Adidas, and Budweiser (Sugden, 2002; Tomlinson, 2005). Even though it is officially a non-profit organisation, in 2014 its financial reserves stood at €1,352 billion (FIFA, 2014). FIFA thus provides an enormous source for wealth and power. Small wonder, then, that its most senior officials have been motivated to use money to obtain power, or to use power to obtain money. Brazilian Joao Havelange, FIFA President from 1974 to 1998, expanded FIFA's membership to a vast number of countries, which were largely impoverished. He subsequently exerted control over these countries by rewarding financial support and patronage (Sugden & Tomlinson, 1998, pp. 144–151). Sepp Blatter, Havelange's protégé and successor, continued this successful strategy (Tomlinson, 2014). According to Mark Pieth, Havelange and Blatter's relationships with national associations established a sort of 'patronage system' in which '[f]riends received personal favours or were able to raise funds for their national associations, their confederations or their local infrastructure in exchange for support for their benefactor' (Pieth, 2014, p. 8). Whereas such practices often took place in a grey area regarding corruption, the so-called ISL affair revealed how senior FIFA officials had taken personal commissions worth around US$100 million in exchange for exclusive marketing contracts (Jennings, 2006). Yet it was not until US authorities stepped in that the world learned about the vastness of corruption in FIFA. In May 2015, US authorities indicted 14 officials on racketeering, wire fraud, and money laundering charges. Seven current FIFA officials (including one FIFA vice-president) were arrested by the Swiss authorities at the request of the US Department of Justice on suspicion of receiving US$200 million in bribes in return for media and marketing rights during FIFA events in North and South America. According to the US Department of Justice, FIFA officials engaged in a '24-year scheme to enrich themselves through the corruption of international soccer' (Department of Justice, 2015).

Besides the enormous commercialisation, the symbiosis between sport and politics is also extremely visible in football. The bidding contests to host the football World Cup have intensified in recent years, with many countries seeking the prestige associated with hosting this event (Cornelissen, 2010, p. 3013). Even though national federations are the official candidates, national governments de facto take part in the bidding race, and invest significant resources to prepare candidacy (Walters, 2011). World Cup bids are often surrounded by controversy.

Recently, serious corruption allegations have been levelled against the winning bids of the 2018 (Qatar) and 2022 (Russia) World Cups. According to a series of articles published by the English newspaper *The Sunday Times*, hundreds of millions of dollars were paid to bribe FIFA officials (Calvert & Blake, 2014). At the time of writing this contribution, US and Swiss authorities are conducting separate criminal investigations into the awarding of these World Cup hosting rights (Gibson, 2015). Yet other countries have also been operating extremely close to the limits of what may be acceptable in order to secure the World Cup hosting rights (Weinreich, 2014). Several countries have been accused of paying lobbyists closely associated with FIFA officials to gain votes and the English 2018 World Cup bid team is said to have presented FIFA officials with US$30,000 in luxury watches (Brown, 2014).

FIFA corruption cases are myriad. The organisation seems to have a tendency to become corrupted. How can this be? While motives for corruption are plenty, a culture of corruption and structural deficits provides an opportunity for opportunistic behaviour. First, FIFA's corrupt culture has been documented extensively by investigative journalists such as Andrew Jennings (Jennings, 2006). Corruption was considered common practice; it was not considered immoral. Former senior officials that have been accused of unethical practices do not seem to demonstrate much shame or guilt (Tomlinson, Sale & Shergold, 2015). Tellingly, even after the litany of corruption-related indictments enveloping FIFA, insiders note that the organisation '[did] not seem to feel the genuine need of urgent reform' (Pieth, 2014, p. 14). Second, for a very long time FIFA has had serious governance deficits relating to transparency, democracy, and checks and balances. Until recently, for instance, FIFA did not have an ethics committee and robust code of ethics. Taking bribes was thus rarely punished and where it was discovered, punishments were often very light. In addition, FIFA did not have term limits installed, which increases the risk of concentration of power. In 2002, former FIFA General Secretary Michel Zen-Ruffinen commented on then FIFA President Sepp Blatter: 'the President, against the statutes, took over the management and administration of FIFA combining both, thereby working with a few persons of his trust only and manipulating the whole network through the material and administrative power he gained to the benefit of third persons and his personal interests. FIFA today is run like a dictatorship' (Zen-Ruffinen in Tomlinson, 2014, p. 133). Recent governance reforms have had a positive impact, though. For instance, FIFA now seems to have a robust ethics committee in place. Yet the organisation still lacks robust, democratic and transparent decision making (Pieth, 2014). For instance, FIFA still lacks state-of-the-art (financial) control mechanisms and the selection of host candidates of the World Cup does not take place according to a transparent and objectively reproducible process, in which bidding dossiers are reviewed independently and assigned a score on the basis of pre-established criteria (Geeraert, 2015). This makes the organisation particularly vulnerable to corruption associated with undue political pressure.

The scandals in FIFA have unquestionably been the most blatant examples of ISF corruption. Yet in November 2015, the IAAF faced similar turmoil when a report issued by WADA found corruption and bribery practices among senior officials relating to the cover-up of doping abuses (WADA Independent Commission, 2015). A second report, issued in January 2016, outlines these practices in detail (WADA Independent Commission, 2016). It describes a culture of corruption within a 'powerful rogue group' led and installed by former IAAF president Lamine Diack. The group, which operated under the aegis of the IAAF, consisted of individuals with familial or close personal ties to Diack (WADA Independent Commission, 2016, p. 8). The report outlines how Diack and other senior IAAF officials deliberately stalled cases of suspected Russian athletes, allowing 'dirty Russian athletes to compete and alter the results on the playing field' (WADA Independent Commission, 2015, p. 10). It furthermore details a strong relationship between Diack and Russian President Vladimir Putin. With evidence of doping involving nine Russian athletes on the table, Diack reportedly explained to an IAAF lawyer that he was in a 'difficult position that could only be resolved by President Putin of Russia with whom he had struck up a friendship' (WADA Independent Commission, 2015, p. 20). According to the report, senior IAAF officials had concrete knowledge of corruption at the IAAF: 'It is not credible that elected officials were unaware of the situation affecting [...] athletics in Russia. If, therefore, the circle of knowledge was so extensive, why was nothing done? Quite obviously, there was no appetite on the part of the IAAF to challenge Russia' (WADA Independent Commission, 2016, p. 46).

The IAAF and FIFA corruption scandals have received global news coverage. The allegations of corruption levelled against smaller ISFs, however, are lesser known. Investigative journalists and whistleblowers have uncovered unethical practices in a number of ISFs. Three are particularly noteworthy. First, Mexican Ruben Acosta allegedly secured US$33 million in personal commissions during his 24 years' reign as president of the International Volleyball Federation (FIVB). He managed to do so thanks to a rule stipulating that, for each contract signed on the FIVB's behalf, he was entitled to 10% of the contract value as a bonus (Hoy, 2005). Second, Tamas Aján, president of the International Weightlifting Federation (IWF), failed to account for the disappearance of an estimated US$5 million of International Olympic Committee grants from two Swiss bank accounts. Reportedly, from 1992 to 2008, all the grants awarded by the IOC to the IWF had been channelled into two bank accounts owned by Tamas Aján (Hartmann, 2013). Third, Hassan Moustafa, president of the International Handball Federation (IHF), allegedly secured a contract worth €602,000 with a German sports marketing company, which later acquired the IHF broadcasting rights. Moustafa is furthermore said to have received over €300,000 in travel reimbursement without presenting receipts – he claims he was unaware of the requirement. Finally, he established a salary raise for himself and the IHF executive board members so that they annually receive around €1.8 million in total, which is more than the IHF total development aid (Ahl, 2009, 2010, 2013).

Conclusion

This chapter demonstrates how specific factors increase the likelihood of corruption in ISFs. Both the commercialisation of sport and the instrumentalisation of sport by politics increase the *motives* for a wide and diverse group to engage in bribery and fraud. Consequently, especially those federations that operate in a highly commercialised and politicised setting and/or because they have a high proportion of board members from corrupt countries are subject to particularly high corruption risks. Yet these factors do not automatically envelop ISFs in corruption. Cultural and structural organisational variables provide an *opportunity* for corruption in ISFs. ISFs that have cultures of corruption and bad governance implemented will therefore have a high likelihood of corruption.

With public institutions at different levels calling for more ethical governance of the world's sports governing bodies, the question is how change can be achieved. The instrumentalisation of sport by politics and the commercialisation of sport are systemic and persistent. Mitigating these trends is therefore impossible. Strategies that decrease the *opportunities* for individuals to commit fraud or take bribes will be the most effective means for ISFs to eradicate corruption. Cultures of corruption are difficult to remove since people's internalised norms and beliefs tend to change very slowly. Attention must therefore be paid to the installation of more solid governance structures, in particular on policies that privilege transparency, democracy and checks and balances. Such structural improvements will not only decrease the likelihood of corruption, they will also prevent cultures of corruption from emerging. Indeed, structural improvements such as the installation of term limits and integrity checks, and female inclusion on decision-making bodies, are known to mitigate cultural problems.

ISFs often do not feel a sense of urgency to reform. In a number of ISFs, the lack of good governance and the presence of cultures of corruption complicate a continuous reflection on governance failures. It is clear those ISFs will only engage in significant reforms when stakeholders jointly increase pressure for better governance.

Recommended further reading

For a more elaborate analysis of corruption in ISFs, see Geeraert (2017). Geeraert (2016b) outlines the governance challenges facing ISFs' increasingly commercialised sporting world. Geeraert (2015) provides a detailed analysis of the quality of governance of a wide range of ISFs. Thibault et al. (2010) focus specifically on the position of athletes in governance structures and Geeraert and Drieskens (2015) explore the limits and opportunities for the EU to control ISFs. Finally, the websites of Play the Game (playthegame.org) and the Sports Governance Observer (sportsgovernanceobserver.org) are recommended for those who wish to learn more about cases of corruption and the basic elements of good governance in sport.

Note

1   In North-America, sport was quickly regarded as a business activity. Consequently, professional sport competitions are organised in closed leagues, which have remained rather national in scope and meaning. ISFs have had little impact on their functioning (van Bottenburg, 2011).

References

AGGIS group (2013). AGGIS Sports Governance Observer. In J. Alm (Ed.), *Action for Good Governance in International Sports Organisations: Final report* (pp. 218–221). Copenhagen: Play the Game/Danish Institute for Sports Studies.

Ahl, C. (2009). *World handball hi-jacked by its president: Structural problems, scandals and an urgent need for change.* Retrieved from: http://www.playthegame.org/uploads/media/Christer_Ahl_-_World_handball_hi-jacked.pdf

Ahl, C. (2010). *Hassan Moustafa and the priority of personal enrichment.* Retrieved from: https://www.jensweinreich.de/2010/01/28/christer-ahl-hassan-moustafa-and-the-priority-of-personal-enrichment/

Ahl, C. (2013). *The despotic regime of the IHF just continues.* Retrieved from: http://www.playthegame.org/fileadmin/image/PtG2013/Presentations/30_October_Wednesday/Christer_Ahl_Play_the_Game_2013.pdf

Andreff, W. (2008). Globalization of the sports economy. *Rivista di Diritto ed Economia Dello Sport, 4*(3), 13–32.

Andreff, W., & Bourg, J.F. (2006). Broadcasting rights and competition in European football. In C. Jeanrenaud & S. Késenne (Eds), *The economics of sport and the media* (pp. 37–65). Cheltenham, UK: Edward Elgar Publishing Limited.

Andreff, W., & Staudohar, P. (2000). The evolving European model of professional sports finance. *Journal of Sports Economics, 1*(3), 257–276.

Ball, C. (2009). What is transparency? *Public Integrity, 11*(4), 293–308.

Barr, A., & Serra, D. (2010). Corruption and culture: an experimental analysis. *Journal of Public Economics, 94*(11–12), 862–869.

Blaug, R. (2014). *How power corrupts: Cognition and democracy in organisations.* New York and Basingstoke: Palgrave Macmillan.

Bovens, M. (2007). Analysing and assessing accountability: a conceptual framework. *European Law Journal, 13*(4), 447–468.

Brannagan, P.M., & Giulianotti, R. (2014). Soft power and soft disempowerment: Qatar, global sport and football's 2022 World Cup finals. *Leisure Studies,* iFirst.

Brown, O. (2014). FIFA Is a Swamp of Greed – Sepp Blatter Claims to be Taking Lead on Ethics But Deserves Nothing But Strongest Ridicule, *Telegraph* (19 September). Retrieved from: http://www.telegraph.co.uk/sport/football/world-cup/11109065/Fifa-is-a-swamp-of-greed-Sepp-Blatter-claims-to-be-taking-lead-on-ethics-but-deserves-nothing-but-strongest-ridicule.html

Calvert, J., & Blake, H. (2014). Plot to buy the World Cup: huge email cache reveals secrets of Qatar's shock victory, *Sunday Times* (1 June). Retrieved from: http://www.thesundaytimes.co.uk/sto/news/uk-news/fifa/article1417325.ece.

Calvert, R.L., McCubbins, M.D., & Weingast, B.R. (1989). A theory of political control and agency discretion. *American Journal of Political Science, 33*(3), 588–611.

Chappelet, J.L., & Kübler-Mabott, B. (2008). *The International Olympic Committee and the Olympic System: the governance of world sport.* London: Routledge.

Chappelet, J.L., & Mrkonjic, M. (2013). *Basic Indicators for Better Governance in International Sport (BIBGIS): An assessment tool for international sport governing bodies.* Lausanne: IDHEAP.

Cornelissen, S. (2010). The geopolitics of global aspiration: sport mega-events and emerging powers. *The International Journal of the History of Sport, 27*(16–18), 3008–3025.

DeBacker, J., Heim, B.T., & Tran, A. (2015). Importing corruption culture from overseas: evidence from corporate tax evasion in the United States. *Journal of Financial Economics, 117*(1), 122–138.

Department of Justice (2015). *Nine FIFA officials and five corporate executives indicted for racketeering conspiracy and corruption*. Retrieved from: https://www.justice.gov/opa/pr/nine-fifa-officials-and-five-corporate-executives-indicted-racketeering-conspiracy-and corruption

Elster, J. (1989). Social norms and economic theory. *Journal of Economic Perspectives, 3*(4), 99–117.

European Parliament (2013). Resolution on match-fixing and corruption in sport, 2013/2567(RSP).

European Parliament (2015). *Resolution on recent revelations of high-level corruption cases in FIFA*, P8_TA-PROV(2015)0233.

European Union Expert Group Good Governance (2013). Deliverable 2: Principles of good governance in sport. Brussels: European Commission.

Fearon, J.D. (1999). Electoral accountability and the control of politicians: selecting good types versus sanctioning poor performance. In A. Przeworski, S.C. Stokes & B. Manin (Eds), *Democracy, accountability, and representation* (pp. 55–97). Cambridge: Cambridge University Press.

FIFA (2014). *Financial report 2014*. Zürich: FIFA.

Geeraert, A. (2015). *Sports Governance Observer 2015: The legitimacy crisis in international sports governance*. Copenhagen: Play the Game/Danish Institute for Sports Studies.

Geeraert, A. (2016a). *The EU in international sports governance: A principal–agent perspective on EU control of FIFA and UEFA*. Basingstoke and New York: Palgrave Macmillan.

Geeraert, A. (2016b). The governance of international sport organisations. In B. Houlihan & D. Malcolm (Eds), *Sport and society* (pp. 413–437). London: Sage.

Geeraert, A. (2017). 'Bad barrels': corruption in international sport federations. In S. Moston and L. Kihl (Eds), *Corruption in sport*. London: Routledge.

Geeraert, A., & Drieskens, E. (2015). The EU controls FIFA and UEFA: a principal–agent perspective. *Journal of European Public Policy, 22*(10), 1448–1466.

Geeraert, A., Mrkonjic, M., & Chappelet, J.-L. (2015). A rationalist perspective on the autonomy of international sport governing bodies: towards a pragmatic autonomy in the steering of sports. *International Journal of Sport Policy and Politics, 7*(4), 473–488.

Gibson, O. (2015). Fifa officials arrested on corruption charges as World Cup inquiry launched, *The Guardian* (27 May). Retrieved from: http://www.theguardian.com/ football/2015/may/27/several-top-fifa-officials-arrested

Gorta, A. (2006). Corruption risk areas and corruption resistance. In C. Sampford, A. Shacklock, C. Connors & F. Galtung (Eds), *Measuring corruption* (pp. 203–219). Burlington: Ashgate.

Hartmann, G. (2013). *IWF president under suspicion of financial mismanagement*. Retrieved from: http://www.playthegame.org/news/news-articles/2013/iwf-president-under-suspicion-of-financial-mismanagement/

Hoy, M. (2005). Volleygate: a showcase of greed and mismanagement. *Play the Game Magazine, 3*, 14–15.

Huntington, S. (2002). Modernisation and corruption. In A.J. Heidenheimer & M. Johnston (Eds), *Political corruption. Concepts & contexts* (pp. 253–263). New Brunswick and London: Transaction Publishers.

IOC (2008). *Basic universal principles of good governance of the Olympic and sports movement*. Lausanne: IOC.

Jackson, S.J., & Haigh, S. (2008). Between and beyond politics: Sport and foreign policy in a globalizing world. *Sport in Society, 11*(4), 349–358.

Jennings, A. (2006). *Foul! The secret world of FIFA: bribes, vote-rigging and ticket scandals*. London: HarperCollins.

Kiewiet, D.R., & McCubbins, M.D. (1991) *The logic of delegation: congressional parties and the appropriations process*. Chicago: The University of Chicago Press.

Klijn, E.-H., & Koppenjan, J.F.M. (2004). *Managing uncertainties in networks*. London: Routledge.

Lejeune, C., & Vas, A. (2012).Comparing the processes of identity change: a multiple-case study approach. Working paper, Université de Strasbourg. Retrieved from: http://www.alba.edu.gr/sites/pros/papers/pros-073.pdf

Levermore, R. (2004). Sport's role in constructing the 'inter-state' worldview'. In R. Levermore & A. Budd (Eds), *Sport and International Relations* (pp. 16–30). London: Routledge.

Luis, J.M., & Stewart, C. (2014). Corruption, South African multinational enterprises and institutions in Africa. *Journal of Business Ethics, 124*(3), 383–398.

MacMullan, M. (1961). A theory of corruption. *The Sociological Review, 9*(2), 181–201.

Mrkonjic, M. (2013). The Swiss regulatory framework and international sports organisations. In J. Alm (Ed.), *Action for good governance in international sports organisations* (pp. 128–132). Copenhagen: Play the Game/Danish Institute for Sports Studies.

Nye, J. (2008). *Soft power and the Beijing Olympics.* Retrieved from: http://www.centerforpublicleadership.org/index.php?option=com_content&view=article&id=113:nye-soft-power-and-the-beijing-olympics&catid=36:cpl-blog

Parliamentary Assembly of the Council of Europe (2012). Good governance and ethics in sport. Resolution 1875 (2012) Final.

Persson, E., & Petersson, B. (2014). Political mythmaking and the 2014 Winter Olympics in Sochi: Olympism and the Russian Great Power myth. *East European Politics, 30*(2): 192–209.

Pieth, M. (2014). *Reforming FIFA.* Zurich: Dike Verlag AG.

Randall, D., & Brady, B. (2011). Fifa accused promises 'tsunami' of revelations at bribery hearing. International alliance of politicians formed to press for reform of discredited governing body. *The Independent.* Retrieved from: http://www.independent.co.uk

Sandholtz, W., & Taagepera, R. (2005) Corruption, culture, and communism. *International Review of Sociology, 15*(1), 109–131.

Sugden, J. (2002). Network football, in J. Sugden & A. Tomlinson (Eds), *Power games: a critical sociology of sport* (pp. 61–80). London: Routledge.

Sugden, J., & Tomlinson, A. (1998). *FIFA and the contest for world football: who rules the people's game?* Cambridge: Polity Press.

Szymanski, S. (2006) *A theory on the evolution of modern sport* (International association of sports economists Working Paper Series, No. 06-30).

Tanzi, V. (1998). Corruption around the world: causes, consequences, scope, and cures. *Staff Papers (International Monetary Fund), 45*(4), 559–594.

Thibault, L., Kihl, L., & Babiak, K. (2010). Democratisation and governance in international sport: addressing issues with athlete involvement in organisational policy. *International Journal of Sport Policy and Politics,* 2(3), 275–302.

Tomlinson, A. (2005). The making of the global sports economy: ISL, the rise of the corporate player in world sport. In M.L. Silk, D.L. Andrews & C.L Cole (Eds), *Sport and Corporate Nationalisms* (pp. 35–66). Oxford: Berg.

Tomlinson, A. (2014). *FIFA (Federation Internationale de Football Association): the men, the myths and the money.* London: Routledge.

Tomlinson, S., Sale, C., & Shergold, A. (2015). FIFA's shameless squad: Hours after being freed from prison for 'exhaustion', suspect Jack Warner parties night away ... as Blatter bleats scandal is revenge for UK and US losing World Cup bids. *Daily Mail* (29 May). Retrieved from: http://www.dailymail.co.uk/news/article-3102072/FIFA-corruption-suspect-Jack-Warner-parties-release-jail-Trinidad-Tobago.html

UK Parliament (2011). Culture, media and sport committee – Sixth report 2018 World Cup bid. London: UK Parliament.

van Bottenburg, M. (2011). Why are the European and American sports worlds so different? Path-dependence in European and American sports history. In A. Tomlinson, C. Young & R. Holt (Eds), *Transformation of modern europe: states, media and markets 1950–2010* (pp. 205–255). London/New York: Routledge.

Voy, R.O., & Deeter, K.D. (1991). *Drugs, sport, and politics*. Champaign, IL: Leisure Press.

WADA Independent Commission (2015). *The Independent Commission report #1*.Montreal: WADA.

WADA Independent Commission (2016). *The Independent Commission report #2*.Montreal: WADA.

Walters, G. (2011). Bidding for international sport events: how government supports and undermines national governing bodies of sport. *Sport in Society, 14*(2), 208–222.

Weinreich, J. (2014). *Macht, Moneten, Marionetten: Ein Wegweiser durch die Olympische Parallelgesellschaft. IOC, FIFA, Bach, Putin, Blatter, Scheichs und Oligarchen*. Berlin: Krautreporter.

Woods, N. (1999). Good governance in international organisations. *Global Governance, 5*(1): 39–61.

MADE IN
EUROPE

ISBN-13: 978-1-4731-4805-1

9 781473 948051

SECTION D

SPORTING

EVENTS

SUSTAINABLE URBAN LEGACIES OF HOSTING THE OLYMPIC GAMES

LARISSA DAVIES

Introduction

In the twenty-first century, major sports events are big business and none more so than the Olympic Games. Proponents of such events, including governments and event organisers, often cite economic, social and physical improvements to the urban environment as a rationale to justify expenditure and gain local support. However, sustainable and positive urban 'legacies' are seldom guaranteed; often they rely on favourable success factors and can take many years to be realised.

This chapter examines the relationship between sports events and urban legacy by drawing upon both theoretical literature and empirical evidence from European cities. Specifically it examines urban legacies associated with hosting the Olympic Games. The first part of the chapter provides a historical overview of the Olympic Games and urban development, and examines the factors necessary for creating lasting positive urban legacies. The second part of the chapter focuses on a case study of London 2012 and how the Games have been used to create an urban legacy in East London. Throughout, the importance of business for sustaining urban legacies in the future is considered.

Defining urban legacy

'Legacy' is a broad term that has become widely used in relation to sports events. However, it is a term that has multiple definitions, meanings and interpretations and despite its widespread usage in the literature, policy and the media, its definition is somewhat elusive (Cashman, 2005). In general terms, it is taken to be 'a tangible or intangible thing handed down by a predecessor; a long lasting effect of an event or process; the act of bequeathing' (Mangan, 2008, p. 1869). Gratton and Preuss (2008) conceptualise legacy as a cube with three dimensions: positive and negative; planned and unplanned; and tangible and intangible. The term legacy is broadly considered to include a wide range of outcomes, from physical elements including sporting facilities and other urban infrastructure developments through to wider environmental, social, cultural, economic, political, sporting, education and tourism-related outcomes (Davies, 2012). For the purpose of this chapter, urban legacy is taken to mean any positive or negative lasting changes to the urban built and natural environment, which result from hosting a major event.

Historical overview of the Olympic Games and urban development

The relationship between major events and urban development is not a new phenomenon. For many years, fairs, festivals, expositions, cultural and sporting events have provided opportunities for cities to invest in infrastructure and environmental improvements (Chalkley and Essex, 1999). In contemporary society, major sports events commonly provide host cities with the opportunity to build new sports facilities and embark on a wider programme of urban development or regeneration. Regeneration is defined as:

> ... comprehensive and integrated vision and action which leads to the resolution of urban problems and which seeks to bring about a lasting improvement in the economic, physical, social and environmental condition of an area that has been subject to change. (Roberts, 2000, p. 17)

In some cases, events are used as the catalyst for larger-scale urban development or regeneration, whereas in other cases they are used to complement or accelerate existing plans. Davies (2010) identifies three broad models of sport-related regeneration, namely 'Sports-led regeneration' where sports events are seen as the catalyst and engine of regeneration; 'Sports regeneration' where sports events are embedded at an early stage into a developing or existing urban strategy alongside other activities; and 'Sport and regeneration' where sports events are not fully integrated at the master planning stage and are often 'added on' at a later stage in the developmental or regeneration process. Other academics have conceptualised the relationship between major events and urban development in different ways. For example, Smith and Fox (2007) discuss the distinction between 'event-led regeneration' – those projects undertaken directly related to staging an event – and 'event-themed regeneration' – those a city voluntarily chooses to pursue in conjunction with an event but are not critical to staging the event. Pitts and Liao (2009) similarly explore the differences between directly incurred event developments (e.g. sports facilities) and those developments a city voluntarily develops (e.g. transport, housing etc.).

There is a long history associated with the Olympic Games and urban development. Since the modern Olympics were revived by Baron Pierre de Coubertin in 1896, as shown in Figure 14.1, the Games have grown considerably. In Athens 1896 there were just 241 athletes from 14 nations, while in London 2012 there were 10,568 athletes from 204 nations. Although the growth of the Olympic Games has now stabilised, the size and scale are now so great that hosting the event has implications for cities that extend well beyond the provision of sports facilities and event infrastructure. Investment in supporting infrastructure such as transport, hotel accommodation, urban landscaping and public realm developments is often required to ensure the effective running of the Games and enhance the image of the host destination for a global audience. As a consequence, the cost of hosting an Olympic Games has become big business and has increased considerably. Not surprisingly, cities now expect a return on this investment in terms of a lasting urban legacy.

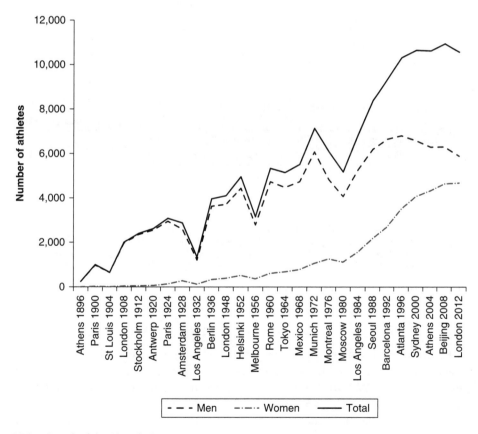

Figure 14.1 Growth of the Olympic Games

Source: IOC (2015)

Essex and Chalkey (1998, 2004) and Gold and Gold (2011) provide a historical overview of the Olympic Games and urban development. Essex and Chalkey (1998) note that since the early 1900s, although not always precisely linear, the summer Olympic Games have had a clear trajectory of increasing impact on the urban environment. Analysis of the Olympic Games and urban impact can roughly be divided into four periods as shown in Figure 14.2.

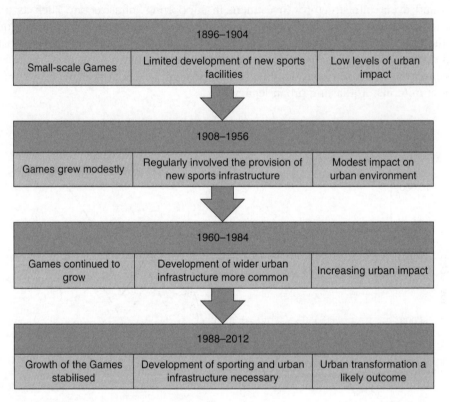

Figure 14.2   The Olympic Games and urban impact

Source: Davies (2012)

While the movement towards the development of more substantial host city infrastructure can be traced back to the 1960 Rome Olympics, it was the Seoul Games of 1988 that marked the beginning of the period which saw the Olympic Games more commonly used as a vehicle for urban transformation and legacy. Seoul notably used the Olympic Games to embark on a wider programme of urban re-planning and reconstruction and used the Games to address the severe economic, environmental and demographic problems of the city (Gold and Gold, 2011). In addition to the sports facilities and the Olympic Village, urban developments in the city included transport infrastructure (three new subway lines), the enhancement of cultural facilities (construction of new venues and refurbishment and repair of historic monuments), an environmental beatification programme (e.g. new parks; improved streets) and improvements to health and hygiene in the city (Essex and Chalkley, 1998).

Although Seoul represented a significant horizon in terms of using the Games to physically upgrade the city's infrastructure and built environment, it was undoubtedly from 1992 onwards and specifically the Barcelona Games, that the Olympics have been associated with more holistic physical, social and economic urban transformation. Barcelona is frequently cited by observers as an exemplar of using a major event for urban transformation and has earned the widely used accolade of the 'Regeneration Games' in recognition of the city-wide social, economic and environmental regeneration that was associated with the 1992 Olympic Games (Coaffee, 2011). For the 1992 Games, sports facilities were constructed and refurbished in two areas of the city (Montjuic and Vall d'Hebron), a large area of brownfield land was reclaimed for the Olympic Village (Parc de Mar), a new marina was developed, and a number of high quality urban architecture and strategic regeneration projects were undertaken across the city to improve the public realm. Transport infrastructure was also improved (e.g. a restructuring of the rail network; development of a coastal road) and a number of complementary social and economic programmes were implemented to improve the quality of life for residents. Barcelona used the Olympic Games as an opportunity to bring forward and fund a number of long-term projects and although Monclus (2011) notes how the city is still criticised for its neglect of social considerations over place marketing and economic considerations, the Games were and still are seen as a good example of using major events as a catalyst for large-scale urban improvement.

The Atlanta Games in 1996 are the exception case in Period 4, in that there were only minor changes to the city's urban infrastructure as a result of hosting the Olympic Games. Essex and Chalkley (1998) explain that this was related to the fact that the local organising committee was formed as a private non-profit making organisation with responsibility only for the development of sporting facilities. They note how the other agencies established for the Atlanta Games were ineffective in producing broader changes to the urban structure. All subsequent Games from 2000 onwards have sought to incorporate significant urban infrastructure developments alongside the development of sports facilities for the event. Sydney 2000, Athens 2004, Beijing 2008 and London 2012 have all used the Olympic Games as an opportunity to transform large urban areas within their respective cities, although urban regeneration has been one of several agendas used as a rationale for hosting the Games. Sydney for example, while using the Games to transform a heavily contaminated area in the west of the city known as Homebush Bay, also used the Games to embrace a sustainability agenda, by incorporating environmental responsibility into the design of facilities and use of resources (Gold and Gold, 2011); Athens used the Olympics to redevelop various areas of the city, in addition to boosting tourism and comprehensively reviewing transport within Greater Athens (Gold, 2011); and Beijing, while using the Games as a catalyst for substantial urban investment, used the Olympics to reinvent China as a participant in the global economy (Cook and Miles, 2011).

While it is clear from the examples provided that most cities from 1988 onwards have experienced significant urban development through hosting an Olympic Games, and many of these urban developments remain long after the Games have taken place, sustainable urban legacies are far from guaranteed. Although some Olympic cities such as Barcelona have gone on to fully integrate Olympic-related urban infrastructure into the city successfully, as discussed in the following section, others such as Athens have been less successful.

Contemporary and future challenges, capabilities and critiques

This section uses examples of previous Olympic hosts to examine some of the factors necessary for creating positive urban legacies. There are three major factors that have relevance to the theme of this book and which present challenges to creating an urban legacy: strategic legacy planning; the long-term viability of venues; and the economic and political context. Each of these factors will be discussed in turn, although they are by no means mutually exclusive.

Strategic and long-term legacy planning

Evidence from previous Olympic cities suggests that one of the key factors in maximising urban legacies is ensuring that there is strategic and long-term legacy planning for the Games. Hobkinson (2002) argues that:

> ... the facilities themselves for sporting extravaganzas such as the Olympic Games, World Cup and Commonwealth Games are not enough and the investment in them is only beneficial if a sustainable plan to regenerate the area and reposition the city is in place to live beyond the flame of the competition. (p. 3)

Preuss (2004) suggests that from an economic and urban development perspective it only makes sense to bid for an Olympic Games if the infrastructure required fits with the long-term plans for the city. Furthermore, if the Olympics can be used to bring forward and accelerate urban developments that were planned anyway, they are more likely to experience positive and long-lasting outcomes.

It is widely acknowledged that the integration of the Barcelona Olympics into the strategic vision and long-term plans for the city was a key factor in its successful regeneration (Coaffee, 2011; Monclus, 2011). Smith, Stevenson and Edmindson (2011) note how the Olympic projects were initially guided by robust urban development plans and subsequently a series of strategic plans that were prepared in conjunction with the Games. Conversely, the organisers of Sydney 2000 were criticised for their lack of attention with regard to broader master planning and this was cited as a factor that resulted in belated regeneration of the area (Brownhill, 2010). In the 'Barcelona model', strategic planning for the Games focused not only on planning and delivering the event, but also on the wider vision and longer-term objectives for the city in the post-Games era. This is widely considered to be a key factor in the sustainability of the urban legacy seen in Barcelona today.

Long-term viability of event venues

In any business, economic viability and performance is a key element of success. A further factor considered important to securing sustainable urban legacy benefits from hosting an Olympic Games is ensuring that the permanent venues have a long-term purpose and are economically viable post-event (Davies, 2011). This is critical to alleviating the economic burden of maintaining the facilities; maximising return on investment and creating employment opportunities for the local community. Furthermore, finding a long-term use for permanent event venues is important for creating vibrancy and footfall to the surrounding area, which is more likely to encourage further related investment (London Assembly, 2011).

There are several examples of Olympic cities that have failed to secure immediate tenants for the permanent venues constructed for the Games. In some cases, this has resulted in so-called 'white elephants' – i.e. venues which are expensive to maintain and whose cost is disproportionate to its usefulness. In a European context, Athens stands out as an example of a host city that failed to secure long-term tenants for its venues in the post-Olympic era and possibly represents the worst example of long-term legacy planning in recent years. The majority of sports facilities, including the national stadium, were intended to be used for public recreation and leisure after the Games. However, bureaucracy and a lack of long-term planning left the Olympic sports complex underused and inaccessible to the public apart from when soccer matches are held at the Olympic Stadium (Kissoudi, 2010). Wrangling about whether the venues should be viewed as a social resource or exploited for their commercial value resulted in many venues being abandoned. While some venues did find long-term usage, for example the Badminton Hall in Goudi became a national theatre, the vast majority of facilities have now fallen into disrepair and whole areas have been fenced off to prevent vandalism (Gold, 2011; Mangan, 2008). Although there are some positive legacies for Athens in terms of transportation, the failure to secure long-term tenants for the majority of venues significantly impacted on the potential urban legacy for the citizens of Athens.

A future challenge for Olympic hosts is to ensure that there is a planned purpose for all permanent structures post-Games or alternatively to consider using a larger number of existing or temporary venues. Paradoxically though, the removal of sporting infrastructure after the Games, while relieving the economic burden, potentially removes the lasting urban legacy, and therefore this needs to be balanced with creating new economically viable and sustainable facilities for the community post event.

Economic and political context

While the previous two factors discussed are within the control of event organisers and urban planners, a factor which is exogenous, but considered by some commentators to be significant in securing a positive urban legacy, is the broader economic and political circumstances under which an Olympic Games and subsequent urban development and regeneration occur. In a study on the impact of the Olympic Games on real estate, Plumb and McKay (2001) argue that context is important and the success of Olympic legacies is often dependent upon the economic and political status of cities. Again, using the example of Barcelona, the 1992 Games took place in a politically stable period '... in conditions that allowed the potential of the Olympics to act as a vehicle for urban development to shine through ...' (Gold and Gold, 2011, p. 45). This impacted positively on private business confidence and investment in Olympic-related regeneration projects. Conversely, unstable economic conditions in Greece and subsequent recession in the global economy have undoubtedly had a negative effect on the ensuing legacy of the 2004 Athens Olympics. A major challenge for Olympic cities is that global economic conditions and the political status of the host country are often different at the time of bidding from those experienced at the time of staging the Games. As a consequence, planning and predicting urban legacies in both scenarios are difficult to establish with any degree of certainty.

The three factors discussed are widely considered to impact on the sustainability of urban legacies. However, the literature suggests that there are other factors which may influence legacy outcomes, including governance of legacy planning; secured public sector investment post-Games; successful place marketing and branding, and meaningful engagement and inclusion of the local community (Davies, 2012). Ultimately, the sustainability of urban legacies from major events is likely to be determined by a combination of factors, which in the end may be unique to each host city.

Case study 14.1: London 2012

While the modern Olympics have historically been associated with urban development, no city since Barcelona has arguably placed legacy and urban regeneration at the heart of an Olympic Games more so than London in 2012. This section will give an overview of how the city has used the Olympic Games to create an urban legacy and reflect on the planning process from a business perspective.

Details and context: Urban legacy planning and London 2012

Urban regeneration was a key part of the London 2012 Games. From the early stages of planning, it was clear that urban regeneration and legacy were an important component of the Games. The Candidate File (2007) stated that:

> The Olympic Park will be created in the Lower Lea Valley, 13km east from the centre of London. This area is ripe for redevelopment. By staging the Games in this part of the city, the most enduring legacy of the Olympics will be the regeneration of an entire community for the direct benefit of everyone that lives there. (p.19)

The Olympic Park is located in East London, on a site which spans across four local planning authorities: Newham, Hackney, Tower Hamlets and Waltham Forest. There were two reasons for locating the Olympic Park in this area of East London. The first was the availability of brownfield land and existing transport extensions to rail and underground systems; the second, as alluded to above, was the high levels of deprivation in the local communities of the Olympic host boroughs. Based on the Index of Multiple Deprivation (IMD), which ranks local areas in England on a range of economic, environmental and social indicators, many areas within the Olympic host boroughs were and are amongst the most deprived quintile (20%) in England and Wales (Host Boroughs, 2009). The Olympic Games were seen as an opportunity to regenerate an area of the city, which for many years has suffered from economic, social and physical decline. As an indication of the importance of urban regeneration to the London Games, it remained a key part of pre-event legacy planning, despite political change in local government in London in 2008 and national government in the UK in 2010.

A core ambition of winning the 2012 Games was to create a platform for a sustainable economic, social and physical regeneration legacy. From a business perspective, a challenge for the London Games was building infrastructure fit for purpose, on time and within budget, which would also be sustainable in legacy mode. The creation of an urban legacy for London required strategic integration of the venues and infrastructure developments into the broader and long-term masterplanning of the area, and a clear business plan for the permanent venues in legacy mode to be economically viable and sustainable.

Building for legacy

As a construction project, the planning and delivery of London 2012 were complex. No major project of the scale planned for the Games had previously been planned and delivered in the UK in such exceptional circumstances on an inner city brownfield site. Carmichael (2012) explains:

> ... the London 2012 construction project was to be delivered at speed, to a non negotiable deadline, on a large scale and previously intractable site, with fixed public funding and uncertain future ownership. (p. 1)

The project presented a significant set of challenges in masterplanning, design and construction for the Olympic Delivery Authority (ODA), the organisation responsible for delivering the infrastructure for the Games. One of the major challenges was delivering two masterplans in parallel: in the short term, to deliver a distinctive Olympic Park to provide a stage for the Games, and in the longer term, to deliver a new urban district. All this had to be achieved under the scrutiny of the UK government, the International Olympic Committee (IOC), the international media and a large number of other stakeholders (Carmichael, 2012). The original budget for infrastructure was £4 billion, although this quickly rose to £9.375 billion (excluding the costs of staging the event; land acquisition and wider regeneration and transport infrastructure).

The infrastructure for London 2012 included a mix of permanent new venues; temporary venues and existing facilities. The Olympic Park, which included most of the permanent venues, was primarily where the urban legacy for London 2012 was created and where the physical change and

(Continued)

(Continued)

local impacts are most likely to be experienced in future. The Olympic Park, subsequently known in legacy mode as the Queen Elizabeth Olympic Park, included the International Broadcast Centre/Main Press Centre and the Athletes' Village, together with five permanent sporting venues. These were the Olympic Stadium; Velodrome; Aquatics Centre; Handball Arena and Eton Manor. Table 14.1 illustrates the legacy use of the permanent venues in the Olympic Park. As shown below, in most cases the venues for London 2012 were reconfigured to reduce capacity and increase flexibility of usage.

Table 14.1   Legacy usage of permanent sports venues on the Queen Elizabeth Olympic Park

Games venue	Legacy venue	Games use	Planned legacy use
Olympic Stadium	The Stadium	Opening and closing ceremonies; athletics. 80,000 seats	Multi use venue: Football (primary); athletics; rugby; various events and concerts. 54,000 seats
Aquatics Centre	London Aquatics Centre	Swimming; diving. 17,500 seats	Swimming; diving; water polo. 2,500 seats
Velodrome; BMX track	Lee Valley VeloPark	Track cycling, BMX. 6,000 seats in velodrome; 6,000 seats at BMX track	Track cycling; BMX; road cycling; mountain biking. 6,000 seats in velodrome
Eton Manor	Lee Valley Hockey and Tennis Centre	Aquatic training, wheelchair tennis. 10,500 seats across several tennis courts	Tennis; hockey. 3,000 seats at main hockey pitch, expandable up to 15,000
Handball Arena	The Copper Box Arena	Handball; goalball; fencing. 6,000 seats	Multi-use venue: e.g. netball; basketball; gymnastics; badminton; fencing; volleyball. Retractable seating, expandable up to 7500

Source: London Assembly (2011); London Legacy Development Corporation (2015)

Sustaining an urban legacy from London 2012: Capabilities, challenges and critiques

It is too early to establish whether the urban legacy emanating from the 2012 Games will be sustainable in the longer term, therefore this section will reflect on the planning process from a business perspective and discuss the potential for sustaining an urban legacy from the 2012 Games in the future.

A key aspect of the approach adopted in London was that legacy planning for regeneration was addressed earlier and more convincingly than in most previous Olympic Games. Masterplanning of the Olympic Park was strategic, taking account of the short-term requirements of hosting the Games and the long-term needs of the local area from the start. Carmichael (2012) suggests that four key strategies emerged in the planning stages, which have contributed to the emerging urban legacy: legacy was 'locked into' the design, planning and delivery process at inception; investment in infrastructure was prioritised as a basis for regeneration; the long-term impact of the Games-time masterplan on the environment was considered from the start; and finally, where there was uncertainty about future requirements within the Park, it was designed where possible to leave long-term options flexible. Furthermore, learning lessons from regeneration projects of the past such as Canary Wharf,[1] the Olympic Park was designed to blend with and complement surrounding neighbourhoods, giving it the best possible chance of integration in the future.

Despite the apparent strengths in legacy planning, a critique of the process is that in the early stages there was considerable uncertainty about the governance arrangements for the Olympic park post event (Davies, 2012). The Olympic Park Legacy Company (OPLC), which later became the London Legacy Development Corporation (LLDC), was not set up until 2009, by which time the ODA was already into its second year of construction delivery. To overcome this, in the interim, the ODA worked with the landowners to design a flexible long-term masterplan, which did not preclude development options (Carmichael, 2012). Seemingly, in the case of London the long-term masterplan was not compromised, although this has been cited as problematic and a reason for slow legacy transformation in other cities such as Sydney (Brownhill, 2010; Davies 2012).

A clear strength of planning for London 2012 was securing a longer-term legacy use for the permanent sporting venues on the Olympic Park. This is important from a business perspective for two reasons: firstly, to prevent the facilities from becoming an economic burden; and secondly, to generate footfall in the Olympic Park, which is necessary to create further economic activity in the surrounding area (Davies, 2011). Nevertheless, planning and securing tenants for the permanent venues in London were not without controversy. There was considerable debate over whether the Olympic Stadium should be used for football. Premier League club West Ham United will be the anchor tenant and move into the stadium from the 2016–17 season. Although the venue will also have the capacity to be reconfigured for multi-use sports events, many commentators felt that the publicly-funded stadium should be retained primarily as an athletics venue. However, evidence from other Olympic cities such as Beijing and Sydney has demonstrated that it is difficult to make a business case for a permanent athletics stadium, whereas there are successful examples of stadia built for major events and subsequently used by football teams. The Ethiad Stadium, built for the 2002 Commonwealth Games and now leased by Manchester City Football Club, is often cited as such. There continues to be ongoing criticism of the use of public money to fund the Olympic Stadium in London and this presents an ongoing challenge for the LLDC (Gibson, 2015).

A further strength of the legacy planning in London 2012 was recognition that there was no demand for many of the facilities required for the Games. Although some use was made of existing facilities, for example Wimbledon for tennis and Wembley for football, 25 temporary venues were built for the 2012 Games, more so than for any previous Olympic Games or global event (Fischer, 2011; Gold, 2012). On the Olympic Park, these included the Basketball Arena and Water Polo Arena, and elsewhere in London included venues for beach volleyball at Horse Guards Parade, triathlon in Hyde Park and horse riding events at Greenwich Park. Several other venues such as the Aquatics

(Continued)

(Continued)

Centre were partially temporary with seating 'wings' that were removed in legacy mode. Critics argue that the construction of temporary venues is costly once dismantling is taken into account and they leave no lasting legacy for the community; nevertheless, there was a strong business case for temporary venues in London. Importantly, the creation of temporary venues, together with the use of existing venues, avoided the financial and environmental problems caused by underutilised and disused facilities seen in other Olympic cities such as Athens.

The case study of London 2012 has largely focused on the legacy planning process, and the key aspects of building a sustainable urban legacy post event, from a business perspective. Hosting the 2012 Games provided an injection of public money to a deprived area, a focused and committed public organisation to deliver infrastructure and a fixed developmental timescale (Carmichael, 2012). Without the Games, it is likely that the brownfield Olympic site in East London would have remained derelict for some time, as private investors would not have tackled the large-scale land remediation and decontamination required for it to be developed commercially, particularly at a time of global recession. The Olympic Games allowed for the planning system to be simplified and developments to be fast tracked. Although beneficial for business investors, critics argue that public consultation time was constrained and in some cases bypassed, marginalising local communities. The Olympic Games have undoubtedly provided a platform for building an urban legacy in East London, but for whom remains to be seen. A significant challenge for policy makers is to ensure that within 20 years, the strategic convergence target of giving the communities who hosted the 2012 Games the same economic and social chances as their neighbours across London, is achieved by improving the standard of living for existing communities, rather than displacing them through the in-migration of a new, younger and more affluent population. Ultimately, the passage of time will determine who the London 2012 urban legacy is for and whether it will be sustainable in the longer term.

Conclusion

The Olympic Games represent a unique opportunity to create physical, economic and social improvements to urban areas. Historically, host cities have used the Games to build new sports facilities and embark upon or bring forward a wider programme of urban development and regeneration. However, as illustrated within this chapter, positive change is not always guaranteed and the sustainability of urban legacies is dependent on various factors, including strategic and long-term legacy planning, the commercial viability of permanent venues post-event and a positive economic climate to encourage inward investment. Cities that have succeeded in creating positive urban legacies have demonstrated strong business acumen in the planning, delivery and operation of infrastructure in legacy mode. They have sought to embed Olympic-related developments into the surrounding area, have a strong commercial rationale for building venues, and importantly, an economically viable plan for their long-term, post-event future.

Ultimately, sustainable urban legacies take many years to be realised and even then, a lack of long-term monitoring and evaluation makes it difficult to establish the specific contribution of the Olympic Games and the counterfactual, namely what would have happened if the Games had not taken place. While the physical transformation of the urban landscape may be clearly visible at Games-time, it can often take 10–15 years to establish whether lasting economic and social legacies have been achieved. From a European perspective the Olympic Games have produced mixed results. Research suggests that the 1992 Barcelona Games has generated a sustainable urban legacy; whereas emerging evidence from the 2004 Athens Games is less convincing. Moreover, despite claims from the LLDC, ODA and various other stakeholders that the 2012 Olympic Games have successfully regenerated East London, it will be a number of years before it is clear whether the Games have contributed to improving economic and social indicators in what are considered to be some of the most deprived areas in England.

The focus of this chapter has been on the business aspect of urban legacies from Olympic Games. However, an important dimension of building a sustainable legacy, which has only been touched upon briefly here, is consideration of the needs and requirements of the local community. A criticism of large-scale, top-down legacy projects such as the Olympic Games is that they marginalise local communities and can lead to the displacement of existing residents with new and more affluent residents. In many host cities, regeneration beyond major events requires private sector investment, which often results in the development of housing and other facilities that are beyond the affordability of existing residents. In such cases, while urban transformation may be perceived as successful from a business perspective, it does little to improve the lives of disadvantaged people or places, which are often the primary focus of major event bids. For the Olympic Games and other major events to create positive and sustainable legacies in the longer term, a permanent sporting infrastructure needs to be accessible to residents in existing as well as new communities, and wider urban developments such as housing and environmental landscaping need to be inclusive and sympathetic to surrounding areas. Urban legacies are still not guaranteed, but the likelihood of sustaining those that are created will be greatly increased.

Recommended further reading

The following contributions may be of interest to those students wishing to read more widely on the issues discussed within this chapter:

Davies, L. E. (2012). Beyond the Games: regeneration legacies and London 2012. *Leisure Studies*, 31(3), 309–337.

This journal article will be of interest to students wishing to know more about the regeneration legacies of Olympic Games. It expands upon the factors that contribute to successful regeneration, discusses the importance of evaluating Olympic regeneration legacies and gives further detail about the regeneration legacy planning for London 2012. The journal article suggests a number of considerations for establishing a framework for regeneration legacy evaluation in the future.

Gold, R. J., & Gold, M. M. (Eds) (2011). *Olympic cities.* London: Routledge.

This book will be of interest to students who want to read further about the changing relationship between cities and the Olympic Games. Of particular interest to students will be the overview of urban legacies of the four Olympic festivals, namely the Summer Games; Winter Games; Cultural Olympiads and the Paralympics. Furthermore the ten detailed case studies from 1936 to 2016 provide students with extensive insight into the challenges faced by Olympic cities.

Smith, A. (2012). *Events and urban regeneration: The strategic use of events to revitalise cities.* London: Routledge.

This multi-disciplinary book will be of interest to students who want to know more about the relationship between major events and urban regeneration. It is a comprehensive text which includes theoretical discussions about why events are important to cities. The book makes extensive use of international case studies of sports and cultural events to explore the merits and problems of event-related public policy.

Note

1   Canary Wharf is a high rise business district in East London. It was built as part of a major policy intervention to regenerate the London Docklands in the late 1980s. Although now considered to be a hugely successful economic development, it was widely criticised for being a 'top-down' flagship project, which did little to improve economic and social conditions for local people (Jones and Evans, 2008).

References

Brownhill, S. (2010). *Literature review: Olympic venues – regeneration legacy.* Retrieved from: http://www.london.gov.uk/sites/default/files/FINAL%20-%20Oxford%20Brookes%20review.pdf
Candidate File (2007). *Volume 1 – Theme 1: Olympic Games: Concept and legacy.* Retrieved from: http://www.london2012.com/publications
Carmichael, L. (2012). *Learning legacy: Lessons from Masterplanning and designing London 2012.* Retrieved from: http://learninglegacy.independent.gov.uk/documents/pdfs/masterplanning-and-town-planning/426150-ll-masterplan-summary-tagged.pdf
Cashman, R. (2005). *The bitter-sweet awakening: The legacy of the Sydney 2000 Olympic Games.* Sydney: Walla Walla Press.
Chalkley, B., & Essex, E. (1999). Urban development through hosting international events: a history of the Olympic Games. *Planning Perspectives*, 14 (4), 369–394. DOI: 10.1080/026654399364184.

Coaffee, J. (2011). Urban regeneration and renewal. In R. J. Gold & M. M. Gold (Eds), *Olympic cities* (pp. 340–359). London: Routledge.

Cook, I. G., & Miles, S. (2011). Beijing 2008. In R. J. Gold & M. M. Gold (Eds), *Olympic cities* (pp. 340–359). London: Routledge.

Davies, L. E. (2010). Sport and economic regeneration: A winning combination? *Sport in Society*, 13 (10), 1438–1457. DOI: 10.1080/17430437.2010.520935.

Davies, L. E. (2011). Using sports infrastructure to deliver economic and social change: Lessons for London beyond 2012. *Local Economy*, 26 (4), 227–231. DOI: 10.1177/0269094211404638.

Davies, L. E. (2012). Beyond the Games: regeneration legacies and London 2012. *Leisure Studies*, 31(3), 309–337. DOI: 10.1080/02614367.2011.649779.

Essex, S. J., & Chalkley, B. S. (1998). The Olympics as a catalyst of urban renewal: A review. *Leisure Studies*, 17 (3,), 187–206. DOI: 10.1080/026143698375123.

Essex, S. J., & Chalkley, B. S. (2004). Mega-sporting events in urban and regional policy: A history of the Winter Olympics. *Planning Perspectives*, 19 (2) 201–232. DOI: 10.1080/0266543042000192475.

Fischer, E. (2011). *London 2012: Temporary Olympic constructions*. Retrieved from: http://www.design build-network.com/features/feature126375/

Gibson, O. (2015). Question of state aid still lingers over West Ham's luxurious new home. Retrieved from: http://www.theguardian.com/football/2015/apr/20/west-ham-olympic-stadium-state-aid-question

Gold, D. (2012). *Why sustainable temporary structures are one of the leading legacies of London 2012*. Retrieved from: http://www.insidethegames.biz/articles/1011205/why-sustainable-temporary-struc tures-are-one-of-the-leading-legacies-of-london-2012

Gold, M. (2011). Athens, 2004. In R. J. Gold & M. M. Gold (Eds), *Olympic cities* (pp. 315–339). London: Routledge.

Gold, J. R., & Gold, M. M. (Eds.) (2011). *Olympic cities*. London: Routledge.

Gratton, C., & Preuss, H. (2008). Maximising Olympic impacts by building up legacies. *The International Journal of the History of Sport*, 25 (14), 1922–1938. DOI: 10.1080/09523360802439023.

Hobkinson R. (2002). *What's the story – more than sporting glory? Manchester and the 2002 Commonwealth Games*. Jones Lang LaSalle. Retrieved from: http://www.jll.com/research.

Host Boroughs. (2009). *Strategic Regeneration Framework: An Olympic legacy for the host boroughs. Stage 1 – October 2009*. Retrieved from: http://www.gamesmonitor.org.uk/files/strategic-regeneration-frame work-report.pdf

IOC. (2015). *Official website of the Olympic Movement – Olympic Games*. http://www.olympic.org/ olympic-games.

Jones, P., & Evans, J. (2008). *Urban regeneration in the UK*. London: Sage.

Kissoudi, P. (2010). Athens' Post-Olympic aspirations and the extent of their realization. *International Journal of the History of Sport*, 27 (16–18), 2780–2797.

London Assembly (2011). *Park life: The legacy of London's Olympic venues*. Retrieved from: https://www.london.gov.uk/mayor-assembly/london-assembly/publications/park-life-legacy-londons-olympic-venues

London Legacy Development Corporation (2015). *Queen Elizabeth Olympic Park*. http://queenelizabetho-lympicpark.co.uk/

Mangan, J. A. (2008). Prologue: Guarantees of global goodwill: Post-Olympic legacies – Too many limp-ing white elephants? *The International Journal of the History of Sport*, 25 (14), 1869–1883. DOI: 10.1080/09523360802496148.

Monclus, F. (2011). Barcelona 1992. In R. J. Gold & M. M. Gold (Eds.), *Olympic cities* (pp. 268–286). London: Routledge.

Pitts, A., & Liao, H. (2009). *Sustainable Olympic design and urban development*. Abingdon: Routledge.

Plumb, C., & McKay, M. (2001). *Reaching beyond the gold: The impact of the Olympic Games on real estate markets*. Jones Lang Salle. Retrieved from: http://www.research.joneslanglasalle.com

Preuss, H. (2004). *The economics of staging the Olympics: A comparison of the Games 1972–2008*. Cheltenham: Edward Elgar Publishing.

Roberts, P. (2000). The evolution, definition and purpose of urban regeneration. In P. Roberts & H. Sykes (Eds), *Urban regeneration: A handbook* (pp. 9–36). London: Sage.

Smith, A., & Fox, T. (2007). From event-led to event-themed regeneration: The 2002 Commonwealth Games legacy scheme. *Urban Studies*, 44, (5/6), 1125–1143. DOI: 10.1080/00420980701256039.

Smith, A., Stevenson, N., & Edmindson, T. (2011). *The 2012 Games: The regeneration legacy*. Retrieved from: http://www.rics.org/uk/knowledge/research/research-reports/the-2012-games-the-regeneration-legacy/

THE COST OF HOSTING INTERNATIONAL SPORTS EVENTS

WLADIMIR ANDREFF

Introduction

Local politicians and decision makers are easy to convince that for a country/city it will be worth hosting an international mega-sporting event. An ex ante study of the economic and social impacts exhibiting a net benefit will finalise the consensus. However, it is nearly impossible to succeed in hosting a mega-sporting event at expected costs and benefits. The economic rationale of this paradox lies in awarding such events through an auction-like procedure which turns out to trigger a winner's curse. In this chapter, we will outline a critical examination of how a winner's curse develops and to what extent its consequences can be managed.

First, the concept of a winner's curse is delineated; its occurrences in the sports economy are pointed out, in particular when hosting sports events. Second, case studies on Summer and Winter Olympics confirm a recurrent winner's curse. Third, and finally, practical implications for how host cities or nations can counteract the winner's curse and better manage hosting international sports events are turned into recommendations for Paris vis-à-vis hosting the 2024 Summer Olympics.

The winner's curse, the sports economy and mega-sporting events

The winner's curse concept emerged in explaining the low returns on investments to companies engaged in competitive bidding that had paid too high a price for oil and gas leases to recoup their expenditures with the revenues from their investment; they had been cursed. Later, the winner's curse was used to understand large takeover premiums in auctions for failed banks. It was noted that in any auction-type setting, where the value of the auctioned object is uncertain but will turn out to be the same for all bidders, the party that overestimates the value of the object is likely to outbid its competitors and win the contest. Auction winners who fail to recognise this possibility are likely to be cursed. Thaler (1994) stresses the asymmetric information across bidders, which leads to an extreme form of the winner's curse in which any positive bid yields an expected financial loss to the bidder. The many occurrences in financial markets comprise the great bulk of the examples in the winner's curse literature. Examples of 'winners' being cursed have also been found in second-hand markets, primarily in the market for 'lemons' where the true value of a second-hand car is uncertain and unknown to the purchasers while hidden by the seller. Akerlof (1970) has demonstrated that with such information asymmetry the market leads to adverse selection and the winning purchaser is cursed.

In centrally-planned economies, investment funds were allocated by central state administration across state-owned enterprises through an auction in a context of information asymmetry and non-transparency. Each enterprise was inclined to 'cheat' with regard to the reality of its investment costs and revenues, underestimating costs and the completion duration of the investment project while overestimating investment revenues. Facing a myriad of 'fantabulous' projects, adverse selection was the most common outcome of central bureaucrats' decisions taken after enterprises' bargaining, lobbying and bribing. Central administration was cursed insofar as it was allocating investment funds to less-efficient projects than expected and state-owned enterprises were cursed, either through cheating, or they were submitting infeasible investment projects and, in practice, were then not able to complete them within the deadline at the ex ante announced cost.

In the sports economy, a winner's curse can emerge in four ways (Andreff, 2014). The first one shows up when several cities compete to host a same team franchise in North American sports leagues (Rosentraub & Swindell, 2002). When looking for a location a team owner is in a monopoly position; cities are the bidders and the prize for the winner is to obtain the franchise being located in its municipal area. Bidders in such an auction-like bargaining process are played off against one another by the team owner. Each competitor bases its bid on how much it expects the team to be worth. If a city overestimates the benefits the team will bring, it overbids for the franchise it would have been better off losing. The key aspect of the winner's curse is that not all cities have the same expectations. When a city wins the bid this basically reflects its optimism about the unknown value of the team due to information asymmetry. Because owners, acting as leagues, have controlled the location of teams so well, the cities are at a bargaining disadvantage and cursed.

A second occurrence happens when TV channels are bidding for a sports league's broadcasting rights (Gratton & Solberg, 2007). The winner's curse results from staging an actual auction and not an auction-like mechanism as in the franchise location story. TV companies usually compete to broadcast a sport event supplied by a single sports organisation (team, league, federation) – thus in a monopoly position. Taking stock of the latter, a sport event organiser offers broadcasting rights on auction that starts with a low bid, which is then raised successively by just small amounts over the previous bid until one bidding TV channel wins. Meanwhile all other bidders give up when the bid rises higher than their own valuation and the maximum reservation price they have claimed to pay. The bidding procedure ends up when the price reaches just above the reservation price of the bidder with the second-highest valuation. The risk of a winner's curse is very high since a TV company has no information about the actual maximum valuation of competitors and thus must overbid to increase its information about rivals' valuation until the price reaches its own valuation. The broadcasting rights have become extremely expensive and prices have increased so much that many TV companies that acquire the rights are hit by the winner's curse. Quite a number of sports rights deals have ended up being unprofitable for the TV channel which translated into financial losses for the TV company that won the bid. Several broadcasters have been cursed because they discovered too late they had overpaid for the rights and were unable to make the acquisition economically viable. For instance, ITV Digital and Kirch Media, after winning on auction for important broadcasting rights were so much cursed that they went bankrupt. To countervail the risk of the winner's curse TV companies tacitly collude or openly merge in such a way as to balance the sporting seller's monopoly power with a monopsony power. Such a countervailing strategy curbs the inflation of broadcasting rights fees whereas its absence fuels a fee skyrocketing trend.

A winner may be cursed in a third occurrence when several teams overbid each other for recruiting the same free agent player in North American team sports, or a superstar player anywhere in European football in the post-Bosman era. In the labour market for talent, team owners are the bidders and free agent or superstar players are sellers of the right to use their talent. For each sale the free agent or superstar player is in a monopoly situation over its talent rights as soon as this player is not substitutable on the pitch. The prize is for the winning team to recruit a player despite other teams' bids. The player auctions the right to use his talent and sells it to the highest bidder while the bids are determined by each team's estimate of the marginal revenue product associated with a given player after looking at his past performance and characteristics (points scored, age, height, experience, etc.). The team that expects the highest marginal contribution of a given player to its revenue offers the highest salary bid. If information about players' characteristics is limited, uncertain and asymmetric across teams, preconditions for the winner's curse are met.

In the context of North American team sports leagues, the winner's curse pertains to trading free agent players whereas in European professional team sports leagues where there is no draft, all players being tradable, the issue is more with players in a monopoly position over their scarce (high quality) talent rights, i.e. superstars. With regard to North American free agent players, overbidding is due to an inherent element of uncertainty in evaluating a player's future marginal worth. Given this uncertainty, the most optimistic team manager will win the bid with an upward bidding bias when many bidders participate. Increasing the number of bidders magnifies the overestimation bias (Cassing & Douglas, 1980). As a result free agents are likely to be overpaid, and the winning team is likely to be cursed. Another assumption is that the market for free agent players shares some features with a market for 'lemons'. Lehn (1984) found that owners lack all the information they need when they make bids and get stuck with injured players at a high price; the market for talent is subject to self-selection of poor quality players just like in Akerlof's market for 'lemons'. In European team sports leagues, the ultimate cause of the winner's curse is the arms race between teams to recruit a superstar player or coach. This arms race is more intense between teams for instance in post-Bosman European football leagues than in North American leagues (Andreff, 2011), so that the winner's curse is more often observed in the former than the latter labour market for talent. However, the winner's curse hypothesis has not been econometrically tested yet for player transfers across European leagues.

The four occurrence of a winner's curse refers to bidding for hosting a mega-sporting event which nearly always comes out with *cost overruns* for the winner (Andreff, 2012). We focus more on such occurrences as the core topic of this chapter while the Olympics is taken as a case in point and dealt with in more detail in the case studies. The IOC publicises the task of hosting and organising the Games within a precise deadline and then it calls for projects proposals. These proposals are not applications for IOC funding; rather, cities are candidates for raising funds from different sources in order to cover the cost of those investments required to host the Games. At the end of an auction-like setting the IOC awards the right to host the Olympics to the most interesting project. The object of such an auction is not to obtain finance allocated by the IOC but to win the status of being the next Olympics host city. A city willing to host the Games commits itself to a heavy investment over a seven-year period and then hopes to benefit from the 'Olympics host city' label which provides a unique capacity for mobilising finance.

The IOC objective, in a monopoly position to award the Games, is to elect every fourth year a host city for the Summer and Winter Olympics, with the expectation that bidding cities will provide projects including all the required facilities and commit themselves to adhering to an operational budget, the minimal precondition for a city to be selected. A complementary objective is the best possible quality of the Games which consists of a guarantee of well-functioning and secure sports contests (quality of sporting equipment, distance between Olympic venues and the Olympic village, and so on), an excellent hosting quality (Olympic village, transportation, hotels), overall security, impressive opening and closing ceremonies, high-quality media and telecommunications and, nowadays, an environmental quality, all prerequisites according to the 20 chapters contained in the bid book. The IOC looks for a project that will benefit from worldwide media coverage, leave a grandiose image of each Olympiad, and an unforgettable memory and indelible marks on the host city landscape. With a view to obtaining a grandiose project, it is in the IOC's interest to fuel overbidding across candidate cities.

The cost of the Olympics is not a decisive criterion in the voting of IOC members. Furthermore, the criterion of minimal cost to some extent clashes with maximising the desired extravagant quality of the Games. For instance, London 2012 was voted at an expected cost (all in $ billion) of 18.3 as against 3.6 for Madrid, 8.9 for Paris, 10.7 for New York, and 11.9 for Moscow. Rio de Janeiro 2016 won with a $9.5bn cost against Chicago 3.3, Tokyo 4.1 and Madrid 4.2. Tokyo 2020 ($3.4bn) won though Madrid was cheaper (2.4). These data exhibit adverse selection in terms of cost.

The crystal clear objective function of bidding cities consists of obtaining the right to host the Games. Each bidding city must promise fixed quantities of the sporting facilities requested by the IOC and a variable quantity of non-sporting infrastructure, focusing on their excellent quality since it will be selected or not on these aspects of its candidature. Since the financial disaster of the 1976 Montreal Games and after Los Angeles 1984 demonstrated that a local organisation committee (LOOC) can end up in the black, the cost dimension of candidatures has become increasingly significant, though not the major decision criterion of IOC voters.

The primary interest of bidding cities is to maximise the qualitative components of their candidature, thereby encouraging ambitious project proposals. After 1984, bidding cities started advertising reasonable or even low costs in parallel with the supposedly unbelievable quality of their candidature. The only way to reconcile an extravagant project with costs that are not exorbitant is, explicitly or implicitly, to cheat, that is, to communicate and to complete the bid book on the basis of costs that are underestimated by different means (omitting the VAT, lowering the Paralympics budget, and so on). Bidding cities naturally overbid upward with respect to the quality and downward with respect to the publicised cost of their project. Such a strategy compares with that of rival enterprises struggling for the allocation of investment funds in centrally-planned economies, except that cities are seeking to be awarded the Games because it is a precondition for mobilising the huge financing necessary for hosting the Olympics. Thus, rival bidding cities are in sync with the principal objective of the IOC, which is to balance outward extravagance with the appearance of reasonable cost, but the host city is cursed.

The IOC's recurrent worries about delayed Olympic building sites can be used as a control variable of the winner's curse. Building delays usually generate cost overruns when it comes to rushing in order to stick to the deadline. Revising building costs upwards (thus revealing initial cost underestimation) or giving up some Olympic building to curb skyrocketing costs is also a tell-tale sign of the winner's curse. Another revealing factor is when the host city obtains extra finance or extra public subsidies, for instance from the government. A financial deficit or an ex post lower financial surplus than expected by the LOOC provides further proof of the winner's curse while a sanction of the latter is a bidding city budget deficit which must be covered with a specific post-Olympics taxation.

Information asymmetry allows the bidding city promoters to play down those less exciting characteristics of the project, namely excessive costs, stark security issues, negative externalities and a possible crowding-out effect. The IOC cannot have a similar in-depth knowledge about each bidding city project and cannot control how accurate or fallacious is the information delivered in the application file, namely about actual costs and externalities. The Olympic site visits by the IOC representatives are not enough to compensate for information asymmetry between bidding city promoters and IOC voters: candidate cities are then compelled to overbid each other, namely in underestimating the costs and overestimating the benefits, in order to obtain the right to host a sports event. Therefore the winner is the most optimistic bidder and is cursed due to the difference between ex ante underestimated and ex post actual costs (overestimated and actual benefits).

Various indices can be checked to verify the existence of a winner's curse in the sports economy (Table 15.1). Here the focus is on hosting the Olympics.

Table 15. 1   Indices of a winner's curse in sports auctions

Mega sporting event	Hosting a team franchise	Bidding for broadcasting rights	Overbidding for players
Cost overruns	Subsidies for new facilities	Swift TV rights fees increase	Growing number of bidders
Ex post project revisions	Luxurious increase in subsidies	TV company financial losses	Salary overpayment/bonus
Delayed completion	Stadium cost overruns	TV company post-bid bankruptcy	Acquiring a 'lemon' player
Extra public subsidy	Slow economic growth	Sport event unknown details	Bid disappointing return
Host city fiscal deficit / debt	Stagnating urban development	Outbidding newcomers	Superstar effect
Lower number of visitors	Lower attendance than expected	TV rights re-packaging	Team's deficit due to payroll

Source: Andreff (2014).

Case studies: The Olympic Games

A first test of the winner's curse is to look at cost overruns in hosting the Olympics. Andreff (2012) provides a long term comparison between ex ante cost – announced in the bid book – and ex post effective cost at the Games closing ceremony or later, from Munich 1972 on. The result is that all Summer and Winter Olympics have been plagued to some extent with the winner's curse apart from Los Angeles 1984. Table 15.2 exhibits an update of this study where the indices of cost overruns are recalculated in 2014 constant euro.

Table 15.2   Cost overruns, ex ante and ex post cost of Summer Olympics since 1984 (in 2014 € billion)

Host city year	Number of de candidate cities	Ex ante total cost candidature file	Ex post total cost Games closure	Cost overrun in %
Los Angeles 1984	1	1.6*	1.6*	0%
Seoul 1988	2	4.0	8.3	108%
Barcelona 1992	6	3.9	10.0	156%
Atlanta 1996	6	2.5	3.3	32%
Sydney 2000	5	2.8	5.4	93%
Athens 2004	5	5.3	11.1	109%
Beijing 2008	5	2.6	32.0	1130%
London 2012	5	4.8	10.9	127%
Rio de Janeiro 2016	4	9.5*	16.5**	74%
expected in 2016***			33.0	247%

* in current $ billion. ** cost reached in 2014.
*** Estimation by Saxo Group Denmark in August 2012.

Source: updated and recalculated in 2014 euros from Andreff (2012).

Ex post total cost of the Summer Olympics is always higher than ex ante announced total cost, the former being a multiple of the latter, two times higher in Seoul, Sydney, Athens and London, 2.5 times higher in Barcelona and 12 times higher in Beijing. Cost underestimation always pertains to investment cost in Olympic sport equipment and non-sporting infrastructure and practically never to the organisation cost – the operation cost of the LOOC which is under tight supervision by the IOC. Yet in 2014, the first signs of a winner's curse were emerging during the preparation of the 2016 Rio de Janeiro Olympics. Ex post final cost might well climb up to 3.5 times higher in 2016 than the cost in the bid book, according to a Saxo Group estimation. Cost overruns as usual!

The 1984 Los Angeles exception confirms the winner's curse analysis; these Games ended up with a financial surplus and no cost overruns. The organisation cost was $546 million and ex post total cost, all investments included, reached $1,592 million. Los Angeles was the unique candidate and thus was not compelled to overbid any competing city with cost underestimation; quite logically, the city did not embark on ex post cost overruns. The 1984 Games had been awarded in 1977, right after the Montreal financial distress so that no candidate showed up for hosting the 1984 Olympics. The IOC had to convince the Los Angeles authorities and accept their candidature on their own terms, including their own costs. Hence no winner's curse and no cost overruns. This is the best exception to verify the winner's curse theory.

The ex post revisions indicator can be witnessed for several Games. The most infamous and costly revision was due to the Montreal Olympic stadium roof which was eventually completed nine years after the Games at an almost six-fold cost increase. In Sydney, two galleries of the Homebush Bay stadium were forgone because of excessive cost. In Beijing, simplifying the 'Bird's Nest' structure of the stadium was a revision that saved 50% of steel costs; the Olympic swimming pool, eventually assessed as too sophisticated, was streamlined. The cost of the London Olympic stadium was revised from $406 million to $850 million while the cost of infrastructures was up by $170 million; the Olympic park inflated by $1,440 million over its initial $5.3 billion bill.

Next, consider the delayed completion indicator. The completion delay of the Centenary Park in Atlanta required additional jobs and overtime work which generated extra cost. In Athens, a number of building sites lagged behind schedule, in particular the new tramway, a circular motorway and a suburban train to the new airport. In January 2004, only one (the Nikaia gymnasium) of the 33 Olympic sites was ready. Then, there was a final investment rush. The completion of several London Olympic sites, including Wembley stadium, was late and the LOOC met with increasing obstacles to availing all sports equipment in due time.

As usual with the Olympics, extra public finance and subsidies have been obtained by the LOOC. Montreal 1976 received overall $1 billion in public subsidies. In Sydney, the riding school obtained an operation subsidy of $676,000 per year and the Blacktown Olympic Park $654,000 per year. The city of Athens never stopped raising public loans when preparing to host the Games and this helped to account for the increase in the Greek public debt. An LOOC deficit does not emerge as often as it should do because extra expenditures are transferred to (or subsidised by) the host city budget and sometimes the region or national government budget. Nevertheless a loss – an operation deficit – has been registered for Munich 1972, Montreal 1976, Sydney 2000, Athens 2004, and probably though unofficially for Seoul 1988 (Preuss, 2004) and slightly for Atlanta 1996. Given the heavy subsidies collected by Barcelona 1992 (and a subsequent $6.1 billion debt), the $3 million official financial surplus is practically fictitious.

The Montreal 1976 debt was reimbursed by taxpayers through an extra local tax ($176 million) and a Quebec provincial special taxation on tobacco ($480 million). Moreover, running Montreal Olympic sporting facilities has created a $13 million annual deficit over 35 years. The city of Barcelona budget had to charge a $1.7 billion repayment to taxpayers. The Sydney Games eventually generated a $168 million debt. New South Wales pays $37.3 million per year to operate former Olympic sites. The Australia stadium is now in financial disarray, and the Superdome and the water sports centre are running at a loss. It is estimated that Greek taxpayers will pay for the Games deficit until 2030.

On the Olympics revenue side there are fewer indices of the winner's curse than on the cost side. Ex ante overestimation of the number of visitors attracted by the Games, in particular foreign visitors, is commonplace. One-quarter of the Atlanta tickets were left unsold. The number of visitors at the Sydney Games was lower than expected. However, one cannot find a major source of the winner's curse in missing or lost revenues.

In the most recent bids, for the 2018 Winter Olympics and after, the IOC has attempted to fight cost underestimation. Each and every investment has to be mentioned and financing has to be secured. Calculations are in both US dollars and local currency and the IOC asks bidding cities for a realistic estimation of miscellaneous and unexpected costs. The outcome of such IOC efforts in terms of alleviating the winner's curse remains to be seen.

Let us now scrutinise in more detail the case of the 2014 Winter Olympics hosted in Sochi. Sochi had won the bid in July 2007[1] over Pyeongchang and Salzburg; its bid book seemed fabulous and its Olympic project was more expensive than in its three previous candidatures. The announced organisation cost, voted by IOC members, was €1.2 billion. However, it was mentioned that the LOOC would not take overinvestment costs. The latter, outside the LOOC budget, were expected to be €7.6 billion in 2007, 60% of which would be covered by Russian government funding. Ex ante total cost was €8.9 billion ($12 billion) overall. From the very beginning, this ex ante total cost was far above those costs announced for Turin 2006 (€4 billion) and Vancouver 2010 (€2 billion).

The promoters of the Sochi Games were justifying such high costs by investment in sporting equipment: 11 new sports arenas and ski resorts, two villages for athletes, one skating rink with views of both the Black Sea and the mountains, and bathing facilities. A 'fantabulous' project was a frequently heard word. This fits even better with non-sporting infrastructures to be built from July 2007 to February 2014. Urban investment in the city of Sochi was especially heavy. Entire city districts were to be renovated and the Rodina hotel as well. An entirely artificial island of 330 hectares, a new airport and a new commercial seaport, a second 67km railway alongside the sea cost, 580km of new roads and a new 63km highway between the airport and the Olympics site, a new motorway to circumvent Sochi traffic jams, an intended 36 km Sochi light metro which was eventually changed for a scaled-down commuter-style railway, the Sochi Aeroexpress, a new press centre, five new big luxury hotels, two new trade centres, one touristic zone, a new motorway tunnel, and additional hotel capacity of 196,000 beds were to be constructed. The production capacity of the electricity power station was to be augmented, and land was to be bought from 3,000 expropriated small owners in view of creating the Olympics park. The Games started with a few unfinished roads, some unfinished construction of hotels and shopping centres, namely in the Rosa Khutor ski resort, rampant water pollution unresolved, malfunctions in the snowmaking equipment while the ski jump had to urgently be redone several times. An Olympics legacy fund of $35 million is supposed to finance the maintenance of sporting equipment after the Games.

A substantial economic impact from such investment expenditures was expected, including a strong attraction of foreign tourists into the region, 6 million people in 2014 instead of 3 million in previous years. In September 2013, Vitali Mutko, the minister for sports of Russia, was still expecting $1 billion of positive spillovers from the Games for Russia. Eventually the number of tourists in the Sochi region increased by 31% (to less than 5 million) in 2014, of which only 10% were foreigners.

The 2014 discounted value of €8.9 billion in 2007 is €16.8 billion.[2] Beyond this amount the total cost in 2014 euro would reveal cost overruns. The Sochi Games total cost reached $33.3 billion in 2010, and $51 billion (€38 billion) in 2014,[3] about 2.2 times higher than the discounted expected ex ante cost. Due to the usual winner's curse, the most expensive ever bid book for Winter Olympics translated into the highest ever effective cost ex post. The cost of the Laura biathlon and ski complex skyrocketed from $500 million up to $2.7 billion whereas the bill for the First Olympic Stadium ballooned from $49 million to $519 million. The Rosa Khutor ski resort was added to the Sochi project after winning the bid, a typical feature of the winner's curse; it was opportunely financed by Interros, a holding company owned by a rich oligarch, Vladimir Potanin – with $36 billion related to non-sporting infrastructure, 96.5% of the funding was public. Eventually at least $23 billion will be paid by Russian taxpayers. All this shows the evidence of a winner's curse. An ex ante cost–benefit analysis of Sochi Games has found a net social cost (social benefits minus social costs) that shows a social deficit of $5.8 billion – in constant 2006 dollars – over 2006–2016 (Pilipenko, 2013).

How to hedge against the consequences of the winner's curse when hosting sports events

Consequently, managing the process of hosting an international sports event is not an easy task for any country/city managers. Would it be possible to phase out or alleviate the unavoidable winner's curse? A response can be looked for a) in a reflection about the allocation of sports events by international sport governing bodies, and b) at the level of each potential host city.

At a governing body level, could one wonder that the IOC would select the cheapest Olympics project from now on? This is obviously wishful thinking. It is unrealistic to trust the IOC to adopt a strategy which would contradict its objective of obtaining the most magnificent Games. Moreover, by calling for the lowest cost, the IOC would in fact fuel an even wider cost underestimation by bidding cities, and thus the winner's curse, instead of phasing it out. In order to exhibit the lowest cost each bidder will cheat more than ever about real costs in the bid book. Another option is that the IOC would fix a maximum cost with a rejection of any bid book running over this cost; the highest probability is that the IOC would receive all candidatures at this maximum cost – with different degrees of cost underestimation from one candidate city to the other – losing cost as relevant information about potential host cities.

Third option: the IOC would finance the Olympics by itself in taking over the major part of hosting costs on its own account; not only would the IOC cover the LOOC operation budget but also the cost of all sporting equipment and a significant share of non-sporting infrastructures. This would have two effects. First, IOC wealth would drastically shrink given that these costs should be covered by revenues (about $6 billion per Olympiad) from sponsorship and TV broadcasting rights derived from the Olympics which, otherwise, are the major sources of IOC finance. Then IOC voters would personally become aware of the real cost of hosting the Games with a hope that their future votes would favour less the 'fantabulous' aspects of Olympics projects and more their genuine costs. As financers, IOC voters would look at and compare each bid book to ex post costs observed in the previous Games and their impact on IOC wealth. As sometimes suggested, tighter auditing of sport governing bodies can facilitate this new behaviour. In times of global economic crisis, the IOC, FIFA, UEFA, etc., are increasingly considered to be wealthy enough to sacrifice part of their revenues earned from mega-sporting events.

The second effect of the IOC self-financing its Games is that the winner's curse will vanish since the IOC should make a unilateral choice on the host city without a bid. The cost of the Games would be aligned on IOC revenues or even below. This would lower the IOC requirements in terms of brand new sport equipment. Again this is wishful thinking because nobody sees any reason why the IOC would renounce the economic benefits associated with its monopoly power over awarding the Games. One sees even less reasons for potential candidate cities to boycott applications for the Games in view of putting pressure on the IOC to self-finance the Olympics.

A last option, in fact THE only credible and efficient solution, would be to uproot the winner's curse by changing the mode of awarding the Games which should no longer be an auction-like setting. Los Angeles' unique candidature without cost overrun is a plea for such a solution. Greece had proposed to host the 1996 centenary Games in Olympia and transform this historic site of ancient Olympiads into a unique and definitive location for Summer Olympics. Such a choice would have put an end to cost overruns forever: no longer would there be the need for new heavy investment in sporting equipment and non-sporting infrastructures, the only costs would pertain to maintaining, refurbishing and modernising existing equipment and infrastructures. However this Olympia candidature tilted against too many economic interests to be retained, namely the interests of the IOC, international sports federations and multinational sponsors.

Moving the Olympics from one site to another accrues abundant monies to the IOC through mobilising sponsors and TV broadcasters – IOC TV rights revenues were up to €3.9 billion for the 2010–2012 Olympiad. There is no chance that the IOC would like to change this. Olympic international sports federations would not support any change either since the IOC redistributes Olympics revenues to them: €140 million from Sydney 2000, €187 million from Athens 2004, €173 million from Beijing 2008, and €382 million from London 2012. Multinational companies that sponsor the Games do really prefer spreading the worldwide exposure of their brands in different big cities around the world rather than being confined once and for all in the same location, albeit Olympia! i.e. Enterprises in construction, transportation, hotel business, catering, and tourism industries would earn less money with a single location than with geographical moves of the Olympics sites and infrastructures every fourth year.

Two emendations of the Olympics awarding process have been implemented or discussed at the IOC. Neither tackles the issue of the winner's curse. One is to favour a rotation of the Olympics host city across continents, i.e. Europe (London), then Latin America (Rio de Janeiro) and Asia (Tokyo) – except that Africa has always been omitted so far. This rule does not uproot the winner's curse and has not stopped cities overbidding from a same or different continent(s). Another envisaged emendation would be to accept a joint candidature by two cities from different countries. The FIFA World Cup was jointly organised in South Korea and Japan in 2002, the UEFA Euro in Poland and Ukraine in 2012 and further Euros after 2016 will be jointly hosted by several countries. However such a possibility does not exclude a competition between different couples – or groups – of joint candidates; the winner's curse would not vanish.

Could a candidate city hedge against the effects of the winner's curse as long as the Olympics are an auction-like award? Recurring recommendations addressed to host cities' managers aim at controlling cost overruns and alleviating other negative consequences of the winner's curse such as: an overoptimistic approach to the bid book must be avoided; cost management must be tight over all the project lifetime; the host city must commit itself to achieve ex post cost–benefit analysis for comparison with the expectations of an ex ante optimistic impact study; extremely rigorous accounting and cost–benefit evaluation methodologies must be adopted in these studies to enable comparison of current costs and benefits with those of cities previously hosting the same sports event.

Some countries have started adopting a strictly normalised and standardised model of cost–benefit assessment. MEETS (2002) is a model which uses normalised profiles of expenditures that makes possible comparable accounting of the economic impact and cost of the different events hosted in Canada. In France, the project of elaborating on a common methodology for ex ante and ex post economic and social evaluation of all mega-sporting events hosted in the country is underway at the DIGES (Inter-ministry Delegation for Mega-Sporting Events), which should be used for cost and impact comparison across different events and over time. At the end of the day, there is no shame from an economic viewpoint for a candidate country/city to renounce if too high costs are expected to overrun any sensible budget. Although these more rigorous methodologies would help management with hosting mega-sporting events, they provide no help to actually hedge against the winner's curse.

What could be the strategy of a candidate city to countervail the IOC monopoly power and divert or partly escape the winner's curse? Imagine that Paris – with regard to the 2024 Summer Games – would take at face value the current doctrine and watchwords of the IOC to stop the growth in size and economic costs of the Olympics. Thus it would apply at a lower cost than all other candidates; and to ensure the city decision makers would commit themselves to achieve hosting the Games without cost overruns (with a 30% margin over the cost announced in the bid book[4]). Then imagine that this commitment would be advertised by the city as the best quality of its candidature. Now the problem is that such a candidature will meet a high probability of being rejected by IOC voters who prefer a more 'fantabulous', more expensive Olympic project. Therefore Paris would face a dilemma or a tradeoff between submitting the first best economic bid committed to no cost overruns while taking a high risk of not passing successfully through the IOC vote. This is exactly the bet that Madrid had lost in submitting a 'low cost, responsible and reasonable' project for the 2020 Summer Olympics; it attracted less votes than the more expensive Tokyo candidature.

The decision has been made in June 2015[5] that Paris would be a candidate to host the 2024 Games. This happened following a favourable televised talk by the President of the Republic in November 2014, a supporting report delivered by the CFSI (French Committee for International Sport) in February 2015, majority votes in favour of hosting the Games passed at the city council of Paris on 13 April 2015 and at the Ile-de-France regional council on 7 May 2015. Could Paris take the opportunity of the current mood created by the exorbitant cost of the Sochi Games (forecast in Andreff, 2013) and an increasing number of candidates resigning before the deadline to succeed in an 'anti-winner's curse' candidature?

In 2012, Rome had resigned from its candidature for hosting the 2020 Olympics due to economic difficulties. More than anything else the cost of the Sochi Games has had, to some extent, a similar effect as Montreal 1976. Only two candidate cities were left as potential hosts of the 2022 Winter Games, Almaty and Beijing, which eventually won the IOC vote. The populace has rejected the candidatures of Saint-Moritz (53% vote against) and Munich-Garmisch-Partenkirchen (between 52% and 60% against in the cities whose residents were voting) in 2013. In 2014, Stockholm gave up after a decision made by its city council, as well as Cracow after a 70% hostile referendum, Lviv due to the military conflict, and Oslo ensuing from the Norwegian Parliament's refusal to vote financial support to the candidature, and despite a 55% favourable referendum. The IOC headquarters were annoyed to see the number of competing cities falling and eventually being stuck with only two Asian bidders. Boston has already resigned with regard to hosting the 2024 Summer Games.

In such a context, an original Paris 2024 bid with the aim of combating the cost overruns that result from an auction-like award of the Olympics would be backed by economists' approval under the following conditions, which are recommendations as well:

a)   Submit a bid book based on realistic, not underestimated costs (nor overestimated positive spillovers). A perspective budget had been publicised by the CFSI in February 2015 with an overall cost of €6.2 billion: organisation cost €3.2 billion, sporting equipment €1.7 billion, and non-sporting infrastructures €1.3 billion. It is neither a very expensive project with a much lower cost than Athens 2004, Beijing 2008, London 2012, and Rio de Janeiro 2016, nor a very cheap one, slightly costlier than Sydney 2000. Needless to say that, if these figures were to be confirmed in a bid book, the last two figures (equipment and infrastructure costs) would be scrutinised by the economists to check whether a winner's curse was emerging.

b)   Paris 2024 should officially commit – through a strong high-level political engagement or even a programme law passed in the Parliament – that there will be no cost overruns, with a 30% margin on current prices, i.e. that the cost will never jump over €8 [current] billion in 2024 (6.2 + 30% = 8.0). This commitment should be the strongest promotional and advertising argument of a Paris candidature, possibly with a slogan like 'the cheapest Games since Sydney 2000'.

c)   The managers of the Paris candidature should make the IOC aware that, if the 2024 Games were to be awarded to Paris, any new IOC demand or requirement as regards sporting equipment and other infrastructures would not be admissible unless they remained within the limits of the €8 billion budget at 2024 current prices. In particular they should refuse in advance to cover cost overruns or a deficit dug by new IOC demands with a call for more public funding. In the absence of an IOC agreement on this point, Paris should abandon hosting the Games since they would no longer be the cheapest since Sydney 2000, except if the IOC would commit itself to finance any cost overruns beyond the initial €8 billion budget.[6]

A final recommendation: Paris and the Ile-de-France region should question their residents about whether they are willing to have the 2024 Olympics hosted on their local territory. One way is to ask them by revealing, through an inquiry, what is the economic value (Walton et al., 2008) they attach as residents to the fact that Paris will host the Games. This is usually achieved by means of a questionnaire circulated to a representative sample of local residents about their willingness to pay for having the mega-sporting event hosted in their area. Those local residents who intend to attend the Games attach a use value to the sporting event. There is also a 'non-use' value for local residents who do not intend to attend but are willing to pay for having the Games hosted in Paris whatever the reason (Paris prestige, individual feel-good, national pride, etc.). Assume that on average each local resident would reveal a willingness to pay of €20 for hosting the Games.[7] Then, multiplying by the number (10 million) Paris and Ile-de-France residents, the economists would find an overall willingness to pay €200 million. It should be crystal clear that, as taxpayers, the residents are not ready to pay, and should not be requested to pay more than this amount in case of an ex post cost overrun or deficit (€200 million is only 2.5% of the aforementioned €8 billion).

Conclusion

Concluding from a political economy standpoint, a more democratic way of questioning local residents about the opportunity of hosting the Olympics in Paris would consist of organising a referendum. The Mayor of Paris Anne Hidalgo publicly announced (in the newspaper *Le Parisien*,

6 April 2015) that she would organise a poll in 2016 about a Paris candidature to host the 2024 Olympics.[8] For sure, she would be welcome to organise it before the deadline for officially declaring a candidature (8 January 2016) or even earlier. Better to know in due time whether Paris and Ile-de-France residents will support hosting the 2024 Games or, to the contrary, will reject this choice as in Saint-Moritz and Munich. In case of rejection, this would mean that resident discontent has risen alongside with and faster than anticipated cost overruns.

Recommended further reading

Andreff, W. (2012). The winner's curse: why is the cost of mega sporting events so often underestimated? In: W. Maennig & A. Zimbalist, eds., *International Handbook on the Economics of Mega Sporting Events*, Cheltenham: Edward Elgar, 37–69.

Kage, J.H. & Levin, D. (2002). *Common Value Auctions and the Winner's Curse*, Princeton, NJ: Princeton University Press.

Zimbalist, A. (2010). Is it worth it? Hosting the Olympic Games and other mega sporting events is an honor many countries aspire to – but why? *Finance and Development*, March, 8–11.

Notes

1   After three candidature failures in 1989, 1993 and 2003 which exhibit how much Sochi was eager to win the auction and thus to overbid.

2   In the Sochi 2014 bid book, the inflation rate from 2007 to 2014 was estimated on average at 5.91% per year. However in the real estate sector inflation has been higher than 100% and prices per square metre went up over those in Moscow.

3   Some evaluations are up to $55 billion – or €41 billion (Müller, 2015).

4   A cost overrun up to 30% in current prices is normally due to local inflation in the host city over the 7-year period of the Olympics preparation as well as to unexpected circumstances always at work in big projects; a 30% overrun can be tolerated in practical terms.

5   Late June 2015, the mayor of Paris officially declared that Paris will be a candidate; this was confirmed by submitting the name of Paris as a candidate city to the national Olympic committee on 15 September 2015.

6   According to the CFSI report, Paris 2024 would be financed by the IOC up to €1.8 billion, by private funding of €1.4 billion, and public finance for €3 billion, i.e. a 52% private (IOC included) to 48% public distribution of finance.

7   An inquiry conducted by T. Belkharoeva at the Russian International Olympic University, Sochi right before the 2014 Winter Games, exhibited that 94% of sampled residents would have been willing to pay for *not hosting the Games* in Sochi, of which 64% declared they were ready to pay more than 5,000 rubles (€90); this would have been the price to pay for avoiding negative externalities which have plagued the residents for years such as delayed building sites, traffic jams, urban disorganisation, noise, pollution and other nuisance.

8   A poll in April 2014 showed that 61% in a sample representative of the whole French population were in favour of hosting the Games in Paris – and 83% of interviewed enterprises. But this is not the proper population to be addressed. It is relevant to question local residents whose opinion may evolve when they become aware of the rising costs of living in a city that is going to host the Olympics.

References

Akerlof, G. (1970). The market for lemons: Qualitative uncertainty and the market mechanism, *Quarterly Journal of Economics*, 89, 488–500.

Andreff, W.(2011). Some comparative economics of the organization of sports: Competition and regulation in North American vs. European professional team sports leagues, *European Journal of Comparative Economics*, 8 (1), 3–27.

Andreff, W. (2012). The winner's curse: Why is the cost of mega sporting events so often underestimated? In: W. Maennig & A. Zimbalist, eds., *International Handbook on the Economics of Mega Sporting Events*, Cheltenham: Edward Elgar, 37–69.

Andreff, W. (2013). Pourquoi les Jeux de Sotchi seront plus coûteux que prévu, *Revue Internationale et Stratégique*, 92, 109–118.

Andreff, W. (2014). The winner's curse in sports economics. In: O. Budzinski & A. Feddersen, eds., *Contemporary Research in Sports Economics*, Frankfurt am Main: Peter Lang Academic Research, 179–207.

Cassing, J., & Douglas, R.W. (1980). Implications of the auction mechanism in baseball's free agent draft, *Southern Economic Journal*, 47, 110–121.

Gratton, C., & Solberg, H.A. (2007). *The Economics of Sports Broadcasting*, Abingdon: Routledge.

Lehn, K. (1984). Information asymmetries in baseball's free agent market, *Economic Inquiry*, 22, 37–44.

MEETS (2002). *Modèle d'évaluation économique du tourisme sportif*, Alliance canadienne du tourisme sportif, Ottawa.

Müller, M. (2015). After Sochi 2014: Costs and impacts of Russia's Olympic Games, *Social Science Research Network*, 25 February.

Pilipenko, I.V. (2013). The Sochi 2014 Winter Olympics – the cost–benefit analysis and ways to improve the project efficiency, *Electronic Publications of Pan-European Institute*, 4/2013,University of Turku.

Preuss, H. (2004). *The Economics of Staging the Olympics: A Comparison of the Games 1972–2008*, Cheltenham: Edward Elgar.

Rosentraub, M.S., & Swindell, D. (2002). Negotiating Games: Cities, sports, and the winner's curse, *Journal of Sport Management*, 16, 18–35.

Thaler, R.H. (1994). *The Winner's Curse: Paradoxes and Anomalies of Economic Life*, Princeton, NJ: Princeton University Press.

Walton, H., Longo, A., & Dawson, P. (2008). A contingent evaluation of the 2012 London Olympic Games, *Journal of Sports Economics*, 9 (3), 304–317.

INDEX

Tables are indicated by page numbers in bold. The abbreviation '*bib*' after a page number indicates bibliographical information in the 'Recommended further reading' sections.

Abramovich, Roman 76, 170, 174, 179
Acosta, Ruben 195
Action for Good Governance in International Sport (AGGIS) 191
Adidas 15, 58, 76
Agergaard, S. and Tiesler, N.C. 39*bib*
Aján, Tamas 195
Akerlof, G. 169, 220, 222
Albertville Winter Olympics (1992) 110
amateurism 57
  and commercial interests 66–7
ambush marketing 88, 108–18
  counter-ambush activities 111–14
  definition 109
  European Championships: Denmark v. Poland (case study) 115–17
  famous cases **111**
  legislation 114
  marketing exclusion areas 113
  see also sponsorship
American Express 110
Andreff, W. 27bib, 164*bib*, 224, 232*bib*
anti-brand communities 8, 128–32

Argenta Running Tour 68
Association of Road Racing Statisticians (ARRS) 67–8
Athens Olympics (1896) 205
Athens Olympics (2004) 207, 208, 209
Atlanta Olympics (1996):
  ambush maketing 110, 111, 113
  costs 224, 225, 226
  number of athletes 205
  urban infrastructure 207
Atlético Madrid 172
Australia 31, 114
  see also Sydney Olympics (2000)
autonomy of sport 188–9
Azerbaijan 189

Babiak, K. and Wolf, R. 141
Balotelli, Mario 115
Barcelona FC 32, 102
  media revenues 99
  revenues 99
  on social media 121, 122, 129
  state aid 162, 163, 173, 176

Barcelona Olympics (1992) 110, 225, 226
  ambush marketing 110
  costs 224, 225, 226
  number of athletes 205
  urban development 207, 208, 210, 215
BASF and 'Sportverein 2020' 86–7
basketball 45, 49, 58, 113, 148, 154
Bayer 04 Leverkusen 122, 157, 178, 182
Bayer AG 178, 182
Bayern München (Munich) 44, 122, 126, 127, 129, 133,
  176, 179, 182
Beckham, David 46
Beijing: bid for 2022 Winter Olympics 230
Beijing Olympics (2008):
  ambush marketing 113
  costs 224, 225, 231
  number of athletes 205
  revenues 229
  urban development 207, 213
BeIN 102, 103
Belgium 26, 60, 61, 62, 67, 68
  football 93, 99, 101, 103, 110, 113
Belkhareava, T. 232
Bendtner, Nicklas 115, 116
Berlusconi, Silvio 174
betting 48, 124
Blatter, Sep 193, 194
Bosman case 31
Bowen, Howard 138, 139
boxing 50–1, 147
Bradish, C.L. and Cronin, J.J. 149*bib*
branding:
  brand/anti-brand communities 8, 123, 126–7, 128–9
  endorsements 45, 49–50
    and doping 52
    FREDD endorser evaluation **49**, 50, 51–2
  and social media 124
  and sponsorship 76–7
Brazil:
  ambush marketing 110
  anti-World Cup demonstrations 137
  media rights 102
  political use of sport 189
  World Cup (2014) 75, 129
Breedveld, K. et al 70*bib*
Breuer, C. et al 70*bib*
Business 2 Business 81

Canada 31, 102, 164, 229
  see also Montréal Olympics (1976)
Cardiff City 99
Carmichael, L. 211, 212

Carroll, A.B. 139, 140
celebrity athletes 45–6, 142
Chadwick, S. and Burton, N. 118*bib*
Chagaev, Ruslan 50
Chappelet, J.L. and Mrkonjic, M. 191
Chelsea FC:
  and Abramovich 67, 76, 170, 176, 179
  and social media 122, 129
China 18, 22, 26, 189
  ambush marketing 113
  football 96–7
  media rights 103
  social media 132
  see also Beijing Olympics (2008)
co-branding 77
collaborative ventures of sports firms 19
commercialization 3–5, 43–53
  and amateurism (case study) 66–7
  and athletes as celebrities 45–6
  and corruption 186, 187
  definition 43
  and doping 47–8
  emergence of 187–8
  exploitation of athletes 46–8
  football 43–5, 47, 76, 155
  and growth of media 187–8
  Klitschkos (case study) 49–53
  and match-fixing 48–9
  Olympic Games 45
  running 64–5, 69
  team sports 155
  and UEFA 43
Connor, J. 46, 47
Cornwell, T. B. 88*bib*
corporate social responsibility (CSR) 79, 137–49
  beginnings of CSR 138
  and capitalism 148
  CSR standards 148–9
  definitions 138
  differing views of 138–40
  French Tennis Federation (case study) 142–7
  key elements 145
  partnerships with business 144, 148
  and sport ethics 140
  and sport values 141–2
  stakeholder theory 139–40
  sustainable development 143, 144
  voluntary and mandatory 140
  whitewashing 139
corruption of ISFs 186–96
  and commercialization 186, 187
  complexity of tasks and rules 188

corruption of ISFs *cont.*
  cultural factors 190, 193, 196
  deficits of governance:
    checks and balances 192
    democratic processes 192, 194
    transparency 191–2, 194
  FIFA and IAAF scandals (case study) 192–5
  instrumentalisation by politics 187, 188–9
  and media 187–8
  organisational structures 191
  origins of ISFs 187
  priniciples of good governance 191
Croatia 116
Crompton, J.L. 118*bib*
cycling:
  doping 48, 141, 147
  media exposure 84
  sponsorship 76
  Tour de France 48, 67, 147
Czech Republic 99, 103

Dartford FC 137
Davies, L.E. 204, 206, 215–16*bib*
Decathlon 20–6
  business activities 22–4
  development of sales turnover **21**
  human resources policy 25
  innovation 24–5
  Oxylane research centre 24–5
  'passion brands' **23**, 24
  retail outlets by country **22**
  service brands 23, **24**
  social charter 25
  values and ethics 25
definition of sport 12
Demir, R. and Söderman, S. 79
democratisation of sport 17
Denmark:
  CSR 140
  handball 34–5, 38, 84–5
  media rights 93
  men's football 99, 103, 115
    soft pricing and subsidies 163
  rowing 85–6
  running 60, 61, 62, 68
  soft pricing 159, 163
  sport and education 37
  Topdanmark 84–6
  women's football 35–6
Diack, Lamine 195
doping 47–8, 52, 186, 189, 195
dual career development 32

economic drivers of sport goods industry 16–17
Elliot, R. and Weedon, G. 39*bib*
Enron 138
Essex, S.J. and Chalkey, B.S. 206, 207
Ethiad Stadium 213
EU free mobility of workers 31
European Commission 3, 163, 173
Everton FC 96, 137
Exxon Valdez 138

Facebook:
  fans-teams interaction 128–9
  football clubs users 121, 122
  privacy protection 134
  and sport brands 124, 128–9
  and sports fan interaction 123, 128
  team-related pages 123
Farrelly, F. et al 78, 85, 88–9*bib*
federations and clubs 57, 58, 66, 229
Ferdinand, Rio 116
Ferrero 148
FIFA: corruption 186, 190, 192–5
Fifa World Cup *see under* football
Filo, K. et al 120, 134*bib*
Finland 60, 61, 64, 68, 103, 140
fitness 3, 51, 52, 58, 60, 63, 64, 65, 68
  sports goods market 12, 13, 20
Fitness Apps 124
football:
  African players 47
  bidding for players 221
  brand communities 127
  Champions League 8, 44–5, 92, 93–4, 99–100, 104,
    161, 169, 175
  Club Financial Control Body (CFCB) 168
  Club Licensing System 168
  club ownership 175
  commercialization 67, 155
  Euro (European Championship) 77, 94, 98,
    115, 229
  European Club Association 180
  European Cup 44, 100
  Financial Fair Play (FFP) 105, 160, 164, 167–81
    aggregate operating results **178**
    break-even requirement 168, 173, 177
    case study: Abramovich as success-seeker 179
    case study: Bayer AG as investor at Bayer 04
      Leverkusen 178
    EU state aid law 173
    growth rates for top clubs **177**
    investments 168, 173–6, 178–9
    objectives 180

football: *cont.*
   settlement procedure 180
   success-seeker investors 175, 179
   'home-grown rule' 31
   investment in playing strength 168–9
   migration of players 30, 31–2, 96–7
      percentage of foreign players in big-five leagues **96**
   and North American team sports 153, 155–6, 164
   open leagues 161
   pricing 159
   profit maximization 153, 154–6
   racism 116
   revenues 154, 156
     growth 167, 177
     and league structures 161
     and losses 156–7, 161, 167
     and media 4, 44–5, 92–106
       competitive balance 97
       distribution of media revenues of big-five
          leagues **98**
       export revenues 95
       extension of fans base 95, 96–7, 104
       Gini-indexes 97, **98**, 99
       growth in media rights of elite leagues 94–**5**
       internet 96, 104
       media rights for club tournaments of big-five
          leagues as percentage of domestic leagues
          101
       non-European markets 100, **101**, 102–3
       revenues of average clubs **99**
       selling of media rights 97, 98
       Spanish LaLiga (case study) 101–3
       time zones 96, 102
       total revenues/media rights proportion **93**–4
   salaries 4, 44, 45, 167, 177
   and social media 121–**2**, 126, 128, 130–1
   social role 79
   social/emotional attachment 161–2
   soft budget constraints 154, 157–64, 168
     accounting 160
     case study: Denmark 163
     case study: Spain 162–3
     credits 160
     crowding out hard budget clubs 171–2
     investments 160, 168, 174
     side effects 170–2
     subsidies and bailouts 160, 170, 172–3
     'too big to fail' 171
   in sport equipment market 13
   trafficking of players 47
   transfer fees 4, 167, 170
   transfers of underage athletes 32

football: *cont.*
   win optimization 153, 154–6, 161, 169
   World Cup:
     anti-brand activism 129
     anti-World Cup demonstrations 137
     and corporate social responsibility 137, 142, 149
     and FIFA corruption 193–5
     and ISO 2021 149
     joint organisation 229
     politics and bidding race 193–4
     Qatar 2022 137
     revenues 75–6, 193
     sponsorship 75–6, 77, 81, 88
       and ambush marketing 109, 110, 111, 112, 113,
         115–17
   World Cup in Women's Football 33
   see also names of clubs
Fort, R. 155
France:
   Albertville Winter Olympics (1992)
   costs of events 229
   CSR 140, 143
   Decathlon (case study) 20–6
   football:
     ambush marketing 110, 111, 113
     financial losses 157
     foreign players 96
     Ligue 1 93, 95, 96
     media revenues 98
     media rights 101, 103
     social media use 121, 122
     World Cup 1998 113
   French Basketball Federation 148
   French Tennis Federation 137, 142–7
   Paris, bid for Olympics (2024) 230–1, 231–2
   Paris Saint-Germain 176
   running 61, 62
   Secours Populaire 148
   sport goods market 14, 20–1
   sport labour migration 30
   Tour de France 48, 67, 147
Franck, E. 164bib, 172, 174, 181*bib*
Friedman, Milton 139
Fuji 109–10

Gaustad, T. 105*bib*
Geeraert, A. 191, 196*bib*
Geeraert, A. and Drieskens, E. 196*bib*
Germany:
   BASF 86–7
   football 44, 103, 127
     ambush marketing 111

Germany: *cont.*
    anti-RB Leipzig activism 130–1
    anti-Wiesenhof activism 131–2
    Bundesliga 92, 93, 95, 96, 128, 157
    foreign players 96
    media revenues 98–9
    media rights 101, 103
    salaries 44
    and social media 128
    use of social media 121, 122
    World Cup 2006 111, 115, 116
   Kitschkos 50–1, 52
   running 60, 61, 62, 67, 68
   social media 134
   sponsorship 83
   sports goods market 13, 14, 20, 26
   sports labour migration 30
Gini, Corrado 97
globalisation and migration 30–9
   and dual career support 35–7
   increase in migration 30
   national protectionist strategies 33, 34
   outsourcing 33–4
   and talent development 31–2, 33, 34–8
   women's football 33–4, 35–7
   women's handball 34–5
Gold, R.J. and Gold, M.M. 210, 216*bib*
Golden Four (G4) 85–6
golf 13, 58, 63
Google+ 124
Google Hangouts 124
Gratton, C. et al 53bib
Gratton, C. and Solberg, H.A. 105–6*bib*
Gratton, C. and Taylor, P. 70bib
Greece:
   football 97, 101
   running 62, 68, 71
   see also Athens Olympics 1896; Athens
      Olympics 2004
Guardian 137
Guinness 110

Hagel, J. and Armstrong, A.G. 120
Hallmann, K. and Petry, K. 70*bib*
handball 34–5, 38, 84–5, 154, 186, 195
Hanover 96 128
Havelange, Joao 193
health:
   and CSR 79, 141, 148
   as driver of sports goods market 15, 16
   health-management programmes 78
   and running 60, 61, 66, 67
   and Sport for All 59
   see also fitness; running

Hemsley, S. 149*bib*
Hibernian 44
Hobkinson, R. 208
Hong Kong 95
Hoye, R. et al 27*bib*
Hungary 60, 61, 62, 68
   football: media rights 103
   'Run for your Health' 67

ICC Cricket World Cup 110
Icebreaker 18
income of athletes 46, 51
   football salaries 4, 44, 45, 167, 177
India 100, 101, 103, 189
Innovation:
   Decathlon 24–5
   as driver of sports goods industries 17
International Association of Athletics Federations (IAAF)
      186, 194–5
International Handball Federation (IHF) 186, 195
International Volleyball Federation (FIVB) 186, 195
International Weightlifting Federation (IWF)
      186, 195
internationalisation of firms 18, 26
internet:
   ease of publishing information 96
   football club promotion 96, 104
   and globalisation 20
   transmission of sporting events 187–8
   ubiquity 122–3
   see also social media
ISO 2021 148–9
Italy, football:
   Serie A 93, 95, 96, 122, 156
   social media use 121, 122
   soft budget constraints 159, 160
ITF (International Tennis Federation) 66
ITV Digital 221

Jackson, S.J. and Haigh, S. 188
Japan 33, 229
Jeanrenaud, C. and Késenne, S. 106*bib*
Jennings, Andrew 194
Jordan, Michael 45
judo 137
Juventus 99

K-Swiss 114
Kage, J.H. and Levin, D. 232bib
Khodorkovsky, Mikhail 179
Kirch Media 221
kitesurfing 16
Klitschko brothers 49–53
   FREDD framework 51–2

Klitschko Management Group (KMG) 50
Kodak 109, 110
Kompany, Vincent 116
Kornai, János 158, 159–60, 170
Kornai, János et al 181*bib*

Lazio 159
Levitt, Theodore 139
lifestyle sports 16, 17
Lillehammer Winter Olympics (1994) 110
London Olympics (2012):
    ambush marketing 114, 115
    corporate social responsibility 137, 148
    cost 222, 224, 225, 229
    number of athletes 205
    urban legacy 207, 210–14
        building for legacy 211–12
        legacy planning 212–14
        legacy uses of venues **212**, 213
        Olympic Park Legacy Company (LLDC) 213
        Queen Elizabeth Olympic Park 211–12, 212–14
        sustaining legacy 212–14
Los Angeles Olympics (1984):
    ambush marketing 109–10, 111, 117
    cost 223, 224, 225, 228
    sponsorship 108–9

McCarthy, J. et al (2014) 134*bib*
McFit 51, 52
McKelvey, S. and Grady, J. 118*bib*
Madrid, bid for 2020 Olympics 230
Maguire, J. and Falcous, M. 39*bib*
Malaysia 97, 100, 101, 103
Manchester City:
    FFP regulations 177
    foreign players 96
    payments for players 170
    private benefactors 174, 176
    revenue 99
    and social media 122
    sponsorship 76
Manchester United 67, 99, 122
Mansour, Sheikh 174
MarketLine industry reports 13
MEASURE network 59
medals, global race for 4, 31
medicalization 47
Meenaghan, T. 79, 118*bib*
mergers and acquisitions 19
Messi, Lionel 32
Miciak, A.R. and Shanklin, W.L. 49, 50
Millet 18, 20
mobile media 77–8, 123
Montréal Olympics (1976) 109, 205, 223, 225, 226

Moratti, Massimo 174
Moustafa, Hassan 195
Müller, Gerd 44
multinational companies 19
MyFootballClub.co.uk 126

NACE standard 12
National Broadcasting Company (NBC) 45
Neale, W.C. 153
Netherlands 60, 62, 63, 67
new sports 17
New Zealand 18
Nike 45, 58, 110, 111, 124, 127, 139
non-profit organisations 57–8
North American team sports 153, 155–6, 164
    bidding for players 221
    bidding for team franchises 220
Norway 35, 93, 94, 100

OBO 18
Olympic Games/IOC 57, 66, 67, 109, 112
    and amateurism 66
    bidding for hosting 222–3, 230, 231–2
    commercialization 45, 109
    costs of hosting 222, 223, **224**
        cost overruns **224**–6
        options for reducing costs 227–31
        Sochi Winter Games (case study) 226–7
    ethics and values 140–1, 147
    growth of Games **205**, **206**
    marathon 59
    political interests in 188–9
    revenue 45
    sponsorship 108–9
    and television 45
    urban legacy 203–15
        Athens Olympics (2004) 207, 208, 209
        Atlanta Olympics (1996) 207
        Barcelona Olympics (1992) 207, 208, 215
        definition 203–4
        economic/social context 209–10
        London Olympics (2012) (case study) 210–14
        models of regeneration 204
        planned purpose for structures 209
        planned viability of venues 209
        Seoul Olympics 206–7
        Sochi Winter Games (2014) 226–7
        strategic and long term planning 208, 210–11
        sustainability of legacies 214, 215
    see also specific Games

Paddy Power 111, 115, 116
participation levels:
    and commercial agents 65

participation levels: *cont.*
    as driver of sports goods industries 16
    and mediatised sports 16–17
Pepsi 113
Peugeot 144
Pieth, Mark 193
Pitts, A. and Liao, H. 204
Pitts, B.G. and Stotlar, D.K. 27*bib*
Poland 115
Pongsakornrungsilp, S. and Schroeder, J.E. 134*bib*
Portugal 115
prize money and doping 48
professional service firms (PSF) 77
PSV Eindhoven 133
Putin, Vladimir 195

Qatar 137, 189

RB Leipzig 130–1
Real Madrid:
    Champions League winnings 44–5, 93
    and private benefactors 179
    revenues 99, 162, 163
    and social media 122
    and state aid 173
Red Bull 130–1
Redmond, S. and Holmes, S. 53*bib*
Reebok 147
relationship marketing 19
Rio de Janeiro Olympics 225
Roberts, P. 204
Romania 103
Rosen 75
Rugby World Cup 111
running 58–70
    clubs and federations 62, 63–4, 65–6, 69
        non-membership in EU countries **62**, 69
    commercial interests 64–5, 66–7, 68, 69
    commercial organization 3
    growth of popularity 59–63
        in EU countries 60–**1**
        reasons 61–5
        waves of events 67–8
    marathons 59, **60**, 67–8
    popularity 59–63
        in EU countries 60–**1**
        non-membership of clubs in EU countries **62**
        reasons for 61–5
    professionalization 60
    social relationaships 65–6
    sport goods market 63
Russia 116, 189, 195
    see also Sochi Winter Olympics (2014)

Salcines, J.L.P. et al 149
Sandler, D.M. and Shani, D. 118*bib*
Scandinavia
    talent development 31, 32, 34–5
    women's football 35–7
Scassa, T. 118bib
Scheerder, J. and Breedveld, K. 59, 70*bib*
Scheerder, J. et al (2015) 70*bib*
scientification 47
Seeler, Uwe 44
Séguin, B. and O'Reilly, N. 118*bib*
Seoul Olympics (1988) 110
    urban development 206–7
Sermanni, Tom 33
Shilbury, D. 27bib
Single European Market 15
size of firms 18
skiing 63
Slack, T. 53bib
Slack, T. and Parent, M.M. 27*bib*
Slack, T. and Thurston, A. 27*bib*
Slagelse Dream Team 84
Slovenia 68
small and medium-sized enterprises (SMEs) 18–19
Smart, B. 53*bib*
Smith, A. 216*bib*
Smith, A. and Westerbeek, H. 70*bib*
Sochi Winter Olympics (2014) 137, 226–7, 232
social drivers of sports goods markets 16
social media 4, 8, 120–34
    anti-brand communities 8, 128–32
        anti-RB Leipzig activism (case study) 130–1
        anti-Wiesenhof activism activism (case study) 131–2
    athletes-sponsors-fans interaction 128
    'Big Five' football leagues **122**
    brand communities 123, 126–7
    branded communities 127
    characteristics 122–3
    definition 120–1
    fan empowerment 128–9
    fan interaction 123, 125, 126, 127
    generating feedback 125, 133
    as marketing strategy 125
    privacy protection 134
    running 58, 60, 63, 66, 68
    social media prism 120–**1**
    and sponsorship 77, 127–8
    sport labour migration 39
    sport-specific factors in relevance 123
    typology of sport-related social media 123–5, **124**
    video sharing 124
South Korea 229
    see also Seoul Olympics (1988)

Spain:
    football 156–7, 159
      deficits 156–7
      government financial support 162–3, 172
      LaLiga 92, 93, 94, 95, 96, 97, 101–3, 162
      use of social media 121–2
    running 60
    see also Barcelona Olympics (1992)
sponsorship 4, 47, 48, 75–89, 108
    and anti-brand activism 129, 130–2
    and branding 76–7
    and channel members 77
    competitor-targeted 81
    and Corporate Social Responsibility (CSR) 79
      BASF and Sportclub 2020 (case study)
        86–7, 88
    growth 109
    and human resource management (HRM) 78, 81
      Topdanmark (case study) 84–6
    impact assessment 83–4
    and media 77–8
    media exposure 84
    negative aspects 88
    partnership contracts 113
    planning process **81**
    professional service firms 82–3
    range 76
    relations and networks 78, 79
    rights bundling 109
    SLIM (Sponsorship-Linked Internal Marketing)
      78, 85, 88
    and social media 77, 127–8, 129
    spending and revenues 75–6
    targets and objectives 79–82, **80**
    see also ambush marketing
Sport for All 59, 67
sport ethics and values 140–1, 147
sport goods market:
    Decathlon (case study) 20–6
    firm-level strategies 18–19
    growth 13, 15–17
    market shares: by country **14**
    market shares: types of sport **13**
    for running 63
    and Single European Market 15
    types of goods 17
sport industry: definition **12**
sporting pyramid 187
Storm, R.K. and Nielsen, K. 161, 164, 164*bib*, 181*bib*
Study on the Contribution of Sport to Economic Growth
    and Employment in the EU (2012) 11
Sugar, Alan 156
Sunday Times 194

Sweden:
    men's football 93, 95
    women's football 35–7
Switzerland 190, 191
Sydney Olympics (2000) 114, 208, 213, 221, 224, 225,
    226, 229
    urban development 207

television:
    advertising rights 113
    bidding for broadcasting rights 220–1
    and doping 48
    growth of 44, 94
    and mobile media 77–8
    and Olympic Games 45
    technology innovations 94
    see also internet; social media
Tencent 132
tennis:
    French Tennis Federation 137, 142–7
      collaboration with ministry of sport 144
      CSR strategy 143–**5**
      French Open 142, 144, 146
      global strategy **146**
      key figures **143**
      partnerships 144–**5**
      pitfalls 146
      Roland Garros 144, 146–7
      sustainable development policy 143
      Yellow Ball campaign 143, 146
    Tennis Europe 66
Thailand 97, 100, 101, 103
Thibault, L. et al 196*bib*
Thompson, P. and Speed, R. 80
Topdanmark 84–6
Tottenham Hotspur 156
TV Sports Markets 101
Twitter:
    football clubs users 121, 122
    and sport brands 124

UEFA (Union of European Football Associations) 66,
    113, 156
    and ambush marketing 110, 113, 115–16
    benchmarking report 156, 167, 173–4
    Champions League 8, 44–5, 92, 93, 99, 100, 104
    and commercialization 43
    Euro (European Championship) 77, 94, 98, 115, 229
    Europa League 8, 98, 104
    European Cup 100
    Financial Fair Play (FFP) regulations 8–9, 105, 160,
      164, 167–81
    football club deficits 156, 167

UEFA (Union of European Football Associations) *cont.*
  home-grown rule 31
  media rights 98, 101, 104, 113
  and not-for-profit sport 58, 66
  and racism 116
  revenues 44, 93–4, 98
  see also football
UK:
  British Olympic Association 148
  football: English Premier League 93, 94, 96, 97,
      98–9, 122, 156
    and FFP 164
    revenues compared with other leagues **99**
    revenues and media 93, 94–5, 96, 97, 98–9, 156
    and social media 122
  Judo Federation 137
  running 60, 62
  sport goods market 13
  see also London Olympics (2012)
Ukraine 115
Ultimate Fighting Championship 147
USA 33, 95
  see also Atlanta Olympics 1996; Los Angeles
      Olympics 1984

Viborg F.F. 163
Viborg HK 84

Victoria Plzen 99
Visa 110
volleyball 186, 195

Weibo 132
weightlifting 186, 195
Wenner, L.A. 53*bib*
Werder Bremen 131–2
West Ham United 213
White Paper on Sport (2007) 11
Wiesenhof 131–2
Wimbledon 58
winner's curse:
  bidding for Olympic Games 222–3
    costs of Olympic Games (case studies)
        223–6, **224**
    forms of 219–22
    indices in sports auctions **224**
    options for alleviating costs overrun 227–31
    Winter Olympics in Sochi 226–7
Wolverhampton 98
World Anti-Doping Agency (WADA) 186

Young and Rubicam 49

Zen-Ruffinen, Michel 194
Zimbalist, A. 232*bib*